BETWEEN THE LINES

BETWEEN
THE
LINES

Readings on Israel,
the Palestinians,
and the U.S. "War on Terror"

EDITED BY
TIKVA HONIG-PARNASS
TOUFIC HADDAD

First published in 2007 by Haymarket Books
P.O. Box 180165
Chicago, IL 60618
773-583-7884
info@haymarketbooks.org
www.haymarketbooks.org

Trade distribution:
In the U.S. through Consortium Book Sales, www.cbsd.com
In the UK, Turnaround Publisher Services, www.turnaround-psl.com
In Australia, Palgrave MacMillan, www.palgravemacmillan.com.au

This book was published with the generous support of the Wallace Global Fund.

Cover design by Jsoh On and Eric Kerl
Cover image of a woman saving oranges from a plantation destroyed by Israeli troops
in Beit Hanoun in northern Gaza Tuesday, May 20, 2003. Using bulldozers the Israeli
troops uprooted thousands of orange trees and other crops before they pulled back to
the edges of the town after a five day seizure in which at least eight Palestinians were
killed and fifteen houses destroyed. AP Photo/Ricardo Mazalan.

ISBN-13: 978-1931859-44-8

Printed in Canada by union labor on recycled paper containing 50 percent post-
consumer waste in accordance with the guidelines of the Green Press Initiative,
www.greenpressinitiative.org

Library of Congress CIP Data is available

2 4 6 8 10 9 7 5 3 1

CONTENTS

Chapter 3. Back to the Essence of the Conflict: Total War—Zionist Left and Right Close National and Class Ranks

Chapter 4. The Case of MK Azmi Bishara: Revealing the True Nature of Israel's Democracy

Chapter 5. From "Defensive Shield" to "Reforming the PA": Jenin's Noble Tragedy

March 2002–February 2003

Chapter 6. Israeli Elections 2003 and the Sweeping Victory of Sharon: What Once Was Will Continue to Be, Only Worse

March 2003

Chapter 7. The Occupation of Iraq: Widening U.S. Hegemony and Its Fallout for Palestine

July 2002–April 2003

The Newest Testament
Yitzhak Laor

O America America, finally you learned
Something from worm Jacob: Fuck
The UN, fuck the Arabs, fear not, America
All our desire is before thee, just tell us:
"Thou Israel, art my servant, I have
Chosen thee." O, America, let us gather
With you by the River of Babylon when
It blushes with Arab blood. (We had one
Victim in the space shuttle, and you
Had such a wonderful visit at the Museum
Of our Holocaust in Washington, D.C.)

Fear not, America, Iraqi babies are just
Babies and we are on your side and
God's on your side. In your honor we were first
To translate your Bible from English, teaching
Our children: "For the oil is the life, and thou
Mayest not eat the life with flesh."
O daughter of Babylon who art to be destroyed
Happy shall be he that taketh and dashes thy little
Ones against the stones. Let Hiroshima be one bedtime
Story out of a thousand and one, let Hanoi
Be forgotten like black slavery, let
The scream of a hundred thousand Iraqi
Mothers freeze for two weeks on CNN screens
In every shopping mall.

"The Newest Testament" was originally published in Hebrew in *Ha'aretz* in the run-up to the March 2003 invasion of Iraq, and was later featured in *Ir Ha-Leviathan* (Leviathan City) (Tel Aviv: Hakibbutz Hameuchand, 2004). The English version was translated by the author, and published in *Between the Lines* No. 21, March 2003.

Foreword

This book contains a selection of articles from *Between the Lines* (*BTL*), a political journal first published soon after the eruption of the Al Aqsa Intifada in late September 2000. *BTL* was published on a regular basis from Ramallah and Jerusalem until September 2003, when it was forced to stop due to difficulties in its material circumstances.[1] Only portions of the articles published in the original journal written by Palestinians, Israelis, and international supporters, in addition to the contributions of the editors, are included herewith. They have been edited for consistency and are presented in roughly chronological order, documenting the major themes and periods that have evolved since September 2000. The last two chapters provide an overview of important developments that have taken place since the journal stopped publication and are composed of articles written by the editors in the period since then. The book's material thus covers events up to November 2006, after Israel's assault on Lebanon. The lengthy introduction constitutes our conceptual and political framework, reflecting on the history of the Zionist colonialist movement and the nature of the Israeli state. It also covers important developments that took place in the Palestinian national movement as the background for understanding the 1967 Occupation, the Oslo process, and its subsequent failure, when *Between the Lines* first began publishing.

This book is thus a first attempt at recording a critical history of the salient trends that unfolded within the 1967 Palestinian, 1948 Palestinian, and Israeli political and social arenas during six years of the Al Aqsa Intifada.[2]

Between the Lines was distinguished from other publications on several levels. As editors, we saw it as our role to provide coverage of Israel's attempts to forcefully repress the Al Aqsa Intifada and to destroy the Palestinian people and national movement—a task undertaken by all Israeli governments, right and left alike. The coverage we provided of these policies and their subsequent repercussions upon Palestinian and Israeli political regimes and societies attempted to incorporate issues and themes all too often ignored by many of even the most progressive analysts and activists, let alone the mainstream media. The void we were attempting to fill was not just informational but also ideological and contextual. *Between the Lines* sought to counter the conceptions that prevail around the Israeli-Palestinian "conflict," portraying it as two "partners" "negotiating peace" or, alternatively, as two peoples fighting since time immemorial, prisoners of their religions and extremists. Such conceptions distort the actual situation on the ground, which is one characterized by the struggles between a colonization project—the Zionist movement as embodied in the Israeli state—and a colonized people—the Palestinians on both sides of the Green Line.[3]

The lack of clarity as to the proper framework in which to understand these dynamics has allowed the world to portray and condemn the ongoing resistance of the Palestinian people as "terror" against the "peace" that Israel is "willing to negotiate." It has also had the effect of ignoring the escalation of the 1948 Palestinian oppression, as though this were an "internal" Israeli issue separate from the "external" issue of the 1967 Occupation.

The need to cut against these false conceptions by providing a holistic framework within which all dimensions of the unfolding "conflict" can be understood couldn't be more urgent. Israel's policies, carried out by both left and right governments, represent the continuation of the Zionist colonialist project, which has aspired to directly or indirectly control all of historic Palestine with the full backing of U.S. imperialism. Furthermore, Israel plays a key role in enforcing U.S. imperial strategy regionally and internationally, particularly in its determined war against "radical nationalism" and democratic trends now subsumed beneath the "war on terror."

Our regular coverage of the escalating oppression against Palestinians in the 1967 Occupied Territories, the persecution of the second-class Palestinian citizens of Israel, and the rapid emergence of a fascist political culture in Israel documented the transformation of the means employed by Israel to achieve its long-held goals. That is to say that *Between the Lines* documented how the "diplomatic option" employed during the Oslo "peace" years (1993–2000) was reverting back to the original Zionist approach toward the Palestinian people—namely, employing forms of total war against the Palestinian national movement that sought to eliminate its potential to resist within the three arenas of confrontation with the Jewish-Zionist state: the decolonization of the 1967 Occupied Territories; the struggle for the democratization of Israel waged by the Palestinian citizens of Israel; and the struggle for the implementation of the right of return for Palestinian refugees.

This perspective runs counter to the prevailing perception that the 1967 Occupation is the root cause of the "Israeli-Palestinian conflict" and likewise, that its solution can be found through a "territorial compromise"—a perception adopted even by many who genuinely seek peace. Rather, it is based upon the understanding that Zionism, led by the Labor movement, has aspired to erect an exclusivist Jewish state in Palestine through colonial settler means. This central premise of Zionism is inherently contradictory to both Palestinian national rights in general and to equality of rights for Palestinian citizens of Israel. Moreover, the neoliberal socioeconomic ideology and Eurocentrism of Israel is contradictory to democracy regarding Jewish citizens as well, particularly vis-à-vis Mizrahi Jews,[4] who make up the majority of the Jewish working class.

No doubt the politics of *Between the Lines* stem from our anti-imperialist and anti-Zionist positions as well as our class consciousness. We believe that these guiding frameworks explain the dynamics of the Oslo agreements as well as the Intifada, the attempts to repress it, and the approach of "unilateralism," which replaced the negotiated "peace years," eventually leading to the "disengagement" from Gaza and the 2006 war on Lebanon. The Intifada has embodied the heroic resistance of the Palestinian popular classes[5] against the machinations of U.S.-funded Israeli colonialism as well as the subcontracted role of the Palestinian Authority in these plans. It is therefore, by extension, the embodiment of popular Palestinian resistance to the interests of U.S. imperialism and to those within the Palestinian national movement who would participate in these interests. This perspective is too often excluded from mainstream coverage and analysis of events. Moreover, the Palestinian discourse surrounding the Intifada that filters into the Western media often reflects only one of the many political currents in Palestinian politics. It is the current that perpetuates the mythology of the peace process, and it has vested political (and

sometimes financial) interests in linking the fate of the Palestinian national movement within the interests of U.S. imperialism. It is also a current that seeks to marginalize the voice of the popular movements that
ignited the Intifada and that have sustained its steadfastness and resistance. This marginalization is made all the worse by the fact that significant elements of the Palestinian resistance leadership is embodied in
Hamas* and all the misconceptions and racist notions this fact tends to
bring with it.

By the same token, the mainstream discourse within Israel and abroad
ignores the fact that Zionism, as the hegemonic ideology of the Israeli
state and society, is constantly reproduced and sustained in the service of
the Israeli-U.S. colonialist project, including the globalized economic interests that underlie it.

Israeli Labor governments have played a central role in introducing
both "peace" solutions and the neoliberal economy, not to mention the
misleading conclusion that there is "no Palestinian partner for peace."
Zionist left/liberals historically created the hegemonic ideology of the
state and continue to articulate justifications for the destructive policies of
all Israeli governments. Their most successful tool has been to frame issues in terms of existential dangers faced by Israel in a way that blurs the
elimination of the structured discriminative nature of the Jewish-Zionist
state, with the destruction of the state itself, of the Jewish people, and ultimately of universalistic humanist values.

Taking their lead from the latter, the Israeli peace camp and progressive movements around the world have tended to focus their protests
throughout the Intifada on the cruelty and atrocities of Israel's policies but
have refrained from putting their support of the ongoing resistance at the
center of their solidarity activities as they would have done (and did) in
the past regarding other national liberation and anticolonial struggles.
Such a solidarity position differs from supporting the Palestinian cause as
a negotiable "human rights issue." It also differs from the widespread
stance that calls for a cessation of violence on both sides. Instead it constitutes identification with the fight for self-determination and national liberation that continues on the ground. It also affirms the growing
solidarity of the Palestinians on both sides of the Green Line with the resistance trends throughout the Middle East, particularly Hezbollah in

---

*Hamas is the Arabic acronym for the Islamic Resistance Movement (Harakat al Moqawameh
al Islamiyya).

Lebanon. Furthermore, the prevailing discourse also ignores the most significant dimension of the daily struggle waged by the Palestinian citizens of Israel demanding national collective rights—this despite the fact that it represents a second front opened from within against the Jewish-Zionist state in the joint struggle of all parts of the Palestinian people against the Zionist-U.S. imperial alliance.

The struggle for genuine peace and—dare we say it—justice and liberation is a long one whose victory is conditioned on the deep transformation of the entire Middle East and its liberation from U.S. imperialism, the Zionist state, and the dictatorial Arab regimes. The ongoing debate surrounding the appropriate solution to the specific issue of Palestine/Israel diverts attention from what we believe is the main mission of progressive forces at this time: educating the world about the reality of Israeli/U.S. imperial and colonial policies while building and uniting the forces in these struggles for a just peace in Palestine and for a better world overall.

We hope that this book can contribute to the crystallization of this strategy and struggle.

Tikva Honig-Parnass and Toufic Haddad
March 2007

Introduction

I. The Emergence of Zionism

Zionism emerged as a project aimed at solving the specific problems that confronted Jews in Eastern Europe.[1] The state-orchestrated discrimination, persecution, and pogroms practiced against these communities in the last quarter of the nineteenth century resulted in their mass emigration to North and South America, with many also ending up in other areas of Europe. Out of the 3 million Jews who left Eastern Europe between 1882 and 1914, no more than one percent went to Palestine.[2] The small Zionist movement that emerged as a nationalist expression of this crisis was thus the product of the particular historical, political, and social circumstances of these Eastern European Jewish communities and not the product of any worldwide Jewish national identity, as is typically claimed by the great majority of Israeli historians.[3] It was, rather, a movement created in Eastern Europe, which embarked on a colonialist project in Palestine by reimagining Jews as an ancient religious community who constituted a nation. Once sculpted, this historical narrative became the essence of Israel's hegemonic ideology, attempting to dominate and marginalize all other narratives of the history of Jews in Europe and elsewhere.

The Zionist narrative determined that the "Jewish nation" had existed for thousands of years and lived as a persecuted minority for almost two millennia in the Diaspora after being expelled from its homeland in *Eretz*

Israel. It further claimed that the Zionist movement was established for the liberation of the Jewish nation, by working for the return of Jews to their homeland, in which they would regain their national sovereignty.[4] Jews in Islamic and Arab countries were not part and parcel of the Zionist movement. The pre-Zionist persecution of Jews in these areas was a marginal issue and certainly did not take the form described by the European Jewish terminology of "pogroms" and "anti-Semitism." The deterioration of relations between Jews and Arabs in the Arab and Muslim world began, on the one hand, with the penetration of European Zionism into the Jewish communities there and, on the other, with the beginning of the ascendance of Arab nationalism, and especially Palestinian nationalism. As the Israeli historian Shlomo Sand emphasizes, the result of the growing contradiction between the two on the question of Eretz Israel/ Palestine resulted in identifying the former Jews of Arab countries as passive collaborators with the European Zionist project, and their lives in their homeland countries became unbearable.[5] Nor did the Zionist movement in the beginning target Middle Eastern Jews as potential members of its colonialist project. Like other colonialist movements, Zionism adopted an orientalist approach towards non-Europeans and emphasized European supremacy over them. Indeed, only after the extermination of the majority of European Jewry in the Holocaust and the prohibition of Soviet Union Jewry from emigrating did the newly established state of Israel turn to bring the one million Jews in the Arab countries in to settle the country.

In addition to being a nationalist product of Eastern European extraction, Zionism consciously envisioned itself from its onset as a bulwark of Europe in the Arab world that would serve the interests of the colonial West. The Zionist movement founder, Theodor Herzl, described the role the Jewish state would play in Palestine as "a portion of the rampart of Europe against Asia, an outpost of civilization as opposed to barbarism."[6] This role would crystallize further both ideologically and organizationally within the Zionist movement, particularly after the issuing of the Balfour Declaration of 1917, an official British letter supporting the establishment of a Jewish state in Palestine. The cofounder of the World Zionist Organization Max Nordau explicitly articulated this role in a July 12, 1920, speech delivered at Albert Hall in London, and which he described years later:

> On stage were Mr. Balfour ... members of the British Cabinet, MPs, and Politicians. I turned to the Ministers and said: During a dangerous moment in the World War [World War I] you thought that we, the Jews, could render you a useful service. You turned to us, making promises that were rather gen-

eral but could be considered satisfactory [a reference to the Balfour Declaration]. We considered your views and were loyal towards your proposals. We only want to continue. We made a pact with you. We consider carefully the dangers and commitments of this pact. We know what you hope to receive from us. We must protect the Suez Canal for you. We shall be the guards of your road to India as it passes through the Middle East. We are ready to fulfill this difficult military role but this requires that you permit us to become powerful so as to be able to fulfill our role. Loyalty for loyalty, faithfulness in return for faithfulness.[7]

Zionism aimed at colonizing the land and establishing an exclusive Jewish state over entire historic Palestine, where the Palestinian Arab people had resided for centuries. This aim was backed by adopting an "organic," ethnic concept of nationalism that had its roots in nineteenth-century central and eastern Europe. This conception defined citizenship on the basis of ethnic ascription and perceived the state as an organic body built on ethnic, cultural, and linguistic homogeneity and embodying the specific historical essence of the ruling ethnic majority. Ethnic nationalism differed from the civic secular nationalism developed in western Europe and in North America, whereby all citizens of the nation–state fully belong to the nation and enjoy equal rights before the law, despite their varying ethnic or religious affiliations.[8]

II. Colonizing the Land

The Zionist Labor movement led the colonization project of Palestine. The socialist discourse and the collectivist structure and ideology of the prestate settler society (known as the *Yishuv*) have typically been portrayed as signifying the socialist era of Zionism, which was replaced by right-wing, capitalist-oriented political forces three decades after the establishment of the state.[9] But as the sociologist Gershon Shafir emphasizes, "The changes that took place in Israeli society after 1967 and the ascent of the Likud to power [in 1977] should be understood not as a transition from a Zionist-socialist society but as a continuity of the colonial project while moving from one colonialist system to another."[10]

Indeed, this widespread portrayal is an entirely misleading conception of how the history of the Zionist capitalist class unfolded with the support of the Labor movement and how it gained such a dominant position in Israel's implementation of Zionist colonialism, including with regard to the peace "solutions" it espoused.[11] It was the necessities created by the specific conditions within which the colonial Zionist project acted that determined the "socialist" veneer of the prestate period: due to the weak-

ness of the private capitalist class of Jewish settlers in Palestine, a collectivist approach to colonization, led by the Zionist Labor movement, was
seen as the most effective way of settling the land and evicting the indigenous population. It was also able to exclude the Palestinians from land
and labor markets. Thus, for example, the collective settlement movement
of the kibbutzim, which has often been described as motivated mainly by
a socialist ideology, was in fact created as an answer to these demands:

> The kibbutz is the clearest expression of the strategy of land occupation and
> labor occupation which was adopted by the Jewish settler workers in Eretz
> Israel. The kibbutz lands were "national," namely owned by the Jewish Na-
> tional Fund, and it was leased to Jews so they could serve a national goal.
> They [the lands] were thus excluded from the framework of the capitalist
> land market. The kibbutz also excluded the employment of its members from
> the capitalist labor market and thus supplied them [the Jewish workers] a
> closed labor market which [served] Jews alone.[12]

The need for the state-in-making to control investment and access to
land and labor markets did not mean that this control was antagonistic to
private capital. On the contrary.[13] This is why the small and weak Jewish
capitalist sector willingly imposed the leading role of the colonization
project upon the Labor faction of the Zionist movement headed by
Mapai—an acronym for the Eretz Israel Workers' Party (the progenitor of
today's Labor Party). Mapai's principal arm was the Histadrut, the General Federation of Workers in Eretz Israel. It thus happened that the umbrella organization of worker trade unions controlled key aspects of
the central tasks that confronted Zionist colonization—economic production and marketing, defense, and control of the labor force—as well as establishing its own industrial, financial, construction, transportation and
service enterprises. These enterprises ultimately formed the core of the
great conglomerates that consolidated after the establishment of the state
in 1948 and that for decades dominated the Israeli economy.

The Zionist Labor movement also played the leading role in creating
the hegemonic ideology of the Zionist brand of colonialism, which from
the beginning sharply diverged from European social democracy.[14] Its
"constructive socialism" rejected the notion of class conflict and stressed
the joint interest of the (Jewish) bourgeoisie and labor force—the "producing" classes—in contributing to the "common good" embodied in the
future state, not to mention the prestate entity.[15]

This version of National Socialism and the worldview and principles
embedded within it became the main tenets of the official ideology and

identity of the state of Israel for decades. It later developed within Israeli political culture by emphasizing the supremacy of the state and its "security" over the principles of individual human and citizen rights, as well as class interests.[16] Up to the very present, it serves as the ideological basis that unifies the left and right wings within Israel behind the principal political policies adopted by all Israeli governments—regarding both the Palestinians and the Arab world and the social economy within Israel. Within this context, the remnants of the collectivist approach of the prestate period still carry weight in economic and social discourse and policies, thus serving the necessities of Israel as a settler society.

A "Pure Settler Colonialism": Liquidation and Expulsion

In accordance with its ethnic nationalist perspective, the aspiration to achieve a Jewish majority in Palestine was a central strategy of the Zionist Labor movement. It underlined the legal and institutional system constructed by the first Labor governments of the state of Israel and developed and implemented since then through direct and indirect policies that aim at fighting the "demographic danger" of losing the Jewish majority in Israel due to the higher Palestinian birthrate.

Creating a substantive Jewish majority in the future state was preferred to the alternative of creating a state with a Palestinian majority, as was the case before 1948. (In 1946, there were 608,225 Jews in Mandate Palestine and 1,237,334 Palestinian Arabs.)[17] The alternative of a Jewish minority governing over a majority Arab Palestinian population would have necessitated establishing a full-fledged apartheid system of racial segregation with dual legal sets—a solution that was rejected by Zionism and especially by the Labor movement that led it.[18]

In the apartheid model of colonization, the labor power of the indigenous people became the main resource to be exploited by the settlers. Hence, the ethnic conflict between the two groups (the colonizers and the colonized) assumed the nature of a kind of class struggle. The South African apartheid system, which represented this model in almost pure form, was based on the exploitation of the vital labor power of the colonized Black majority by the white settlers at least as early as the eighteenth century, when gold was discovered. Apartheid was a device for keeping the exploited natives—the majority of the population—as part of the same economy and therefore essentially also of the same society, but without actually admitting it and without giving the former rights of citizenship. Officially, the natives were citizens of fake states, the Bantustans. But as Moshe Machover rightly emphasizes, the last thing the architects of the apartheid state wanted was a real departure of the Black Africans, whose labor power was vital to its economy.[19]

The Israeli economy, however, from the inception of Zionist colonization, was not dependent on Palestinian labor in the same way that the South African economy was dependent on Black African labor. The Zionists adopted a model of "pure settler colonies," similar in ways to that in North America, New Zealand, and Australia, whereby the native population was to be exterminated or expelled rather than exploited as cheap labor.[20] Already early in the history of the Zionist movement, its leaders recognized that mass expulsion of the Palestinian population was a necessary condition for the future purely Jewish "Land of Israel," thereafter becoming a consistent element in the thought of the Zionist forefathers.[21] The organic nationalism they adopted supplied the ideological rationale needed for the ethnic cleansing later committed in 1948. But this was not on the agenda as long as the Zionist movement was under the control of the British mandate: the *Yishuv* was a minority within this British colony, without the full capacity to implement its plans regarding the indigenous Palestinian residents. However, the Zionist leadership waited.[22] Until politically and militarily expedient circumstances would permit for this (*she'at kosher*), policies of separation were to be implemented between the *Yishuv* and the indigenous Palestinian residents of the land. This included excluding Palestinians from the land and labor markets, and banning Jews from buying goods produced by Palestinians (*"kibush h'karka," "kibush h'avoda," and "tozeret haaretz"*).[23] Two main organizations that were in charge of implementing these nationalistic segregation policies—the Histadrut[24] and the Israel National Fund—continued to play their role in serving the Jewish population alone, after the establishment of the state, and have done so up until the very present.

The opportunity to expel the Palestinian people emerged in the 1948 War, which followed the U.N. Partition Resolution of November 29, 1947. The Zionist movement accepted the U.N. decision only declaratively since it contradicted the central Zionist aim of an exclusive Jewish state on the whole area of historic Palestine.[25] According to the U.N. Partition Plan, the proposed Jewish state had an almost equal number of Jews and Palestinian Arabs (498,000 Jews and 497,000 Palestinian Arabs) and would have been, in effect, a binational state.[26] Moreover, were it not for the mass expulsions of Palestinians from the areas conquered in the 1948

War, the percentage of Jews within the frontiers that followed the 1948 War would have been much smaller. This is because the Jewish state considerably expanded beyond the borders allocated to it by the U.N. Partition Plan.[27] Hence the Zionist movement took the opportunity created by the "fog of war" and the period thereafter to commit the mass expulsion of the Palestinians. These events have come to be known as the *Nakba*—the Arabic word for "catastrophe"—in Arab historiography.

Thus, Israel's Jewish majority was achieved in an area that was far larger than the area allocated to it by the U.N. Partition Plan (78% of Palestine as opposed to 54%) and was the product of a campaign of mass ethnic cleansing that today is well documented by international, Arab, and Zionist historians. Between 750,000 and 900,000 Palestinians were expelled or forced to leave their homeland,[28] while all means were employed not to let the refugees return, even if they left their villages for only a short period of time.[29] At least 418 Palestinian villages and 11 Palestinian cities were depopulated in the 1948 War, while as many as 532 villages in total would be depopulated as the cycle of ethnic cleansing continued up until 1959.[30]

III. The Early Years of Israel: Initial Stages of State and Class Formation

Legal Infrastructure: Judaization of the Land

After the 1948 War, only 132,000 Palestinians were able to stay put on their land or within the borders of the newly established Jewish state.[31] These Palestinians (hereafter referred to as 1948 Palestinians, or Palestinian citizens of Israel) were immediately placed beneath a military governorate that lasted until 1966. The latter quickly made efforts to confiscate the majority of their lands, handing them over to Jewish settlements according to "lawful" procedures.[32]

The legal infrastructure laid down in the first years of the state was inspired by the felt need to avoid an explicit apartheid regime with officially separate legal systems for Jews and Palestinians. This was done because the mainstream Zionist movement understood the importance of sustaining a democratic facade to its colonial project, in order to gain the legitimacy of the international community and despite the dispossessive policies it was carrying out against its Palestinian citizenry.[33] Hence a formal democracy was established that claimed to apply equal rights to the Palestinians who remained within the borders of Israel. They were granted citizenship and formal equality before the law, including the right to run for and vote in the Knesset and, at least theoretically, the right to organize on political lists which participated in general elections.

The Law of Return of 1950, which is recognized as a fundamental principle of the state of Israel, "possibly even its very *raison d'être* as a Jewish state,"[34] is one of the only Israeli laws that overtly grants a basic human right only to Jews. It grants the right to Jews from all over the world to settle in Israel as an *oleh*,[35] which applies also to Jews who have already settled in the country or who are born in it. This definition has its most significant implications in distinguishing between Jews and Palestinians not only in regard to the right to enter and settle in Israel but also regarding the basic rights and benefits that derive from full citizenship. Needless to say, it also served to prevent the return of the Palestinian refugees (dispossessed of their lands and homes in the 1948 War) who were dispersed throughout the West Bank, Gaza Strip, Lebanon, and Syria and as "internal refugees" within Israel itself.

The other Basic Laws enacted between 1948 and 1952 enabled the Judaization of land and resources and their continued domination and control within Jewish hands, all within a single legal system.[36] In subsequent years an intricate language of laws developed, further allowing for the systematic preference of Jews and discrimination against the 1948 Palestinians.[37] A special way to circumvent a situation in which state laws explicitly discriminated against Palestinian citizens was found through granting "national institutions"—as opposed to state institutions—a free hand to act in the interests of Jews alone. This was usually implemented through legislation that directly designated certain matters to the authority of the prestate colonizatory institutions (such as the Jewish Agency and the Jewish National Fund) that continued to exist after the creation of the state. With the power of the state behind them, these institutions, which claimed to represent the interests of the "entire Jewish people," could now fulfill their role of "Judaizing the land," without restriction. Thus, for example, the allocation of "state land" to the Jewish National Fund (JNF) ensures their retention in Jewish hands alone, preventing them from ever being sold to non-Jews, according to the fund's internal bylaws.

However, before the legal structure for a "normalized" discriminative political regime was laid down, the new state hurried to delimit it within the framework of a declared "state of emergency," which has also lasted until the very present. This in and of itself emptied the Zionist regime from full equality, as formally promised to its citizenry in the Declaration of Independence. Dozens of emergency laws and regulations, most of which were legalized by the British Mandate, are still in use today, while their amendments have become an integral part of the Israeli legal system.[38] Of course, the state's incorporation of emergency measures into its daily functioning violates the norms of international law, including the imposition of collective punishment and arbitrary deprivations of liberty. Beneath the "security" pretext conferred by the perpetual "state of emergency," these laws were activated to root out the emergence of any determined national identity or movement that might arise from within the Palestinian citizenry. They could also be used to extinguish any solidarity these forces might develop with those in the Jewish anti-Zionist Left who identified with challenges to the Jewish character of the state.[39]

Thus a permanent emergency situation, beneath which the irregular situation of "suspension of the rule of the law within the legal framework," prevails in Israel to this day. According to Frantz Fanon, this is a permanent situation in colonial occupations: the colonial sovereign declares an "emergency" situation, thus removing itself from the rule of law and turning the "emergency rule" into a constant paradigm.[40] In the post–September 11, 2001, era, what was perceived previously as an exceptional "emergency situation" has turned into a regular working method for Western regimes as well, directed primarily toward internal populations of non-European ancestry.[41] Israel, however, never waited for the legitimacy of the "official" antiterror campaigns of the Western states. For decades it has derived its legitimacy from its self-described context as a "democracy in an emergency situation," presumably enforced to defend itself from its Palestinian and Arab enemies. With the onset of the 1967 Occupation, this legal infrastructure was extended to draw from and incorporate the existing "emergency regulations" that also existed in the formerly Jordanian-annexed West Bank and the Egyptian-administered Gaza Strip.

Jewish Religion as the Ultimate Legitimacy

Zionism's need for religious legitimacy, based upon the notion of the "return" of the Jewish people to its homeland to regain its lost sovereignty, has had a decisive impact on its ideology, culture, and social and political institutions both in the prestate period and in the state of Israel today.

In the political culture of the postcolonial order, says Baruch Kimmerling, the Israeli settler society is plagued by the question "Why precisely here?"—why did Zionism choose Palestine, despite the fact that it was populated by the indigenous Palestinian people? The answer to this question, he says, has been supplied by Jewish religion. "Thus," Kimmerling concludes, "not the nation nor its culture could be successfully built outside the religious context, even though its prophets, builders and fighters have seen themselves as entirely secular."[42]

The myths of the Divine Promise, namely the promise of God to Abraham that the land would be given to him and his offspring till eternity, has served as the "ultimate legitimacy" for Zionism. Jewish religion and tradition supplied Zionism with the capacity to mask its nature as a colonialist project by granting it the image of a "return to Zion."

The decisive step in the process of establishing the centrality of religion in the identity of the Jewish state began with the "Status Quo" Agreement. The latter was forged between the orthodox non-Zionist Agudat Israel movement and the leadership of the Jewish Agency, headed by David Ben-Gurion, the leader of Mapai, and took place in the run-up preparations made for the establishment of the state. This agreement contributed to laying the foundations of the nonseparation of religion and state in Israel, which was later embodied in its legal system. Accordingly, certain state legislative and judicial powers have been transferred to the realm of the religious establishment, which makes its judgments according to Halachic law. For example, all aspects of the major areas of marriage and divorce are dealt with according to Halachic interpretation, based upon the Orthodox current of Judaism. Jewish-religious elements have also been incorporated into other areas of legislation as well.[43] Additionally, there are statewide and local laws that consist of public norms also based upon the Halacha.[44]

Class Formation

The early years of consolidating the legal and institutional basis of the Jewish-Zionist state, together with the de-Arabization of the land, were also the years in which the state was involved in a process of escalated economic development and in its internal class formation. The class structure was built on national and ethnic divisions as follows:

The emerging capitalist class was comprised of European Jews or their descendents (hereafter Ashkenazi Jews) who represented the great majority of the prestate settler community and its leadership. They were the major benefactors of the vast investments that the state made in its first years in employment, education, housing, and direct and indirect encouragement of the local business sector. The state directed virtually all capital transfers (from German reparations and foreign Jewry) to favored business groups involved in the "national project." These "allied" groups were owned mostly by elements of the Labor Zionist movement, as represented by the Histadrut and its other wings. In return they undertook industrialization projects and investment in areas designated as crucial for the development of the economy.

By the late 1960s, these favored business groups had coalesced into five large conglomerates or holding companies (Hapoalim, Leumi, Koor, Cal, and IDB Holdings) that came to dominate the economy in both its financial and industrial sectors. All but one of the "Big Five" (IDB Holdings) had their origins in the prestate colonization period and were linked to wings of the Zionist movement. These large conglomerates formed a kind of umbrella within which the private capital of selected families allied to the state and the Zionist movement could be nurtured and grow. The state's systematic policies aimed at nurturing a capitalist class were implemented through encouraging these key families and international capital (mainly from North Americans, particularly those with historical ties to the Zionist movement) to undertake joint projects and investments with the state and quasistate enterprises (such as the Histadrut and the National Bank [Bank Leumi]).[45]

Israel's emerging working class was also divided along national lines between Palestinian citizens (1948 Palestinians) and Jews from Arab countries and their Israeli-born descendents (hereafter referred to as Mizrahi Jews). The 1948 Palestinians were all but excluded from employment in the public sector (because it was said to consist of "strategic" industries) and from state- or Histadrut-controlled economic enterprises.[46] They were thus forced to seek employment in the private sector, which lacked the relatively better work conditions and fringe benefits that Mizrahi workers could achieve in the public–Histadrut sector.[47] The systematic policies that were implemented by all Israeli governments, aiming at the dedevelopment of the Palestinian "sector" in Israel (concentrated primarily in the Galilee and Triangle regions), made them dependent on the Jewish economy both in terms of jobs and in terms of purchasing basic life necessities. Their villages became and remain commuter communities while most of their lands have been taken by the state and allocated to nearby Jewish settlements.[48]

The national division of the working class was supplemented by a division within Jewish wage laborers on ethnic lines, between Mizrahim and Ashkenazim. The first wave of Israeli industrialization began in the late

1950s and was led by the Zionist Labor movement through its control of the apparatuses of the state. It was facilitated by the massive immigration of Jews from Arab countries, a large proportion of whom were settled in small, so-called development towns, in remote corners of the country, which had meager economic bases and few resources for real development. Usually these towns were composed of nothing more than a state-subsidized industrial plant that turned the Mizrahim into a cheap and dependent labor force. Together with Mizrahi immigrants who were settled in pre-1948 Palestinian cities, towns, and neighborhoods (such as Jerusalem, Haifa, Jaffa, Acre, Lydd, and Ramleh), the Mizrahim came to constitute the bulk of the Jewish working class, mostly in blue-collar jobs, whether skilled or not. The Histadrut's failure to defend their rights, both historically and up to the present, has contributed to the gaps in salaries between professions occupied by Mizrahim and Ashkenazim—a division that exists even within the same grades and profession. The dominant orientalist ideology of the Ashkenazi elite, which presented the Mizrahim as descendents of undeveloped countries and inferior cultures, has supplied a justification for their lower positions in the economy and society. Unlike the Palestinian citizens, however, the Mizrahim did play a central role in developing the "strategic" branches of Israeli industry in the 1960s.[49] In contrast, Ashkenazi laborers were (and still are) concentrated as employees within the big conglomerates, overwhelmingly populating its management structures while enjoying high salaries and formidable social benefits. Their unions form the backbone of the "thirteen strong labor unions" that gradually emerged after 1948 and enjoy strong Histadrut support up to the present.

IV. The 1967 Occupation: Outlining the Future Map for a "Peace" Settlement

The Israeli victory in the 1967 War completed the "unfinished task" of the 1948 War by bringing Israeli rule to the entire territory of historic Palestine.[50] The defeat of the Pan-Arabist forces in that war eliminated the "radical nationalist" threat that Egyptian President Jamal Abdel Nasser had symbolized. This victory was a tremendous service for the United States and for the tyrant regimes of the oil-producing states in the Arabian Gulf, as explained by Noam Chomsky:

> Remember how Saudi Arabia [the most important oil producing state in the world] was at that time on the verge of war with Egypt [under Nasser]. . . . In general, Israel's services in the Middle East have established the close Israeli-American alliance and confirmed the estimations made by the American in-

telligence [community] as early as 1958, that the "logical answer to confronting 'Radical nationalism'"—that meaning independent secular [Arab] nationalism—is "support of Israel," which is the only reliable base for the U.S. in the region (alongside Turkey, which began its close relationship with Israel in the same year).[51]

Israel was thus recognized as a strategic asset for U.S. policy in the Middle East, resulting in huge economic and military support to it. This support made Israel a regional military powerhouse, further widening the gap between it and the surrounding Arab states significantly. In the coming years Israel also began to supply secondary services to U.S. imperialism, such as helping the Reagan administration circumvent congressional limitations regarding the mass terror campaigns waged in Central America and facilitating the evasion of the international trade embargo placed on the apartheid regime in South Africa.[52]

Thus a central thrust of the joint interests between U.S. imperialism in the Middle East since 1967 and Zionist colonialism as embodied in the state of Israel has always been to abolish the Palestinian national movement as a central pillar in the campaign to do away with Arab nationalism and the democratic forces that threaten U.S. hegemony in the region. Israel's goal of preserving both direct and indirect rule over entire historic Palestine has also meant the definitive establishment of the state of Israel as an outpost of U.S. imperialism. Preserving the "Jewishness" of the state and ensuring that it is thoroughly entrenched and protected are natural corollaries to this imperial logic.

Israel's enlarged military industry also enabled it to become competitive in world markets. Before 1967, the scope of the local economic activity was relatively low, and exports comprised primarily agricultural products and finished diamonds. But after 1967, growth rates greatly increased and Israel became not only a regional military power but also a military-industrial power. Later the "defense" industry brought about the growth of a local high-tech industry that brought Israel into the club of states at the forefront of technological development.[53]

The Allon Plan: The Basis for All Israeli Political Solutions

It is within this overarching framework that we must come to understand the "peace" proposals that have been submitted to the Palestinians, initiated by either side of the U.S.-Israeli alliance, both historically and up to the present. All such proposals have had similar goals, which aim at serving both Israeli and U.S. hegemonic interests. From the Oslo Accords in

1993, through former Labor Party Prime Minister (PM) Ehud Barak's offer at Camp David in 2000—all have sought to eternalize Israel's dominance over the 1967 Occupied Territories under the pretext that Israel would make "substantive concessions" in search of "historic compromise." This pretext facilitated years of fruitless political negotiations, all the while that "facts on the ground" deepened Israel's control over the 1967 Occupied Territories, worsening each "offer" submitted to the Palestinians from one "peace plan" to the next.

U.S./Israeli "peace proposals" have all adhered to principles laid down by Yigal Allon, the admired commander of the Palmach,[54] who outlined Israel's strategic priorities for what to do with the West Bank and Gaza Strip once they were occupied in June 1967. As deputy prime minister in the Levy Eshkol (Labor) government, Allon submitted his plans for a political settlement to the government as early as the beginning of July 1967. Since then it has come to be known as the Allon Plan[55], welcomed by the U.S. government and even by former French Prime Minister François Mitterrand.[56]

The Allon Plan was devised under the necessity to solve the "dilemma" that Israel confronted due to the 1967 Occupation. Unlike the 1948 War, in which two thirds of the indigenous people were expelled, most Palestinians in the newly occupied areas (who numbered more than one million) remained on their land after 1967. (Hereafter, the Palestinians in the West Bank and the Gaza Strip will be referred to as 1967 Palestinians).[57] Although the aspiration to expel the Palestinians loomed steadily in Zionist thought after the 1948 ethnic cleansing, the international circumstances at the time of the 1967 War, together with its short length (six days), did not allow the Labor "pragmatists" then in power to use "the fog of war" to repeat the massive expulsions witnessed in 1948.[58] Nor, for that matter, did circumstances permit the carrying out of the "unfinished business" of the Palestinians who survived the 1948 Nakba and who had remained on their land, now within the borders of the state of Israel.

Given that left and right Zionists shared (and still share) the conviction of an exclusivist Jewish state based on the principle of "separation" between the two peoples, both became preoccupied with the concern of losing the "Jewish majority" if the newly occupied territories remained under Israel's control. This emergent concern was now added to the already existing concern regarding the Palestinians inside Israel whose survival within the state had not been planned for.[59] However, at the time, it was the issue of the 1967 Palestinians that most concerned the Israeli establishment, given the fact that the 1948 Palestinians were largely defeated and terrorized by the military governorship they had lived under between 1948 and 1966.[60]

The presence of the Palestinian population in the 1967 Occupied Territories made the "demographic problem"—namely the fear of losing the Jewish majority—a much more urgent issue for the Zionist Left than for the Right. The Zionist Labor movement has always been concerned with the "democratic" and "enlightened" image of the Zionist colonial project and of the Jewish state, which they believe a Jewish majority provides. Hence it rejected the approach of the Zionist Right, which supported the full annexation of the 1967 Occupied Territories, without the felt need to grant citizenship to the occupied Palestinians. Furthermore, the extent to which the Zionist Left has been prepared to base its policies regarding Palestine upon the dictates of various U.S. administrations has traditionally been much greater than that of the Right.[61] Hence the Left's adherence to the Allon Plan was also based upon the United States' belief that its principles were the condition for the "stability" it sought in the Arab world, including in Palestine.

The Allon Plan was meant to replace, for the time being, "transfer" as a solution for addressing the "danger" of the Palestinians who resided in the areas Israel had occupied through war and intended to permanently control, whether directly or indirectly. Its basic premise called for some form of amputated Palestinian self-rule, called "autonomy." These areas were to be determined based upon the Zionist Left's traditional approach, which upheld the principle of demographic separation between Palestinians and Israelis, with Israel seeking to maintain maximum territorial control over as small a Palestinian population as possible.

Allon thus devised a plan that permitted Israeli control over the West Bank and Gaza Strip but that also preserved the "Jewish nature" of the expanded state of Israel and its democratic reputation. It proposed a partial annexation of around 35 to 40 percent of the 1967 Occupied Territories to Israel, while leaving the remaining areas of high Palestinian population density to fall beneath either Jordanian rule or some form of Palestinian self-rule, enclaved within the new frontiers of Israel. Allon advocated the fragmentation of these areas with Israel definitively controlling a frontier strip stretching roughly fifteen kilometers in width west of the Jordan River (the Jordan Valley). It also foresaw the annexation of the Old City of Jerusalem and the extension of the eastern boundaries of Jerusalem to the Jordan River. This was seen as necessary so as to divide the West Bank into two separate enclaves to the north and south of Jerusalem, linked by a narrow corridor controlled by the Israeli Army.[62] As for the Gaza Strip, Allon advocated that it not be returned to Egypt but rather be attached to the West Bank enclaves, "with rights of circulation, but without creating a corridor," while keeping Israel's control of the south of the Strip so as to control access to the Egyptian Sinai, which it borders.[63]

Allon understood that such a "peace" settlement dictated by Israel could not be accepted by the Palestinian national movement as long as it preserved its national liberation goals and identity. Consent to these plans could be granted only by a collaborative leadership, although even this was problematic, as such a leadership also needed to be armed with the "authority" needed for its decision to be credible.[64] Such a Palestinian leadership simply did not exist in 1967, nor for many years thereafter.

Thus, the Allon Plan was not meant to supply an immediate solution to the 1967 Occupied Territories. On the contrary, it envisaged a prolonged occupation that would incrementally annex lands via the building of settlements, so as to physically occupy the territory that Israel sought to control directly in any final agreement. If Israel were ever forced to negotiate its policies, the Allon Plan foresaw drawing out the negotiations until a collaborative leadership would emerge that could sign on to the aspired agreement of surrender. This strategy was adopted by all successive Israeli governments from 1967 up to September 2000.

The policies administered by the military rule imposed over the 1967 Occupied Territories included the strangulation of Palestinian economic development, thus making the Palestinians fully dependent upon the Israeli economy and turning the 1967 Palestinians into a source of profits for Israeli markets and services, as well as a source of cheap labor. The smooth flow of Palestinian workers into Israel became a source of surplus labor power, which also served to keep down the wages of low-paid Israeli workers.[65]

In 1985, the Shimon Peres government (Labor), together with the cooperation of the Histadrut, implemented an Economic Stabilization Plan that introduced neoliberalism onto the political and economic scene according to the "advice" of the International Monetary Fund (IMF). Like the structural adjustment policies implemented in other developing countries, the Israeli version included cuts in the state budget and social services, privatization, and depression of workers' wages. But in Israel, the policies of privatization and of transferring resources to the business sector constituted an essential turning point in the state-led class formation. Namely, it gave rise to the emergence of private capital as a class independent from the state. As the political economist Adam Hanieh confirms, this shift was marked by the privatization of state-owned and quasi-state enterprises—the network of companies controlled by the core conglomerates, as well as the relaxation of governmental control over capital markets as a means to attract foreign investment. The Israeli economy thus departed from the old system, in which the state sheltered and promoted capital accumulation within the big conglomerates. By opening the door for the process of privatization, a new era began in which the emergent capitalist class was given control over the key sectors of the economy, as well as a more distinct, direct intervention in Israel's policies regarding the Palestinian question. The new "free-market" economy and the rise of the new independent capitalist class was only the last stage in the long process in which the traditional procapitalist approach of the Zionist Labor movement and the Labor Party governments which succeeded it was finally openly disclosed.[66]

Despite what seems a contradiction, the diminished economic role of the state and the adoption of neoliberal ideologies have not weakened Israel's hegemonic Zionist ideology. Its emphasis upon the submission of individual interests and rights to "collective" goals remains as durable and powerful as ever.[67] This is because the requirement to mobilize support for its colonial and militarist missions buoyed and motivated the continuing bias toward policies that incorporate some forms of social protection. Thus the aspirations for a liberalized economy shared by both Right and Left in Israel was "compromised by its coexistence with traditional Zionist convictions that require a substantial role for the state in expressing collective tasks and the collective will."[68] These have put some restraints on the development of an extreme free-market economy, as witnessed in other countries that have passed structural adjustment policies in accordance with the IMF. It should also be stated that the financial aid the U.S. government has provided Israel has been instrumental in subsidizing the Israeli economy: since World War II the United States has supplied Israel with more aid than any other country (more than $140 billion, in 2004 dollars) and currently supplies $3 billion in direct assistance each year (roughly one-fifth of the U.S. foreign aid budget), worth about $500 a year for every Israeli.[69]

In any respect, as long as the cost of Israel's occupation of the West Bank and Gaza was not high in comparison to the profits it brought, the developing capitalist class supported Israel's direct military control and the emergent settlement map according to the main principles outlined by the Allon Plan.

However, the eruption of the Palestinian Intifada in December 1987, which lasted for six years, signified that the time had come to reassess the Israeli means of controlling the Palestinians and their land. Israeli capitalists, acting through their traditional mouthpiece of the Israeli Labor Party, gradually realized that due to the inevitable Palestinian resistance, the costs of direct occupation were rather high. The Arab boycott and impediments to foreign investments were blocking Israel's industrial integration into world economic globalization.[70] Thus already by the beginning of the 1990s, the Manufacturers' Association of Israel—a powerful organization of local industrialists—called for a settlement with the Palestinians, without excluding the idea of establishing a Palestinian state.[71]

The political and social elites also "lost their belief in an approach which relied upon confrontation and enforcement and understood that the cost of the occupation is higher than its fruits."[72] Hence Prime Minister Yitzhak Rabin and Foreign Minister Shimon Peres willingly accepted the U.S. and World Bank dictates (also supported by Israeli industrial circles) to adopt the peace agreement embodied in the 1993 Oslo Accords, which was intended to remove these obstacles.[73]

V. 1993–2000: The Oslo Accords and the "Years of Peace"

The Oslo Accords, signed on the White House lawn on September 13, 1993, amounted to an updated version of the Allon Plan.[74] They were based on the assumption that a Palestinian leadership needed to legitimize the planned "autonomy"="separation" framework envisioned by Allon. The PLO had "ceased to be the PLO"—the condition set by Allon for recognizing it as a partner for negotiations.[75] "There has been a change in *them* not *us*. We are not negotiating with the PLO, but only with a shadow of its former self," noted Shimon Peres.[76] And indeed, in the context of the "New World Order" that emerged after the fall of the Soviet Union and the 1990–91 Gulf War, the greatly weakened Palestinian leadership, led by Yasser Arafat and the Fateh party (which since 1982 had been based in distant Tunisia), was more ready to accept a plan of surrender and serve as subcontracted collaborators with the U.S.-Israeli scheme.[77]

In return for Arafat's commitment to repress Palestinian resistance to the occupation witnessed in the 1987 Intifada, the Palestinian Authority (PA) was permitted to run the areas of highest Palestinian density with a form of self-rule that was disingenuously called a "Palestinian state in the making" by much of the international community.[78] Furthermore, it gradually became

apparent to proponents of the Allon Plan within the Labor Party establishment that the "Arab-free" areas it was carving out in the West Bank could
even be extended beyond the 35 to 40 percent they had formerly conceived
of annexing to Israel. By 1993, the Palestinians had already been dispossessed of about 50 percent of their lands in practice, because they had been
designated as "[Israeli] state lands," security zones, and "land reserves for the
settlements."[79] Labor Party circles began to talk of Oslo as the "Allon Plus
Plan"—namely, more land for Israel and further fragmentation of the West
Bank. The number of encircled Palestinian enclaves increased, thus tightening Israel's control over the entire 1967 Occupied Territories and blocking
the prospect for a viable territorially contiguous Palestinian state.[80]

All this became conditioned upon retaining the economic dependency
of the 1967 Occupied Territories upon Israel, while blocking their ability
to produce or export products that would compete with Israeli products,
as stipulated in the Paris Economic Agreement of 1994. As Shlomo Ben
Ami noted, "The Oslo Accord has actually determined a basic neo-colonialist assumption, of living one within the other for eternity. . . . The
Paris Accord is one of its expressions. Instead of turning the sight of the
Palestinian economy to the East, to Jordan and to the Arab world, it fix-
ated it within an almost absolute dependency upon Israel. The Accord has
created a prolonged colonial situation. It assumed that even in a final
peace between us [Israel] and the Palestinians, a structured condition of
dependency, of inequality between the two entities, will exist."[81]

The paradigm of a "New Middle East" that the Oslo process was intended to give rise to was elaborated by none other than Shimon Peres, the
old Labor Party leader, who, together with PM Yitzhak Rabin and PLO
Chairman Yasser Arafat, won the Nobel Peace Prize for their role in
putting together the Oslo Bantustan solution. Peres articulated his vision
of Israel's role in the global market economy by outlining its integration
within the framework of "regional communities." He summarized the plan
as follows: "To erect the sewing workshops in Gaza (or in Tulkarem [in the
West Bank] or Amman [in Jordan]) administered from Tel Aviv, while the
owners reside in New York."[82] Israel was designated, on the one hand, the
role of integrating into the Middle East, so that it could become a base for
the activity of multinational corporations, while, on the other hand, it
planned to develop an advanced high-tech industry, solely under the ownership of multinational corporations—though overwhelmingly American.

The disingenuously titled Oslo "peace years" indeed benefited the Israeli capitalist class, as foreseen by its architects. Among other things, they

enabled a large flow of investments into Israel from the United States, primarily in the high-tech and agriculture sectors (but in fact, in all branches of the economy as well), thus tightening the cooperation between foreign and local capital. These benefits were explicitly celebrated by Nehemia Stresler, a conservative economic commentator for the Israeli daily newspaper *Ha'aretz,* which has traditionally acted as the mouthpiece of Israel's business community: "The turning point for the Israeli economy was on September 13, 1993, when Yitzhak Rabin signed the Oslo agreement. Within a short time, the world changed its attitude toward Israel. . . . The Arab boycott was canceled, thirty states renewed their diplomatic relations with Israel, foreign investments reached the level of several billion dollars a year, exports went to countries where Israel previously had no foothold, and the Israeli economy began to grow at a dizzying rate of 7 percent in 1994 and 6.8 percent in 1995, with unemployment declining to a welcome low of 6.6 percent of the workforce."[83]

Oslo and the Palestinians

The implementation of the Oslo version of Allon's plan facilitated the construction of the monstrous situation on the ground that inevitably gave rise to the Al Aqsa Intifada and finally to the collapse of the Oslo framework itself, following the Camp David summit in July 2000. There were two aspects of this situation, both of which were direct consequences of the Oslo Accords and the subsequent agreements reached between Israel and the Palestinian Authority thereafter:[84] the situation in the West Bank and Gaza vis-à-vis the Israeli occupation, and the internal Palestinian setting with regard to the PA.

Deepening Israeli Occupation

After almost seven years of the negotiated process, only 17.2 percent of the West Bank and 58 percent of the Gaza Strip fell under the "full" autonomy of the PA—territories designated as "Area A" under the Oslo Accords, which included the major Palestinian cities of Jenin, Nablus, Qalqiliya, Tulkarem, Ramallah, Jericho, Bethlehem, Hebron,[85] and the cities and refugee camps of the Gaza Strip—but excluding Jerusalem.[86] Israel designated these areas of highest Palestinian population density as areas whose civilian and security aspects would be under PA control. However, the Israeli Army's redeployment from the Palestinian cities took place only to the settlements and military bases that were entrenched on the borders of these concentrations themselves and along the main access roads on which they depended for connection with one another and to the outside world. Israel also maintained the "right of hot pursuit" into the Area As, in moments when it claimed it needed to arrest a fleeing attacker seeking refuge there. Otherwise, the great majority of the West Bank lands (82.8 percent) that remained under direct Israeli military occupation were categorized as "Area B" (under Israeli "security" authority and Palestinian "civil" control) and "Area C" (under full Israeli authority, both "security" and "civil").

These forms of division of the West Bank and Gaza constituted a "matrix of control"[87] that was erected and imposed by Israel throughout the Oslo era, facilitating the complete immobilization of the Palestinians by controlling key points on the matrix. They thus collectively acted (and continue to act) as a straitjacket pinning in Palestinian communities, preventing them from carrying out any normal social and economic existence. The Palestinian enclaves were enclosed within a network of settlements and their extended "master plans"; major Jewish settler roads to "bypass" Palestinian towns and villages; army bases and industrial parks at key locations; closed military areas; "nature preserves"; control of aquifers and other natural resources; an extensive internal checkpoint system; and control of all border crossings with Jordan and Egypt.

The military legal system in place across the 1967 Occupied Territories also facilitated the further dismemberment of these areas. The planning, permits, and policies in Areas B and C entangled the Palestinian population in a tight web of restrictions, including the zoning of land as "agricultural" in order to freeze the natural development of towns and villages; a system of building permits, enforced by house demolitions, designed to confine the population to its constricted enclaves; land expropriation for (solely Israeli) "public purposes"; licensing and inspection of Palestinian businesses; and prohibition of and restrictions on movement and travel, among others.

In sum, Israel's policies aimed at consolidating its grip upon as much Palestinian land as possible (particularly over strategic mountainous areas, water resources, fertile plains, quarries, etc.), integrating these regions into Israeli infrastructure networks (through 480 kilometers of "Jews only" settlement bypass road, and Israeli electricity and water grids), while using strategic planning as a weapon against the development and integration of Palestinian localities.[88] The subsidies Israel provided to Jewish settlers in the West Bank and Gaza facilitated the doubling of the number of settlers between 1993 and 2000,[89] under both Labor and Likud governments. In this respect the Oslo "years of peace" represented the most escalated settlement drive in the history of the 1967 occupation. The annexation policies were most severe with respect to Jerusalem, which was incorporated into Israel through a massive double ring of settlements that entirely cut the city off from its organic connections to the rest of the West Bank. This transpired in conjunction with Israel's historical policies in the city, which has resulted in the mass revocation of the residency rights of at least 60,000 Palestinians from East Jerusalem since 1967.[90]

But it was not merely Israel's settlement policies that continued during Oslo; its military ones did as well. Although substantial repressive measures were subcontracted out to the newly created Palestinian Authority, at least 364 Palestinians were killed by the Israeli Army or settlers between September 1993 and April 1999, and thousands were detained and imprisoned.[91] Israel also engaged in clear provocations during this period, assassinating important nationalist figures and field leaders—primarily from the Islamist movements, but also from within Fateh.[92] Moreover, the Oslo years witnessed Israel demolishing 740 Palestinian homes, 300 in the area of Jerusalem alone.[93] Needless to say, despite the media spectacle of the "peace process," Israel's oppressive colonialist policies were carried out both before and after Rabin's assassination in November 1995 and were clearly hostile to Palestinian national aspirations to end the occupation—the primary reason why many Palestinians had initially supported the Oslo process in the first place.

The Palestinian Authority

Not by chance, the internal Palestinian setting that developed during the seven "peace years" saw the emergence of a corrupt, authoritarian, and repressive regime in the form of the Palestinian Authority. This was in no unsubtle way the result of the Oslo Accords themselves, a substantial part of which dealt with "security considerations." (In fact no mention of the word "occupation" is found in the Oslo Accords, or in any other Palestinian-Israeli accord.) The former Israeli military and prison headquarters located in every Palestinian city (which in some cases had been the same facilities used by the Jordanian, Egyptian, and British militaries in years past) were now handed over to the PA, while basic Kalashnikov rifles were provided to its security chiefs and their men. Upward of nine different security service apparatuses were established, funded and trained by the

United States and European Union, under the pretext that they were the basis of "building the future Palestinian state." And indeed, for some time, the "strong police force" aspired to under Oslo fulfilled the role designed for it. Political dissenters (primarily Islamists, but also from the Left and even within Fateh itself) were intimidated, censored, imprisoned, and in some cases even killed.[94] Perhaps the worst example of this took place on November 18, 1994, when PA police opened fire on protesters in Gaza, killing fourteen, in events that came to be known as Black Friday.[95]

The security apparatuses, which accounted for 70 percent of public sector jobs, were also accompanied by an oligarchy of economic elites closely tied to the PA and often directly linked to the security chiefs themselves. Together with the neoliberal arrangements created by the Paris Economic Agreement of 1994, a thin tier of Palestinian capitalists, allied to the Israeli upper classes, arose, while creating ripe grounds for political and economic corruption and nepotism.[96]

The majority population of villagers, urban poor, and those who depended upon work in Israel were directly affected by the geographic, political, and economic regime Oslo brought about. "Per capita income fell by 17% between 1994 and 1996. In 1998, the number of people living in poverty—those earning less than $2.10 per day—was 37.2 percent of the population in the Gaza Strip and 15.4% in the West Bank. Unemployment, which before 1993 hovered at 5 percent, soared to over 28.4% in the Occupied Territories in May 1996."[97]

The neocolonial—in fact, the *strictly* colonial—arrangements being erected were directly overseen by repeated delegations of U.S., EU, Israeli, and U.N. representatives and diplomats, who met and courted the security chiefs and economic barons of the PA during Oslo. And not so much as a peep was heard by these forces insinuating "corruption" in the PA. As the veteran journalist Graham Usher would later note, "the PA did not need a 30,000 strong police force to facilitate the economic, social and political development of its 2.6 million people [as designated by the Oslo Accords]. A police force of this size was only needed to keep the lid on a people in the absence of such development."[98]

A Brief History of Retreat

The economic, political, and social decadence of the PA witnessed during the Oslo years was but the final stage in a long line of historical retreats of the PLO beneath Fateh tutelage.

The PLO was initially formed in 1964 as an appendage to Jamal Abdel Nasser's pan-Arabist project, which called for the unification of the Arab world, the liberation of Palestine, and the return of Palestinian refugees. But the early PLO did not embody the self-mobilization of Palestinians inasmuch as it was an attempt by Nasser to contain and control Palestinian political activity taking place throughout the Diaspora. After the defeat of Nasser in the 1967 War, Yasser Arafat and his Fateh movement maneuvered to take over the structure of the PLO and to assert its political independence from the broader geopolitical struggles of the Arab world and Israel.

At this stage, Fateh, like all Palestinian groups, called for the liberation of Palestine and was the first to launch attacks against Israel in 1965. Fateh saw the 1967 Arab defeat as an opportunity to unify the Palestinian people under a single political banner (a reconstituted PLO) and to assert the Palestinian cause as a struggle for national liberation and self-determination, rather than as a "problem" of disparate groups of refugees caught up in the struggles of pan-Arabism. Influenced by the guerrilla struggles of the Vietnamese and Algerian liberation movements, Fateh saw armed struggle as the necessary tool for achieving Palestinian ends. Though it made efforts to establish cells in the West Bank immediately after the 1967 War, they were quickly discovered by Israel (which had the Jordanian intelligence archives), and the PLO was forced to set up bases of operation in neighboring countries.

This forced an important dynamic upon the national movement that would affect it for years to come: how to navigate the complexity of a national liberation movement in diaspora while maintaining its political independence. The PLO needed to organize and train cadres and sought to conduct operations within the political geography of an Arab world whose ruling classes were suspicious of and sometimes hostile to the revolutionary potential of the Palestinian struggle itself, as well as the effect it could potentially have on their own populations. Aware of these tensions, Fateh articulated a strategy that argued that the liberation of Palestine did not require changes in socioeconomic conditions in the Arab world or the (re)building of an anticolonial, pan-Arab movement. This political outlook contrasted sharply with the left wings of the Palestinian movement, which were calling for the incorporation of class and socioeconomic dimensions into the liberation movement and its agenda. But the victory of Fateh's line within the PLO was ultimately consolidated in the amendments made to the National Charter in July 1968. Though seemingly radical in character, the changes actually laid the basis for delimiting the revolutionary potential of the national movement to suit the interests of the Arab and international ruling classes it sought approval from. The Marxist political scientist Gilbert Achcar describes the nature of these changes, using them to show how ultimately the national movement cut itself off from ideas and strategies that might genuinely have had the potential to exert force against Israel and its imperial backers:

> The Charter was made more radical, but in terms of the ideological limitations of Fateh: "Armed struggle is the only way to liberate Palestine." . . . The accent was put on an "armed revolution" of the Palestinian people that the Arab states had a duty to support, notably by giving material aid. The nationalist maximalism that characterized Fateh at the time shows up in the Charter's new Article 21, which rejects "all solutions which are substitutes for the total liberation of Palestine." It combined with an explicit rejection of any inter-Palestinian class struggle perspective or political struggle against the Arab regimes. This sociopolitical conservatism, a meeting ground between the bourgeois PLO and petit bourgeois Fateh, was the essential reason for the support given to Fateh by most of the Arab states. "The PLO shall cooperate with all Arab states," stipulates Article 27 of the charter, it shall not interfere in the internal affairs of any Arab state.[99]

The "meeting ground" Fateh found between its interests and the interests of the Arab regimes was problematic and contradictory. The Palestinian national movement from its inception had been forged within a historical crucible that was based upon and catalyzed by conceptions of pan-Arabism, anticolonialism, and anti-Zionism. However, the reactionary oil-producing states of the Arabian Gulf, from which the PLO received its finances, together with Jordan, where the PLO was based until 1970, were just as much a part of the Western-backed regional order as Israel was. Their dependence upon Western military support for their own survival meant that there were always political conditions set for the PLO's activity and for their continued support for it.

The PLO's policy of "noninterference" in the internal affairs of any Arab state (despite the fact that the Arab states never refrained from intervening in Palestinian affairs) also positioned the national movement on a certain political footing that would expose it to the efforts of Israel to exploit these contradictions. Israel understood that the interests of the Arab ruling classes in maintaining their hold upon power *always* superseded any populist aspiration for the "liberation of Palestine" made by Arab leaders, genuine or otherwise. It thereby forged a policy against the surrounding Arab countries that attempted to force the Arab elites to either curb or destroy Palestinian national activity themselves or to risk losing yet more territory to Israeli expansionism.[100]

Thus, after the events of Black September in 1970, when thousands of Palestinian revolutionaries were massacred at the hands of the Jordanian King, resulting in the PLO's expulsion from Jordan to Lebanon, Fateh cofounder Salah Khalaf articulated the conclusion the movement was forced to draw:[101] "[I]t was only too evident that the Palestinian revolution could not count on any Arab state to provide secure sanctuary or an operational base against Israel. In order to forge ahead toward the democratic, inter-sectarian society that was our ideal, we had to have our own state, even on a square inch of Palestine."[102]

This line of political thought was eventually crystallized at the twelfth session of the Palestinian National Council in June 1974. It was there that the "Ten-Point Program" was adopted, understood to be a "Program of Stages" calling for the incremental establishment of a sovereign West Bank–Gaza state, with Jerusalem as its capital, and the return of the refugees as mere "stages" on the road towards full liberation.

From that point on, the PLO began internalizing a logic of liquidating the liberation essence of the Palestinian movement. Although it was argued that statehood was only the first step in a broader struggle, it was also clear that this would come only at the price of making certain concessions of principle: accepting the colonial partition of Palestine into a Jewish and Palestinian state; implicitly acknowledging the legitimacy of Zionism; accepting the tainting of Palestinian resistance as terrorism; while accepting the regional Arab order (which Palestinian refugees, together with the Arab masses, were forced to live beneath).

Fateh's success in convincing the considerable portions of the Palestinian people to support (or at least not to forcefully resist) such a strategic shift was undergirded by Fateh's domination over the PLO's financial resources and Arafat's undemocratic practices within the organization. The long road to Oslo therefore began, based upon a belief that it was impossible to specifically target Zionism and its alliances with imperialism in principle or to build forces that could do this both in the Arab world and abroad. Instead, Fateh chose to passively acquiesce to this order, because it was "realistic" and conformed with its class view. The false logic of "pragmatism" would tie the hands of the Palestinian movement for decades to come, while cutting it off from its natural organic political constituency.

Said Hammami, one of Fateh's primary ideologues, fleshed out the rationale behind this strategic shift in a telling interview with Moshe Machover, cofounder of the anti-Zionist Israeli socialist organization Matzpen, held in London in 1975:[103]

> We demand the establishment of a Palestinian society, a Palestinian author-
> ity, a Palestinian state on any part of Palestine that we can liberate. . . . This
> would draw the poison out of the hatred [between Palestinians and Israelis].
> This would relax the exaggerated alarm of the Israeli Jews; this would reduce
> the tension among the Palestinians, and then give it time. . . . In ten or fifteen
> years, the Israeli Jews will find out what nice people we are—and I really be-
> lieve in this. They will realize that we are not monsters, but people like them.
> . . . [W]hat is more important than all this is that the progressive organiza-
> tions among the Palestinians and the Israelis will have a much better atmos-
> phere for struggle, for a dialogue.[104]

Hammami's seemingly good intentions naively overlooked the alliances Israel had forged with imperialists, who supported the Zionist
state out of calculated geopolitical considerations and the services it could
render them. It also ignored the deeper workings of Zionist ideology, as
pointed out by Machover in the same interview:

> Opposition to the creation of an independent Palestinian state is a question
> of principle for the Zionist leadership. . . . The entire legitimacy of the exis-
> tence of Israel as a Zionist state has never been based on the right of self-de-
> termination of the Jews who live there, but on the so-called historic right of
> the Jews of the entire world to Palestine. From the starting point, to ac-
> knowledge that another people exists in Palestine who can legitimately lay
> claim to this country would amount to undermining the legitimacy and self-
> justification of Zionism.[105]

The contradictions inherent in the strategic shift of the national movement would be further compounded by resounding failures and deficiencies
in other areas. The petrodollars the PLO received from the Gulf states provided for the creation of an enormous bureaucracy, which, over time, would
develop its own interests and inertia. These interests would increasingly
weigh in on the Palestinian decision making process, surfacing particularly
in times when the national movement was in retreat and aiding in the lowering of the ceiling of the minimum political demands that the PLO would
accept from Israel and the United States. Then there was the inability of
the Palestinian Left to form a genuine independent revolutionary project
(either within or outside the PLO). Though there are many reasons for this
failure,[106] it ultimately resulted in its major factions effectively supporting
the quest for a staged approach, the acceptance of a two-state solution, and
a retreat in the expectation of revolutionary change in the Arab world.

All this should be contextualized within the understanding that the
national movement was entirely unprepared to take up the challenges it
faced upon its (premature) launching immediately after the 1967 War, resulting in it lurching into politically inconvenient circumstances time after

time[107] and sustaining political retreats year after year. The extended accumulation of these factors, together with the context of world forces after the 1990–91 Gulf War, ultimately paved the way for the PLO to accept the Oslo Accords, negotiated in secret.

Oslo was therefore not merely a case of the PLO "selling out" but the unfolding of the limitations and contradictions of the Fateh-led PLO's political worldview, combined with the political bankruptcy of its Left currents:

> The PLO claimed that it represented the interests of all Palestinians. In reality, it has always served the interests of the Palestinian bourgeoisie, especially this class's desire to form its own mini-state through negotiations and compromise with the U.S. and Israel. It has never wanted to rely on mass struggles of Palestinian or Arab masses, which could endanger the stability of both itself and its Arab allies. This fear of mass rebellion from below . . . explains why the PLO has always had a contradictory attitude towards mass struggles. On the one hand, the PLO needs some form of struggle to pressure Israel into making concessions. On the other, it has to constantly try (sometimes unsuccessfully) to keep any such struggles, especially the Intifadas, under its own control.[108]

Oslo and the 1967 Palestinians

The Palestinians in the 1967 Occupied Territories had never been directly exposed to these elements of the diasporic movement and moreover seriously began mobilizing into mass political parties only in the early 1980s, after the PLO's exile from Lebanon to Tunisia in 1982.[109] Although the 1987 Intifada included within it the expression of independent organizing after years of disconnection from the historical leadership of the national movement, its struggle still maintained direct links to the PLO as "the sole representative of the Palestinian people." This demand was legitimate insofar as Israel had tried to create and foster local collaborating elites that were independent of the PLO and did not have a nationalist agenda.[110] But this mantra was also historically abused by the PLO to suppress the unfolding of genuine independent organizing by local actors, disaffected and discontented with the largely defeated and flatulent bureaucracy the PLO had become and its inability to relate or address their concerns. The accumulated degeneration of the Palestinian struggle, witnessed most prominently in the PLO's signing of the Oslo Accords, and the subsequent behavior of the PA between 1993 and 2000, laid the basis for precisely how the Islamic brotherhood movement, and later Hamas, siphoned these energies into itself, thereby striking deeper roots in Palestinian society, where once it had found very little fertile soil.

Thus, with the return of the historical national leadership to territorial Palestine, local political actors were organizationally ill equipped for the extent of the degeneracy that the PLO had undergone in diaspora. They were likewise unprepared to confront the destructive consequences of Oslo upon their social, economic, and indeed national existence.

Within this context, the Palestinian social and political settings under Oslo underwent dramatic shifts. First and foremost, class divisions deepened tremendously, including within the constituencies of the political parties themselves and particularly among Palestinian society's weakest and most exposed sectors: the refugees, villagers, and workers formerly dependent upon employment in Israel. Popular discontent with the negotiated process would also repeatedly manifest itself in outbursts of anger directed against the Israeli occupation[111] and through the repeated demands for political, financial, and organizational reform of the PA. All, however, were repeatedly rebuffed by the PA, often in a hostile manner.[112]

Additionally, it should be noted that the traditional political structures of the Palestinian national movement that existed in the Occupied Territories and were historically tied to the PLO began to witness a process of delegitimization, atrophy, and collapse. These structures, including the traditional political parties (Fateh, the Popular Front for the Liberation of Palestine [PFLP], the Democratic Front for the Liberation of Palestine [DFLP], and the People's Party [the former Communist Party], and their auxiliary organizations, proved themselves entirely impotent or ineffective in countering the destructive consequences of the Oslo process on Palestinian life. While Fateh had largely dissolved and incorporated itself into the PA after Oslo, the Palestinian Left was split between those who supported the Oslo Accords (the People's Party and the Palestinian Democratic Union [FIDA]) and those who rejected them (the PFLP and DFLP). But even the latter were not serious about organizing a counter-Oslo movement. Their demoralization and ideological disorientation after the fall of the Soviet Union were but the last stage in a long process of their own distancing from any radical strategy, leaving them incapable of mobilizing their constituencies around building an alternative to Oslo.[113] Their sociopolitical vision and class consciousness were nebulous at best. Furthermore, the undemocratic nature of the parties themselves and their bureaucratic and nepotistic natures, which alienated new talent and failed to train, educate, and mobilize their constituencies, was a recipe for failure. This left the door open for much of the traditional Left leadership to be co-opted financially and/or politically while the grassroots cadres abandoned their parties en masse. The traditional Left leadership became a form of token loyal opposition to the PA and Oslo, often within the framework of Western-funded nongovernmental organizations (NGOs). Grassroots forces who were members of these parties became atomized, depoliticized, and alienated from their traditional parties and leadership.

Likewise, the full absorption of the mainstream nationalist Fateh party into the PA would also result, over time, in large class and political divisions within its ranks. Although popular discontent with the Oslo process was gradually leading many grassroots Fateh actors into the conclusion that the "peace process" was a prolonged dead end and that it served only to obfuscate the nature of the Israeli occupation while squandering the international sympathies brought about by the mass struggle of the 1987 Intifada, they lacked the resources and the significant political clarity or will to organize outside their mother party, which, for all intents and purposes, was leading these disastrous policies in the form of the PA.

It was primarily Hamas that combined a clear oppositional stance to Oslo within a social and political platform that attempted to both resist Israel and take up the enormous social and class questions that were being left unaddressed by the PA, Fateh, and the Left. Armed with substantial financial resources (something the Left failed to develop other than through grants from Western governments and institutions) and the occasional suicide operation (which harvested the growing anti-Oslo/anti-Occupation frustrations among the Palestinian masses), the political conditions were ripened to affirm Hamas's platform and activities by default and practically irrespective of its religious content.

Israel: Preparing for War Against the Palestinians

The realization that the Oslo solution did not work and that resistance to the Israeli occupation would not stop began at least as early as the latter half of the 1990s, particularly after the events known as the Tunnel Uprising. In September 1996 the Israeli Likud PM Benjamin Netanyahu opened a controversial tunnel that passed beneath the Al Aqsa Mosque compound, which was believed by Palestinians to threaten the integrity of the structures above. More important, however, Palestinians at the time were growing increasingly frustrated with the negotiated process and with Israel's manipulation of it to reinforce Israeli colonial policies. A massive eruption of protests exploded on September 26–27, 1996, in which eighty

Palestinians and fifteen Israeli soldiers were killed. In an attempt to quell the uprising, Netanyahu ordered the use of Apache helicopters and army tanks, providing a harbinger of the military technologies and operational strategies to come when the Al Aqsa Intifada would break out in 2000.[114]

The Tunnel Uprising prompted the U.S. and Israeli military to collude in the creation of a secret plan known as Operation Field of Thorns chronicled the by Zurich-based, anti-Zionist Israeli freelance researcher Shraga Elam in a prescient article published soon after the outbreak of the Al Aqsa Intifada.[115] Elam discloses the plan elaborated by Anthony H. Cordesman, the Middle East "expert" at the influential Center for Strategic and International Studies (CSIS) in Washington, D.C.—an institute with strong affiliations with the CIA.[116] The Field of Thorns Plan aimed at confronting Oslo's inevitable collapse and the uprising it would likely usher in, replacing the Oslo "peace track" with a war strategy of dispossession, elimination, and ethnic cleansing. The detailed operations it recommended the Israeli army carry out, were to serve as provocations to escalate the war against the Palestinians, leading to the elimination of the Palestinian Authority (PA) and the "forced evacuations of Palestinians from sensitive areas."[117] Field of Thorns has been incrementally implemented since September 2000, its tempo depending on green lights from the United States as confirmed by the unfolding of the events since 2000 until the barbaric offensive against Gaza and Lebanon in 2006.[118]

The detailed means recommended in the Field of Thorns operation compiled by Elam include:

• Massive reinforcement of IDF [Israeli Army] troops at points of friction.

• Use of other forces to secure settlements, key roads, and terrain points.

• Use of helicopter gunships and snipers to provide mobility and suppressive fire.

• Use of extensive small arms, artillery, and tank fire to suppress sniping, rock throwing and demonstrations.

• Bombing, artillery strikes, and helicopter strikes on high-value Palestinian targets and punish Palestinian elements for attacks.

• Search-and-seizure interventions and raids into Palestinian areas in the Gaza Strip and West Bank to break up organized resistance and capturing or killing key leaders.

- Selective destruction of high-value Palestinian facilities and clearing of strongpoints and fields of fire near Palestinian urban areas.

- Mobilization and deployment of armored and other land forces in the face of a massive Palestinian rising.

- Use of armor and artillery to isolate major Palestinian population areas and to seal off Palestinian areas, including many areas of Zone A.

- Introduction of a simultaneous economic blockade with selective cut offs of financial transactions, labor movements, and food/fuel shipments.

- Use of Israeli control of water, power, communications, and road access to limit the size and endurance of Palestinian action.

- Regulation and control of media access and conducting a major information campaign to influence local and world opinion.

- Use of military forces trained in urban warfare to penetrate into cities if necessary—most probably in cases where there are Jewish enclaves like Hebron.

- Carrying out "temporary" withdrawal of Israeli settlers from exposed and low-value, isolated settlements like Hebron.

- Arrest of PA officials and imposition of a new military administration.

- Forced evacuations of Palestinian from "sensitive areas."

Cordesman, a well-informed and well-connected Israel supporter, explicitly affirms that the Oslo Accords were inherently incapable of doing justice to the Palestinians and that Israel's stance would not change, thus resulting in continued Palestinian resistance for years to come:

> Even if a peace settlement can now be reached, it will still leave major problems and the near certain threat of at least low-level continuing violence. Any compromise acceptable to both sides must leave Jerusalem and the West Bank deeply divided. Much of the West Bank would remain under Israeli control and at least the greater Jerusalem area would remain open for Israeli settlement. No peace can meet the economic and political expectations of the younger Palestinians for years to come.[119]

However, as Elam notes, since the potential for violence as an integral part of this unjust "solution" exists for a long period of time, and "because Israel is not ready to make any real concessions, or as Cordesman says 'cannot' make them, the CSIS Report puts the Palestinian before a terrible choice between two alternatives: either there must be 'peace with violence' or war."

But since "peace with violence" is conditioned (according to the United States) on a full puppet Palestinian leadership—a role Arafat already refused to play—the war alternative remains the sole "solution" to the continued resistance.

VI. Return to the Original Zionist Strategy: Liquidation of the Palestinians as a People

Indeed, the recognition that the Oslo Bantustan solution did not work and that resistance to the Israeli occupation would not stop facilitated a reversion to the historical Zionist approach of elimination and ethnic cleansing. A pretext, however, was needed to convince the world that forsaking the "negotiations strategy" of Oslo was inevitable.

The Camp David Charade: Creating the Pretext for War

This pretext was supplied by the charade of the Camp David summit in July 2000, which served to paint the Palestinians as "rejectionists." Labor Prime Minister Ehud Barak, together with then U.S. president Bill Clinton, staged the summit in a way that made it look as though Yasser Arafat turned down the "most generous offer submitted by any previous Israeli government."

However, during the months prior to Camp David, Barak had already explicitly admitted that the alternative to rejecting his proposal would be "a bloody confrontation which will bring no gain [to the Palestinians]."[120] Such a perception prepared the ground for a *causus bellum* that would implicate the Palestinians in advance if a conflagration were to arise. It thus laid the groundwork for legitimizing ending the Oslo process and Israel's transition into full-scale war against the Palestinian people.

To justify the strategy of war, which would replace the former approach of political negotiations, Arafat's rejection of the Camp David proposals had to be presented as entailing an "existential danger" to Israel. Thus Israel misleadingly framed this rejection as disclosing a "deep-rooted unwillingness" to accept the existence of Israel and to live in peace with it.

There were, however, no grounds to substantiate this prevailing narrative composed by Barak with the active help of the U.S. administration and international media, on the one hand, and the Zionist Left parties (Labor and Meretz) and Zionist liberals, intellectuals, and academics, on the other. Revelations from the inner circles of both the U.S. and Israeli negotiation teams, published or leaked to the written media, disclosed various aspects of the Camp David fraud as early as 2001.[121] Furthermore, the Israeli daily *Ha'aretz* revealed more such evidence in June 2004, based upon an interview with Amos Malka, head of the General Intelligence Services (Aman) from mid-1998 to the end of 2001—the period in which the Al Aqsa Intifada began.[122] Malka rejects the claim that Arafat refused to recognize Israel, instead affirming that "the assumption [of the General Intelligence Services] was that Arafat preferred a political process, that he will do anything he can to achieve it, and only if he reaches a dead end, will he turn to the alternative of violence. But this violence was only designated to rescue him from the dead end, to motivate international pressure [on Israel] and to receive extra mileage [time]." Moreover, Malka emphasizes that this estimation was expressed in a government meeting in which he warned the Labor PM, Ehud Barak, that Arafat could not accept Barak's proposal, due to be presented at Camp David.

Indeed, Arafat and the PLO had openly recognized "the right of Israel to exist" in 1988 through the acceptance of U.N. Resolution 242 and on many other occasions thereafter when he explicitly adhered to this position in the Oslo framework. Moreover, the symbolic and ideological part of the Oslo Accords, which deals with the mutual recognition between the PLO and Israel and which was the condition for Israel to sign it, implies the PLO's recognition of the Jewish state.[123] What Arafat rejected in Camp David, however, was precisely Israel's attempt to do away with recognizing the right of the Palestinian people to self-determination in an independent state within the 1967 borders.

The "End-of-Conflict" Scheme

Much of the subsequent discussion surrounding the Camp David summit of July 2000 has also ignored the most significant condition that PM Ehud Barak introduced into his proposal, knowing full well that Arafat could not accept it—namely, the demand that the sides sign "a final agreement" accompanied by a Palestinian declaration of "an end to conflict."[124] This stipulation in fact implied that the Palestinians would lose all legal standing for future claims based on U.N. Resolutions, which would be nullified in exchange for the legally binding new agreement. Moreover, Barak specifically demanded that the new agreement legally replace U.N. Resolution 242, which stipulated the withdrawal of Israel to the pre-1967 border,[125] thus negating the basis upon which all prior Palestinian consent to "peace proposals" had been founded—the conception of "land for peace," embodied in U.N. Resolutions 242 and 338, and the implementation of U.N. Resolution 194, calling for the return of 1948 Palestinian refugees to their lands and homes.

However, the demand to "end the conflict" and negate all previous U.N. resolutions not only implied conceding the legal basis for future Palestinian claims, including the right of return. It also functioned as a demand to surrender recognition of the Palestinian cause as embodying the national collective consciousness, memory, and identity of the Palestinians as a people, who were dispossessed from most of their homeland in 1948, not only from certain percentages of territory occupied by Israel in 1967. At its core was the demand to negate the historical anticolonial context and national essence of the Palestinian movement.

Although since 1993, Arafat had traversed a long way in collaborating with the previous U.S.-Israeli "peace proposals," he could not agree to this new demand, which Barak insisted upon as a condition for agreeing to the Bantustan state he proposed at Camp David. For Barak, however, the demand to nullify U.N. resolutions served to redelineate the boundaries of the "Israeli-Palestinian conflict," which the "peace process" had blurred since Oslo—namely, the existential contradiction between Zionism and Palestinian national rights, disclosed by the continuous resistance of the Palestinian people to Israel's attempts to eternalize its occupation, particularly throughout the "peace years."

Thus, the very demand for the explicit declaration of a "final solution" facilitated the opening of a new era in which the slogan that "there is no partner" for peace would end the search for what used to be claimed was a mutually agreeable political solution. It would also usher in a new phase of prolonged war against the Palestinian people aimed at their elimination—socially, nationally, and, as much as possible, physically as well.

The Spark: Reaping the Whirlwind

Given the ripeness of the geo-political setting that had been prepared throughout the Oslo accords and particularly in the wake of the "failed" Camp David summit, with no thanks to the complicity of much of the corporate Western media, all that remained for moving on to the option of total war was the "spark" that would ignite the powder keg. This spark came at precisely 7:30 a.m. on Thursday, September 28, 2000, when Ariel

Sharon, then the chair of the right-wing Likud opposition party, stepped onto the Al Aqsa Mosque compound with two thousand Israeli security force personnel, declaring "I have come here with a message of peace."

Sharon's choice of the Al Aqsa compound was not incidental, nor was it merely a question of "testing Israeli sovereignty over the area." Indeed, Sharon was aware of the significance of the Al Aqsa compound to the Palestinian, Arab, and Muslim world and was certainly aware as to how it had already acted as a lightning rod of popular Palestinian protest, both during the Oslo era (the above-mentioned Tunnel Uprising in September 1996) and previously (particularly in 1990, when nineteen Palestinians were killed there under the government of Yitzhak Shamir in the run-up to the Gulf War).

Days before Sharon's visit, a senior PA negotiator, Saeb Erekat, had been sent as a personal envoy from PA president Yasser Arafat to plead with Ehud Barak to prevent Sharon's well-publicized coming visit. The PA correctly feared that such a provocative measure would ignite the situation on the ground. But the Palestinian protest fell on deaf ears.

The following day (Friday) after Sharon's visit, Israeli police under the jurisdiction of the minister of internal security, Shlomo Ben Ami (of the Labor Party), were sent to surround the compound after the midday prayers. Seven worshipers (including one Palestinian citizen of Israel) were subsequently killed and dozens were wounded in the ensuing yet predictable conflagration. The Al Aqsa Intifada would thereafter spread like wildfire throughout the 1967 Occupied Territories. The forceful reaction to the breakout of the Intifada and Israel's attempts to militarize it, in accordance with the Field of Thorns plan, signified the opening up of the bloody era of Israel's prolonged wholesale war against the Palestinians and the latter's valiant resistance to it, which continues to the present, when these lines are written (October 2006).

Support by Israeli Capitalists

Ehud Barak's all-out war strategy, which was soon continued beneath PM Ariel Sharon (who won the 2001 elections when heading the Likud and later led the new party Kadima in 2006), represented a return to the traditional Zionist approach to the "Palestinian question" of elimination and ethnic cleansing. It was thus a distinct break from the deviation of Oslo's "years of peace," when the Israeli political and military establishment believed that a form of apartheid solution in the 1967 Occupied Territories could indeed be worked out. The renewed war strategy has explicitly been articulated by this establishment, as a continuation of the Zionist struggle of 1948 for Israel's very existence, which the Palestinians refuse to come to terms with. The Zionist Right and Left have closed ranks and supported this war strategy, which has rapidly unfolded under overt U.S. protection and the support of the European Union. Indeed, the U.S. "war on terror" and the occupations of Afghanistan and Iraq have provided the necessary framework for Israel to greatly advance its actions against the Palestinians as the "natural" extension of these policies locally.

The essence of this war is that of elimination—not necessarily a one-time mass expulsion, which nonetheless remains the most preferred approach to solving the "Palestinian question." The current means used to revive Zionism's original extermination and ethnic cleansing approach has amounted to a "silent" ethnic cleansing (or "low-intensity war") through the destruction of the very fabric of social and political life and through daily killings, economic warfare, starvation, and severe restrictions of movement of persons and goods, as well as "removing" populations from areas that have been annexed to Israel.

This strategy gained the support of Israel's capitalists for several reasons.

First, the economic role the 1967 Occupied Territories played for Israeli capital declined greatly because globalization and the end of the Arab boycott after Oslo made the Palestinian market for Israeli exports less relevant. By 2000 the way was opened for Israel to become the high-tech center of the Middle East. Second, global production and imported foreign workers replaced Palestinian workers, since the latter were prevented from entering Israel since the early 1990s due to Israel's closure policies. By then, however, the influx into Israel of cheap Palestinian workers had effectively decimated what remained of Jewish organized labor and its demands. Israeli capitalists have subsequently gained an unprecedented power vis-à-vis Jewish organized labor. The Histadrut, as an organization that had economic and political power, lost even its potential capability to lead struggles for increases in wages and improvements in working conditions.[126] These dynamics served to remove any opposition the Israeli capitalist class may have had in transitioning into the current war strategy. Palestinians finally became truly "unnecessary," just as in the prestate period, and their "exclusion" (i.e., ethnic cleansing) was no longer blocked by any economic considerations initiated by the Oslo peace track.[127]

CHAPTER 1

The Outbreak of the Al Aqsa Intifada and Its Early Development

September 2000–January 2001

Introduction

The Intifada's eruption on September 29, 2000, showed the widely felt need amongst the Palestinian popular classes to reject the apartheid reality created under the Oslo Accords and to dam the corrosive effects of the Oslo process on the Palestinian national movement itself. The widespread willingness of these classes to resist the Israeli occupation and to forge a new reality on the ground capable of achieving their long-denied goals was not, however, matched by the organizational, political, and ideological preparedness of the traditional structures and leadership of the national movement. Unlike those engaged in struggle on the ground, the Palestinian Authority saw the Intifada not as the rejection of the Oslo framework but rather as a tool for improving its conditions. Furthermore, the political and social bodies on the ground associated with the PLO and its constitutive parties, which in years past had acted as the vital organs of the national movement under occupation, particularly during the 1987 Intifada, had so deteriorated and/or become bureaucratized, that they were simply unable to offer any substantial support for or experience to the new currents of political energy to which the Intifada gave birth.

Lacking the structures to determine the Intifada's goals, tactics, or leadership, and within the context of Israel's closure policies and massive killing of unarmed demonstrators, conditions were created for popular experiments in armed operations that represented the nucleus of future guerrilla warfare. These developments, however, would be exploited by Israel to conflagrate the situation on the ground, so as to implement its own planned polices.

Israel's policy of incitement was also directed at the Palestinian citizens of Israel, who had immediately identified with the outbreak of the Intifada in the 1967 Occupied Territories. The killing of thirteen Palestinian citizens in the early days of the uprising was intended as an unequivocal message directed against the process of strengthened national identification of 1948 Palestinians and the desire to challenge their inequality in the Jewish-Zionist state by demanding collective national rights.

The repression of both Palestinian citizens of Israel and those in the 1967 Occupied Territories was in no unsubtle way facilitated by the Zionist Left, which supported Barak's claim that "We have no partner to negotiations," after the failed Camp David summit in July 2000. The path of forsaking the 'peaceful approach' embodied in the 1993 Oslo Accords accumulated ever-greater intensity as years went by, ultimately reaching the level of participating in a united political framework with the right wing and together launching increasingly brutal campaigns against the Palestinian people. The academics, intellectuals, and wide ranks of Peace Now—the largest peace movement in Israel, which supported the Oslo Accords—led by public figures from the left of the Labor and Meretz parties, hurriedly stripped themselves of the virtual liberal identity they had adopted during the Oslo years. They now granted moral legitimacy to the attempts of the Labor-Meretz government headed by Barak to crush both the strengthened nationalism of the Palestinian citizens of Israel and the popular resistance of Palestinians in the 1967 Occupied Territories.

Barak and the Israeli Left were so successful in dehumanizing and vilifying the Palestinians and their leadership in these early days that they blurred the reasons that distinguished them from the Right in the eyes of the Israeli public. The ground was thus prepared for Barak's demise and the coming ascendance of the Likud, headed by Ariel Sharon.

Going Up in Flames

Graham Usher[*]

The "Intifada al Aqsa" ended its first month amid armed Palestinian attacks on Jewish settlements [in the 1967 Occupied Territories] and an Israel poised to "broaden" its [Labor-led] government in readiness for what many are already describing as a long war of attrition. Israel's aim will be to quell the most serious Palestinian revolt in thirty-three years of occupation. The outcome will determine the scale, nature, and terrain of the future conflict. The only certainty is that both are going to be structured by the ruins and realities of Oslo.

The Terminus of the Barak-Clinton "Peace Proposals"— The Sharem el-Sheik Summit

That concept of "peacemaking" probably breathed its last at the Sharem el-Sheikh summit on October 17, 2000—a last-ditch effort born in flames and almost immediately shot down in them.[1] The cause was a massive Israeli escalation of force against the Palestinian Authority (PA) following the killing of two Israeli soldiers by a Palestinian mob in Ramallah on October 12, 2000. In a "limited response," the Israeli Army launched aerial and sea rocket attacks on Ramallah, Gaza, Nablus, Hebron, and Jericho, leaving millions of dollars' worth of damage to property and at least forty-five Palestinians injured, most of them civilians.

Over the next three days a procession of diplomats, U.N. Secretary-General Kofi Annan, EU representative Javier Solana, British Foreign Secretary Robin Cook, and, by phone, Egyptian president Mubarak and King Abdullah of Jordan, prevailed on Arafat to impose some semblance of "calm" on his fractious, outraged people. It was left to President Clinton to plead with Israeli leader Ehud Barak to exhibit even a flicker of interest in "resumed negotiations" with Yasser Arafat, the man he holds responsi-

---

* Graham Usher is a journalist and the author of *Palestine in Crisis: The Struggle for Peace and Political Independence After Oslo* (London: Pluto Press, 1995 and 1997), *Dispatches from Palestine: The Rise and Fall of the Oslo Peace Process* (London: Pluto Press, 1999), and, with John Torday, *A People Called Palestine* (Stockport, UK: Dewi Lewis Publishing, 2001). This article first appeared in *Between the Lines* no. 1, November 2000.

ble for the "violence" in the Occupied Territories and whom he had long buried as a "partner for peace."

But Arafat has only slightly more control over this Intifada than he had over its 1987 predecessor. And Barak was unwilling to do even the minimum to restore some kind of order to the Occupied Territories. Both before and during the [Sharem el-Sheikh emergency] summit [of October 17, 2000] he refused to withdraw Israeli forces from Palestinian civilian areas, lift the siege on the West Bank and Gaza, or accept an international investigation into the causes of the violence. In their stead, Clinton was left to read an unsigned "statement," mouthing platitudes about returning things to "where they stood" on September 28, 2000, before Ariel Sharon decided to demonstrate "Jewish sovereignty" over the Islamic holy sites in occupied East Jerusalem.

Clinton's statement was received by settlers shooting dead a Palestinian near Nablus and Palestinians opening fire on Gilo settlement in East Jerusalem. And a veritable explosion over the weekend of October 21–22, with fifteen Palestinians killed and over four hundred wounded, as clashes and gun battles erupted in Nablus, Gaza, Hebron, Ramallah, Jenin, and Tulkarem. By October 27 the Palestinian toll stood at 142 dead and over 5,000 injured, many of them critically, 77 percent of them from live ammunition wounds to the head and upper body. By way of comparison, this represents 15 percent of all casualties from the 1987 Intifada. The difference is that that Intifada lasted six years. This one has lasted barely a month.

The Sharem el-Sheikh "compromise" [for "calm" and to return things to where they stood before September 28, 2000] was also rejected publicly at a Fateh-led march in Ramallah on October 17 and in a statement issued by the Palestinian National and Islamic Forces (PNIF) the next day. Both described the summit as a "failure" that did not meet the Palestinians' "minimal expectations" and called for a continuation of the "people's peaceful Intifada until sovereignty and independence are achieved." The people heeded the call and ignored the "calm" demanded by the world.

From Popular Intifada to Guerrilla Tactics

The PNIF is an umbrella movement made up of all the factions, laying down a calendar of mass protests and actions similar to the way the Unified Leadership gave form and direction to the 1987 uprising.[2] But there are differences.

The first is that this time the umbrella covers both the PLO factions[3] and the Islamist movements of Hamas and Islamic Jihad. The second is that few dispute that the driving force behind this revolt is Arafat's Fateh movement and particularly its grassroots organization, the Tantheem.[4] "Fateh is manifestly leading the uprising, partly because it has access to the guns and partly because the other factions—including Hamas—have lagged behind the spontaneous actions of the masses," admits Ghazi Hamad, editor of the Islamist *Al-Risala* newspaper.

But the organization of this uprising remains as inchoate and diffuse as Fateh itself, with the direction as much determined by the decisions of local leaders as by any orders from "above," even if the "direction" is determined by senior leaders. For example, on October 19, Fateh activists fired on settlers and a busload of Israeli tourists near Nablus, leaving one Palestinian and one settler dead. Arafat reportedly ordered a cease-fire so that the tourists could be evacuated and dispatched a squad of his police to enforce it. These forces, however, withdrew after being fired on by the Fateh militants, who were then joined by hundreds of Palestinians from Nablus to take up the battle against the settlers.

Insofar as there is strategy behind Fateh's leadership, it has been expressed less by the PA officials than by grassroots leaders like West Bank Secretary-General Marwan Barghouti [see interview with Barghouti below] and the head of Fateh's ideology department, Sakhar Habash. Modeling themselves on the final phase of Hezbollah's resistance in Lebanon,[5] they have described the present revolt as "peaceful civilian protests" combined with "new forms of military actions" against soldiers and settlers in the Occupied Territories. And the longer the revolt continues, the more the second is going to take precedence over the first, if only because of the fractured, cantonized geography Oslo has imposed in the West Bank and Gaza [which will have the effect of localizing oppression and resistance dynamics].

Consciously or spontaneously, this movement is starting to happen, as the armed actions radiate out from attacks on [Israeli] military settlements like Netzarim, implanted in the heart of Gaza, to more guerrillist hits against peripheral settlements such as Gilo near Beit Jala, Pesagot near Ramallah, and Gush Katif in Gaza. In all cases, says Habash, the aim is to "persuade the settlers that they would be safer within the Green Line than beyond it."[6]

Reality Check

It is a drift that Israel is determined to crush, as it braces Israeli public opinion for what could be an extremely bloody showdown with the Palestinians. "Basically the conflict now has become a reality check," says one analyst, who refused to be attributed. "The Palestinians are demonstrating—seven years after Oslo—that they still live under the most brutal occupation. Israel is demonstrating—five months after its withdrawal from south Lebanon—that it cannot be defeated, not militarily, politically or diplomatically."

What results from this clash of wills is anyone's guess. . . . But the Palestinian national consensus is now loud and aired by just everybody from the PNIF to Jibril Rajoub [head of the Preventive Security Services in the West Bank, the apparatus established according to the Oslo Accords, to take over Israel's task of repressing Palestinian resistance]. It involves a commitment to a negotiated solution but only on the basis of international legitimacy and only under a wider "internationalized" umbrella, embracing not only the U.S. but also the U.N., the Arab League, the EU, and Russia.

Given Israel's certain refusal of these terms, there will be enormous public pressure on Arafat either to declare a state or at least to try to realize "Palestinian sovereignty" beyond the military, geographical, and civilian configurations imposed on the Occupied Territories by the "Oslo process" [i.e., beyond the 17 percent of the West Bank designated as Area A under "full" PA control]. Israel's response to such an "abandonment of the peace process" is known. It will impose Oslo by force of arms, "unilaterally separating" from the main Palestinian civilian areas (excluding the settlements within them), blockading the Jordan Valley, and annexing the main West Bank settlement blocs and perhaps also Gaza's Gush Katif bloc.[7]

At that point, it is difficult to see how the Intifada could become anything other than a fully-fledged struggle for independence. The real question is, what would Arab states, the U.N., the EU, and others then do? Would they condemn Israel's unilateral imposition of a "long-term interim agreement" predicated on Palestinians having limited autonomy or perhaps a "state" in about 40 percent of the West Bank and 70 percent of Gaza? Would they use the various and vast diplomatic, economic, and legal instruments they have at their disposal to provide the Palestinians with international protection and insist on Israel's withdrawal to June 4, 1967, lines? Everything about the last twenty-seven years suggests the world would not do any such thing. Everything about the present Intifada and Israel's brutal response to it tells us the alternative is going to be the "Lebanonization"[8] of the conflict within the Occupied Territories and, perhaps, regional war beyond them.

The Tantheem Wild Card*

Toufic Haddad

Sundown, October 7, 2000. Doha neighborhood, just south of Bethlehem. Droves of people have been making their way up this dilapidated hillside to pay their respects to the family of Mustapha Fararjeh (22), shot and killed two days earlier from a nearby Israeli military position. Some say he was just in the wrong place at the wrong time. Others maintain that he was throwing rocks at settlers' cars on the nearby bypass road. His family receives the convoys of many of the 30,000 well-wishers who participated in his funeral procession the day before.

A group of twenty-five masked men march into the funeral tent. Some are dressed in army fatigues, while others wear vests with military accoutrements. Most brandish M16 automatic rifles while some carry less traditional sawed-off automatic weapons. They pay their respects to the family and make a short but fiery speech about how the martyr's blood has not been spilled in vain and his death shall be revenged.

These men represent the Tantheem, the Fateh-based paramilitary group whose Arabic name means "the Organization." Many of the recent exchanges of fire that the Occupied Territories have witnessed and that the international media have been keen to report (as though there were a semblance of equal forces squaring off) have been attributed to them. Israel has repeatedly laid blame on the Tantheem for the "cycle of violence" and called upon the PA to disarm it. Yet these demands are little more than bluff: Israel, as well as the PA, knows that disarming it is impossible as its members are the rank and file of Arafat's primary constituency.

Who Are the Tantheem?

The emergence of the Tantheem on the Palestinian scene is quite recent, dating back to the 1994 arrival of the PA in the Occupied Territories. It was then that the establishment of the PA came hand in hand with the establishment of an elaborate security and intelligence network—a precondition Israel made in the Oslo Accords. During an August 30, 1993, Knesset speech [two weeks before the signing of the Accords], then Is-

---

* This article first appeared in *Between the Lines* no. 1, November 2000.

raeli Prime Minister Yitzhak Rabin called upon the creation of "a reality whereby internal Palestinian security will be in Palestinian hands. . . . They will rule by their own methods, freeing—and this is most important—the Israeli Army soldiers from having to do what they will do."[9]

Had Rabin lived longer [he was assassinated by a right-wing Israeli in November 1995], he would have been proud of his own forethought when it was fully actualized. The PA gladly collected the Intifada-tested ranks of the West Bank and Gaza Fateh movement into its myriad security services. In fact, the PA security services accounted for 70 percent of the public-sector jobs and were dominated by Arafat-loyal strongmen.[10] The role of the security services involved several tasks, most important of which was the maintaining of the political (then largely Islamic) opposition in check. But their work also involved following up on known Israeli collaborators, monitoring the black-market arms trade, and keeping tabs on criminal activity. The Fateh cadres newly inducted into the PA security services were prime candidates for accomplishing this task, given their knowledge and experience of the local scene. Occasionally, however, the nature of their work, together with the lack of serious accountability within the Fateh family, led to many of their personnel becoming involved in the arms and stolen-car trade themselves.

The significance of these forces began to shift with the visible decline of the "peace process," beginning during the tenure of Benjamin Netanyahu (Likud) in 1996. Fateh cadres found it increasingly difficult to defend themselves against popular accusations that the PA was performing poorly at the negotiations table and at the same time was becoming perceived as corrupt abusers of power on the street. Furthermore, the national conscience of many Fateh cadres was becoming infused with a sense that there was something drastically wrong with the political trajectory of the PA. During the Jebel Abu Gheneim/Har Homa settlement crisis in March 1997,[11] an emergency session of Fateh's Higher Committee was held in the town of Beit Sahour [near Bethlehem]. The Fateh general-secretary in the West Bank, Marwan Barghouti, commented after the meeting that "Many Palestinians—including from inside Fateh—are questioning whether we made the right choice of peace with Israel. . . . At the Beit Sahour conference some Fateh cadres called for a return to the armed struggle. This was not the majority view—but there were voices, and we cannot ignore them."

Barghouti himself began calling for drastic changes in PA tactics as early as this same crisis: "We are demanding that the PLO cease all nego-

tiations with Israel. We are also calling for an end to all security cooperation between Israel and the PA. We cannot and will not defend Israel's security unconditionally."[12]

This was the nest within which the Tantheem was born. The Tantheem became the populist front of the Fateh rank and file, many of
whom constituted the PA security services, but also many of whom had
budding concerns that the PA strategy impeded rather than aided Palestinian national interests. By projecting a radical image as the defenders of
national rights and armed with the guns at their disposal, the Tantheem
were able to put a wedge between the popular perception of Fateh being
indivisible from the PA.[13] Along the way, they were able to clarify the divisions within Fateh between those who were loyal to the Palestinian
cause and those who defended PA corruption. Their participation in
demonstrations—be it during local nonviolent events (predating the outbreak of the Al Aqsa Intifada) or more recently as active participants in
armed clashes with Israel—has gained a cautious respect from the Palestinian masses. Still, however, looming in the back of popular consciousness is the understanding that Fateh was also responsible for the tragedy
of Oslo. In this sense, the demonstrations raging throughout the Occupied Territories are Fateh's redemptory trial by fire, in an attempt to realign itself in the camp of the Palestinian masses.

The Tantheem Leadership

The Tantheem is unofficially led by Marwan Barghouti, though it is well
known that the fractious nature of the security services is also reflected in
its own organization.[13] The overwhelming majority of Tantheem cadres
are also highly influenced by local heroes of the 1987 Intifada within areas
where Fateh has been historically strong. The important distinction to be
made here is that the Fateh rank and file prefers to give its allegiance to
local, well-known leaders from the Occupied Territories, as opposed to
those who returned with the PA following the Oslo agreement.

It is also important to note that because of the loosely knit nature of
the Tantheem, it is not as though it can be "turned on or off," as Israel implies when it demands that the Palestinian Authority "stop the Tantheem." One leader in Ramallah might call for a calming of the situation,
while another in Gaza might call for its escalation.

The current explosion of events across the Occupied Territories
brought the Tantheem to a crossroad. When Marwan Barghouti con-

firmed in 1997 that there was "not a majority" of "voices" within Fateh who called for armed struggle, he was speaking in an age when wide swathes of the Palestinian people were only beginning to awaken to the inability of the Oslo process to address their historical rights. Three and a half years later, a crystallized popular consciousness has demanded alternatives. The Tantheem represents part of that alternative, and it is extremely significant that it emerges from perhaps the last significant remaining constituency within Palestinian society that defended the Oslo "peace process." Thus, the PA lacks the power to squelch demonstrations particularly because its own constituency (Fateh and the Tantheem) has taken that power away from it.

Since the Intifada's eruption, Barghouti has acted as its self-appointed spokesperson, giving countless interviews, advocating the observation of general strikes, and calling for the boycott of Israeli products, an end to joint Israeli-Palestinian patrols (which had been in operation since the arrival of the PA in 1994), popular participation in solidarity demonstrations, and the blocking of settler bypass roads.

His ascension to the forefront reflects his own acumen in reading the Palestinian political map in the Occupied Territories. Barghouti appreciates that the Palestinian people will not accept a return to the humiliating cycle of negotiations before the Intifada broke out. Furthermore, he recognizes the vacuum of power that exists in the succession of the aging Arafat. His past as a known Fateh student leader at Birzeit University who was deported before the 1987 Intifada, together with his firebrand rhetoric during the recent events, positions him well as a Palestinian leader, especially when compared with the coterie of Arafat sycophants despised even within Fateh.[14]

More than anything, the emergence of the Tantheem during the Al Aqsa Intifada is an indication of a trend of internal questioning within Fateh. What was once the PA's subcontracted strong arm has now evolved into a wild card that threatens Israel, the PA, and indeed the unity of Fateh. Marwan Barghouti knows that when he calls for a boycott of Israeli products, it is the PA that has been the foremost importer of such products through its private monopolies. Israeli political commentators have recognized such splits and bicker about whether the situation is part of a larger Arafatist plan or whether Arafat is indeed powerless. In many senses, whether Arafat supports or opposes the radicalization of the Tantheem is irrelevant: for him or anyone else to attempt its subduing would mean political suicide.

Changing the Rules of the Game

An Interview with Marwan Barghouti, Secretary-General of Fateh in the West Bank*

Toufic Haddad

One enters the Fateh Central Headquarters building in El Bireh (near Ramallah) hardly expecting it to be so dilapidated. Its dingy stairs cause one to ponder the suggestions of Israeli media pundits who figure this top-floor apartment to be one of the central headquarters of current events in the Intifada. It has taken no fewer than eight telephone calls advising "to call back later," before the promise of a half-hour interview with Marwan Barghouti is finally granted. The "close aide" (read: bodyguard) who confirms this information does so over a telephone connection that is so clearly tapped that one can virtually hear the convergence of several intelligence gathering agencies fighting for their ears at the speaker.

As the secretary-general of Fateh in the West Bank and the man identified as the political spokesman for the Fateh paramilitary grouping Tantheem, Marwan Barghouti remains somewhat of a mystery. How much of a genuine challenge to the current Palestinian political regime and how much power he actually commands is not quite known. It is, however, clear that one can hardly ignore his presence on the political map in the wake of recent events.

Three young men walk into the office helping a fourth who limps in on crutches. They look at the foreign journalists waiting in line for their turn to see Barghouti and begin to speak in Arabic among themselves:

---

* Marwan Barghouti is from the village of Kobar near Ramallah. A former student leader of Fateh at Birzeit University, he was exiled to Jordan in 1987 and was permitted to return to the Occupied Territories only in 1994. He has since acted as the secretary-general of Fateh in the West Bank. In 1996, he was elected to the Palestinian Legislative Council for the district of Ramallah. In April 2002, he was arrested by the Israeli Army, after which he was tried, convicted, and sentenced to five life sentences. Barghouti refused to recognize the court's legitimacy and demanded instead that "the occupation be put on trial." On November 30, 2004, Barghouti declared himself a candidate for the Palestinian presidential elections, challenging fellow Fateh candidate Mahmoud Abbas (Abu Mazen). He subsequently retracted his nomination before elections took place after coming to a political understanding with Abu Mazen, who went on to become PA president. This article first appeared in *Between the Lines* no. 4, February 2001.

"I'm thinking about going to the press about this if things aren't resolved." When I ask what the problem is and what they are doing here, one of them explains: "We are from a village outside Ramallah [in Area C, under full Israeli control]. Over three weeks ago there were clashes with the [Israeli] Army, and our friend here [the one on crutches] got shot. We carried him through the valley to get him to the main road so we could get him some medical attention. We suspected the army already wanted us, and indeed soon after we came to Ramallah we heard that they had raided our homes and beat our family members to see if they knew where we were. We are now stranded in Ramallah without a place to stay, without money, and we don't even know whether we will be able to return to our village. Every time we go to the PA for help, they tell us to 'go talk to so and so,' or they simply lie and say that 'things are in process.' We decided to turn here. They say Barghouti can help."

Barghouti keeps himself tucked away in a secluded part of the office, sitting in front of a massive picture of the Dome of the Rock and gradually taking in the long line of each day's visitors. Assistants are constantly whispering things in his ear, handing him mobile phones, or changing the satellite television station so that he can time himself better when doing a live interview. His answers to most questions are well-versed sound bites that speak to the person in the street. In fact, it is difficult to get Barghouti to switch out of sound-bite mode and even more difficult to get him to concentrate on one thing at a time. Amid constant interruptions, this interview was carried out in an effort to gain insight into what Marwan Barghouti is all about.

Q: What are the goals of the Intifada?

A: The goal of the Intifada is to put an end to the Israeli occupation. This is a very clear goal, and there is consensus on that to mean independence. . . . The Intifada will not stop until there is an end to the occupation of the entire Occupied Territories and the establishment of an independent Palestinian state on 1967 borders.

Q: What is your strategy for achieving this goal?

A: To continue the Intifada, meaning the resistance of the occupation by all means. It is the shortest way to achieve independence and to make the Israeli occupation pay a high price. Eventually Israeli public opinion will change its mind. This is our strategy: to fight.

Q: Do you feel the Palestinian people are prepared for this?

A: Yes, absolutely. The leadership is not prepared, but the people are prepared.

Q: In what way do you find the leadership not prepared?

A: I don't think they put enough efforts, abilities, and power into this Intifada.

Q: What do you think should be the balance between negotiations and diplomacy on the one hand and the Intifada on the other?

A: We are not against negotiations in general because we do believe that at some point, we will reach the stage where we will have to negotiate. But we do not believe in negotiations on the same basis as they have been operating for the last seven years.

I think this Intifada asked to change the rules of the game, and it did this. First of all, everyone has to understand and recognize the condition that in order for the negotiations to be a success, there is a need for the continuation of the Intifada and the resistance. There will not be any fruit of these negotiations unless this Intifada continues. Second, there is a need to again put U.N. resolutions on the table and not to get caught up in meaningless details [in negotiations] about this street here and that corner there. As far as I am concerned, all we have to talk about is the timetable for the implementation of the U.N. resolutions. Finally, we have to change the sponsorship of the talks. We should not leave the Americans alone [as "facilitators" of negotiations]: they are not fair, they are not honest.

Q: Yet the PA went directly back to negotiations [in Taba in January 2001][15] on the basis of the exact same conditions that existed before.

A: Unfortunately. They are wasting a historical opportunity to correct the direction of negotiations. Still, however, we feel that the chance is still there [to change the rules].

Q: What does that say about the ability of the PA to represent the people?

A: I think every leadership has to deal with the people's opinion. And in general, throughout the Arab world, leaders ignore their public's opinion. In this, the PA is a little better than the Arab regimes, but not by much....

It [the PA] tried to achieve independence, and it failed. Now the Intifada has broken out. I believe it has to change its mind and play by a new set of rules. Unfortunately, it has not done this till now. Partially, it deals with the Intifada and its demands, but it is not enough. We will judge a final agreement by whether it fulfills Palestinian national aspirations or not and will consider any agreement that violates Palestinian red lines as an illegitimate agreement.

Q: In this light, how important is democratization of the Palestinian national movement in achieving national aims?

A: I think a very important relation links the two. Since the Oslo agreement, and when I took up my position as secretary-general of Fateh in the West Bank in 1994, we started the process of democratizing our institutions [Fateh]. During the first twenty-seven years of Israeli occupation, most of our activities were underground and secret, so the process of democratization could only come after Oslo [when the Israeli Army withdrew from the major Palestinian cities]. We have so far succeeded in convening 172 local conferences, representing more than 120,000 Fateh members throughout the West Bank. For the first time, these people elected their own leaders as well as their local committees. This was an effort toward hosting a national conference that we plan on having. Unfortunately, the Central Committee and leadership of Fateh are not satisfied with this idea, because it would mean that new leaders from a new generation will come to power.

I believe democratization is part of our struggle for independence and must be used as a means to strengthen our organizations. All political factions must begin this process, though I acknowledge that this is still not enough.

Q: Do you feel it is time for general elections to be held to get a more representative national leadership?

A: Right now I think it would be technically difficult to have elections. One month ago, though, we did call for an Intifada government. This means allowing all Palestinian factions that are united (and this is the first time they are all working together on the ground) to have representatives that will formally adopt the Intifada as the policy of the government. This is a good solution until we are somehow able to have general elections, which we will of course support.

Q: What was the response from the PA to your calls for an Intifada government?

A: It criticized and refused this, but the people have welcomed the idea.

Q: This seems to be the situation that we are always in?

A: Yes, it's stalemate.

Thus an Apartheid Regime Develops

Azmi Bishara[*]

It seems that recent events are leading to the completion of a comprehensive apartheid regime within the borders of Israel as well as in the 1967 Occupied Territories. With regards to the security forces' behavioral patterns, the Green Line has been blurred. The police forces have clearly institutionalized two different ways of oppressing demonstrations, as well as two different forms of imprisonment and detention—one for Jews, the other for Arabs. Hand in hand with this are the entire Israeli media, which have been mobilized for the benefit of the security forces to incite the Jewish community against the Arab one—defining it as the enemy. The representatives of the Israeli Left are tongue-tied. The majority of the Israeli public (as revealed by the polls) express understanding with mobs that attack Arabs in Israel, thus creating the conditions for the establishment of a full-fledged apartheid regime.[16]

All at once, the secondary contradictions within Israeli society, together with its party divisions, became irrelevant. All contradictions have withdrawn to the background because of the "Arab problem." It turns out that when the state is not a state of all its citizens, equality becomes a mere illusion and maybe even a fraud. When a policeman is confronted with a demonstrator who is a Palestinian citizen, he does not use "discriminating means" to control him; he simply behaves toward him as an enemy.

The fact is that every time Arab citizens were murdered in Israel, the Left, or the so-called Left, was in power and the Right was in opposition:

---

* MK Dr. Azmi Bishara is a Palestinian citizen of Israel and leads the National Democratic Assembly Tajamu' Party in the Israeli Knesset. He frequently writes for *Al Hayat* (London) and *Al Ahram Weekly* (Egypt). This article first appeared in *Between the Lines* no. 1, November 2000.

the massacre at Kufr Qassem (1956)[17] and Land Day (1976),[18] together with the recent events—all took place under Labor governments. This so-called Left has always backed the security forces, strengthening them and abandoning the Arab citizens and the notion of citizenship in general. For years Arab citizens have been complaining about the conduct of police commanders of the Northern Districts, Alik Ron, but nobody in the Left would listen. The minister of interior security [in the Labor government headed by Ehud Barak], Professor Shlomo Ben Ami, embraces him and gives him his complete backing. The recent demonstrations inside Israel, in which fourteen people[19] were killed and hundreds of youngsters were wounded, are not the first in which shooting took place in recent years. There have been demonstrations in Al Ruha, Um Al Sahali, and other places. Though hardly any demonstration in the Arab sector manages to pass without shooting [from the Israeli police], all remains quiet in Israel. The recent events are not a turnabout but a case in which quantity has changed into quality. All this time the Israeli Left did not exist. There was complete silence at the time of the shooting in Lydd, where I personally was wounded.[20] Furthermore, no sound was uttered when Police Commander Alik Ron used violence toward demonstrators protesting against the implementation of Israel's house demolition policy [of houses of Palestinian citizens of Israel].

It is the paternalism of the Israeli Left that leads it again and again into arrogant conduct. Not only does it hold the wrong positions, but— and here as opposed to the Right—it also expects the Arabs to accept these positions. That is why the Left becomes disappointed and angry whenever Palestinians in Israel come out to the streets in protest for their rights, and that is why they look for "agitators" to pin the blame on. We, who support equal citizenship and liberal positions; we, who are struggling for a civil-democratic line of equality, have suddenly become "extreme agitators" against the state of Israel.

Israeli liberalism is shocked only when a right-wing mob sets out to kill Arabs. It so happened that the Left awoke only after the massacre in Nazareth during the October events. It started with a Jewish mob from Nazareth-Ilit [Jewish Upper Nazareth, built on lands confiscated from the adjoining, Arab Nazareth] running wild but ended with brutal violence against Arabs on the part of the police. The only thing that the Left did was to organize a delegation to visit the bereaved families. However, it is unacceptable that the Left become a representative of one clan that comforts the other. The brutal behavior demonstrated toward Arab citizens reflects the same values that enable such unrestrained brutality in the Occupied Territories. The same goes for the absolute silence and even the explicit support of the Zionist Left, of all the steps taken by the Security Forces—a silence that continues even in the face of more than a hundred killed and thousands wounded in the recent demonstrations in the Occupied Territories. Also there, the events started in the wake of the police action when they fired without any justification at people who were praying at the Al Aqsa Mosque.[21]

These unprecedented brutal steps, to which the use of helicopters and tanks was later added, won general agreement among the Israeli public—fully accepting the Israeli version of the peace process and the reasons for the failure of the talks in Camp David ("We have no partner for peace") and the behavior of the army in the Occupied Territories.

Both inside and outside the Knesset, we [NDA—Tajamu'] said that Barak's program, which was celebrated at the time of his victory in the last elections [May 1999] cannot be a basis for peace. We reiterated this position before Barak left for Camp David and naturally after it. So why does the Left seem so surprised? What is indeed surprising is the surprise of the Left, which continues to be addicted to the wrong information and to images of images. But nobody wanted to listen because everybody [in the Zionist Left] was so pleased that [Benjamin] Netanyahu [then head of the Likud party] had been beaten in the [1999] elections. Instead, the Zionist Left strengthened the anti-Arab line. The Zionist Left gambled on a peace based on the existing relation of forces and did not set up principles of justice and equality. That is the reason it did not confront Israeli public opinion on the terms for a just peace and, instead of criticizing Barak's initiative, supported and aided the accusation made against the Palestinians who opposed an agreement based on an apartheid state, divided into cantons.

The Left, with the "security" argument written on its flag, brought militarists to power and did not give one thought to the significance of the "political" steps taken by them in the last months. Today we are witness to the results of this attitude. And all this is taking place after no voice was raised throughout the previous year against the policy of massive settlements, against house demolition, against the expulsion of people from their homes, and against continuing restrictions on movement and labor [in the 1967 Occupied Territories]. These processes were beyond Barak's government's areas of interest in its first year. This also was the case with the question of Syria and Lebanon: it was possible to withdraw from Syria and Lebanon with a peace agreement.[22] But the Israeli Left celebrated the unilateral retreat of Israel from Lebanon [which took place in May 2000] instead of exerting pressure on [Prime Minister] Barak, who constantly ignores any moral criticism of his program, to achieve a comprehensive agreement.

I view the war that Israel declared on the Palestinian Authority as the continuation of the same policies [it carried out in the past], now implemented by different means. That has been the political trend of Barak from the beginning. It boils down to the ultimatum that Barak gave the Palestinians [at Camp David]: either everything or nothing—either Arafat immediately puts his signature to Barak's conditions for a final status agreement, concerning the "Four Nos" as he had presented them since his election campaign—or nothing, namely war. These four principles include: no to Palestinian sovereignty over East Jerusalem, no to a withdrawal to the June 4 [1967] borders, no to the dismantling of settlements (with 80 percent of the settlers under Israeli sovereignty), and a definite no to any debate concerning the right of return or any just solution to the refugee question. That is the reason that the popular uprising was so predictable. The non-"moderate physical pressure"[23] now being exerted on the Palestinian population, including threats on the life of Arafat, is a continuation of the diplomatic pressure that began after the [failure of the] Camp David summit. Barak and his supporters were pleased with his diplomatic achievements and with his success in presenting Arafat as the recalcitrant one who refuses to accept his "generous offers." They were convinced that they would be able to force an agreement on the Palestinians. Very few joined us during those months when we tried, time and again, to make it clear that no Palestinian would accept such an ultimatum and that this was a dangerous policy that would lead to war. Sharon's rush to Al Aqsa Mosque with the consent of Barak is only a small detail in these happenings.

We have always said that there are three possibilities for an agreement. The first is a two-state solution, namely, the establishment of a Palestinian state within the borders of 1967, including Jerusalem, without the settlements. The second possibility is that of a comprehensive solution of living together in one democratic state. The third is an apartheid reality. Anyone who refuses to accept one of the first two solutions consequently leads to the third—apartheid. The Israeli Left did not really accept the principle of two states. What it supported was an agreement based on cantonization of the Occupied Territories. On the other hand, it is still shocked by the very possibility of one shared democratic state, based on national and citizenship equality. Therefore, it itself is leading to apartheid, namely, it practically supports the third option although it calls it a Palestinian state.

The obvious conclusion that the Israeli Left has to draw from these recent events is not to indulge in a kind of hypocritical and beautified despair but to begin a real soul-searching and self-criticism. In this context, we call upon the Israeli Left to regain control and express determinedly its objection to the government's policy, to struggle against apartheid, against the systematic oppression of the Palestinian population, and against Barak's "peace plan." The principles of this policy will only worsen the situation and bring about its escalation. It is not enough simply to call "the two sides to the discussion table." The Left must clearly declare the set of morals and values needed for any agreement.

Not only will the Israeli Left have a lot to do. Both in the Arab world and in [Palestinian] society, many missions await us. The declaration of war on a whole nation has left us with scorched earth, which enables an irrational political discourse to take over, sometimes that of a religious war. This discourse has not yet chosen the colors with which the national uprising will be painted, but such a danger is looming, mainly in public opinion and in parts of the Arab media. The national and democratic forces in Arab society must not ignore these phenomena. Difficult as it may be, we must tackle them even during the most painful process of decolonization.

Gender, Class, and Representation in the Al Aqsa Intifada

An Interview with Eileen Kuttab[*]

Q. What can explain the limited role that women are playing in the present Intifada?

A. This Intifada is limited to direct confrontations on military barricades

---

[*] Eileen Kuttab is a longtime left activist in the women's movement and the director of the Women's Studies Center at Birzeit University. This article first appeared in *Between the Lines* no. 3, January 2001.

on the borders of major cities where Area A [under PA control] meets Area B or C [under Israeli control]—places where refugee women cannot go, and where village women are not located. The geographic location of the confrontation makes a big difference—it's not that women don't want to struggle. It also has unfolded into a guerrilla war, which itself limits the role of women.

Recently, however, we see that more women are getting involved in confrontations, including students and village women. But this is only a mere shadow of what they were in the previous Intifada.

Q: Does the women's movement participate as a movement in this Intifada?

A: After the first Intifada, the women's movement lost its connections to the grass roots. In the early 1990s and especially after Oslo, women's issues became institutionalized, professionalized, and NGOized. The political parties [which supported and were linked to women's initiatives in the 1987 Intifada] declined and collapsed. This resulted in an overall sense of a political vacuum that women—as other social sectors—have experienced. Recently, the Women's Technical Affairs Committee [WTAC—an umbrella of women's committees and professional organizations] held a meeting in which they were asking how they could participate in the Intifada and be effective. But the problem is that they [the women's organizations] have separated women's issues from the political and national issues, which in turn deepens their marginalization from the grassroots struggle.

Because the women's movement has lost its ties with the grass roots, not to mention the political parties, they are not able to mobilize women from wider strata on issues of concern to most women. WTAC is more of a bureaucratic leadership that promotes campaigns, hosts delegations of solidarity, holds press conferences, and tries to help families of martyrs in different ways. However, when these NGO women want to go to a village and talk about women's mobilization, they have great difficulty. The people are depressed and frustrated; they see corruption all over and identify these [NGO] women as an elite. They therefore challenge their capacity to speak with them [the village women] about their problems and advise them what to do to solve them. Most intellectuals and political activists in NGOs have become detached professionals who cannot represent people and their issues.

I have repeatedly said that the issue of class is becoming more and more of a variable in the national struggle. In the past the class issue was never a clear category of separation between the masses in the national struggle. When we used to talk of national liberation and the national movement, there was a kind of a unity among us. Now, how can you build unity when [since the establishment of the PA] a certain elite has been promoted with privileges and benefits and when the class interests of these elites are even defining and determining the scope of national rights? This is a major problem.

I couldn't even participate in the conferences and panel sessions that I have been invited to speak at by various NGOs. How can I approach the people? And what do I tell them? It's very embarrassing, because we intellectuals are not doing anything for the Intifada. I don't even know how to define myself anymore. It is clear that in times of uprising, one's identity can be defined only through one's role and participation in the people's struggle. At present, we don't have that.

Q: What you are talking about in the women's movement is reflective of wider phenomena throughout the Palestinian "civil society sector." How was it possible to get to this stage? Why did Palestinian "civil society" so easily become a self-serving enterprise that lost its popular basis and legitimacy?

A: I believe the problem is structural and ideological. Funding now is becoming increasingly conditional on the bureaucratization and "professionalization" of the NGOs. Among other things, there is constant emphasis on "transparency," "accountability," and so on. This means that in order for any organization to receive funding it must be an institution with relatively sophisticated mechanisms to ensure these things. These imposed structures promote a self-serving elite that can barely relate to people's issues or empower people unless they are run by activists who are very class conscious.

Now, because the political parties have collapsed, especially the Leftist parties, and their ideology has also been shaken, many people are embarrassed to address the class dimension as a clear category of analysis. The elite claims that this analysis [in terms of class] will compartmentalize people and that now is not the right time to do it. In my opinion, however, this is a necessity. The "human rights" approach (of most Palestinian NGO activity) is not enough in our case. Because if we look at things closely, we realize that even the national issue has become compartmentalized and divided into unequally distributed privileges. How, then, can you neglect the issue of class as a valid concept? In this context, gender is very related to class, because when we are talking about women, we must ask ourselves who are the women we are talking about and what kind of issues we should promote in order to address their needs.

Another main factor resulting in the loss of the women's movement's connection to the grass roots is the links it forged with the PA: women's NGOs changed their agendas to address policy makers and to promote women's rights as part of "democratic governance." To do that, you have to present your views and positions in a way acceptable to the PA. Oftentimes, because you become obsessed with women's issues and rights in a lobbying forum, you become alienated from the people you are supposed to be representing. When you target policies, you target "state" institutions and their hierarchy. And the women's movement keeps forgetting that when seeking any serious changes in any policy, it needs genuine popular input to be the pressure group from the bottom of the pyramid.

Q: If this is indeed what the current situation demands—that the women's issue return to the grass roots and that there be no separation between gender and national issues—how can you do this when you already have admitted the isolation of the women's movement in institutionalized elitist NGOs?

A: The main thing women need to do is to go back to the political parties. The opposition democratic parties must prove themselves now, or they will be forgotten by their constituencies. These parties need to go back to their people and mobilize them on all the different issues—not just the political issues, but also the democratic issues. The left parties have a large role to play at this stage as a real opposition. They need to control the national agenda so that no marginalization of the core issues like the right of return is permitted. But at the same time they have to exert pressure to implement equal redistribution of resources and stop the trend of increasing marginalization of the poor, peasants, workers, and women in a dependent economy linked to Israel and global markets.

Q: Can the parties do this in their present state?

A: The parties themselves are there, though I can't really say that they are functional. . . . After the Intifada erupted, there was a wave of seminars and workshops that took place. The first one, I believe, was held by Muwatin [the Palestinian Institute for the Study of Democracy] and had a full hall. All the intellectuals in the West Bank attended because they wanted to see what they had to do and sought to share the analysis and discourse about what is happening, largely because they found themselves in a dilemma of having no structure or tool to mobilize them. This means that these people have not lost their commitment to the Palestinian issue. But most of them are out of political parties at this stage. They are waiting for somebody to take their hand and guide them onto the right path. The problem is that regaining a structure that is purely PFLP or DFLP [the two main Palestinian left factions][24] is not going to happen. It will more likely take the form of building a democratic bloc that can bring together all the people who share some basic concepts and principles that will become the basis for future work.

We always used to say that we wanted a state. But we don't want any state. We want a democratic state because we have struggled for a long time now and people deserve to be rewarded with good governance. We also used to say that that we would not follow the path of the Algerian women, who, after liberation, went "back to the kitchen" and are now suffering the consequences of an oppressive fundamentalism that has demolished their achievements. We were very clear with what we wanted, but the question is "Why are we losing it now?"

We need a democratic bloc to put forward a program. This cannot be done alone. We must start from the basics because people have lost confidence not only in the PA but also in the political parties, not to mention the various social movements as well as the women's movement. That is why there is a need to rebuild the consciousness and confidence of the people, and this will take time. It's not something that can be solved by simply going to a seminar room for a workshop.

No Substitute for a Popular Uprising

Salah Abdel Jawwad[*]

On November 5, 2000, an open panel session on recent developments in the Intifada was held in Ramallah, sponsored by Muwatin, the Palestinian Institute for the Study of Democracy. The event was well attended by wide sectors of the academic, political, and community leadership of

---

* Dr. Saleh Abdel Jawwad is a professor of history at Birzeit University and lives in El Bireh in the West Bank. This article first appeared in *Between the Lines* no. 2, December 2000.

Ramallah and Birzeit University, as well as members of the National Democratic Assembly (Tajamu') Party from inside Israel. The following article is an edited transcript of the presentation of Saleh Abdel Jawwad, a history professor at Birzeit University.

We are presently engaged in a battle of such gravity without really knowing what we want: What is our strategy? Do we have a plan or not? What are we going to do with the economic situation? What is the Israeli strategy? This lack of knowledge is not only limited to major and strategic matters but also includes simple and tactical aspects as well. We must confess to our own lack of knowledge.

Lessons of the Past: The Militarization of the Intifada

The important lesson we should learn from the history of our struggle relates to military actions and their dimensions.

It is my feeling that we must go back to a popular and peaceful-natured Intifada, with the possibility of adding to this studied military action that would not give justification for a comprehensive Israeli response.

The use of weapons, as has been displayed throughout the current Intifada, plays into the enemy's hands and hence into the conditions and rules which it sets. It gives the Israelis justification to talk about armed confrontations "between two sides" and to use deceiving terminology such as "war" that perpetuates this false image of the situation.

What are the dangers of military action? First, it gives justification for the enemy to use its military force—tanks, planes, etc. to quell an Intifada, which is popular in essence. It gives it justification to completely destroy the economic infrastructure and to redraw maps through temporarily or permanently displacing the population. If Palestinians want to shoot, this is an option—I do not exclude this option. But as I have said, this has to be done in a studied manner and from certain areas. In all cases, it should not involve us in total confrontation.

Palestinians have legitimate and symbolic motives to carry arms. But the wide presence of arms excludes large sectors of the people from the struggle. Contrary to the first Intifada, women are almost completely absent from today's confrontations. In my opinion, the urge to use weapons leads to reinforcing an undemocratic trend in society. We need to suffice with confrontations that take the nature of the resistance of an unarmed population that seeks national liberation from an occupational army and settlers.

Possibilities of Continuing the Struggle

Let me now address the question of whether we can continue the Intifada. First, let us see what the Intifada has achieved until now.

The Intifada has reaffirmed something that was forgotten—that the West Bank and Gaza are occupied land. Since the Oslo Accords and because of them, this issue has been absent [from international discourse].

A second accomplishment of the Intifada has been its ability to clearly expose the fact that there is no possibility for peace with the [Israeli] settlements and without the return of Arab Jerusalem [which Israel has annexed] to the Palestinians.

Third, the Intifada achieved the solidarity of the masses in the Arab world and to a certain degree an international solidarity.

I must, however, warn that these achievements are not concrete. Some of these need reinforcement, while others are still in the process of becoming.

As for the accomplishments within the Arab world, this indeed is a great thing. However it is important to transform these demonstrations and popular rage into action. A similar popular Arab rage happened in 1948—from Aden (Yemen) to Masqat (Morocco). But when the war began, there were no more than four thousand volunteers in Palestine. The same thing happened during the Gulf War in 1990. Most Arab masses supported Iraq—but how do you transform this into a logical plan of action?

Having acknowledged the achievements, we must also stress their incompleteness and need for reinforcement. It can be said, for instance, that Palestinian national unity has been achieved: but what are we unified over? It has not been clear until now. We need a new program approved by the Authority and the opposition. Without it, there is no possibility of continuing.

What do we want from the Intifada? Do we want to improve the conditions for negotiations? Or do we want independence? With negotiations or without? Here we must specify a strategy. But this strategy must be compatible with our capabilities.

As a transitional step, we must reassess and reformulate new conditions for confrontation. The process involves basically gathering your forces, assessing what has happened, eliminating the causes of the armed explosion that the Israelis wanted, and then trying to think of how you want the Intifada to be. In my opinion the Intifada cannot continue successfully without change and reform.

Among other things, there is a need to activate [the democratic] apparatuses that are completely inactive at present. The Palestinian Legislative Council [which functions as the PA's elected parliament] has no presence or role in what is taking place. This situation cannot continue within the existing context. The question must be raised as to how we can truly begin a process of reform in the midst of this battle. I believe we can, and we must.

CHAPTER 2

A Likud-Labor Gangster Government After Sharon's Victory in the 2001 Elections: Provocative Escalations, Defiant but Handicapped Resistance

January–October 2001

Introduction

The ground for Sharon's victory in the February 6, 2001, Israeli elections was prepared during the months of the Labor government tenure, chaired by Barak and with the enormous help of the Israeli Left. The latter provided full support for Barak's oppressive measures against the Palestinians in the 1967 Occupied Territories and inside Israel, accompanied by its traditional role-play of supplying a progressive face to the Zionist project, including its most appalling policies. It was thus actively involved in manufacturing the consent needed for implementing the coming horrors of the unified Likud-Labor government, headed by the most suitable person for this job, Ariel Sharon.

The disclosure of the true face of the Zionist Left regarding the Palestinian citizens of Israel, combined with the latter's significant strengthening of national consciousness, brought about the unprecedented united position of boycotting the prime ministerial elections of February 2001. The underlying message of the boycott confirmed to the Israeli establishment and the Zionist Left that a new era had opened in their relations with their Palestinian citizens. Not only did the Palestinian citizens refuse to act as a "supplement" to the policies of the Left Zionist parties in the Knesset or, for that matter, seek to merely "punish" them for their approach toward the Palestinians as a matter of sheer power politics. Rather, their disengagement from these parties signified a deep understanding of the essential contradiction between their interests and those of the Zionist Left, including its most liberal currents. That is to say that their fight for the complete democratization of Israel is in fact the fight against the Jewish "identity" of the state—the central premise of Zionism, to which the Israeli Left is wholeheartedly committed.

The Palestinian Authority, however, did not share the political disillusionment of the Palestinians in Israel and instead sent messages in which it tried to convince the heads of their parties to vote for Barak. The PA continued its traditional ignoring of the wide consensus between Right and Left in Israel around the Zionist colonial project, its embodiment in the Jewish state, and its political solution for the 1967 Occupied Territories. It failed to see that both currents came to share similar policies: the elimination of the PA and its institutions, on the path to doing away with the Oslo framework, on the one hand, together with the attacks against the political radicalization of the Palestinians in Israel, on the other. Moreover, it failed to see that these policies were doomed to develop into a full-fledged campaign of liquidating the national movement as an inevitable outcome of the continued resistance of these two parts of the Palestinian people to the war declared against their national identity.

This war became increasingly brutal as the Intifada escalated. Israel actively upgraded its means of oppression, including widening its use of military assaults, besiegement, and house demolitions while beginning the systematic assassination of Palestinian activists. The initial approval Zionist liberals gave to these "surgical pin-point prevention operations" carried out by the Israeli Army, which supposedly "eliminate (specified) ticking bombs," gradually grew to providing legitimacy to the mass killings of activists, often with their family members or mere passersby. Indeed by 2006, the pretext for such killings was so used that it included targeting the areas where potential resistance could take place, with the use of hourly artillery fire. Needless to say, the death of Palestinians became a daily phenomenon (see Chapter 10).

The approval of the Zionist Left thus played a central role in conditioning the Israeli public to accept the law(-lessness) of the gangster state in general and its future military actions, which senior Israeli commentators had already begun to discuss openly as the coming "severe blow" (later implemented in the West Bank in the massive assault Operation Defensive Shield launched in March–April 2002 (See Chapter 5).

In the meantime, the post-Oslo "unilateral" era opened with the adoption of the apartheid "Separation Wall" plan, initiated by the Labor Party and designed to dispossess ten of thousands of Palestinians from their lands, while de facto annexing them into Israel as part of the large settlement blocs. By joining the escalated "demographic phobia" of Israel losing its Jewish majority across entire historic Palestine, the Zionist Left provided moral justification to the process of ethnic cleansing that the building of the wall was known to usher in, together with all the other calamities that awaited the Palestinians in coming years.

With the increased facistization of Zionist elites against both 1948 and 1967 Palestinians, with the cooperation of his partners from the Labor Party in the united war government, and with the support of the Left in general, all that remained for Sharon was to wait for the pretext that would enable him to receive the "green light" from Washington for implementing the later stages of the Field of Thorns plans (see Introduction).

Within this context, Palestinian grassroots forces braced themselves for the challenges that lay ahead. A loose operational field unity began to coalesce as the resistance attempted to carve and widen a niche between the Occupation's blows and the bourgeois "state-building" current in the PA, intent upon redirecting the Intifada back into the previously defeated framework of negotiations. Though great gains were made to develop a grassroots resistance dynamic and discourse capable of marginalizing these elites, the overall equation of the national movement was unenviable. Split among different discourses and tactics, and with Arafat cynically overseeing both currents, grave questions arose as to the Intifada's capacity to achieve Palestinian rights in its current form and the dangers that such conditions portended.

These dangers were further compounded in the wake of September 11, 2001. Just as the United States immediately set out to exploit these events to accelerate its pursuit of its geostrategic imperial interests, so too did Israel hasten to act similarly in its own "war against terror," indeed acting as the very extension of U.S. interests locally. The enormous escalation in Israeli oppression that these events ushered in forced the exposure of the authoritarian nature and differing class interests represented in PA. The United States, however, had already determined that the PA under Arafat had completed its role and needed to be fundamentally restructured if it were ever to serve a role in its plans again.

Election 2001 Results:
Disappearance of the Israeli Left,
Reappearance of the Good Old Zionist Consensus[*]

Tikva Honig-Parnass

The Israeli political arena is perceived by most observers in the Israeli, Palestinian, and world spheres as sharply divided into two main blocs, led by the Zionist Labor and Likud parties. These two blocs are considered to represent the classical division of "Left" and "Right," which presumably includes, in its Israeli version, opposing positions towards the Palestinian-Israeli conflict: the "peace camp," which is assumed to support massive territorial concessions and a Palestinian state, on the one hand, and the "nationalist camp" which strives to establish Israel's rule throughout entire historic Palestine while denying civil rights to its Palestinian subjects, on the other.

Moreover, judging from the recent election campaign for prime minister, it becomes rather clear that this perception actually also prevails within the so-called Israeli Left itself. Even the radical parts of the Israeli "peace camp" called for voting for Barak (Labor) before the election, as the "lesser-evil" alternative when compared with Sharon (Likud). All this despite Barak's preplanned burial of the Oslo negotiations framework and his bloody attempts at repressing the Intifada and with it the solidarity of Israel's Palestinian citizens (detailed in Chapter 1). It is therefore important to refute this false and misleading perception, which prevents the growth of a genuine Left capable of struggling for social and political transformation of the Jewish-Zionist state—an essential condition for the fulfillment of Palestinian national rights, not to mention democratic rights for all citizens.

The Shared Neoliberal Ideology and Policy of Left and Right

To begin with, it is important to underscore that both left and right blocs do not embody any significant differences in socioeconomic interests, as is classically attributed to the division between "social democratic" and "con-

---

[*] This article first appeared in *Between the Lines* no. 5, March 2001.

servative" or "right-wing" politics. Rather, it has been the Labor governments that, from the mid-1980s on, willingly accepted the dictates of the United States and the World Bank and began implementing neoliberal policies aimed at integrating Israel within the processes of capitalist globalization. (See elaboration and references in the Introduction.)

The right-wing governments of the Likud, which at various times since 1977 have exchanged power with the Labor Party, adopted neoliberal policies initiated by the latter, with both also representing the Ashkenazi composition of the Israeli economic, military, and political establishment. Their similar policies brought about the strengthening of free-market economics, reduction of government expenditures on infrastructure and education, privatization of health and welfare services, breaking the organized power of workers, and freezing or reducing employees' wages, which in recent years have come under stiff competition from foreign workers. The income gap in Israel has thus become one of the largest in the Western world. The top income bracket now lives on an annual income twelve times larger than the bottom, in comparison to 8.6 times ten years ago.

The government of Barak (Labor), the sworn disciple of Thatcherist economics, followed through with the Labor Party's long-held objection to a minimum-wage law. He also opposed raising the present minimum wage; intends to annul the rights of tenants in public housing (most of whom are Mizrahi Jews), and called for limiting social benefits to those whose wages are less than the official minimum, thus inflicting even more hardships upon the working class and the poor, the majority of whom are Palestinian citizens and Mizrahi Jews.

The consensus between Labor and Likud regarding the economy is comprehensive and explains their silence concerning these issues during the election campaign. Both Barak and Sharon were interested in continuing the process of dismantling the welfare state in the service of big capital. And indeed, the meeting that took place shortly after the elections between representatives of the capitalists (who financed the Labor campaign) and Sharon, at his ranch in the Negev Desert, left them extremely satisfied. Sharon, after all, promised to continue with neoliberal economic policies of the Labor Party.

The fact that the two largest Zionist parties represent similar class interests is reflected in the real meaning of their seemingly different approach to the solution for the "Palestinian-Israeli conflict." Big capital traditionally supported the Labor Party because it believed that a neoliberal economy was conditioned upon a peace agreement like Oslo, which was led by the Zionist Left (see the Introduction). On the other hand, Likud leaders have argued that free-market economics can flourish in principle at the same time that the war against the Palestinians continues. Thus, while their similar attitudes toward economic policies are openly expressed, this is not the case with the political process. In regard to "peace," the deception regarding their differing positions—claimed to be "the most severe rift in Israeli society"—is sustained by both camps.

The Shared Final-Solution Plan of Left and Right

And indeed, although the positions of Left and Right regarding the peace process in the framework of the Oslo Accords are professed to be contradictory, the policies on the ground of all Israeli governments, both Labor and Likud, have been the same. All exploited the Oslo years to implement the Israeli goal of perpetuating its rule over the 1967 Occupied Territories and preventing the possibility of a viable Palestinian state, by means of an escalated mass settlement and bypass road construction policy.

During the February 2001 election broadcasts and interviews, Barak announced that if Arafat insists, as at Camp David in 2000, on the right of return and on sovereignty over the Temple Mount (the Al Aqsa Mosque compound), his (Barak's) government, if elected, would keep the commandment "We are here and they are there"—namely, forced "separation" between the two populations, Israeli and Palestinian.[1]

The "separation" principle traditionally adopted by the Zionist Left, together with the fundamental Zionist goal of "preserving a Jewish majority," are, and have always been, racist justifications for perpetuating Israel's control "over there," as evidenced through the Israeli settlement and bypass road map. Furthermore, the rationale of the principle of a Jewish majority can easily lead to the conclusion that there is a need to transfer (expel) the Palestinians from the Occupied Territories, and from inside Israel as well. This was understood by MK Rehavam Ze'evi, head of the extreme-right Transfer party.[2] When responding to some members of the Knesset from left political parties who opposed joining a government with him in it, Ze'evi commented, "Barak has even adopted the slogan, 'We are here and they are there.' The only difference between us is where the 'there' will be. On the whole, it is only a matter of moving the border a few kilometers to the east."[3]

The departure of senior Labor Party leaders from the Oslo framework was reflected in the explicit declarations made by Shimon Peres (the minister of foreign affairs in Sharon's Likud-Labor unified national government established after the elections), which call for an interim agreement or a partial agreement of the kind Barak spoke of in his "here and there" speech. This is a departure from what had been the official Labor Party position calling for a "final" agreement in the framework of Oslo and in line with the Sharon and Bush administrations' attitude toward an agreement with the Palestinians (see Chapter 1).

The Oslo process, which from the onset was one of the greatest deceptions in modern history, is now dead and buried. Its supporters, in a roundabout way admit that "it is the concept of Oslo that has collapsed"—namely, "the idea to bring people here from Tunis, give them a territory, and impose on them to keep order and security for us—and believe it will work" (Shlomo Ben Ami, minister of internal security and foreign minister in Barak's government).[4]

The progressive political commentator Haim Baram adds, "[Israeli 'dove' Yossi] Beilin[5] sold the public the illusion that it is possible to achieve peace at the lowest price, with a united and expanded Jerusalem under Israeli sovereignty and with eighty-one settlements within the Palestinian areas. Beilin himself tried to sell Abu Dis to Arafat as a capital, claiming that this neighborhood/village is Jerusalem. Since the missionaries in black Africa bought stretches of land, each of them the size of entire Europe, in return for some glass beads, never has there been such a transparent attempt to buy peace and general Arab acknowledgment at such a cheap price."

Labor's Crawling to a Unified Government

Indeed, the "disappointment" about the Oslo process, as well as the essential affinity in positions with the Likud, explains the Labor Party's crawling to participate in the national unified government established by Sharon after the Likud victory in the elections. They are thus ready to provide "legitimacy" to the new government headed by Sharon—the worst war criminal of the entire Israeli leadership—which is also composed of Rehavam Ze'evi, head of the Transfer party. Upon its establishment a decade earlier, the Transfer party platform had even been sharply rejected by MK Benny Begin (Likud, son of former prime minister Menachem Begin) who argued, "What do we mean when we use the word 'transfer'? Even if we add the words 'willful' or 'consensual,' as Ze'evi is doing, the plan is to starve, to thirst, to burden and to frighten the Arabs of West Eretz Israel [between the Jordan River and the Mediterranean] until they willingly leave."[6]

But today it is difficult to find any significant difference between this understanding of what Ze'evi's conception of transfer means and the policies implemented by the Labor Party headed by Barak—policies that include dimensions of ethnic cleansing inherent within them, behind the pretext that suppressing the Intifada is the condition demanded for renewing "peace negotiations." Both are proof of the fact that the peace camp the Left claims to represent is empty of any unique content that could prevent a unified government with Likud.

Indeed, alongside the similar neoliberal ideology of the Labor and Likud parties, both are committed to Zionism and its corollaries: a Jewish state with "a solid" Jewish majority; continuation of existing institutions that fulfill the goals of encouraging and subsidizing the immigration of Jews to Israel; and the structural discrimination of the Palestinian citizens. These commitments are featured in the first draft of the "Guidelines of the Unified Government" which state:

> Article 6.1: The government of Israel will place the Zionist national agenda at its top priorities.
>
> Article 6.2: The government will act, together with the Jewish Agency and the World Zionist Federation, to encourage immigration to the country, to intensify the Jewish-Zionist education of the young generation in the Diaspora . . . to fortify the unity of the Jewish nation around Israel, and to ensure the Jewish, Zionist and democratic nature of Israel.[7]

Ashkenazi Middle-Class "Left" versus Mizrahi Working-Class "Right"

The majority of the peace movement in Israel has traditionally committed itself to supporting the rule of the Labor Party and to preventing the ascent to power of the "nationalistic camp" headed by Likud. However, the blurring of boundaries between Left and Right regarding the economy and the Palestinians is accompanied by what seems to be the "unnatural" constituencies of these two blocs.

The Mizrahim, who make up the majority of the Jewish working class (second to the Palestinian citizens, who occupy much lower echelons of the working class),[8] have been committed to voting for the Right over the past three decades, while the Ashkenazi big-business circles and middle classes support the Left. Thus, in the recent elections for example, in upper-middle-class communities such as Kfar Shmaryahu and Ramat Hasharon, Barak received 75 percent and 62 percent of the votes, respectively, while in the "development towns" of Sderot and Ashdod[9] (the majority of whose populations are Mizrahim), he received 13 percent and 9 percent, respectively.

These differences in voting patterns reflect the Israeli situation in which belonging to the left/peace camp entails not so much different political positions but a shared "cultural identity" among the affluent Ashkenazim, who aim at retaining their hegemonic position. This is often manifested in their racist, orientalist positions wrapped in a self-perception of their own "rationalism," "secularism," and "democracy" counterposed to the "backwardness," "traditionalism," and "primitiveness" that they attribute to the orthodox supporters of the Right.[10] However, an examination of these self-perceptions reveals that the main object of left Ashkenazis' hatred is neither the secular Right (of Likud) nor the religious Right (embodied in the National Religious Party [Mafdal], which leads the settlement movement) but the Mizrahi religious party Shas and the forces it has come to represent. In their understanding, Shas embodies a potential threat to Ashkenazi hegemony, simply because it is an expression of the self-organization of Mizrahim that could lead to the challenge of Ashkenazi elites. For this reason, neither of the right-wing parties of Likud or Mafdal were disqualified from joining the coalition government that Barak tried to set up after his victory in the 1999 elections. But the racist slogan "Just not Shas" (demanding that Shas not be allowed to join the government) became the mantra heard from the Zionist Left and big business at the time.

Moreover, the self-professed secularism of the Zionist Left is misleading. Its secularism has nothing to do with a worldview based upon democratic values or centered on freedom of conscience and religion.[11] On the contrary, the goals of Zionism were, and still are, perceived today as justifying the subordination of individual rights to the needs of "the nation and the state"—the "*Jewish* nation-state" and its "security." Genuine commitment to humanist and universal values is thus inevitably weakened because these "state and national needs" discriminate against the Palestinians in Israel *by definition*. It is further weakened toward Jews as well, due to Zionism's anchoring in religion, which supplies the legitimacy for choosing precisely Palestine for colonization. Hence Israelis are doomed to live in a semitheocratic regime in which there is no separation between state and religion—a "Theodemocracy," according to Baruch Kimmerling.[12] The Rabbinate has been granted the monopoly jurisdiction over family and personal affairs, and religious symbols, norms, and legislation have permeated central areas of social life.[13] (See Chapter 9.)

The Zionist Left claims to attack Shas on the grounds of its religious orthodoxy. But this intentionally ignores the fact that the majority of Shas supporters are not Orthodox at all. Rather, their support for Shas stems from their protest over the years of cultural, political, and economic marginalization of Mizrahim at the hands of the Israeli establishment, headed by the Zionist Labor movement. The Zionist Left aims to present the struggle against this movement as "the battle between the forces of enlightenment versus those of darkness," thus delegitimizing Mizrahi attempts at protest and organization in the framework of the Shas movement.[14]

The Betrayal of the Zionist Left

Throughout the seven years since Oslo, the extraparliamentary, Zionist Left–supported Labor Party dictates in the negotiations with the Palestinians, while being virtually silent about the massive increase in settlement building. Moreover, even the more radical parts of the Left, largely the followers of Hadash (the front headed by the Communist Party, whose members are largely Palestinian citizens) and Meretz (the Civil Rights party, considered to be left of the Labor Party), refrained from declaring that the peace process *was* occupation and oppression in disguise. They hence did not focus their struggle upon delegitimizing it. This helped preserve the misleading conception of the peace process as aiming to fulfill the national rights of the Palestinian people. Thus, when the time came, the entire rank and file in the peace camp was ripe to accept Barak's version of the failure of the July 2000 Camp David talks, adopting his claim that "there is no partner to peace." Furthermore, when the Intifada broke out two months later, most of them accepted—either explicitly or through silence—the brutal means of attempting to suppress it.

Despite the mass killing of more than four hundred Palestinians, including thirteen Israeli citizens, under Barak's government during the first three months of the Intifada, the Left called for "voting Barak" in the recent election. They even depicted him as "the man who can ensure the implementation of the peace process." The traditional commitment to the Zionist Labor movement was shared by even more radical circles of the Left. Intellectuals and academics known for their genuine adherence to the mission of a "just solution" were revealed to have accepted the virtual deep rift between "Left" and "Right" as representing positions of "peace" versus "war." They furthermore accepted the assumption that Barak "went further than any politician before him in presenting compromise sugges-tions to the Palestinians." A telling example is the position adopted by professor Ze'ev Sternhell, a genuine social democrat who revealed in his book "Nation Building or a New Society," the quasifascist nature of the "National Socialism" adopted by the prestate Zionist Labor movement.[15] He too called to vote for Barak, claiming that Barak "had freed himself, as Rabin and Peres did previously, from the myth to which he was captive: the myth determining that Israel, due to its technological and military power, has the ability to force the Arab world to accept its terms."[16]

Hadash, which had also accepted the Clinton-Barak proposals at Camp David, delayed its call to cast a blank ballot instead of voting for Barak until a few days before the elections. In doing so, it went against the majority of the remaining Palestinian leaders in Israel, who called for—and carried out—a complete boycott of the elections.

The connection to the Labor Party, which is still rather strong amongst the Hadash leadership, is reflected in an interview given by Hadash MK Muhammad Barakeh two days after the elections, in which he almost apologized for calling upon voters to cast a blank ballot: "We continued speaking to [PM] Barak's ministers until the last minute [in the hopes that a deal could be reached between Hadash and the Labor Party, allowing for the former to support the latter's campaign], but they left us no alternative [and we were forced] to accept the blank ballot, which is the worst option that a person can reach."[17] Thus, Hadash did not actively participate in the historic turning point in the political behav-ior of the Palestinians in Israel, who united to express their alienation from the Jewish-Zionist state. (See Azmi Bishara in this chapter.)

Strengthening of the National Consciousness of Palestinians in Israel

It was amazing to see the massive response of the Palestinians in Israel to the call to boycott the elections and their disregard for the Hadash position—the party that used to win the traditional support of 1948 Palestini-ans and that has never challenged the Jewish definition of the state. Eighty-two percent of 1948 Palestinians did not vote at all, and of the 18 percent who did vote, only a few percent obeyed the Hadash call to cast a blank ballot.

This massive boycott of the Palestinian citizens indicates their liberation from the traditional loyalty they historically had shown to the Zionist Left. It may turn out to be a step forward in strengthening their Palestinian national identity and their readiness to struggle for their collective rights as a national minority in their homeland. The slogan of collective rights raised by the National Democratic Assembly (Tajamu') and Adalah (a dedicated legal organization fighting for the rights of Palestinian citizens) is a large step for this community. It transcends the demand for individual civic rights for 1948 Palestinians (as traditionally called for by Hadash) or even the right to "cultural autonomy," which sections of liberal Zionists have recently been willing to adopt. Rather, this new slogan constitutes a challenge to the Jewish-Zionist nature of the state of Israel, which refuses to acknowledge that any other national group besides "the Jewish people," is entitled to full citizenship.

The disconnection of the Palestinian citizens from the Zionist Left constitutes the removal of a central source of its legitimacy, which served as a fig leaf for its actual approach to the Palestinian national movement and the apartheid nature of the Jewish-Zionist state. This disconnection is the primary condition for the Israeli Left becoming able to grow into a genuine antioccupation and antiapartheid movement that together with the Palestinians, will fight for the de-Zionization and democratization of Israel.

Boycotting the Elections: Crystallizing of Palestinian Citizens' National Consciousness[*]

Azmi Bishara

On February 4, 2001, two days before the Israeli elections, the Bisan Center for Research and Development held an open panel session in Ramallah on the implications and scenarios of the Israeli elections for prime minister. Following are excerpts of MK Azmi Bishara's (National Democratic Assembly [Tajamu']) lecture explaining the position and thinking of the Palestinian citizens of Israel in this election.

[*] This article first appeared in *Between the Lines* no. 4, February 2001.

Before proceeding to talk about the reasons for the Tajamu' call for boy-cotting the coming elections, I will try to explain the general context in which this call takes place. By context, I don't mean the political mood in the street, which is a result of the clashes that took place at the beginning of October 2000 [in which thirteen Palestinian citizens were killed by the Israeli police]. This popular political mood is important and we will invest in it, but it is not an appropriate justification for making this decision. Our decision not to vote in this election is a political, rational, and prag-matic decision and not an emotional reaction to frustrations with Barak or revenge for the killing of our martyrs.

Saying No

Why are we abstaining? Why are we saying "No" to Barak and "No" to Sharon in these elections?

To begin with, the national movement has been committed to devel-oping itself by trying to mobilize a national consciousness and accumulat-ing a national experience among the [Palestinian] people [in Israel]. The results of these endeavors were reflected in the popular upsurge of Octo-ber 2000, in the interaction with our people in the West Bank and Gaza—and in the increase in the adherence of the young generation to our national identity, which has emerged after a long period of what we call the period of "Israelization."

This building of a national movement would have been damaged if we had belittled this current upsurge and voted for Barak, who bears the main responsibility for the recent crimes. Building this national move-ment is more important than voting for Barak and also more important than the difference between Barak and Sharon—and I am aware of the difference between them. Our decision to abstain is made despite the fact that we *do* see the difference between Barak and Sharon.

This is our viewpoint as a national movement. We differ with our brethren in some other movements in the Arab arena. There are those among them [a reference to the Communist Party, Hadash] who hold that the Arabs in Israel are part of the class struggle within Israel. They hold that the Arabs in Israel constitute a reserve power for the Zionist Left and for Israel to become a socialist or democratic state, and that through this struggle it is possible to solve the problem of nationalism.

To begin with, there are real doubts as to whether the Communists themselves are involved in any class struggle. But this, in any respect, is not compatible with the tribal-ethnic structure of Israel and the need to organize the Arab citizens [within it].

What is important is the perspective I am speaking from. Am I speaking from the perspective of the struggles between the "Right" and "Left" within Israeli society, or am I speaking from a totally different perspective, namely, the development of the national Palestinian political awareness? I can see the achievements and results we have attained in building this identity. Will I now just stop all of this and say that there is a more important struggle than building the national movement because there is the danger of Barak losing? Should we just vote for him and deliver a blow to our own national awareness and accumulated experience?

Boycotting the elections is a political stance, not an ideological stance. Elections for a national minority which is excluded from the definition of the state as a Jewish state are a tool—a tool which can be used either to vote or to abstain. However, only those who have the right to vote in the first place have the right to abstain. So, paradoxically, abstention from voting is the use of the same tool as voting. I do not see this as yielding an acquired civil right.

Some of the officials in the Palestinian Authority did not understand our position because they have a way of thinking, may I say, more affected by the Zionist Left—with whom they interact more than with us. So they listen to them more than they do to us. I emphasize that this applies to some officials in the PA, as there are others who have thought differently.

The Demise of Barak and the Pathetic Zionist Left

Yossi Sarid [chairman of the left Zionist Meretz party] gives us advice that the "Arabs should vote." Yet when Barak was forming his coalition [after his victory in the 1999 elections], Sarid preferred the Likud over Shas in the government coalition [which Meretz joined].[18] Moreover, he was willing to quit the coalition over the issue of an electricity generator being transported on a Saturday.[19] Does this person [Sarid] want peace? An electricity generator is more important than the coalition or peace [that the coalition Meretz was in claimed to strive for]? And then he comes to the Arabs saying, "Forget the thirteen people killed, they are not important." But your generator [being moved] on a Saturday is important and you are willing to bring down Barak for it? Only we are not important. Each of your [the Israeli Left's] issues in Israeli society is more important than the Arabs inside Israel, and you are ready to bring down Barak for them. Sarid was ready to have Mafdal—the settlers' party—in a government and not Shas because he was afraid to lose secular votes to another secular party, Shinui.

Barak lost on many fronts in Israeli society. He bore the defeat of Lebanon but tried to portray it as a victory. But it is impossible to portray a withdrawal in the middle of the night from a country without a peace agreement as a "victory." It can only appear as a defeat. And no doubt it affected the morale of the Arab peoples, including the Palestinians.

There is not one issue that Barak did not prove a failure in, largely due to his arrogance, which in politics turns out to be sheer stupidity. It quickly became apparent how many times the Palestinian people turned overnight from not being a "partner" [for peace negotiations] to returning to being a "partner."[20] Furthermore, in this same time frame, Israel proved that the only thing it understands is force. If you will recall, according to the PA and Israel, there was "progress made in Taba." The statement released after Taba declared, "We were never so close to a final solution in all our history." So between Camp David [July 2000] and Taba [January 2001], "progress" was made. This can be explained only by the effect of force—the power of the people—the Intifada. The Israeli claim against the Arabs that "they understand only the language of force" is turned against Israel: "Israel understands only the language of force." Barak proved this to his people, and with this, he frustrated his people with his security theories, which dictate no concessions when confronted by force. "Security" turned into his weak point. Additional to this was the discontent of the "supporters of peace'" who elected him to "achieve peace" in which he also failed. On both sides his supporters abandoned him.

The Jewish State—the Arab Vote

We have our own agenda. We have been a people on the brink of losing our identity. Up until 1996, there were 60,000 Arab members of the Labor Party. There was a necessity to begin a formidable process of struggle in order to "Palestinianize" and "Arabize" the people to hold fast to their land and their everyday civil rights. We had to convince people through hard work that it is also our right to intervene in the [overall] Palestinian cause and show our solidarity with our Arab nation and with the Palestinian people. Then to think that we are asked to put all these issues aside and use our electoral powers to tip the scales for one camp against another in Israel, on the issues of "peace and war." Has Israel ceased to be a Jewish state? Is it really a state for all its citizens?

This is a Jewish state and if the right wing is the majority, as it seems to be even under Barak, we must confront this.

Voting for the Labor Party now—after what happened and despite it—will lead the Labor Party to be assured once and for all that, whatever happens to Palestinian citizens, "they are sure to vote for us." We are therefore not talking so much about revenge for what happened [in October 2000, when thirteen Palestinian citizens were killed by the Israeli police] but about taking care of the generations to come. If we let it pass this time, it would give a "green light" for any prime minister from the Labor Party to understand that "the Arabs give extreme and threatening speeches at funerals, but in the end, they always come back." This has dangerous and bloody consequences for how this state will deal with us during demonstrations in the future. We cannot allow this. We cannot just say, "Let it go."

We [Israeli Jews and Palestinian citizens] live together. Will this state one day become a democratic secular state for all its citizens? We will struggle for this democratic cause. It might take two or three generations, or it may not happen at all—we don't know. It must, however, be clear to them that the lives of our youths are not something we have tolerance for losing. No. We are like the Zionists. Each one of us is important, and each person who killed one of the thirteen must be punished, even if we have to make our children and their children memorize their names over and over again. You can't just say, "Forget it, they're gone." They are not gone.

Zionist Principles of Separation and Ethnic Cleansing at Their Peak on Both Sides of the Green Line*

Tikva Honig-Parnass

The majority of the Israeli establishment, including the Left, has lost faith in obtaining the consent of the present Palestinian leadership for the institutionalization of an apartheid regime throughout historic Palestine—a goal central to the Oslo Accords. However, very few on the Left are willing to openly admit this, tending to do so only in rare mo-

---

* This article first appeared in *Between the Lines* no. 10, September 2001.

ments of truth. MK Yossi Beilin, who is one of the forefathers of the Oslo Accords and a onetime senior leader of the Labor Party, provided one such example in a recent interview published in *Ha'aretz*, conducted by senior analyst Ari Shavit.[21] Beilin confirms his commitment to the traditional principles of the Zionist Left regarding "separation" from the Palestinians and the need to maintain a "Jewish majority." He also acknowledges that his support for the "two-state solution" in the framework of Oslo was based on the argument that it is "the only way to save the Jewish state from an Arab majority."

However, after Shavit questions whether Beilin thinks "the Palestinian national movement in general and Arafat in particular will accept deep down the existence of a Jewish state inside the Green Line," Beilin answers, "Deep down, I don't know." He admits that Zionism is an obstacle to the Oslo solution: "What we have to understand as a Zionist movement is that we are doing a very, very unnatural thing here. . . . We are returning after two thousand years . . . claiming our right to establish a state of our own here . . . when there are other people here, who say they do not accept that idea, that it is against their will." Soon enough, however, he withdraws from his understanding of the Palestinian political position, retreating to the racist, orientalist perception that Palestinian resistance to Israel's dictates is motivated by irrational hate. Beilin describes the relationship that developed with the Palestinians around Oslo as a very thin layer of ice, that "when it here and there breaks, you suddenly see the hatred welling up from the depths of the ocean and threatening you. That is hard, [and] it is hard for me too."

Typical of the Zionist Left's continual preaching of an unrealistic solution, Beilin ends his interview with the concluding statement that there is no other choice but to continue "thickening the ice." No wonder this hopeless approach, which subsequently underlies that of wider circles in the Zionist Left, fails to convince Israelis to change their position regarding the national rights of the Palestinian people. Hence the number of those hanging around to share Beilin's conclusion decreases daily. Refusing to give up the apartheid framework that sustains the Jewish state, as well as the disastrous planned solution for the 1967 Occupied Territories, inevitably leads to adopting the choice of Sharon.

The conclusion drawn from the conviction that there is no prospect for ending Palestinian resistance is explicitly expressed by Israeli military circles: they supply justifications for continuing the path of a prolonged war undertaken by Sharon's government, through their emphasis on the traditional Israeli claim of the "external threats" posed to Israel's security by Arab states and forces that do not submit to U.S.-Israeli dictates. Furthermore, according to the senior commentator Amir Oren, who is close to the "security establishment," the situation "may even deteriorate within this period, in the wake of a possible escalation in the North [of Israel] to a regional war, confronting Hizbullah and Syria."[22]

The steps aiming at destroying the PLO and the entire Palestinian national movement have thus picked up the pace. This was reflected in the assassination of Abu Ali Mustafa, the secretary-general of the Popular Front for the Liberation of Palestine (PFLP) on August 27, 2001—the most senior figure Israel has killed so far during the Intifada, the head of the second largest faction in the PLO. It thus fell in line with the cabinet's decision of July 4, 2001, regarding the assassination of the Palestinian leadership.[23] A reflection of the U.S. "green light" given to this policy was publicly expressed by the U.S. defense secretary Donald Rumsfeld, who in a CNN broadcast on September 9, 2001, justified "Israel's use of American arms for pinpoint prevention operations" and defined these operations as "self-defense." However, until the oppressive measures against the Palestinians yield a leadership that will fully collaborate with Israel's schemes, the Likud government, headed by Sharon, has adopted the "pragmatic" tradition that has been coined by the Zionist Labor movement since it led the colonization project in Palestine—namely, committing daily actions on the ground whose cumulative significance transforms into strategic political achievements over time. This approach is implemented today through the separation wall scheme.

Unilateral Separation in the 1967 Occupied Territories: The Wall

August 2001 witnessed the emergence of a new version of Israel's desire for "unilateral separation" as an alternative to the political negotiations approach. Negotiations, by definition, imply some "concessions" and minimal references to past agreements, such as the third redeployment, stipulated by the Oslo Accords but never implemented by Israel.[24] Now, under the pretext that "there is no partner for peace," Sharon has adopted the Labor plan regarding the need for a "separation wall"; namely, building a massive wall that will separate the future Palestinian cantons from the areas Israel seeks to annex, thus creating the infrastructure of an enforced solution upon the Palestinians.

Those who initiated the plan and are leading the public campaign for it are some of the very same Labor leaders known for their "enlightened moderation" and for their support for Oslo.[25] This includes Minister Dan Meridor (Center), Minister Dalia Itzik (Labor), and MK Haim Ramon (Labor). As in previous times, left Zionist intellectuals have hastened to contribute their expertise and moral respectability for legitimizing the claimed "separation" between Palestinians and Israelis. Thus, Shlomo Avinery, a political science professor at the Hebrew University (who served in Rabin's Labor government as director of the Israeli Foreign Ministry), recently expressed the traditional self-righteousness of the Zionist Left and its dehumanization of the Palestinians, which justifies the enforcement of this racist, unilateral separation:

> The Palestinian side is not ready for an historic compromise. They see the negotiations process only [as a means] to implement their demands and not as a painful process of give-and-take. The wide support of the Palestinian public and their leaders for the terror against [Israeli] civilians proves that the other side is indifferent to the universal values enshrined by the Israeli Left ... which has never believed in intentional assassination of children.[26]

As in the past, the Zionist Labor Party's most bitter policies are wrapped in hypocritical and misleading discourse. Thus Avinery promises that the separation wall project will "enable today to put an end at least to most of the occupation," despite the fact that he knows full well that large areas will be annexed to Israel and that virtually nothing will remain of the West Bank but a fragmented collection of Palestinian enclaves. In doing so, he willfully ignores the details of the proposal presented by his political colleagues, such as MKs Ramon and Meridor, who revealed that the wall will leave approximately 150,000 settlers in Israeli-controlled areas—namely, the big settlement blocks of Ariel, Ma'aleh Adumim, and Gush Etzion[27] and the Jordan Valley, "needed as a military line facing a possible eastern front."[28]

On June 8, 2001, the cabinet confirmed the plan put forward by Sharon and the heads of the army for the "seam *zone* deployment," which differs from the Labor Party proposal only in terms of the amount of territory it will bite away from the future Palestinian cantons. The commentator Amos Harel emphasizes the massive ethnic cleansing operations to be committed in the areas included within it: "The thousands [of Palestinians] who inhabit the villages in these areas will be compelled to leave. ... They will be permitted to cultivate their lands only if they coordinate in advance [with the military authorities] and have the appropriate confirmation."[29] Moreover, within this zone the army will issue more lenient open-fire directives against Palestinians.[30]

Left and Right Shared Anxiety: "The Demographic Danger"

The initiators of the various versions of the plan to impose "separation" on the Palestinians were overwhelmed by a common concern: how to immediately confront the "demographic threat"—that is, losing the Jewish majority in the exclusivist Jewish state, which is the very essence of the Zionist project. The concept of "separation" adopted by the Zionist Labor movement since its inception was a code word used to uproot the Palestinians in the prestate period and later acted as a justification for the 1948 Nakba in terms of the "existential need to establish a exclusivist Jewish state." The same principle has been applied by its successors from the Zionist Left and self-professed "liberals" as the supreme value to justify all versions of a political solution to the Israeli-Palestinian conflict.[31]

However, during the "good old days" of the Oslo process, they managed to remove the elements of the "demographic danger" from the center of the discourse on "separation" to some extent. Instead they chose to hide them behind justifications of "ending the occupation" and "recognizing Palestinian rights." But not anymore. The demographic discourse and policies have returned to the forefront, armed with the full legitimacy conferred upon them by the Zionist Left.

Haifa University professor of geography Arnon Sofer, who for years was considered a persona non grata in "progressive" circles, has now become the ideologue of the unilateral separation scheme. The figures presented in a booklet he published in 2001 regarding the estimated future increase in the Palestinian population created panic in wide circles of the political establishment, including the Zionist Left.[32] His figures indicate that by the year 2020, 42 percent of the population living between the Jordan River and the Mediterranean Sea will be Jewish, while 58 percent will be Arab. (The total population will be 15.2 million people.) The separation map that Sofer suggests "to prevent the disappearance of the Zionist entity," leaves 30 to 40 percent of the West Bank, including the Jordan Valley, under Israeli sovereignty "until the Palestinians agree to return to the negotiations without shooting."[33] Among other policies, he suggests an "exchange" of territories whereby the settlement blocs will be annexed to Israel and the Triangle area[34] inside Israel will be transferred to the "independent" Palestinian areas.

The intolerable ease with which this blatant racism, expressed by Sofer for the last twenty years, and adopted by many who supported the Oslo Accords, was expressed by the senior *Ha'aretz* commentator Avirama Golan:

> No one is bothered by the looking at Palestinian citizens through "evil-planning wombs" [of Palestinian women]; no one is shocked at Sofer's suggestion to determine a "Singapore Law" that will control births, because of concern over the high birthrate among the non-Zionists, which presumably will increase poverty. . . . The argument that the impoverished Arabs are turning Israel into a Third World state permits the Left to swallow the demographic frog without suffocating.[35]

The perceived need to strengthen the Jewish identity of the state and the discriminative policies it implies toward its Palestinian citizens has become an urgent issue for the so-called liberal political and intellectual elites in Israel. As *Yediot Ahronot's* senior commentator Nahum Barnea correctly emphasizes, "Ministers, from the prime minister down, often in private talks, say that the most severe problem on their agenda is that of Israel's Arabs."[36]

It has increasingly been recognized that the plan for a peaceful, accepted apartheid solution throughout entire Palestine that was intended to be implemented through the Oslo Accords has reached a dead end. In the new era opened with the attacks of September 11, 2001, Israel will be given a free hand to follow its chosen war path.

The Policies Recommended By Mainstream Zionist Elites: Dispossession, Transfer, and Blatant Capitalism[37]

An indication of the extent to which the notion of "transfer" of Palestinians from both the 1967 and 1948 areas has become a legitimate opinion openly expressed in ever-widening strata in Israeli society, far beyond its traditional base in the extreme Right, can be found in its inclusion in the agenda of the country's most prestigious conference. In March 2001, *Ha'aretz* reported on the Herzliya Conference, which more than three hundred people from the Israeli academic, economic and security professions attend yearly—the supposed "center of the center."[38] This conference is so well-respected in academic and political circles internationally that it attracts many of the most esteemed figures in these areas from around the world, year after year. This year's conclusions were compiled in a document entitled "The Balance of National Strength and Security in Israel: Policy Directions," presented in mid-March 2001. The document's call for uprooting and expelling Palestinians reveals the economic-social interests of Israeli elites who had reverted to the traditional Zionist approach toward the Palestinians: not integrating them as part of the Israeli economy as a cheap labor force but rather liquidating or expelling them.[39]

As the sociologist Yossi Dehan remarks, "The document resembles a pamphlet of the members of the [fanatical right-wing] Kahana Hai movement more than a document written by academic and security personnel. Moreover, even they [Kahana Hai] would have reservations about parts of the convention recommendations as too extremist."

Dispossession and Transfer

The document makes a number of significant recommendations regarding the Palestinian citizens. Among them is the suggestion to encourage Jews to settle in areas that are "demographically problematic"—especially the Galilee, the Jezreel Valley, and the Negev—*inter alia*, "in order to prevent a contiguous Arab majority that will geographically divide the country." It also calls for adopting the aforementioned idea to transfer Arab blocs of population to Palestinian sovereignty, including the little Triangle, East Jerusalem, and concentrations of Bedouin dwellings in the northern Negev.

Regarding the 1967 Occupied Territories, the authors are even more blatant: "If the Palestinian population of the [1967 Occupied] Territories does not curb its rate of increase, it will be necessary to find some place for resettlement outside the state of Israel (perhaps to the east of the Jordan [River])."

Of course the motives for transfer are "humane." One of the document's contributors, Dr. Uzi Arad, commented, "The Palestinians have made a decision that they want the highest rate of natural population growth in the world, but they don't have the means to support it. They are all crowded together in a tiny area. So what should those who are really interested in their welfare do? Leaving them in the Gaza Strip means sentencing them to a life of misery."

Hypocritically, the document insists that the decision to adopt the semitransfer policy toward the Palestinians in Israel will be made "democratically." Asked if the shift to Palestinian jurisdiction will be imposed on Israeli Arabs living near the Green Line, despite their known objections, Arad answered, "In a democratic state, it is the majority that determines where the national borders are. Just as the government can decide to withdraw from territories in Judea and Samaria [the West Bank], it can decide on land exchanges anywhere else in the country."

Retired Brigadier General Shlomo Gazit, a former Intelligence Branch director of the Israeli Army and president of Birsheva University, was more explicit than the composers of the document regarding the means needed to implement what appears to be a "rational," "peaceful" solution to the demographic threat. He argues that in order to preserve the Jewish character of the state, "it seems that only an emergency regime and abandoning the democratic game can perhaps resolve the problem."

Brutal Capitalism

The economic ramifications of losing the Jewish majority to the Palestinian citizens is presented without shame: "Israel's growing Arab sector is endowed with socioeconomic characteristics that will turn it into a millstone around Israel's neck. A very small percentage of the Arab population participates in the work force, whereas its consumption of public services greatly exceeds its relative share of the total population."

However, underlying the approach to the Palestinians is a comprehensive brutal capitalism that inevitably aims at marginalizing poor Jewish circles as well.

The sociologist Yossi Dehan, who criticizes the Israeli brand of brutal capitalism, says, "[A]s in the jungle, so in real life: only the strong survive." Therefore, Dehan says, the report recommends strengthening the strong: "[Report:] In order to preserve a qualitative advantage and lay the groundwork for an advanced technological society, we will have to invest heavily in the education of the stronger population." In view of the country's limited resources, "it will not be possible to invest simultaneously in two areas at once—closing gaps and fostering excellence."

And what about the social solidarity the Zionists need in order to implement their colonialist goals?

These experts cynically assume that they can continue to manipulate the working Jewish masses for a long time. Dehan says, "To those who fear that ignoring social gaps will harm not only the weak sectors but also the objective of social solidarity, Arad offers reassurance: according to the findings, the social gaps [among Jews] that exist today have not made people less willing to 'do something for the country.' There is no proof that the weaker sectors are less motivated in this respect than the strong sectors." Dehan concludes, "It is difficult to find another democratic country in which three hundred of the academic and security elite will compose such a simplified, racist, antidemocratic and reactionary document. . . . This document indicates that the threat to the democratic nature, moral image, and Jewish inheritance is located in the center of the heart of the Israeli establishment, among the band of ex-generals, advisers in the 'war on terrorism,' ambassadors, and professors who are active in increasing the 'national strength' of Israel."

Whose Intifada—Theirs or Ours? On the Growing Popular Alienation from the Palestinian Leadership

An Interview with Husam Khader[*]

Toufic Haddad

Q: September 28, 2001, marked the first-year anniversary of the beginning of the Al Aqsa Intifada. Can you evaluate where we stand?

A: The Intifada, generally speaking, is a blessing (*khair*). It has been able to return the Palestinian issue to its natural place, emerging from a state of deep desperation regarding the political process, which Israel used as a

---

[*] Husam Khader is a refugee from Jaffa whose family was forced into exile in 1948. He grew up in Balata refugee camp in Nablus (the largest refugee camp in the West Bank) and gradually emerged as a leader of the Fateh movement. Khader was exiled in 1986 and returned to Palestine only in 1994. In 1996 he was elected as a Fateh party candidate to the Palestinian Legislative Council for the district of Nablus. In December 1999, Khader was a signatory to what became known as the "Petition of 20," which represented one of the first organized attempts by 1967 Palestinian community leaders to voice their grave concerns regarding the trajectory of the PA within the negotiated process. He commands widespread respect throughout the West Bank, particularly in the refugee camp populations, as an independent and critical voice within Fateh. He is also the founder and director of the Committee for the Defense of Palestinian Refugee Rights, based in Balata camp, which is also where his family resides. In the early-morning hours of March 17, 2003, Khader's house in the Balata refugee camp was raided and trashed by the Israeli Army and he was subsequently arrested, tried, and sentenced to seven years in prison.[40]

This interview was conducted on October 5, 2001, in Balata refugee camp, in an effort to shed light upon the status of the current Intifada one year after its launching. It originally appeared in *Between the Lines* no. 11, October 2001.

guise to evade its commitments [under the Oslo Accords]. The Intifada has also come as an expression of the refusal of the Palestinian street to accept the humiliating conditions of Oslo's "security" clauses and the other negative consequences Oslo was having within the Palestinian setting, including the absence of law, order, and transparency in our public institutions, as well as high levels of administrative, financial, and political corruption.

In this sense, the Intifada has been able to accomplish a great deal: it has been able to return the spirit of popular resistance (*moqawama al sha'biyeh*), armed resistance (*moqawama musallaha*), and martyrdom to the Palestinian political dictionary; all had been made "illegal" in the previous phase [in the Oslo era and under the Palestinian Authority].

Furthermore—and this is very important—the Intifada was a victory for the "nationalist current" (*al tayar al watani*) within the PA, at the expense of the "economic current," which had tied its fate to Oslo (*tayar Oslo al iqtisadi*). The representatives of this current have for the past seven years negotiated with the Israelis while simultaneously pursuing individual economic interests in exchange for providing collective security for Israel.

This victory [of the nationalist current] was an extremely important accomplishment. National unity has been able to take form in unprecedented ways. The Intifada was also able to end many of the internal tragedies witnessed in the pre-Intifada era, the most important of which were the closing of the Jericho casino and the end to the process of political arrest [of opposition group members by the PA].[41] These, in my estimation, have been the greatest achievements on the local level.

From here, we hope that the national current will continue its efforts and escalate the Intifada on two fronts: first, by confronting and resisting the occupation and its manifestations through all available means; second, by undertaking the process of reorganizing and realigning the internal Palestinian front.

Q: PA Minister of Information Yasser Abed Rabbo was recently quoted as saying, "Israel wants the Palestinians to forfeit Oslo and all the subsequent agreements. It wants us to lose the areas we already have. So it is in our best interests to stress our commitment to all the agreements and commitments signed."[42] What do you say to this?

A: The previous year confirmed what we were already aware of: that Oslo has no basis and that the peace process in its entirety is an illusion. Though there are small Palestinian gains that have been obtained by way of the negotiations and that we are trying with all our might to protect while Israel tries hard to cancel them, Oslo, with its previous conditions, has ended and is over, whether Yasser Abed Rabbo is willing to confess to its death or not.

I believe we must address the principle of what we want if we are to go back to the negotiations table or not: Do we want to return to the previous Israeli-imposed negotiation conditions? Or do we want to return with strong nationalist convictions with the desire to continue the peace process, accepting nothing less than the implementation of U.N. Resolutions 242, 338, and 194? The responsibility of the portfolio of public relations [which Abed Rabbo is responsible for] in the PA was to make sure that the world knew that Israel violated every agreement with impunity and thus, we, as Palestinians, cannot be expected to be committed to any of the demands that Oslo imposed upon us.

But the PA has no political media strategy. This is something the Intifada has made only too clear. You have instead an institution—the Ministry of Information—directed by Yasser Abed Rabbo to highlight his own political career. He and the others like him within the leadership who believe in the framework of Oslo support it because they see it as an opportunity for personal benefit and for economic exploitation of the Palestinian people. For them, the continuation of Oslo provides the opportunity to grab even more. The greatest tragedy, failure, and lost opportunity will be if the Intifada ends with the realization of part of our goals, and this "mixed lot" remains in place.

Q: What, then, is the leadership strategy in the current stage? The people are suffering and paying a very heavy price to live, let alone to resist.

A: I do not think that there is going to be a clear Palestinian strategy, at least in the present context. Since the very first days of the onset of the Palestinian revolution [the post-1967 Palestinian movement], the traditional leadership has acted upon a reactive basis. Not once has this leadership taken a proactive stance that is authoritative and well planned, nor is it capable of producing a strategy. There is a clear inconsistency between the official political narrative and what the people speak of and call for. One hopes that the free will of the Palestinian people will eventually direct the order of things and not those who place their wagers upon Israel, Egypt, Jordan, or the CIA.

Q: Do you believe that the PA is really serious when it talks about the return to negotiations as suggested by the Americans?[43] Is there any degree of tactics in these calls?

A: To my great dismay, yes, they are serious—far more than need be. We must realize that there is a very strong current [within the PA leadership] that applies pressure, scares Arafat, and provides him with information that is filled with lies, attempting to daunt him. This current attempts to impress upon Arafat that he will be held accountable for any bullet fired against the occupation and that his life is in danger if he does not end the Intifada. In this respect, I feel as though this current has been successful in leaving its fingerprints upon Arafat's statements and speeches.

Allow me here to declare unequivocally that from a nationalist perspective, Arafat is the leader of the nationalist current within the PA, even within the shadow of the previous seven years of Oslo. He has acted as the point of balance between the "nationalistic" current and the "Oslo economic current"—between the nationalism of our cause and those who would surrender our rights and create a Lahad regime in the area.[44] The Palestinian national factions,[45] as well as the decent and honest people within the PA, are unable to gain access or impose their conditions and intentions upon Arafat.

We are living in a state of charged emotions, all the while that attempts are being devised to break the Intifada. There is a tacit agreement between the Oslo economic current and the Israeli occupation forces, including their [the Israeli] military intelligence. This agreement seeks to sweep away all honest nationalist field leaders and operatives to prepare the groundwork for what will come after the breaking of the Intifada and its cessation. This period, like the seven years of Oslo, will be characterized by self-interest of the elite—monopolies [on products in the Palestinian market, controlled by specific Palestinian capitalists with connections to Israeli capitalists], VIP status [allowing for unimpeded travel both within the Occupied Territories and overseas], and co-optation, all in exchange for the collective security of Israel and the forgoing of our national right to establish a state, with Jerusalem as its capital and the return of the refugees. These representatives of the Oslo economic current—and I do not exaggerate here—have an interest in the continued subordination of the Palestinian economy to Israel and the destruction of Palestinian national industry so it won't compete with their monopolies and privileges and the exploitation of our society in the post-Intifada era.

Q: What do you say to the critique that in the early days of this Intifada, protests had a more "mass popular character to them" that diminished after the first few months, while the "militarization of the Intifada" became more pronounced?

A: In the previous Intifada [1987–1993], the Israeli occupation army was in the heart of our cities, villages, and refugee camps, thus requiring nothing less than a direct and wide-scale popular confrontation to this form of occupation.

But today the Intifada is confronted with a geographical reality imposed by the regionalism of Areas A, B, and C that has brought about the inutility and ineffectiveness of the previous forms of demonstration seen in the first Intifada. Now the Israelis are outside our cities and we need to go to them if we desire to confront them. The soldiers themselves are so well equipped and defended that they are capable of killing you at any time. At least when Israeli soldiers were within our cities, there was a chance that they could be hit and possibly hurt. The Intifada has sought, in part, the alternative of armed struggle to help in the achievement of breaking the occupation.

The fragmentation that took place in the West Bank and Gaza under Oslo was the genius of the Israelis [see Introduction]. It is also evidence of the foolishness of the Palestinians who agreed to the scheme, who could not see that this plan was designed to prevent any unified popular action. This only shows that the Israelis were thinking years in advance, while the Palestinians were thinking of the privileges the political agreements would bring them.

At the same time, it is wrong to think that this Intifada is strictly military and not "popular." The popularity of this Intifada is witnessed in existing events that the people can participate in—be they days of commemoration, funerals, boycotts and so on, in which often tens of thousands of people from all social strata are involved.

However, from the beginning of the Intifada I have been saying that the presence of the PA, and its attempts to stop the growth of a balancing or alternative body capable of leading the Palestinian street, has left us without "national unity," but with a loose collection of factional leaders and field operatives. Rather than strategy leading the Intifada, it is the continued spilling of Palestinian blood that hardens the people's resolve to continue to resist.

Nonetheless, I believe that ultimately it will be the Palestinian faith in our cause and our willingness to sacrifice ourselves on the path toward accomplishing our rights and justice that will redeem us.

I hereby confirm my emphatic support—an opinion I do not shy away from—of [armed] confrontation of the occupation—be it soldiers or settlers—within the 1967 Occupied Territory boundaries. It is a natural and legitimate right. I should also say that I have strong reservations about martyrdom operations that target civilians within the boundaries of 1948 Occupied Palestine.

Q: Where does this place the role of the internal front in this Intifada?

A: The internal front is of utmost importance. The feeling of desperation that has resulted from a lack of harmony between Yasser Arafat and the field operatives is increasing. So is the call of the various political factions and powers for genuine unity and rectification of the political, administrative, and monetary strata. These matters relate directly to the people's willingness to sacrifice themselves for the cause. People are asking a very important question: Who is it that will benefit from and reap the harvest of this Intifada? In the shadow of the presence of the corrupt structures and individuals represented in the Oslo economic current, I say there is no utility in struggle. However, if this struggle is an indirect means to trample upon those individuals—to do away with them, isolate them socially, and boycott them entirely, this would be something very important to achieve.

Q: This Intifada and its spokespersons have emphasized the goals of the Intifada to be the establishment of an independent state along the 1967 borders, with Jerusalem as its capital. Though lip service may be given in certain instances, it is clear that the issue of the refugees has been marginalized out of a tacit feeling that it is unrealizable as a goal of the Intifada. What are the prospects, given the current nature of the Intifada, to achieve these goals?

A: First let me be clear by saying that I do not believe that the Intifada in its current form and reality is capable of achieving even the goal of establishing an independent state with Jerusalem as its capital [let alone the goal of return]. The Intifada in its current form—including its types of resistance, the internal front, the loose coalition of political parties on one side and the PA on the other, and so on—is not capable of accomplishing the nationalist project for which it was created and for which the people rose in resistance.

As far as the PA is concerned, this Intifada is being conducted to improve the conditions for and prepare the groundwork to be in the best position for when the decision is made to return to the negotiations table.

However, if the Intifada is to set for itself the goal of national liberation, as the people demand, we must organize ourselves differently. We have to engage the entire PA security agencies and all the groupings and factions of the people to participate in a new and creative armed struggle, anticolonialist and antioccupation in nature, that involves the attacking of Israeli interests and presence everywhere. It is well known that the PA [security services], after an entire year of the Intifada, has yet to actively participate in it. Thus, for example, at least eighty-five Palestinians from the various security services have been killed throughout the course of the Intifada: Fifty-four of these have been killed [by the Israeli Army while] simply doing their jobs, sitting at checkpoints or in barracks. They were not killed in confrontations; they were killed by being shelled by Israel. If those eighty-five had instead been killed in the process of armed confrontation with Israel, the reality of the Intifada would be a hundred steps ahead of where it is today. Instead we have a situation where Israel is hunting and picking off our men within the national security forces and our honest political leadership like rabbits.

The PA and the Oslo economic current continue to want the young free-spirited and courageous fighters from the first Intifada who joined the security services to be a private army for the defense of a group of thieves and their personal interests. They do not want from these young military heroes—many of whose lives were characterized by great sacrifices for the national cause, including prison sentences [in Israeli jails], political arrest, torture, suffering, and injury—to take a role in the process of national liberation. These people [the Oslo economic current] still bet upon the return of the situation before the present Intifada, endeavoring to ensure that Palestinians remain entangled in the Israeli occupation in exchange for their own monopolies and privileges.

As for the marginalization of the issue of the right of return, it requires nothing less than the formation of a new Palestinian political party and resistance movement that will engage in a fiercer and more widespread resistance. It will have to overarch the Palestinians within Palestine and those beyond its borders, particularly the residents of the refugee camps, who have always formed the nucleus of any Intifada.

The Ends of the Scorched Earth[*]

Toufic Haddad

Very soon after the September 11, 2001, attacks it became only too evident that a new campaign was about to be waged against the Palestinian people and their cause in an effort to isolate them within the media's newfound bipolar world of "civilization, justice, and good" versus "barbarism, terrorism, and evil." Any and all efforts to elucidate the nuances of gray—let alone speak of the reality of a people under occupation and Israel's relentless assaults against them—would quickly be swept away in what has become an international barrage against the most elementary human values, freedoms, and rules of logical integrity. What wasn't immediately clear to Palestinians, however, was the extent to which Israel would go in trying to force the Palestinians into the camp of "terrorists." Neither was it clear to what extent the PA would go in its attempts to deter this from happening.

The Ceaseless Fire Cease-fire

Sharon's unified government gleefully stole the opportunity created in the haze of the rubble of New York and Washington, D.C., to pummel the Palestinians. The destruction wrought in Jenin, Ramallah, Hebron, Rafah, and Jericho in the following two weeks resulted in thirty-two Palestinians killed and scores more injured. Once the dust had settled somewhat, however, immense international pressure was exerted to bring about a cease-fire on September 26, 2001, declared in part so that the United States could more easily assemble its "antiterror coalition" [in preparation for its attack and occupation of Afghanistan]. But in the wake of the long list of particularly brutal Israeli assaults against Palestinian cities and villages, the declaration of cease-fire between Arafat and Israeli Minister of Foreign Affairs Shimon Peres [Labor] in the Likud-Labor unified government was made to ring hollow—especially regarding its Oslo-like incantations of "full security cooperation," the exertion of "maximum efforts to sustain the declared cease-fire," and the "beginning of the lifting of the closure."

And hollow it was. Less than two kilometers from where Peres and Arafat were meeting at the Gaza International Airport,[46] Palestinian re-

---

[*] This article originally appeared in *Between the Lines* no. 11, October 2001.

sistance forces in Rafah on the Egypt–Gaza border had dug a tunnel beneath an Israeli military installation and blew it up, injuring five Israeli
soldiers, one critically. By the time Peres left the area, Israel's scorched
earth campaign would begin, resulting in seven Palestinians being killed
and seventeen houses being demolished within twenty-four hours.

Privy to the fact that they would pay dearly if the situation did not abate,
the PA began efforts to cool the ire of the Palestinian resistance forces, if not
out of loyalty to the Peres-Arafat cease-fire, then out of an increasing sense
that events on the Palestinian street were becoming uncontrollable. After an
Israeli woman from the settlement of Teqoa near Bethlehem was killed on
September 24, 2001, the PA temporarily appeased Israeli security demands
that a well-known Tantheem member from Bethlehem, 'Atef Abayat, be arrested for supposedly being involved in the shooting attack. The PA
promptly complied, presuming it would win valuable points in the "war on
terror." The only problem was that as soon as word arose of Abayat's arrest,
the Bethlehem-based Tantheem offered the PA its own ultimatum: either
release Abayat immediately or mortars would be fired upon the nearby settlement of Gilo. Abayat was promptly released by the stated deadline.[47]

Livid regarding his decreasing control over events, Arafat personally
issued orders for the changing of the PA police chiefs in the Bethlehem
and Rafah areas. In the case of the latter, Arafat also issued a request to Israel that he be allowed to move an additional four hundred to six hundred
PA security personnel from the north of the Gaza Strip to Rafah in the
south so as to "better fulfill his part of the cease-fire."

But the momentum of Palestinian resistance could not be deterred so
easily. On the night of October 2, 2001, a Hamas cell composed of
Ibrahim Rayan (17) and Abdallah Sha'ban (18) (both from Jabaliya
refugee camp near Gaza City) penetrated the Israeli settlement of Elai
Sinai in the Gaza Strip. The prolonged four-hour raid on the well-forti-
fied settlement left two settlers dead and fifteen settlers and soldiers injured, in addition to the death of the two Palestinian youths who
conducted the operation. This operation followed a similar attack a
month earlier conducted by the Democratic Front for the Liberation of
Palestine (DFLP) on the Israeli bunker position of Gan Ur in Khan Younis that killed three Israeli soldiers. Both attacks shredded the illusion of
Israel's defenses in the Gaza Strip and most likely will prove to be among
the events that force Israel out of the Gaza Strip.[48]

The PA's reaction to the event was predictable but particularly backstabbing to the feelings of the Palestinian street, which widely supported

the operation. While stating its commitment to the cease-fire, the PA openly condemned the attack on Elai Sinai *even before the operation had been completed*—i.e., while the Palestinian militants Rayan and Sha'ban were engaged in a shoot-out with Israeli soldiers within the settlement borders.

And it wasn't just the Islamist factions who were pushing the envelope: three days later, Natheer Hammad, a Fateh activist from Jenin, dressed up as an Israeli soldier and opened fire at the central bus station in the Israeli city of Afula near Nazareth, killing three and injuring fourteen, before being gunned down by Israeli police. The operation was the first time, at least since the early days of the Intifada, that Fateh had conducted a military operation within the Green Line, breaking its traditional concentration upon soldiers and settlers within the 1967 Occupied Territories.

Growing Class Rifts: Murder at the Islamic University

The momentum Palestinian resistance activities have developed and the street's support for them in the shadow of a crippling Israeli siege policy have placed the PA in an uncomfortable position. With the increasing price the Palestinians are paying for their resistance, the resolve to continue and achieve the aims of the Intifada, particularly among the most marginalized classes in Palestinian society (the refugees, the villagers) becomes further entrenched, while their willingness to compromise—even to hear of a return to negotiations—decreases. This bodes ill for elements within the upper and middle classes linked to the PA (both economically and in the "security" realm), who have recently shown themselves intent upon using the pretext of September 11 to shift the Palestinian movement back into the theater of negotiations, in light of the "New World Order" part II, being constructed by the U.S. administration. It was precisely these elements that took advantage of popular Palestinian protest against the American-led assault on Afghanistan on October 8, 2001.

The Islamic University in Gaza decided to hold a demonstration in protest against the war against Afghanistan. A member of the student council later interviewed recalled, "We have held hundreds of events throughout the course of the Intifada, and not one required permission, certainly not to voice our protest against the American strikes. For that reason we were surprised to see the [PA] riot police. They didn't ask us to break up the demonstration. They just came after us with clubs."[49] The demonstrators were beaten back to the university campus, where many students from the nearby Al Azhar University (considered to be Fateh dominated) began participating in the unfolding events as well. The demonstration quickly escalated from batons to tear gas and live bullets that sprayed the crowds. Three people were killed, including a thirteen-year-old boy, while dozens were wounded.[50]

Once word of events circulated, the streets of Gaza were set alight. Angry groups of Palestinian youths, many from the poorest sections of Gaza, attacked symbols of the PA and the class of wealthy profiteers associated with it, including burning down police stations in Sheikh Rudwan and Shati refugee camp, in addition to the PA Civil Aviation Authority and the Palestinian Airline Company. Jabaliya camp, Nusseirat camp, Khan Younis, and Rafah witnessed similar fury as the night continued.

Intent upon pinning blame for the events upon the perennial scapegoat Hamas, the PA police claimed that "unknown masked men began firing from within the university upon the students and police, forcing police to act in the same manner"[51]—a claim the university administration vehemently denied. The police also claimed that the demonstration was "chaos that threatened the life of citizens" and that "those who organized the demonstration bear full responsibility for what took place for holding this unlicensed, unlawful event."[52]

But the PA wishes in vain that the targeting of student protestors in Gaza was a problem it faced solely with the Islamist factions. Wide swathes of the popular classes (significant portions of which are associated with Fateh) participated in the Gaza events, perceiving it to be the straw that broke the camel's back. The frustration on the street had reached an extreme within the context of Israel's unending assaults against it, a taxing resistance campaign, and the endless cynicism of the PA, which constantly tries to manipulate the Intifada in the service of its stated objective (the "return to negotiations").

Indeed, the basic centers of power—be they financial, political, or related to decision making—within the PA polity have yet to be reshuffled, despite the fact that the Intifada created the illusion that this might be the case or at least was an issue that was to be addressed at a later stage. The "surprise of riot police," no doubt trained by courses offered by the European Union and the CIA since 1994, was a rude awakening to the Palestinian masses. Its clearest message was that no significant internal Palestinian change has yet to occur. This forces these classes to ponder more deeply the relationship between "internal" and "external" liberation in the context of their resistance and struggle.

While Israel beamed in approval, assuming it had succeeded in its long-sought desire to foment internal chaos among Palestinians—a process of questioning has been set into motion for the national movement whose answers are far from clear. This internal questioning was voiced well by the editor of the *Al Istiqlal* newspaper,[53] Ala Al Suftawi, who in the wake of events in Gaza had the following to say: "The people are prepared to offer tens of thousands of martyrs upon the alter of the Intifada until liberation and independence . . . but they are not prepared to lose one soul in a losing battle with their brothers in the police force. . . . What's important is, why did those [who shot] from within the PA kill these people [in the demonstration]? The answers are clear and are on the tongues of even the simplest folk. The smile on Peres's face can give a primary answer, to which we must add that the PA failed in its test during the resistance (*moqawama*) and in the Intifada, just as it failed the political and negotiation tests. How long, then, shall we wait at the mill, awaiting flour that has not come for a long time? . . . It is clear that there are basic realities that must inevitably be determined before the people and the political parties and powers: there is no avoiding undergoing a serious process of thinking and reevaluating the role of this Authority and its structures in a serious and comprehensive way."[54]

Is it any surprise that within the reality of the unresolved struggle for who invests in and who reaps the fruits of the Intifada, Suftawi's audacity in expressing this popular emotion brought him arrest by the PA and the shutting down of his paper?

CHAPTER 3

Back to the Essence of the Conflict: Total War— Zionist Left and Right Close National and Class Ranks

Introduction

The sidetrack Zionist colonialism took with respect to the "Israeli-Palestinian conflict" during the 1990s, as embodied in the Oslo apartheid solution, ended with the Palestinian rejection of Barak's "generous offers" at Camp David in July 2000 (see Introduction). Israel's alternative strategy to the Oslo framework was then publicly disclosed in August 2002 by Army Chief of Staff Moshe Ya'alon, who declared a bloody policy of indefinite war against Palestinian nationalism, which might include expulsion "if needed." The goal of this war was also explicitly presented as the need to inscribe in the Palestinians' consciousness their complete defeat and to expunge all remnants of national collective identity by liquidating any basic social existence that might enable the pursuit of liberation.

The Israeli political-military establishment's realization that the Palestinians would not accept the subcontractor security role assigned to Arafat or surrender the right of return as demanded at Camp David in July 2000, together with the increased challenge of the Jewish definition of the state by Palestinian citizens in Israel (see Chapter 4), brings the pre-1948 Zionist understanding of the essence of the "conflict" as an existential contradiction between Zionism and Palestinian nationalism to the forefront. This explains Ya'alon's candid reference to the possible need for the original "solution" of doing away with the indigenous Palestinian population, which indeed was practiced by the Zionist brand of colonialism both in 1948 and, to a lesser degree, in 1967.[1]

This collective understanding aroused the urgent need among the Zionist Left and Right to reunite around their shared commitment to the definition of Israel as a Jewish state and to its "security" as a supreme value that overrides the absoluteness of human rights and democratic procedures. The efforts to close ranks between Zionist liberals/Left and the Right, witnessed in this period, took place in dozens of joint meetings that also aimed at preserving the class and ethnic hegemony of the Ashkenazi elites.

Many Zionist liberals, including those within academia, contributed their "enlightened expertise" as a justification for this process. Loyal to their traditional political affinity to the United States as the bastion of democracy, they willingly joined the discourse of the "war on terror," even explicitly saying that "it is no time for democracy." This served to justify the assassinations carried out against Palestinian activists, while excluding any moral considerations from the discourse surrounding them or the other daily human rights violations in the 1967 Occupied Territories. The Israeli High Court also supported this when it rejected the appeal demanding cessation of the assassination policy, thus becoming partner to the facistization process of Israeli society.

Israel's long-term goals pursued in this period dictated its opposition to the possibility for a cease-fire, which could in turn lead to "immature" political negotiations (with this opposition later finding its more complete expression in the "unilateral" strategy (see Chapter 9). Likewise, the irrelevant and even hypocritical plans for a "partial solution" publicized in this period by various Labor Party ministers and MKs, together with Palestinian figures, did not suggest anything that hadn't already been rejected by the Palestinians. The never-ending meetings and declarations by Peres (Labor) and others, with European bodies and the Quartet, which continued during these months (providing the semblance of "peace-seeking diplomacy") were in any case obsolete in light of Israel's redefinition of the "conflict" in terms of eternal war.

A Society Stripped of Its Democratic and Moral Pretensions[*]

Tikva Honig-Parnass

As the atrocities in the 1967 Occupied Territories reach unprecedented levels, the large majority of Israeli society has increased its support for Sharon's policies, and calls upon him to inflict even harsher measures against the Palestinians. A recent poll showed that 85 percent of the Jewish public support the means used in repressing the Intifada.[2]

No Time for Democracy

Moral considerations have completely disappeared from public discourse in Israel. When a few public figures on the Left recently began expressing their criticism of the assassination policy, they did so based on pragmatic considerations alone—namely, its "inefficiency" in terms of being able to reduce the rate of Palestinian military operations. Below is an account of the true moral corruption of the political and cultural elites, which was recently featured in B. Michael's weekly column in *Yediot Ahronot*.

> The written press cynically reports as a matter of fact about the meetings of the "three elders" [of the unified government] (Ariel Sharon [Likud], Shimon Peres and Benjamin Ben Eliezer [Labor]), who "confirm each time the suggestion of the name of the next Palestinian to be assassinated." There is also a lively public debate, as befits a democratic society. Leaders and professional surveys study public opinion regarding the "liquidation policy"—a "policy" of institutionalized public hangings. Intellectuals, academicians, and ordinary citizens who care participate in an active and determined manner in the cultural polemics on the subject of "Liquidations—For and Against." Democracy at its best, indeed.[3]

The Israeli High Court itself has increasingly become a partner to the accelerating facistization of Israeli society. Indeed, for decades the High Court acted as the arm of the occupation regime, conferring legitimacy on Israel's atrocities in the 1967 Occupied Territories. However, while actually ignoring the Fourth Geneva Conventions, for example, it made sure to base its decisions on interpreting them in a way that "exempts" Israel from violating human rights. Furthermore, the High Court has made ef-

---

*This article first appeared in *Between the Lines* no. 13, February 2002.

forts to give the impression that it is an objective and professional body that serves the rule of law and justice. This month, however, this fortress of "Israeli democracy" adopted the blatant "security" language of the crowd in legitimizing assassinations.

On January 29, [2002], the High Court rejected the appeal submitted by MK Mohammad Barakeh, the chair of the Hadash faction in the Knesset,[4] and Siham Thabet, the widow of Dr. Thabet Thabet (former secretary-general of Fateh in Tulkarem, assassinated in January 2001), demanding the cessation of Israel's assassination policy. Attorney Nahla 'Atiya (a Palestinian citizen of Israel) argued that an act of assassination needs a court order and asked the High Court to issue an interim order to stop the assassinations until a decision about the appeal is reached. She also mentioned the two categories of "soldiers" and "civilians," who, despite the differences between them, "deserve the defense of the law." Below is the discourse that developed in the courtroom:

Judge Matza: But there is a third thing named terror. It is the enemy of all humanity. All states relate to terror as a joint enemy.

Attorney Atiya: And who decides who is a terrorist?

Judge Matza: Certainly not the court.

Attorney Atiya: But there is also the right to live. The killing of a human being is forbidden and should not be committed clandestinely.

Judge Kheshin: Tell this to those who send terrorists to the center of Jerusalem or to the Dolfinarium [a nightclub in Tel Aviv in which twenty-three Israelis were killed by a Hamas suicide bomber standing in line to enter on June 2001].

Judge Matza: Do you want the minister of defense to be issued a permit by the court before every pinpoint preventive operation [the Israeli term used for assassinations]? This issue is not within the court's jurisdiction.

Judge Kheshin (*sarcastically*): Maybe you would like us to discuss this in court in the presence of both sides [Palestinian and Israeli, before confirming each assassination]?[5]

After Attorney Atiya argued that if the state had succeeded in detaining Mordechai Vanunu and Mustafa Dirani outside its borders,[6] Israel can also catch wanted Palestinians in Area A (the areas technically under Palestinian civil and security control[7]) and bring them to trial in Israel, Judge Kheshin responded, "It is my son who enters this area, and I don't want to endanger him. Your son, my lady [referring to Attorney Atiya, whose son is a Palestinian citizen of Israel and does not serve in the army], does not enter Area A [and thus is not in danger]."

Professor Shlomo Avinery, the internationally renowned political scientist who heads the Institute for European Studies at Hebrew University,[8] joined other peaceniks disappointed by Oslo and now actually justifies violations of human rights along the U.S. model, adopted after September 11, 2001. Avinery writes:

> When a democracy sets out to war, its public discourse changes. For instance, the issue of human rights. Since September 11, 2001, people in the United States have been in prison under administrative detention. Their names are not known. Some of them have no access to a lawyer. And for those who are permitted to meet with a lawyer, the court allows listening in on them. The American public does not take to the streets in order to defend these people. The Americans are also changing the immigration laws in a way that clearly goes against people of Muslim origin, and the public accepts it.[9]

Stripped of Minimal Solidarity with the Working Classes and the Poor

But it is not just in regard to Palestinians in the 1967 Occupied Territories where the moral degeneracy of the Israeli political and social establishment is exposing itself. The public discourse on the socially cruel 2002 budget, which hits most forcefully the Palestinians in Israel and Mizrahi Jews as well as the poor and disabled, reveals an additional dimension of the moral bankruptcy of the Israeli state and society. The main victims of the neoliberal policies of the government (see Introduction) lack political power in terms of parties or trade unions that could in principle fight against the "free-market" policies. The Jewish parties in the Knesset and in the government coalition have long abandoned even the pretense of speaking on behalf of the entire working class or watching out for the interests of the Palestinian national minority. Instead they fight to cancel the proposed budget cuts for the specific social sector that is their supposed constituency in the next general elections. Their indifference toward the plight of disabled civilians (as distinct from disabled soldiers, who are well taken care of by the army authorities) is summarized below by the commentator Mordechai Gilat. The former have been demonstrating day and night for the last fifty days in the lobby of the Ministry of Labor and Welfare, demanding a raise in their 1,740 shekel per month (approximately U.S. $385) allowance:

> The truth should be said to the disabled; you are a kind of nuisance to most MKs and the government. You are a headache to the "socially oriented" ministers of Shas, Likud, and Labor. You are a pain in the ass to those who pretend to be the representatives of the proletariat. You are second-rate citizens,

people whom the elected leaders prefer neither to see nor to listen to. . . . There is no money for you.[10]

The very fact that the self-organized strike of the disabled has been the only long, determined strike launched against the annual budget indicates the heightened stage of dismantling any independent working-class organization and ideology in Israel. At the beginning of January 2002, many Israeli NGOs and research centers were involved in two mass demonstrations against the cuts in the 2002 budget, which increased unemployment, and in support of the striking disabled. This came as a refreshing phenomenon that filled to a certain extent the vacuum created by the total disregard of the political parties of the deteriorating condition of the working classes and the poor. However, these solidarity actions were entirely isolated and received no support from the Left, namely Labor or Meretz.

The extent and type of support the disabled have received from the Histadrut (the umbrella organization of workers) illustrate this body's true position on neoliberal policies and ideology. MK Amir Peretz, secretary-general of the Histadrut and chair of its Am Echad (One People) party,[11] refrained from mobilizing the large, powerful public-sector trade unions, whose members enjoy high salaries and whose interest the Histadrut traditionally serves (see Introduction), to campaign against the budget. Nor did he mobilize the unions to carry out any acts of solidarity with the disabled strikers, whom he always expresses warm words of support for. Instead, Peretz initiated a kind of charity activity, issuing a call on the public to make contributions to the disabled—this despite the fact that the disabled have stated their disdain for this type of initiative, emphasizing that they are asking not for charity but for their rights.

Indeed, the arrogant rule of the powerful capitalist groups and the political establishment is still largely based on their success in mobilizing the commitment of the Jewish (mostly Mizrahi) victims of their policies to Zionism and "state security." Both have been significant tools in economically and socially pacifying the oppressed Mizrahi Jews, who have been misled to believe that a commitment to Zionism and "security" will gain them acceptance into "enlightened" Ashkenazi Israeli society. The role of betrayal that intellectuals have played in exploiting the working class and the poor seems even greater here than elsewhere.[12]

Zionist Left and Right Unite in Defense of the Ashkenazi Capitalist Jewish State[*]

Tikva Honig-Parnass

Traditionally, Ashkenazi "liberal" intellectuals and academics in Israel have been connected to the Zionist Labor movement and have played a role in sustaining the hegemonic Zionist ideology of the state. Together with their mother party, Labor, they have long since abandoned the idea of social solidarity and instead support neoliberalism disguised beneath the banner of "freedom and progressiveness."

The two largest parties, Likud and Labor, rather than representing, at least to some extent, different social classes and strata, overwhelmingly represent the interests of the dominant economic groups. This is why they can continue to participate in a unified government following Sharon's victory in the 2001 elections with only secondary internal power considerations threatening to end the coalition.

By the same token, the intellectuals and academics of the liberal/Left Zionist elites, most of whom are Ashkenazi, are now capable of joining even the most extreme nationalist Right in order to preserve their hegemony, which is nourished (and has been nourished) by the interests of those who, in the last analysis, they collectively serve: big capital and the wider Israeli bourgeoisie.

Continued Efforts of the Zionist Left to Close Ranks with the Right

Precisely because the Zionist Left identified with the bloody oppression of what was a mass popular uprising in the first two months of the Intifada; precisely because the inevitability of "militarization of the Intifada" became a matter of time, which would fall into line with the preplanned strategy of bringing about the conditions for Israel to launch a total war against the Palestinian national movement; precisely because of the determination of Palestinians in Israel not to surrender their strengthened Palestinian national identity and challenge to the Jewish-Zionist state—

---

[*] This article first appeared in *Between the Lines* no. 13, February 2002.

precisely because of all of these things, an urgent need arose to reunite around the Zionist tribal fire. The cracking of Zionism's hegemonic self-righteous ideology, which is conditioned on the subdued acceptance of Palestinians, has induced a sense of panic resulting in hurried attempts to close ranks around the definition of Israel as the "Jewish-Democratic" state.[13]

This was reflected in the repeated phenomenon of unprecedented measures whereby liberal Zionists and those on the Right, and even the extreme Right (both secular and religious), jointly participated in tens of events that took place in universities, research institutes, and individual projects and discussion groups, attempting to emphasize their collective increased adherence to the "Jewish state."

Dan Margalit, a senior political commentator on the three main Israeli television channels and the daily newspaper *Ma'ariv*, dedicated his column in the latter to describing at length this phenomenon:

> Precisely because the [Israeli Jewish] academia—actually only part of it—was aware of the difficult conditions Arabs [Palestinian citizens of Israel] live in, they [the academics] are also more frustrated than other parts of the [Israeli] public by the Arabs' refusal to compromise on the Jewish-Zionist aspect. Among the liberal academia, more and more voices are heard arguing that in a final political agreement based on the establishment of a Palestinian state in the West Bank, there is a need to examine the possibility of transferring Um El Fahem and its surrounding villages to the jurisdiction of this state, without of course moving even one Arab from his home. . . . If I had been Arab, I would have seen in an ever-widening part of the moderate and liberal Jewish academia—who until recently have been allies with the just demands of the [Palestinian] minority—the nut that is hardest to crack. [This is] because the strengthening of the most seclusive trends among Arabs regarding the state looks more and more suspicious to them [the liberal Israeli academia].[14]

Failed Attempts to Receive Palestinian Citizens' Acknowledgment of the Jewish State

In some of these meetings, organized by institutions that deal with the issues of democracy and human rights in Israel, liberal and national religious[15] Zionists have confronted Palestinian citizens in an effort to bring them to declare their acceptance of the Jewish definition of the state of Israel.

Margalit focuses on one of these meetings, which he describes as "The most serious, significant, and sad effort [to confront the problem]." It took place in 2001 at the Israeli Democracy Institute, where joint marathon discussions were organized under the title "The Jewish-Arab

Rift," headed by Professor Ruth Gavison (former chair of the Association for Civil Rights in Israel (ACRI) and professor at the School of Law of the Hebrew University) and Dr. Adel Man'a (from the Van Leer Institute in Jerusalem).

The discussion group was of a most "moderate political composition of participants," whose defined aim was to sign a joint Jewish-Arab covenant upon its culmination. The Jewish side included, among others, certain people who in Israel are considered truly liberal—individuals like Professor Mordechai Kremnitzer (School of Law, Hebrew University, well known for his determined fight against violations of human rights), Philosophy Professor Edna Margalit-Ulman (Hebrew University), and Sociology Professor Sami Samooha (Haifa University), "both of the peace camp," alongside secular right-wingers like Moshe Arens (former minister of foreign affairs [Likud]), Dr. Eli Reches, an "expert in Arab affairs," Tel Aviv University, and Rabbi Yoel Ben Noon (a "moderate settler").[16]

The Palestinians attacked the policies of discrimination and dispossession of Israeli governments against the Palestinian citizens and declared that "they have no trust in the Israeli establishment." The Jews in the discussion group poured forth concessions and moderation, ranging from economic and social equality to replacing the current Jewish-Zionist national anthem with one acceptable to the Palestinian citizens as well.

However, the impasse that ended the discussion was a suggestion by Professor Kremnitzer to have the final joint covenant state that "the Jewish people had actualized their natural right to self-determination in Israel, where full equality between its citizens will be established."[17] According to Margalit, the response of the majority of the Palestinian group was negative. Dr. Man'a stated that he could not accept "this issue of 'two states for two people,' as though the Arabs are put in a cage in the West Bank and Gaza Strip in which only there they are allowed to be Palestinians." Kremnitzer, who was disappointed by the Palestinian position, said, "If the Arabs don't agree even to that, there is no way to continue." Furthermore, Sami Samooha scolded his Arab colleagues as though they were children, saying, "They [the Palestinian citizens] do not confront the question of living in a Jewish state. All the time the Jews have to justify [the fact] that this is a Jewish state, while the Arabs do not conduct the [necessary] thinking. They do not deal with this [the Jewish state] on the intellectual level."

Margalit reports on another failed attempt to achieve a joint perspective regarding the identity of the Jewish state and the Palestinians' citizenship status within it. This meeting between Israeli and Palestinian MKs and public figures, which took place in Haifa University, was organized by the Haifa branch of the Institute for Democracy, in the hope that the Palestinian MKs would show more readiness than the Palestinian intellectuals in the previous meeting. However, this did not happen. It became even clearer to the Left politicians that the Palestinian participants fully support the recent strengthening of the Palestinian demand for national collective rights:

> MK Ofir Paz-Pines [Labor] suggested confirming in a Knesset law that the Declaration of Independence, which was written by Ben-Gurion on the day of the establishment of the state of Israel, be the introduction to a constitution [which Israel is yet to have] that promises full equality of rights to all its citizens. . . . However, Paz-Pines concluded, Jews tend wrongly to assume that the Arabs demand that Israel become the state of all its citizens. [But this too is not enough (for Arabs)]. They have national collective demands [as well].

This is why these progressives have escalated their search for allies, even among the most extreme right wing, aiming to close ranks around their essential common perspective: defending the nature of the capitalist, Ashkenazi, Jewish-Zionist state. This was most recently seen in the Kineret Covenant.

Internal Unification: The Kineret Covenant for Defending Zionist and Class Hegemony

This month [February 2002], figures from across the Jewish political spectrum signed the pretentious Kineret Covenant, which declared the wide common denominator of their Zionism. The list of participants who conceived of the covenant, together with its signatories, included, on the one hand, many who had long been among the most vocal representatives of the Oslo "peace" framework—public figures such as Professor Yuli Tamir (former minister of absorption under Barak's government and a teacher of political science at the Hebrew University) and Dov Lautman (ex-chair of the Manufacturers' Association of Israel). On the other hand, the Kineret Covenant included signatories and supporters from the fanatical right wing, including Brigadier (Reserves) Efi Eitam (from the National Religious Party (Mafdal), who calls for greatly expanding the settlements and for reoccupying the West Bank and annexing it); Geography Professor Arnon Sofer (the foremost Israeli academic warning about "the demographic danger of Arabs in Israel"); Emuna Allon (a settler journalist representing the most extreme current within the settlers' movement); and several rabbis, including the above-mentioned "moderate settler" Rabbi Yoel Ben Noon.

And, yes, the list of signatures also includes the names of a number of Mizrahim, most of whom belong to the principally Ashkenazi "peace camp." Their signatures contribute to the misleading feel of a "multicultural, across-the-political-spectrum" document that pretends to unite all Jews for the collective benefit of all Israeli citizens.

The covenant repeats the core tenets of Zionist ideology: that Israel is "the national home of the Jewish people" and that it is a "Jewish and democratic state." However, not a word is said about the occupation and settlements and their implications for the covenant's commitment to the unspecified "principle of self-determination of the Palestinians and its expression in a nation-state."

Under the heading "The State of Israel Respects the Rights of the Arab Minority," the covenant calls for "the need to immediately implement the principle of civil equality in those areas in which non-Jewish citizens [not the "Arab-Palestinians"] are discriminated against and neglected." However, in light of the statement presented beneath the heading "The State of Israel Is a Jewish-Democratic State," the covenant states that "in order to ensure the continuity of the existence of a Jewish-democratic Israel," it is necessary to continue to preserve a "substantive Jewish majority" which in both itself and its implications is the core of the Israeli form of apartheid.

The underlying motive of the Kineret Covenant is, in fact, its call for the preservation of the status of the hegemonic elites and the Zionist ideology that legitimizes it. As Dr. Sami Shalom Chetrit, notes:

> Question: What is the connection between the left Zionist Professor Yuli Tamir and the extreme-right-wing, fascist Brigadier (Reserves) Efi Eitam?
> Answer: They are both motivated by fear. Namely, what connects a nationalistic Zionist, who is a fanatic settler-occupier, to a secular, liberal Ashkenazi-Zionist woman is the panic that their control of the European anti-Mizrahi Zionist state will slip through their fingers. . . . And what is most notable is the fact that this panic is precisely the same panic that brought about the current fascist government [Likud, headed by Sharon] and that this Ashkenazi-Zionist covenant enjoys full ideological backing by the current nationalist regime. This is the regime that is ready to jail people for expressing their political opinion (as indicated by the accusation sheet against MK Azmi Bishara[18]), for whom the disabled are merely social nuisances, and for whom the workers have become redundant and harmful. This is the regime that has given its consent to this shameful document.[19]

Zionism's Fixation: War Without End[*]

Tikva Honig-Parnass

The decision to replace the negotiations framework of Oslo and return to the original Zionist approach of total war between Zionism and the Palestinian national movement was explicitly declared this month [September 2002] by the new Israeli Chief of Staff, Moshe Ya'alon. The presentation of Israel's political strategy by a representative of the military indicates both the significance of this statement and the nature of Israeli democracy. The military echelons and security industry in Israel have determined policy for years, acting behind the front of a formal democracy with the backing of all Israeli governments. However, a declared state of war entails disclosing the leadership position of the security echelons in Israeli politics as well as openly disregarding democratic values and procedures.[20]

The Israeli Chief of Staff: A War Without End

Below are lengthy excerpts taken from Ya'alon's interview with *Ha'aretz*.[21] They should be seen as most significant in terms of representing the policies implemented by Sharon's unified government while providing guidelines for what has become the emerging narrative in wide swathes of Israeli society. This includes the Zionist Left, which uses it to support the policy of all-out war against the Palestinians.

1. Palestinians as cancer

Ya'alon: The characteristics of that threat [the Palestinians] are invisible, like cancer. When you are attacked externally, you can see the attack, you are wounded. Cancer, on the other hand, is something internal. Therefore I find it more disturbing, because here the diagnosis is crucial. If the diagnosis is wrong and people say it's not cancer but a headache, the response is irrelevant. But I maintain that this is cancer. My professional diagnosis is that there is a phenomenon here that constitutes an existential threat.

---

[*] This article first appeared in *Between the Lines* no. 18, October 2002.

Q. Does that mean that what you are doing now as chief of staff, in the West Bank and Gaza Strip, is applying chemotherapy?

A. There are all kinds of solutions to cancerous manifestations. Some will say it is necessary to amputate organs. But at the moment I am applying chemotherapy, yes.

2. The Palestinian aim is to liquidate the Jewish state

Ya'alon: I maintain that the story is not occupation [of the West Bank and Gaza Strip]. The story is nonrecognition of the right of the state of Israel to exist as a Jewish state. . . . He [Arafat] saw Oslo as a Trojan horse that would enable the Palestinians to enter Israel and September 2000 [when the Intifada erupted] as the moment of emergence from the belly of the horse.

Today, too, the ideology of Fateh is to bring about Israel's disintegration from within. What they are after is not to arrive at the end of the conflict but to turn Israel into a Palestinian state.

Q. In other words, the goal of Arafat and Fateh is to liquidate Israel by stages?

A. Of course. Not to reach an agreement and not to arrive at the end of their claims, in order to preserve the conflict and to let time run its course according to the phased theory.

3. Therefore we are back to 1948 and before

Ya'alon: There has not been a more important confrontation since the War of Independence [the 1948 War.]

Q. It's that critical?

A. Yes. I have no doubt that when this period is viewed historically, the conclusion will be that the War of Independence is the most important event in our history and the present war the second most important.

Q. Even more important than the Six-Day War [1967 War] or the Yom Kippur War [1973 War]?

A. Of course. Because we are dealing with an existential threat. There was an Israeli attempt to end the Israeli-Palestinian conflict by means of a territorial compromise, and the Palestinian reply was war. So it brings us back to the confrontation of the prestate [period], the partition proposal, and the War of Independence. . . . The Palestinians have returned us to the War of Independence. Today it is clear that the state of Israel is still an alien element in the region.

4. This time, however, there must be nothing less than a change in Palestinian consciousness

Ya'alon: The facts that are being determined in this confrontation—in terms of what will be burned into the Palestinian consciousness—are fateful. If we end this confrontation in a way that makes it clear to all Palestinians that terrorism does not lead to agreements, it will improve our strategic position. On the other hand, if their feeling at the end of the confrontation is that they can defeat us, our situation will become more and more difficult.

Therefore, I say that we must not disregard the weighty meaning of this confrontation. When you grasp the essence, it becomes clear what you have to do: you have to fight for your life.

5. An eternal war without any agreed solution

Ya'alon: [Any Israeli withdrawal] will give a push to the struggle against us. Even if it appears tactically right to withdraw from here or there, from the strategic perspective it is different. That was my argument when the question of withdrawing from Joseph's Tomb [in Nablus] was raised.[22]

Q. If this is, as you say, the Palestinians' position, where is all this leading? How long are we to live by the sword?

A. I refer people who ask what the end will be to a well-known quotation of the late Moshe Dayan.[23] When he was asked in 1969 what the end would be, his reply was the biblical sentence "Do not fear, my servant Jacob." Dayan said that the emphasis should be on the path and not on the goal, on the process of the struggle and not on the final destination. As human beings we want a solution now. But "nowism" is a false messiah. It is the mother of all sins.

Growing Support for "Existential War"

Moshe Ya'alon sets forth a definition of Israel's goal in its war against the Palestinians that can never be achieved: a deep transformation in Palestinian identity and consciousness regarding the recognition of the premises of Zionism. He explicitly admits that the inevitable ends of such an abstract goal will be that no true process of political negotiation will be carried out and that the war track that replaces it is likely to develop into a war for the liquidation and/or expulsion of the Palestinian people in light of their continued resistance. In saying this, Ya'alon contradicts the misleading claim of the Labor Party regarding the present escalating bloody offensive against the entire Palestinian population—namely, that it is the necessary means of paving the way to renewing the political process with a more "realistic leadership."

However, Ya'alon would not have dared express his positions publicly without being aware of the roaring silence of the liberal intellectual elites in the face of the nationalist-religious-militarist positions that now openly dictate the Likud-Labor unified government policies and public discourse.

The arrogance of this head of the military junta even receives direct backing from the growing adoption of his narrative by many of the intellectual elites who "feel disappointed by the Oslo framework," which they enthusiastically supported.

Thus, no less abstract and unattainable than Ya'alon's goal is that of the world-renowned Israeli "liberal" Shlomo Avinery, professor of political science at Hebrew University. Avinery, in fact, demands that the Palestinians accept the legitimacy of Zionism as a condition for any political process to begin with. Moreover, he justifies this demand by identifying it with the demand for "the right to exist"—the conceding of which led to the Oslo Accord's failure:

> But whoever looks into the mounds of agreements that Israel signed [after Oslo] will be shocked at the extent to which the Israeli negotiators neglected the ideological infrastructure of the conflict. . . . Neither the Israeli experts on security, nor the economists and legalists who accompanied the negotiations for many years, ever understood that the way to historic reconciliation is not only through security and economic cooperation arrangements but in a principal transformation of the Palestinian position with regard to the state of Israel and its legitimacy. Therefore they did not insist on a position that an absolute condition for the process to continue should be the deep *ideological* change in the Palestinian position as it is expressed in textbooks, media, and speeches.[24]

Avinery's position reflects the growing tendency to explicitly define the "existential war" against Palestinian nationalism in terms of the battle over the Jewish-Zionist definition of the state and the principle of a "Jewish majority," which is perceived as central with regard to even the areas in the West Bank that Israel plans to annex.

Likewise, Ya'alon's arguments gain further moral sustenance from the self-professed liberal judicial and intellectual elites, which have retreated from any semblance of an absolute commitment to human rights. Thus,

Ruth Gavison, professor of law at the Hebrew University, the former chair of the Association for Civil Rights in Israel (ACRI), a senior colleague in the directorship of the Israeli Democracy Institute, and a recipient of the Jerusalem Prize for her fight for human rights, recently commented that "Manning checkpoints, clamping down closures, and even destroying houses from which shooting at soldiers takes place are legitimate military steps. Also, the killing of those who are about to commit attacks on Israelis or of those who send them [to these operations] are not acts over which the black flag [of illegitimacy] is waved."[25]

With the growing moral corruption of many in the intellectual elites[26] spreading, the likelihood that wider circles of Zionist liberals or Leftists will inevitably come to support the "eternal war" waged against the Palestinians, explicitly declared by the military and the Right, increases too. Likewise, the terrifying consequences this implies for the Palestinian people become all the more stark, as the "total war" embedded in the very nature of Zionist colonialism comes to the fore.

CHAPTER 4

The Case of MK Azmi Bishara: Revealing the True Nature of Israel's Democracy

Introduction

The democratic participation of Palestinian citizens of Israel in the state's formal political processes is always held up to Western audiences as evidence of Israel's true democratic nature. However, the escalated persecution of this citizenry by the state in recent years, and the development of the legal framework aimed at stripping them of significant aspects of their political rights, show just how shallow these assurances are. The case of MK Azmi Bishara, to which this chapter is dedicated, reveals the true nature of Israeli democracy.

The increased oppression of Palestinian citizens should also be seen as part of the all-out war launched against the Palestinian national movement (see Chapter 3). This war does not aim solely at bringing the Palestinians to accept Israel's dictates regarding the 1967 Occupied Territories; it also demands that they accept the "Jewish state," which is the central premise of Zionism, and surrender the right of return, as a condition for any "peace agreement." The ideological dimension of this war thus calls for the surrendering of the most significant indicators of Palestinian national identity and unity.

While the Palestinians in the West Bank and Gaza are involved in a struggle against the occupation regime that is largely a battle to survive and remain on their land, the Palestinians in Israel carry on a daily politi-

133

cal, legal, and ideological campaign that increasingly challenges the Jewish and Zionist identity of the state. Hence, the return to the pre-1948 definition of the conflict has also placed Palestinian citizens in the orbit of this war—a war the Zionist Left until recently defined as solely focused on the 1967 Occupied Territories. This return has meant that the concept that Israel was a "democracy" with a "civil society," which was a part of Zionist Left discourse during Oslo (and which was promoted as a way to ignore the structural inequality of Palestinian citizens), has now been shattered. Moreover, the difficulty experienced by self-professed liberal circles in Israel (including the High Court) to justify clinging to the contradictory definition of Israel as both Jewish and democratic is also increasing.

Thus, the indictments of treason and support for terrorism leveled against MK Azmi Bishara should be seen in the context of disclosing the Israeli strategy of escalating the campaign against Palestinians in Israel and their leadership. It embodies, in a nutshell, Israel's "second front" in its war of forcing the Palestinian people to accept Zionism and the Jewish state.

Bishara and the NDA—Tajamu' have been justly recognized by the Zionist establishment, including the Left, as the initiators and leaders of the process of strengthened national identification of Palestinian citizens. This includes their solidarity with their brethren in the 1967 Occupied Territories and their own struggle against the foundations of the Jewish-Zionist state, which does not recognize them as a national minority residing in their homeland but only as various religious sects (Muslim, Christian, etc.). Bishara, who is in the vanguard of democratic forces among Palestinian citizens, is thus perceived, from a "Zionist perspective," to be "a most dangerous person." This makes him a "wanted" target as Israel attempts to do away with what remains of the political content and basic freedom of 1948 Palestinian citizenship.

Although the charges against Bishara were ultimately dropped by the Supreme Court on February 1, 2006, this did not mean that the campaign against the self-organization of 1948 Palestinians ended. While this campaign had been restrained in the past by the attempts of the Supreme Court not to violate the fundamental right of Palestinian citizens to participate in the political process, the wording of the Court's decision in Bishara's case and the draconian clause 7(a) of the election law, which the Court accepts in principle, provide clear warnings to 1948 Palestinians, about what lies ahead.[1]

Accusations of Treason Leveled Against MK Bishara, Supported by the Left*

Tikva Honig-Parnass

On June 5, 2000, in Um el Fahem, MK Azmi Bishara of the National Democratic Assembly—Tajamu' (hereafter NDA—Tajamu') participated in a mass commemoration of the 1967 War. Soon after, on June 10, Bishara attended a ceremony in Qirdaha, Syria, that signified the one-year passing of former Syrian president Hafez el-Assad. On both occasions, Bishara made statements regarding the need for the Palestinian and Arab nation to resist Israel's policies and dictates, drawing forth a stormy reaction against him from the entire Israeli political spectrum.

The statement made in Um el Fahem concerned the legitimacy of Hezbollah's resistance in Lebanon. His statement in Syria called upon Arabs to support the Intifada. In Bishara's words:

> The Israeli government came into power determined to shrink the realm of resistance by putting forth an ultimatum: either accept Israel's dictates, or face full-scale war. Thus, it is not possible to continue with a third way—that of resistance—without expanding this realm [of resistance] once again so that the people can struggle and resist. Nor is it possible to expand this realm without a unified and internationally effective Arab political position. This is precisely the time for such a stance.[2]

On July 1, 2001, the Israeli police recommended the indictment of MK Bishara on violation of various sections of the penal code, including, among others, Section 99 (Treason and Assisting the Enemy) and Section 114 (Contact with Foreign Agents Affiliated with the Enemy).[3]

It was Bishara's speech in Syria that aroused the most public outrage in Israel. The Knesset called for holding a special plenum to discuss the police's accusations and decided to transfer the subject to the Knesset Committee for Internal Affairs to consider whether Bishara's parliamentary immunity should be lifted. Hysterical accusations of treason were repeated in this session, where MKs called for banning Bishara and the NDA from the next elections. The Left, Center, and Right, both in the

---

* This article first appeared in *Between the Lines* no. 12, December 2001. For comprehensive updated information on the accusations and defense of these trials, see the Adalah Web site www.adalah.org/eng/bishara.php.

Knesset and in the public at large, were equally condemning of Bishara. Hebrew University Political Science Professor Shlomo Avinery, known as a liberal dove, compared Bishara's speech in Syria to an act not less than collaboration with the Nazis.[4] Meretz MKs Yossi Sarid, Zehava Galon, and Ran Cohen competed among themselves as to whose condemnation of Bishara would be harshest. When the chair of Hadash,[5] MK Mohammad Barakeh answered a journalist's question regarding "Bishara's strong orientation to Syria," he implicitly justified efforts to rescind Bishara's Knesset immunity so that he could be put on trial: "We [Palestinian citizens] cannot angrily decry violations of our immunity as Israeli members of the Knesset and be silent at the violation of immunity and functioning of members of parliaments in other places [in the Arab world]."[6]

Moreover, Barakeh joined the widespread racist calls for preventing the NDA—Tajamu' and the northern branch of the Islamic movement from participating in the Knesset elections, while intentionally blurring the difference between their "nationalisms." The traditional submissive stance of the Israeli Communist Party, which has consistently striven to prove its patriotism, is expressed in Barakeh's words:

> [Bishara's] delusions about Arab nationalism and Islamic fundamentalism in the Israeli parliament is hypocrisy and doublespeak, and it is time to stop it. . . . I can understand people who are aspiring to bring back Arab nationalism and the glory of Islam, but this should not be done in the Knesset. You are entering the Knesset in order to legislate laws, to speak from the supreme Israeli platform, to influence political decision making in Israel. What we have here is a great hypocrisy. I say to Bishara, "Don't lie to the people. . . . In national terms we are Palestinians, but when you are talking in the context of Israeli citizenship, you cannot hold to this and at the same time complain that the state does not grant you rights. You even feel disgusted to utter the name of the state, and still you want rights. There must be a limit to this cynicism."[7]

Except for a handful of committed Jewish democrats,[8] not one liberal publicly defended the content of Bishara's words, "No to war and no to surrender,"[9] which you might expect to be the stance of any self-respecting social democrat.

Against this background it is no wonder that Bishara's immunity as a Knesset member was revoked on November 11, 2001. The way was thereafter paved for him to stand trial on charges levied by the attorney general Elyakim Rubinstein, for "supporting terror organizations" and "incitement to terror."

Once again, the Israeli Left reinforced the illegitimacy of the expressions of national consciousness by Palestinian citizens, defining them as "nationalist extremism." It thus joined the larger campaign against the Palestinian citizens of Israel and their emerging struggle against their structural discrimination in the Jewish-Zionist state.

Alongside the deepening of national identification and solidarity among the Palestinian citizens of Israel, there is an everspreading demand for national collective rights, initiated by the NDA. This demand is a top priority for the younger generation, which is dissatisfied with simply demanding equality of individual political rights, which are supposed to be automatically granted to any immigrant group that acquires citizenship in a Western country.[10]

The demand to recognize the Palestinians in Israel as a national minority in its homeland is a challenge to the Jewish state, which does not recognize any other nationality but the Jewish nationality. The assumed threat from these demands and Bishara's central role in their articulation is well recognized by the senior *Ha'aretz* commentator Uzi Benziman:

> Bishara is an eloquent and impressive person. From a Zionist perspective, he is also a dangerous man. He is the most consistent and zealous [leader] in the Arab sector who represents the perception that denies the Zionist logic inherent in the establishment of the state of Israel. He founded [the NDA—Tajamu'], which [as of August 2002] has only one member in the Knesset. But his viewpoints are increasingly taking root among the young generation.
>
> Bishara aspires to turn Israel into "a state of all its citizens"—namely, to get rid of all the Jewish and Zionist elements from the definition of the state. He aspires to replace them by another world of values—civic and nonnationalistic. Bishara is the vanguard of the current that Dr. Dani Rabinowitz and Dr. Khawla Abu Baker name in their new book *The Stand-Tall Generation.*[11] This is an ever-widening current, which demands *collective* equality of rights—and not only *personal* [rights]—for the Arab citizens of the state[12] [emphasis added].

The concern that this demand has raised is being followed by government-initiated legislation and regulations aimed at destroying the political and social organization of Palestinian society.[13] It also aims to provide the legality for escalating the theft of lands under the campaign of "Judaizing" the Galilee and Negev.

Not "Democracy Defending Itself" but Nationalism Attacking Democracy[*]

Azmi Bishara

On November 12, 2001, one day after the Knesset revoked his immunity, MK Azmi Bishara [National Democratic Assembly—Tajamu'] held a press conference in Ramallah [in the West Bank] addressing the lifting of his parliamentary immunity. Following is a transcript of his presentation, followed by reporters' questions.

The revoking of my immunity [as a member of the Knesset] is an unprecedented step in Israel's history since its establishment in 1948. Though the immunity of a Knesset member was removed in seven previous cases for criminal offenses, it has never been removed for political statements or positions. The revoking of my immunity is a dangerous step for democracy because normally Knesset members are elected precisely in order to present their political positions.

One thing, however, I wish to draw your attention to is that this is not an issue of freedom of expression, which is how people, especially in the Western media like to present it. This is so because if I weren't Azmi Bishara and if I weren't a Knesset member representing a political force [of Palestinian citizens], I think the Israeli establishment could endure the ideas I have expressed [in Um el Fahem and Syria]. In Israel, people can say the sorts of things I said, and even sharper things have been said in the past. So the issue is not the content of what I said, nor is it an issue of freedom of expression. It is a political issue.

Indeed, Israel was never a liberal democracy but a Jewish-Zionist democracy. The Arabs in Israel are considered guests—tolerated guests in the best case, but always under suspicion and considered to be a "fifth column." At present, however, a political campaign is being launched within the Israeli establishment and the Knesset aiming to redraw the boundaries of Israeli democracy so that certain political ideas and forms of political empowerment among the Arab community in Israel are excluded. The present campaign aims to further limit the political representation of the

---

[*] This article first appeared in *Between the Lines* no. 12, December 2001.

Arabs in Israel because it presents challenges to the Jewish democracy that it cannot withstand or endure.

The pretext of this campaign regards two statements I made: the first which was made in Um el Fahem, concerned the legitimacy of the resistance in Lebanon. The second related to a speech I gave in Qirdaha, Syria, calling upon the Arabs to support the Intifada as the third option, which refutes the option of total war, on the one hand, and Israeli political dictates, on the other. This was considered "incitement to commit acts of violence by the enemies of Israel against the state." This accusation is false, and we're going to prove that in court. But again, it is not what I said that really worries them. They use my words as a pretext to fight what they call the "radicalization" process of the Arabs in Israel, which started with the emergence of the NDA—our political current.

I believe that the current judicial process is a political process targeting our legitimacy—trying to delegitimize Arab political organization and participation in the political process. The fact is that the Arabs in Israel are gaining assertiveness and self-confidence in both spheres of political life: that of their national identity (emphasizing the fact that they are Arabs and Palestinians) and that of their civic issues (emphasizing the need for equal rights with the other citizens of the state of Israel). These two processes are represented by the NDA: on the one hand, we began opening up to the Arab world and to the Palestinians [in the 1967 Occupied Territories], trying to build ties, and on the other, we began calling for the transformation of Israel into the "state of its citizens," or the de-Zionization of Israel. Our claim is that equality and Zionism contradict each other.

That is why the NDA and Azmi Bishara were diagnosed as a mobilizing factor in a process contradictory to that which took place in the 1980s, known as the "Israelization" [of the Palestinians in Israel]. Instead what we are witness to is a Palestinization process, if you want.

We firmly believe that the Israeli intelligence services [the General Security Services—Shabak] played a considerable role in this case. It is they who made the initial diagnosis and later published it in Israeli newspapers. It is one of the rare moments in the history of the state where the Shabak openly released its reports to the media. The daily newspaper *Ha'aretz* published their [the Shabak's] report on the role of the NDA [in fomenting the October Uprising] and mentioned my personal responsibility [in this radicalization process]. Avi Dichter, head of the Shabak, even personally addressed the Committee of Foreign and Security Affairs in the Knesset and reported to it on this matter. This is also the first time that the head of the Shabak has done such a thing regarding the conduct of a Knesset member. Actually, this is a case of involvement of the security agencies in the affairs of the parliament, a matter that places a large question mark over the entire claim of Israeli democracy.

In Israel, the case is being presented as though it were "democracy defending itself" in order to find admiration among liberals in the West. However, the campaign being waged against me and against us as Arabs and Arab Knesset members has nothing to do with "democracy defending itself." This is because, first and foremost, the majority in today's Knesset has nothing to do with liberal democracy. [Moreover,] most of that majority is composed of people who are declaratively nondemocrats. *It is not we but they* who are calling for turning Israel into a nondemocratic state. Therefore what we are witnessing is not "democracy defending itself." It is nationalism attacking democracy, while we are "democracy defending itself."

We are passing a very important crossroads. It is important for the Arabs in Israel to win this battle. We don't want to play the role of the victim. We go with the spirit and mentality aiming to win, not to lose. The political activity that has lately developed among the Palestinians in Israel is very disturbing to the Israeli government. We must thus proceed and continue with this kind of political activity despite attempts to criminalize and excommunicate us. It must be noted that the most important element in this process is one that aims to intimidate the Arab population and terrorize it so that in the future people will be afraid to support national democratic leaderships. . . . There is thus a need for a national unity that overrides all political differences, thus warding off attempts to characterize and divide the Arab population into moderates and extremists. Everyone is aware of these attempts, and that is why things are beginning to take the form of an all-encompassing confrontation—a public and national [Arab] issue and not merely something that relates to one party or individual.

The Arabs in Israel are not willing anymore to accept the dictates regarding the kind of leadership they should have, as was the case during the military governorate [between 1948 and 1966]. They are not going to tell us how to participate in the political process. It's either democratic Arab participation or no participation at all. We have already proved that we are able to [boycott the elections]: in the last prime ministerial elections [2001], we called upon the public not to vote, and they did not vote [see chapter 2]. So if they dictate to us what leaders we are to have or to exclude the NDA from the electoral process, they will be committing a very grave mistake: a new history of Israel will begin in which it will become a full fledged apartheid state.

Questions from the Floor

Q: How do you evaluate the response of the Israeli peace camp to the issue of the lifting of your immunity?

A: The Zionist Left is undergoing a process of dissolution, not merely on the level of [the size of] its popular support, but also on the fundamentals of its moral integrity.

The Zionist Left has been divided into two parts: that which supports the lifting of my immunity and that which objects to it, for reasons they say have to do with "the need to preserve Israeli democracy." Both divisions, however, embarked upon an incitement campaign that was more violent and vitriolic than that of the Israeli Right. They did not defend the NDA or the Arabs—God forbid. They defended "democracy." MK Yossi Sarid [then chair of Meretz] said, "Azmi Bishara is a supporter of Hezbollah, he has links with so and so . . . but despite all this, I am against the lifting of his immunity." I would prefer if he had voted in favor of lifting my immunity. Thanks a lot for that great act of solidarity! He presents all the theoretical justifications so the Right is able to attack me but tries through his "solidarity" to prove his moral superiority over me [that he must defend democracy]. This is the racism of the Zionist Left. I am confident that I am more a democrat and a liberal than MK Yossi Sarid and his likes, and I am not in an existential need of having the Zionist Left on my side. This is perhaps the thing that disturbs them the most about the whole phenomenon of the NDA and Azmi Bishara.

Q: If this is your position regarding the Israeli Left, how do you expect to achieve anything? Do you expect to be going back to the Knesset, or are you rethinking the whole idea of participation in this body?

A: There is a great debate concerning whether participation in the Knesset is the means of achieving real change [for 1948 Palestinians] or whether all it can provide is compromises.

This is something Israeli parliament members never understand: it's not as though they made a compromise to allow us Arabs into the Knesset. Rather, it is we who made a compromise in our very decision to enter the Knesset. I believe the NDA is the only current on the contemporary scene of Arab political parties that underwent a serious internal debate as to whether we should participate in the Knesset. Yet everything that has been taking place recently confirms the correctness of our decision. It confirms that trying to balance the daily struggle within the Knesset for equal rights with our nationalist positions has presented the largest and most unprecedented challenge to the Jewish-Zionist state. No one in the history of the state has been incited against the way we have been. This provides evidence of the extent of the challenge we have been posing.

Q: Do you think a campaign will begin against other Palestinian members of the Knesset?

A: The Arab Knesset members have become used to the treatment of them and their immunity as a mere formality. In practice, de facto speaking, many of them have been beaten during demonstrations; there is constant incitement against them; and threats on their lives are made on a daily basis. In explaining what my parliamentary immunity [really] means, I always give the example that I was shot in the shoulder two years ago by the Israeli police and no one was arrested, nor was even one police officer investigated. What, then, does this immunity mean exactly? My house was attacked by three hundred thugs who intended to burn it down during the October Uprising [in 2000], and the police were there. Not one person was arrested.

We know very well that in the prevailing public atmosphere in Israel, "immunity" is really a formality of whether they can or cannot bring you to trial. And now they have brought me to trial. So even the formality is now removed. Six other Arab Knesset members are currently undergoing investigation—meaning two thirds of the Arab MKs.

This is the process that is going on, and which continues to snowball. I do not think they will remove the immunity of all Arab Knesset members. They will check, through my case, if this deterrent [the indictment and trial] is useful or not as a form of intimidation for the rest. That is why we believe the best thing to do in challenging it is for people not just to say, "We defend his right to immunity" but rather "We agree with what he said, and we are not afraid to say it." This is very important, and more and more Arabs are doing that now.

Azmi Bishara: Model Citizen

Adi Ophir[*]

In order to understand the removal of MK Azmi Bishara's parliamentary immunity, one must view the act in the general context of the Israeli occupation regime. For that reason, one must also examine the transformation of that regime that has taken place since the Oslo Accords.

The Oslo Accords created and institutionalized a gap between the de facto situation in the West Bank and Gaza Strip—occupation—and the de jure situation—the peace process. Many people did not believe in this gap, but it offered a chance (indeed, it was only a chance), of gradually changing the de facto situation. However, most of the Israeli public, including many moderates, did not understand what the widening gap between the de facto situation and de jure talk meant for the Palestinians. Then Barak came and divested himself of the principle of gradual movement. He wanted peace now. Everything, now. He destroyed the rules of the game, which permitted the existence of a scrap of a chance for progress. In the summer of 2000, the Camp David peace talks collapsed. The game was up. Gradually, with the vigorous assistance of the Intifada, all the playing fields were shut down. In February 2001 [when Ariel Sharon came to power], the whole team was sent home. The election of Sharon and all his actions since then have only one, unchanging meaning: there is no longer a gap between de jure and de facto. The actual state of occupation is the desired situation, legally and formally. There is no political horizon, no process, no negotiations, nothing except the occupation.

Nevertheless, one important thing remains from Oslo and from the two Intifadas—the one that gave birth to Oslo and the one that buried it: recognition of the temporary status of the occupation. No one speaks seriously any longer about the permanence of the occupation. The temporary character of the occupation is both the de jure and the de facto situation. That temporary character is the new law of the occupation. Violent Palestinian opposition both imposes that law and forces that law to be brought to light. Since it broke out, it has been entirely clear—even to those who

* Dr. Adi Ophir is a professor of philosophy at the Institute of History and Philosophy of Sciences at Tel Aviv University. This article first appeared in *Between the Lines* no. 12, December 2001.

did not understand it earlier—that everything is temporary. But that temporary character exacts a dreadful price in Israeli responses. The army temporarily enters Area A [beneath full Palestinian Authority control] and temporarily leaves Area A; there is a temporary closure, temporary transit passes, and their temporary cancellation, and, in temporary fashion, there is a policy of assassinations, and the rules for opening fire are temporarily changed, and then they are changed again. Only two things escape from the changes in time and the temporary movement: the dead—who are dead forever—and the settlements. While the occupier constantly plays with temporary measures, everything, simply everything—everything that moves, everything that lives—becomes dependent upon the arbitrary decisions of the occupier, who knows that he is always playing with borrowed time, which is actually stolen time, the time of others. This occupier runs amok, almost without boundaries, for everything, or almost everything, is temporarily permitted: everything goes, every crime, every form of violence, because the temporary nature of things gives it, as it were, authorization—the temporary authorization of an emergency situation.

What alternatives do the occupied have in this situation? Most of the Jews of Israel think that because the Palestinians refused to accept "the generous offer" that the powers that be wanted to impose on them, they must gird their loins with patience and continue to talk *ad infinitum*. But since February [2001] at least, if not before then, the Palestinians have had no one to talk to and nothing to talk about, aside from cosmetic changes in the way they are ruled, to agree to change the situation of occupation back from temporary to permanent. The occupation continues, and the violence continues, and the expropriation continues. What alternative do the Palestinians have? The liberal tradition of political thought in the West, the tradition upon which also the Israeli legal system is based, and the tradition of political action in the West (the tradition that Zionism itself, which defines itself as the movement of liberation of the Jewish people, sought to belong to)—that tradition says that in such a situation, the occupied have no choice. They have no choice but to resist. Their resistance to the occupier is their moral right. Their violent occupation to the occupation is a direct result of the violence of the occupier himself. Violent opposition of this kind may not be moral, and it may not be wise—in certain conditions it may be improper from the moral point of view precisely because it is not wise—but according to the legal and political tradition to which most of the Israeli political leadership subscribes, there is no doubt that this resistance is legitimate. The Palestinians have no alternative but to resist.

Today it is forbidden to say these simple things aloud. There are only a few Israeli Jews who are prepared to say openly today that they understand this resistance and support it, even if they cannot in any way agree to the criminal forms that it sometimes takes. Most Israeli Jews cannot admit today that the Palestinians have no choice. That is too threatening. That makes every Jewish victim into a vain victim. That undermines the effort at mobilization that the new form of warfare demands. Therefore, they say that they, the Jews, have no choice. They turn the tables, for they are experts at that, and they present themselves as someone who is once again fighting with his back to the wall. This is the war that they know how to wage best, so they have to present every war as involuntary. Palestinian resistance in all its forms, from the most criminal acts of terror to the most heroic and honorable struggle, must be presented as an existential threat to the state of Israel and the entire Jewish people. In this situation, one must concentrate on the Jewish victims and look away, systematically and intentionally, every time Palestinian victims appear. As for the daily victims of closure, there is nothing at all to talk about. Other victims are given military code names; "targets for liquidation" or "collateral damage." This systematic blindness is contagious. Every day you find more and more people around you who have been infected with the bacillus of that blindness. The blinder we become, the greater is our dread and the greater is our willingness to stand behind the most dreadful crimes. Israeli Jews must be blind so that they can agree to the new form of struggle against the Palestinians. They have to be nationalistic so that they can live at peace with the war, with the assassinations, with the starvation and the curfew. It is important to understand—nationalism did not give birth to the new form of occupation; the new law of the occupation, the law of the temporary status, was what caused nationalism once again to become a state religion.

Palestinian citizens of Israel were swept into this process in October 2000. They, too, had no choice. How could they have stayed at home while their brothers were resisting and being killed? How is it possible not to understand that? The violent, disproportionate police response led to the death of thirteen citizens. Some of them were apparently murdered in cold blood. Exactly as on the other side of the Green Line, here, too, the new form of violence required a new form of justification. The Palestinian citizens were retroactively marked as a threat. In some cases, this is liable to be a self-fulfilling prophecy. It is impossible to erase—neither Jews nor Palestinians should do so—the cases, very few meanwhile, in which Israeli Palestinians joined the cycle of armed struggle and volunteered to carry out acts of terror, including suicide bombings. That terror was precisely appropriate to the new category prepared for the Israeli Arabs by the nationalistic hegemony—a return to the days of the fifth column and the enemy from within, a return to the days when it was possible to represent the Palestinian citizens of Israel as an existential threat.

Exacerbation of relations between Jews and Palestinians within the Green Line is decidedly in the interest of the Right. It makes it possible to blur the distinction between the civil struggle of Palestinians on the Israeli side of the Green Line and the Palestinian liberation struggle on the other. Extremism makes it possible to create a public atmosphere that will accept not only the removal of leaders and parties that represent the Palestinian public in Israel from the Knesset but also the severe blow to the democratic representation of that public. The removal of one leader or party is liable to cause a chain reaction in the Palestinian community in Israel that ultimately will exclude that community from the process of elections. Without Palestinian voters, the rule of the Right is ensured for at least another generation.

Thus we see a combination of ideological motives, the main burden of which is nationalist mobilization in order to justify the new form of the occupation regime, and political motives, the main burden of which is to see fewer Palestinians in the parliamentary arena. In any case, the result is the demonization of the political leadership of the Palestinian public and the delegitimation of its civil struggle. That is why it is so important [for them] to point out the support of non-Jewish citizens for terror that supposedly intends to destroy the state of Israel. However, the Palestinian citizens support the struggle for national liberation, not terror. Terror is a pattern of action that contradicts the socioeconomic situation, the state of mind, and the moral consciousness of the majority of Palestinian citizens of Israel. The opposition of Israeli Palestinians to the Israeli occupation regime, their opposition to fifty years of discrimination in a state that is prepared to award them defective citizenship and that is not prepared to recognize them as a national community, that opposition is a model of civil opposition. That is what the new Jewish nationalism finds so hard to swallow.

It is hard to swallow the civic virtues of the Palestinian citizens, not only because their civil opposition spoils the place prepared for the Arab in the new national matrix. It is also hard to swallow because the civility of this opposition threatens the distorted conception of citizenship in the Jewish national state and its very ability to conceal over time the inherent contradiction between the Jewish and democratic elements in the Jewish national state. No one represents that threat better than Dr. Azmi Bishara. Azmi is a model citizen, an intellectual who can teach lessons in citizenship and run a school of democracy for most of the members of the Knesset. Yet he is represented today as a threat to the Israeli regime. The need to brand Azmi and present him as unacceptable is clear. This is part of the retroactive justification of the Jewish nationalistic mobilization. It is also part of the struggle to rebalance the political map after the enormous rightward drift. If it is possible to present the Arab Left as having crossed the line of legitimacy that a democratic Jewish regime is prepared to tolerate, it is, as it were, possible to present the Right at the opposite end of the spectrum as saner. The entire center bloc has slipped to the right, where the consensus resides today. At its extreme, beyond the pale, are a small number of Jews, Jewish terrorists, Kahanists who were outlawed, and, on the other side, a few Arab public leaders who incite their community to violence. Only the blind would buy a picture like that. Only the deaf would listen to that tune. However, nationalism blinds the eyes and deafens the ears.

Yet, on second thought, we have to admit that Azmi Bishara really is a threat to the new Israeli order, the nationalist order that has made permanent the temporary status of the occupation. That regime has actually made an apartheid system here, or at least set up all the conditions for the consolidation of an apartheid regime. Azmi Bishara represents the vanguard—or perhaps the rearguard—of democracy defending itself. He shows the Zionist Jew the nationalistic boundaries of his liberalism. Bishara's insistence on a democratic form of Arabic nationalism appears dangerous to them. They cannot bear it. It forces Zionists to admit that their nationalism is higher on their list of priorities than democracy. It forces them to recognize how narrow their conception of democracy is and how systematically it is distorted.

Today the democratic minority in the Jewish society needs to cooperate with Azmi and his friends in order to continue their struggle against Jewish nationalism with all its consequences and to defend the chance of rehabilitating a democratic regime in Israel. Today the democratic majority on the Palestinian side needs the cooperation of the democratic Jewish community to defend its civil status and to save their civil achievements.

The motives are different, and the points of departure are different, but the interests are common.

High Court Decision to Qualify Bishara for the 2003 Elections: An Equivocal Victory[*]

Tikva Honig-Parnass

The definition of Israel as "a Jewish-Democratic state" was first included in the Basic Laws of 1992–1994. Since then, the Knesset has made it de rigueur to include this phrase in any future Basic Law it contemplates passing.[14] Granting constitutional significance to this definition aimed at constructing a safeguard against any legal attempt to change it. However, the very content of the phrase, which has since prevailed in both judicial and public discourse, has in fact tied the definition of Israeli democracy to the aims and principles of Zionism. It thus blocks attempts to introduce any liberal meaning into the notion of Israeli democracy in a manner that could be congruent with universal standards of the rights of citizenship and equality.

The strengthening of national consciousness among Palestinian citizens has further increased the political and legal establishment's concern about emerging political forces that would struggle in democratic ways to transform the Jewish state into a state of all its citizens. Hence the state has consistently scrutinized the basic citizenship rights that allow individuals and groups who do not accept the notion of the Jewish state to participate in the political process and to run for elections to the Knesset.

The recent amendments introduced into the Disqualification for Elections Law and the use of it against Palestinian leaders in Israel points to the escalation of this process.

Disqualification for Elections: Section 7A[15]

In 1984 the Knesset added section 7A to the Basic Law of the Knesset. This section states:

---

[*] This article consists of excerpts from an article that first appeared in *Between the Lines* no. 20 (February 2003).

A list of candidates shall not participate in the Knesset if its aims or actions, expressly or by implication, point to one of the following:
(1) Denial of the existence of the state of Israel as the state of the Jewish people;
(2) Denial of the democratic nature of the state;
(3) Incitement to racism.

Furthermore, according to an amendment attached to the Knesset rules, the Knesset Presidium may not allow the presentation of a bill that is "essentially racist or denies the existence of the state of Israel as the state of the Jewish people" to the Knesset.[16]

The emergence of the National Democratic Assembly—Tajamu' (NDA—Tajamu) as a political movement has created a qualitative change in the political and security establishment's approach toward the political activity of Palestinian leaders. The NDA both expressed and contributed to the strengthening of Palestinian and Arab national consciousness and emphasized the implication of the Jewish-Zionist state in creating the structural inequality of Palestinian citizens.[17] Furthermore, its call for national collective rights, and for state recognition of the Palestinians in Israel as a national minority, began to be embodied in daily fights in the legal arena by Adalah, the Legal Center for Arab Minority Rights in Israel, under the directorship of Attorney Hassan Jabarin.[18] This piqued the concern of the Israeli establishment, including the Zionist Left, which rightly saw in these demands and this organizing a full-bodied challenge to the nature of the Jewish state.

Thus, a second amendment to Article 7A of the Basic Law was passed in May 2002. Candidates could now also be disqualified for "supporting an armed struggle of an enemy state or a terrorist organization against the state of Israel." Another innovation in the Article 7A amendment enables the Central Elections Committee (CEC)—the body headed by a Supreme Court judge that authorizes party lists eligible for participation in Knesset elections—to disqualify not only a list of candidates but also a single candidate in the list.[19] No sooner was this legal infrastructure created than the Israeli establishment found the opportunity to use it in the run-up to the 2003 general elections.

In an unprecedented move, Attorney General Elyakim Rubinstein submitted a motion to the CEC, calling for banning the NDA—Tajamu' party list from participation in the state elections.[20]

Without shame, Rubinstein declared that, among other sources, he based his motion to ban NDA—Tajamu and its leader, MK Azmi

Bishara, upon the research of Nadav, the head of Shabak's "Research Department Regarding Palestinians in Israel." The latter had argued that:

> The central goal of NDA is the negation of Israel as a Jewish and democratic state and support of the armed struggle carried out by terror organizations against the state of Israel. . . . The NDA has a systematic and clear program whose main theme is to change the Jewish character of the state of Israel and to replace it with a Palestinian state.[21]

On December 30–31, 2002, the majority of CEC members voted to ban the NDA list, and MK Bishara and MK Tibi, from participating in the elections.[22]

On January 9, 2003, an expanded Supreme Court panel of eleven justices, who reviewed the disqualifications and heard Adalah's appeal against the decision to ban the NDA, overturned the decision of the CEC, rejecting the requests to disqualify the NDA, MK Bishara, and MK Tibi from participating in the elections. In the majority opinion, Supreme Court Chief Justice Aharon Barak stated that, while Dr. Bishara's statements did amount to supporting *a terrorist organization*, his speeches did not constitute support *of armed struggle* by a terrorist organization, in this case Hezbollah. He also stated that the Court must be very careful when ruling on whether or not to limit the freedom of expression of MKs. Barak further noted that the law's language is very general and vague regarding what constitutes supporting the armed struggle of terrorist organizations.

However, in its substantive, written decision submitted in these cases, issued on May 15, 2003, the Court did not rule on Adalah's arguments relating to the violation of the separation of powers. Nor did the Court provide any interpretation for the new provision of "supporting terror." Instead, it adopted an evasive stance, arguing that the disqualification motions presented no factual basis upon which to disqualify the candidates or the parties from participating in the elections.[23]

What we are thus witnessing are the desperate attempts of the High Court to continue its discourse of adherence to some formal dimensions of democracy. So far it is refraining from calling for the disqualification from participation in elections of those who challenge the Jewish state. But by their very support of Article 7A, the High Court plays a significant role in the comprehensive campaign aimed at intimidating the Palestinian citizens from openly challenging the premises of Zionism. Thus, in fact, the discourse that denies the legitimacy of the Palestinians' democratic struggle for full national and collective equality and the threat that it embraces already plays the role of reducing their freedom of full participation in the political process.

Moreover, the limited support given by Zionist liberals to the Supreme Court's hesitant decision is expressed in the *Ha'aretz* editorial of January 10, 2003. It welcomed the High Court decision not to disqualify Bishara and praises the High Court's values of freedom of opinion and tolerance for the NDA's ideological and political positions, which are outside the Israeli consensus, as expressed in its ruling. However, the editorial concludes with a warning to Palestinian MKs that implies a conditional legitimacy given to their participation in the Knesset:

> ... Although from a formal legal perspective, there was no place for another ruling, one cannot ignore the fact that in the expressions that are attributed to Bishara and Tibi, they have come dangerously close to the boundaries that can be tolerated. Let's hope that these MKs and others similar to them will learn the lesson when [in the future] they will ask to be members of the [Israeli] legislature.

Here, as in a variety of cases confronting Zionist liberals, an unequivocal adherence to universal values is blocked by a commitment to the exclusivist Zionist approach. The shaky, conditioned citizenship of Palestinian citizens in their eyes, as expressed in the *Ha'aretz* editorial, puts in doubt the future prospects for resisting attempts to legalize the exclusion of Palestinians from the political arena. Bishara, the NDA, and the "stand-tall generation" of the Palestinians in Israel are perceived as challenging the basic values of Zionism and the Jewish state, even among progressive Zionists:

> Israeli Arabs will continue to perturb the Jewish majority because they are aware of the built-in conflict between Israel's definition as a Jewish state and its claim to be democratic. Using the democratic tools that the state gives all its citizens, the Arab minority is fighting not only for its right to full equality but to have an impact on the components of the state identity and national symbols. As this struggle continues to heat up, the Jewish majority will have to contend with positions and demands it will find hard to swallow—positions that are inherently opposed to the Zionist conception of the state.[24]

CHAPTER 5

From "Defensive Shield" to "Reforming the PA": Jenin's Noble Tragedy

March 2002–February 2003

Introduction

Between September 11, 2001, and April 2002, Israel killed no fewer than 630 Palestinians while assassinating forty key Palestinian grassroots activists.[1] In many of these assassinations, Israel's timing and choice of targets consistently and deliberately sabotaged Palestinian efforts to achieve or maintain a cease-fire.[2] While such provocations were designed to escalate the situation on the ground, bringing it to a point of no return, they also sought to forcibly push the Intifada and Israel's repression of it within the skewed logic of the U.S. "war on terror." Although Palestinian resistance forces were privy to the dangers of this escalation and indeed attempted to focus their tactics and targets to avoid them,[3] these efforts were always encumbered by the continued savagery of Israel's escalations[4] and the lack of a centralized command structure within the resistance itself. The discernable rise of Palestinian suicide operations inside the Green Line during this period, which is now a tactic adopted by almost all resistance factions (despite representing less than 0.6 percent of all Palestinian attacks during the Intifada),[5] together with the daily classic guerrilla operations against soldiers and settlers, set the stage for allowing Israel and the United States to implement what they had long been planning.

Israeli provocations finally reached a climax on March 27, 2002, when Abdel Basset Odeh (25), a Hamas operative from Tulkarem, blew himself up at the Park Hotel in Netanyahu, killing himself and twenty-nine others. The unprecedented number of Israeli deaths, which took place on the eve of Passover, provided a sufficient pretext for the Israeli Army to launch its planned "big blow," which it disingenuously titled Operation Defensive Shield. Within a mere twenty-four hours, Israel mobilized 20,000 reserve soldiers and promptly engaged in a massive assault that brought about the full reoccupation of all Palestinian Area As in the West Bank (except Jericho). Over the course of the next forty-five days, Israel killed 413 Palestinians and detained more than 6,000 others for various periods of time.[6]

Though careful to situate its justification for this operation within the boundaries of "defensive action," which sought to dismantle the Palestinian "infrastructure of terror," the Israeli Army deliberately targeted the educational, health, and civic infrastructure of Palestinian society—essentially everything that permitted the self-organization and sustainability of Palestinian life and national resistance. This included the Ministries of the Interior, Transportation, Public Works, Agriculture, Education, Higher Education, Culture, Finance, Civil Affairs, Industry, Information, Supplies, Social Affairs, and Local Government and the Health Directorate of the Ministry of Health—all of which were systematically attacked, looted, and made inoperable. Targets also included human rights NGOs, informational archives, and databases, as well as significant historical and archaeological sites—a specific type of destruction that results in further long-term social and political disintegration.[7]

The aftermath of this destruction redefined Israeli colonial policies against the Palestinians, definitively destroying what remained of the minimal "achievements" of the Oslo Accords: the PA hereafter no longer "enjoyed" any autonomy in Area A, as the Israeli Army now invaded and left these areas as it pleased; Arafat became permanently confined to the ruins of his compound in Ramallah, remaining there until his death in November 2004; and the daily death and devastation wrought upon Palestinian society became entirely normalized.

The brutality of Operation Defensive Shield was typified in the Jenin refugee camp, where large sections of the camp were simply flattened, despite a valiant resistance waged there by local forces. One Israeli Army bulldozer driver later recounted the destruction of the Jenin camp in a chilling testimony he gave to the Israeli daily *Yediot Ahronot*:

> For three days, I just destroyed and destroyed. The whole area. Any house
> that they fired from came down. And to knock it down, I tore down some

more. [The Palestinians] were warned by loudspeaker to get out of the house
before I came, but I gave no one a chance. I didn't wait. I didn't give one blow
and wait for them to come out. I would just ram the house with full power, to
bring it down as fast as possible. I wanted to get to the other houses. To get as
many as possible. Others may have restrained themselves, or so they say.
Who are they kidding?

   I am sure people died inside these houses, but it was difficult to see, there
was lots of dust everywhere, and we worked a lot at night. I found joy with
every house that came down, because I knew they didn't mind dying, but they
cared for their homes. If you knocked down a house, you buried forty or fifty
people for generations. If I am sorry for anything, it is for not tearing the
whole camp down.[8]

While the PA failed to offer any resistance to Israel's massive invasion
of Jenin—or of any other Area As—local forces in Jenin organized for
their own self-defense and sense of personal and national honor. The contrast between the PA's passivity and the heroism of Jenin's fighters became
permanently inscribed in Palestinian popular consciousness, accelerating
the alienation of these classes from traditional party and established national movement structures.

The enormous destruction inflicted by Operation Defensive Shield
was followed by international diplomatic initiatives (led by the United
States) for "reform" of the PA. These efforts gathered pace with U.S. president George W. Bush's foreign policy speech of June 24, 2002, in which
he called upon the Palestinians to elect new leaders "not compromised by
terror" and to "build a practicing democracy, based on tolerance and liberty."[9] Only after the "Palestinian people have new leaders, new institutions, and new security arrangements with their neighbors" would the
U.S. "support the creation of a Palestinian state, whose borders and certain
aspects of its sovereignty will be provisional until resolved as part of a final
settlement."

Rather than revamp the already skewed and nonexistent negotiated
process, the drive for "reforms" merely acted as a scheme to complete the
political goals of Israel's military offensive: namely, to finally do away with
Arafat; to establish the conditions for an alternative and totally submissive
Palestinian leadership; and to reestablish the infinite conditionality of the
Oslo Accords, allowing for Israel to continue its assaults against the national movement and its colonization of Palestinian land.[10]

As the issue of "reforms" became the new tool used to advance U.S.-
Israeli interests, the serious questions that Operation Defensive Shield
and the "reform process" posed related to Palestinian leadership, strategy,
tactics, and resistance failed to be addressed. Instead, the long-standing

Palestinian grassroots demands for genuine reform were further marginalized, as PA elites became totally preoccupied with their own political survival, inducing internal rifts within Fateh and calls for marginalizing Arafat himself.

On the Israeli Operation, the Resistance, and the Solidarity of the Palestinians in Israel

An Interview with Jamal Zahalqa[*]

Tikva Honig-Parnass

On Operation Defensive Shield

Q. What are the aims of Operation Defensive Shield?

A. The operation constitutes a qualitative upgrading of the war of attrition against the Palestinian people. The Israeli media and politicians launched an unprecedented propaganda campaign in advance so as to convince the public that the operation was inevitable. At present, they take care to explain that similar operations in the near future will be necessary as well.

The central aim of the operation is to sustain the Israeli occupation in the West Bank and Gaza Strip. Since it is impossible to convince the Palestinians to accept this, the only way is to use force and more force, violence and more violence.

Sharon wants to drag the Palestinians into a comprehensive confrontation in which he can take advantage of Israel's enormous military superiority over the Palestinian population and the small resistance forces armed with only light weapons. The Israeli political and military establishment believes that "Operation Defensive Shield" and similar operations in the future will make it possible to achieve a military end to the conflict.

---

* Dr. Jamal Zahalqa is one of the founders of the National Democratic Assembly—Tajamu' and formerly was the director of Ahali Center for Community Development. In January 2003, Zahalqa became a member of Knesset on the NDA—*Tajamu'* list. This interview was first published in *Between the Lines* #15, May 2002.

Such operations are designed to achieve the intermediate goals of re-covering the deterrence power of the Israeli Army and to restructure the reality in the West Bank and Gaza Strip. These are intermediate goals on the way to achieving Israel's strategic objective of abolishing Palestinian resistance by destroying the Palestinian national movement. Sharon is at-tempting to continue the job done in the Lebanon war [in 1982] when he tried but was unsuccessful in abolishing the PLO. In the recent operation, he aimed at destroying everything while leaving only shards of a local Palestinian leadership that will agree or be forced to agree to collaborate with his plan to restructure the reality in the Occupied Territories.

Q. How do the aims of Defensive Shield integrate with the plan to solve the question of the 1967 Occupied Territories after the collapse of the Oslo process?

A. Sharon wants to liquidate any centralized and nationwide Palestinian expression in order to reach arrangements with local leaders after dividing the West Bank and Gaza into separate enclaves. But even prior to Opera-tion Defensive Shield and to Sharon's reign, and while the operation was taking place, an effort was made to destroy the infrastructure of the PA and of Palestinian society in general, so that Palestinians will have to be involved in rehabilitation activities for a long time instead of in organizing resistance to the occupation.

Both PM Sharon and Minister of Foreign Affairs Peres (Labor) want to implement plans for long-term interim settlements that consist of in-stitutionalization of the apartheid system in the 1967 Occupied Territo-ries. This is in effect their joint political base. And indeed, when compared to South Africa, Israel has been involved in forming an apartheid situation that equals the worst phases of the history of apartheid in that country. Thus, in parallel with the preparations for the military op-eration, Israel began reviewing its plans for restructuring the situation in the Occupied Territories. The "buffer zones" along the 1967 border, around the settlements, and in the Jordan Valley will leave the Palestinians with very limited municipal areas, and even these areas will be under Is-raeli control, which will govern the passage between them.

Israel is attempting to create a situation in which all aspects of daily life will be under its control. According to this logic, Palestinians will not have any choice but to enter into negotiations with Israel—negotiations that are not planned to bring about a political solution to the occupation or to relate to the principal issues of refugees, settlements, Jerusalem, and so on, but will be over issues of water, electricity, freedom of movement, commerce, export, import, and so on. The interim settlement that Sharon is planning will be enforced by military means and by establishing facts on the ground.

Q. What are the prospects for blocking the implementation of Israel's plan to destroy the fabric of Palestinian society and the national movement? What strategy should be undertaken to achieve the goals of the Intifada?

A. The opposition to Sharon in Israel is weak, and part of it is quite miserable. The situation can change only if Palestinian resistance to the occupation continues. Jenin refugee camp has shown the entire world—and especially the Palestinian people—the power embodied in a stubborn and determined resistance to the occupation forces. The Palestinian people are ready to take up a no-choice battle for their life and future. The Israeli military operation has not broken the Palestinian spirit of resistance. Never before have the Palestinian people been imbued with the determination to stand steadfast and struggle as they are today, in all social strata and throughout the entire Occupied Territories.

It is important to remember that the Intifada has been not only a reaction to Israeli violence but a struggle for national liberation aimed at driving out the occupier and building Palestinian independence. Contrary to the illusions of the Oslo process, the basic assumption inherent in the Intifada is that the end of occupation will bring about peace, not that peace will bring about the end of occupation.

On that basis it is possible to build a strategy that envisions a wide popular struggle, not only that of small organized groups affiliated with various political factions. It may well be that the Palestinian people do not have the power to end the occupation in the near future. However, they are capable of bringing about the failure of Israel's objectives and plans. The Palestinian leadership has a decisive role in the current stage. It must push for unity on all levels and outline a unified, wise, efficient, and determined strategy of struggle capable of stopping Israel's plans.

On Palestinians Inside Israel

Q. We have been witness to the escalated campaign against the Palestinians in Israel in general and the persecution of the National Democratic Assembly (NDA) and Azmi Bishara in particular. How is it connected with the aims of the attack on Palestinians in the 1967 Occupied Territories?

A. Israel has set out to launch a battle that aims to annihilate the entire Palestinian national movement. Therefore the Palestinian national movement inside Israel, with the NDA movement at its center, is also the target of the Israeli establishment. It is the same battle as in the 1967 Occupied Territories, only with different names that express the different agenda and means: the name of the operation in the West Bank is Defensive Shield and the slogan of the attack on us here [inside Israel] is Defending Democracy. There is no bigger lie than that. It is actually chauvinist nationalism defending itself from democracy. This is confirmed by the very words of the legal adviser of the government, Elyakim Rubinstein and ex–prime minister Ehud Barak. Both have described the struggle to turn Israel into a democratic state for all its citizens that the NDA initiated as *the* most dangerous position, which must be fought with utmost determination and by all means.

The direction of the trend that has taken place in the last few years within Israel is clear: the state is becoming more Jewish and less democratic. Even in its distorted and limited perception, the aspirations of the Zionist Left for a political settlement with the Palestinians and for peace with the Arab world that began to develop in the first half of the 1990s have been replaced by aspirations for internal Jewish unity and peace with the Right.

The current wave of attacks on the Palestinian population in Israel began before the Intifada, although it escalated after October 2000. The chauvinist nationalist campaign, the increase of racism, and the demographic phobia of losing the Jewish majority are pushing toward the institutionalization of apartheid, not only in the 1967 Occupied Territories but in regard to the Palestinian national minority in Israel as well. This is a most dangerous process, which must be revealed and fought against before full-fledged apartheid evolves.

Thus, although the "demographic phobia" has always been an important axis in Israeli politics, it recently burst onto the center of the political stage and public discourse and became an obsession rooted in all social strata of Israeli society. In the eyes of many, the demographic question of the Palestinians inside Israel is even more difficult to resolve than the issue of the 1967 Occupied Territories. This is because it is possible to "separate" from the Palestinians in the Occupied Territories through some form of political settlement or by way of institutionalizing an apartheid system there, without necessarily introducing a dramatic change into the political or legal structure of Israel. This, however, is not the case with the situation inside Israel.

The "problem" concerning the Palestinian citizens of Israel is not merely described with respect to their "quantity" but also relates to their "quality." The political and security establishment in Israel is aware that if the Palestinians are divided and unorganized, the "quantity" danger will be reduced and it will be possible to control them. But if the process of national identity develops and the building of national institutions continues; if the awareness of their civil and collective rights continues to increase and the readiness to struggle and confront the authorities strengthens, it will confront a very severe challenge [to the Jewish nature of the state] that it has not previously known.

The emergent reactions to the double nature of the "danger" that Palestinian citizens constitute are as follows. The suggestions to solve the "quantity" problem revolve around various forms of transfer, such as the plan to annex the Triangle communities[11] to the future Palestinian state (see Chapter 3). As for the "danger" of the strengthening Palestinian national consciousness [the "quality" problem], the establishment has turned to depicting this trend as "extremization" while persecuting its leadership.

This is an expression of the current trend, whose aim is twofold: to minimize Palestinian citizens' political rights and to restructure the boundaries of Israeli democracy so that those who do not qualify according to the criterion of accepting Israel as a Jewish state, or do not join the prevailing Israeli discourse regarding Palestinian resistance, will be excluded from political legitimacy. This is reflected in the new amendment to the election law, which does not leave any doubts with regard to these intentions (indeed explicitly declared) of the ruling coalition in Israel (see Chapter 4).

Q. The Palestinians in Israel have been playing an active role in the protest against the military assault on their brethren in the 1967 Occupied Territories during Operation Defensive Shield. What are the dimensions of these activities? Who is leading them? Does the semiofficial representative body of the Palestinians in Israel—the Follow-up Committee—play an active role in organizing them?[12]

A. The brutal crimes that Israel has committed during Operation Defensive Shield have raised tremendous anger among the Palestinians. The Palestinian street in Israel was boiling with rage and searched for ways to act. Two general strikes were declared, and mass demonstrations took place all over the country. It just so happened that Operation Defensive Shield began very close to Land Day, which the Palestinians in Israel (as

well as in other places) commemorate every year on March 30.[13] This year
the extent of participation on that day, in demonstrations in Sakhnin in
the Galilee, in Kufr Kana in the Nazareth area, and in Rahat in the South
(Negev/Naqab), was enormous. Tens of thousands took to the streets to
express their protest against Israel's crimes and their support for the Palestinian struggle. In demonstrations that took place a week later in all Arab
localities, the popular participation was even greater. The police did not
enter the villages and towns, letting the demonstrations pass without serious confrontation. It seems that a decision had been taken not to open a
"second front" with the Palestinians in Israel, as happened in the first
week of the present Intifada, in October 2000, when the police killed thirteen Palestinian citizens.

The Follow-up Committee tried to avoid calling for strikes and
demonstrations and objected to widening the campaign. Various political
forces and heads of municipalities have been under pressure by the Israeli
authorities and were afraid that things would get out of control. However,
the fact that the Follow-up Committee is the only framework of cooperation among political forces, local municipalities, and public leaders in general created a dilemma among radical political forces. On the one hand,
these forces wanted to escalate the struggle, but on the other, they considered it important in the current circumstances to keep the unity of the
campaign. This was also the will of the wider Palestinian public. Thus a
serious attempt to put pressure on the Follow-up Committee to widen the
protest and to escalate the campaign was only partially successful.

An important additional activity of the Arab Palestinians in Israel was
the collection of contributions, food, medicines, and medical equipment for
the West Bank. In each village and town at least one committee was active
in organizing these contributions. Huge quantities of these supplies were
transferred to the Occupied Territories despite the many difficulties confronting the organizers at the time the military onslaught was at its peak.

It is important to emphasize how the supplies were not distributed
through a centralized bureaucratic body [affiliated with the PA] but were
sent directly to the villages, neighborhoods in cities, towns, and refugee
camps. The real needs of the people were identified through direct con-
tacts established between the aid committees inside Israel and activists on
the ground in the West Bank. The estimation is that the contributions
collected in April 2002 were of tens of millions of dollars, which is a
tremendous sum for a population of one million people whose economic

status is rather difficult. This was a genuine popular project in which almost the entire Palestinian population participated in the unified endeavor to contribute emergency aid to their brethren in the West Bank and Gaza.

Q. Are these various demonstrations and contributions merely an expression of solidarity with the sufferings in the 1967 Occupied Territories, or do they also indicate the political radicalization of the Palestinians in Israel, as expressed in supporting the resistance movement— the Intifada? Are there differences between the extent of solidarity witnessed during the 1987 Intifada and the present?

A. The demonstrations and the variety of other solidarity activities express both the anger and the political radicalization of the Palestinians in Israel. It is their political radicalization that nourishes and strengthens the struggle against the occupation and against the dirty war launched against the Palestinian people.

People were searching for ways to do something and were running from one demonstration to another. In between they were involved in collecting contributions and food. No doubt, the expressions of solidarity and identification with this Intifada have been much more significant than those witnessed during the 1987 Intifada. In the decade that passed since the 1987 Intifada, many developments took place among the Palestinians in Israel: the development of a higher national and political consciousness; of greater readiness to struggle; of taking a critical approach to the Israeli media and choosing instead to receive information and analysis from Arab satellite stations; and of the total distrust in forged and enforced coexistence. All these phenomena, in addition to many others, brought the Israeli orientalists and Arabist "experts" to conclude rightly that national identity and national consciousness have steadily increased in recent years. They have "accused" NDA—Tajamu' of being responsible for this development and of course Tajamu' admits to the accusation.

The Democratization Reforms Scheme:
The United States and Israel Publicly Join Hands
on the Road to Liquidating Palestinian Nationalism*

Tikva Honig-Parnass

On May 30, 2002, the *Ha'aretz* commentator Aluf Benn reported on the arrival of a senior U.S. security delegation to Israel the previous day. The delegation came to participate in talks on strategic and military cooperation between the two states within the framework of the U.S.-Israeli Defense Policy Advisory Group (DPAG), which had not met since October 2000:

> The talks will encompass all joint issues between the US and Israel [namely]:
>
> • Joint plans: Joint [military] exercises of the IDF and the American army, exchange of intelligence and research and development projects;
>
> • Regional issues: The threats from Iraq and Iran, and cooperation between the security [authorities] of Jordan, the PA, and Asia;
>
> • Review of the situation in Indochina, and planned projects for selling Israeli arms to India.[14]

Israel's long-established role of serving U.S. interests in the Middle East as well as in the broader region of Southeast Asia[15] continues at full pace in the era of the "war on terror." This is also true regarding the war Israel is waging against the Palestinian national movement, embodied in its bloody attempts to repress the Intifada, which is of utmost importance to American interests. The destruction of Palestinian nationalism is considered a model for fighting what author Noam Chomsky calls "radical nationalism," meaning any buds of independent nationalism in the Middle East and throughout the Third World. This gives Israel a rather free hand in carrying out its appalling oppressive measures, as long as such measures are executed within the framework of the general U.S. strategy—which Labor Party governments in the past, and Sharon's government today, have been prepared to abide by.

---

* This article first appeared in *Between the Lines* no. 16, June 2002.

The measures of increased oppression adopted since the end of Operation Defensive Shield include the army's daily incursions into cities and villages; days and even weeks of curfew; and the daily killing and mass arrests of Palestinians (more than 7,500 of whom are now in Israeli prisons). The political and military establishments are aware that continued short military incursions cannot end Palestinian resistance. Therefore, Israel has ended any semblance of Palestinian autonomy and returned to full direct "security control" of all areas of the West Bank, thus doing away with the last remnants of the Oslo agreements. But since the reinvasion and security control are not officially defined as "reoccupation," Israel is not only destroying and preventing the functioning of the Palestinian social services systems, but also avoiding its own responsibility to provide them. Israel claims that the security control/reoccupation is accomplishing what Arafat failed to do under the Oslo Accords—namely, "liquidating terror."

These operations constitute the continued Israeli efforts to break the will of the Palestinian resistance and to do away with the Palestinian national movement. Such a goal requires much more than the demolition of the infrastructure of the resistance itself. Israel has set out to crush the entire Palestinian society, including its basic collective and individual infrastructures, and turn them into human dust—desperate, submissive, atomized individuals who will "agree" to U.S.-Israeli dictates. At the same time, these policies aim at strengthening the institutionalization of the Israeli version of an apartheid system, including its fragmentation of the 1967 Occupied Territories into enclaves with checkpoints and permit systems for crossing from one locality to another.

The Impetus Behind Settlement Escalation with U.S. Consent

Settlement and bypass road construction are essential to ensure Israel's control of all of historic Palestine. In the year since the formation of Sharon's coalition government with the Labor Party in February 2001, at least thirty-four new settlements and eighty new "lookout positions" have been built.[16] Furthermore, in the first week of June 2002, work began on a new Jewish "neighborhood" composed of hundreds of homes on a site near Jabel Mukaber, south of Jerusalem. The Israeli Ministry of Housing also publicized its intention to build 957 additional housing units in the 1967 Occupied Territories, largely within "Greater Jerusalem," which spreads from the outskirts of Ramallah in the north to Bethlehem in the south.

The senior *Ha'aretz* commentator Akiva Eldar rightly notes that "these [new settlements] have not surprised the Americans, who know that the Israeli annexation continues galloping, under the auspices of a defense minister and foreign affairs minister (both from the Labor Party) who do not lift a finger against the settlements."[17] A B'tselem[18] report from May 2002 confirms the true nature of Israel's policies:

> Israel has created a regime of separation and discrimination in the Occupied Territories. This regime enables the settlers to sustain separate planning institutions and two legal systems: a military system for the Palestinians and a civic system for the Israelis. The [Israeli] High Court grants this unique phenomenon legal approval, either by legitimizing flawed actions of the government and the army or by refusing to interfere and thus prevent the harm done to Palestinians.[19]

U.S.-Israeli Schemes for a More Collaborative Palestinian Leadership

It is against such a backdrop that one should assess the U.S. pressures to introduce "reforms" in the PA headed by Arafat. The U.S. administration shares the conviction that the collaborative role assigned to Arafat in the Oslo Accords is over. Now, under the pretext of "democratic reforms" in the PA, a more submissive and collaborative authority and leadership are being sought to replace Arafat's regime.

As in the past, the two partners—the U.S. and Israel—share a deep understanding of the principal dimensions of the reform scheme and its implications for the comprehensive strategy to fight the Palestinian resistance. The respected Israeli researcher Meron Benvenisti comments, "When the regime of isolated cantons and economic and administrative chaos is institutionalized, a corrupt system will be erected that will make the old system look like the height of transparency. This is so because according to the prevailing perception, nursing the greediness of the Palestinian leadership to be is an incentive to fill the role of collaborator and strengthens the interest in the continuation of the indirect occupation."[20]

Sharon and Bush: A Unified Front

During talks with Sharon on June 10, 2002, (George W.) Bush accepted Sharon's unrealistic conditions that full Israeli security needs and essential reforms in the PA be met before political negotiations resume. He even went so far as to disingenuously claim that these demands "consist of building the institutions that will enable the establishment of the Palestinian state."[21] Following the visit, Bush confirmed a "deep understanding" between himself and Sharon. "Sharon and Bush: A Unified Front" was the large-font headline of a report published in the Israeli daily *Yediot Ahronot* the day after the meeting.

As to the fate of Arafat, Bush and Sharon agreed that "as long as Arafat is around, there is no chance for a settlement." The members of the unified government, except the minister of foreign affairs, Shimon Peres (Labor), have long since set out on a voyage whose main aim is the removal of Arafat. However, the Labor Party prefers the "political" path to getting rid of Arafat, as presented by the Israeli intelligence establishment:

> The intelligence reports to the government that Arafat's position is continually deteriorating. The earth is shaking beneath him, but the conditions are not yet ripe for sending him away. In the intelligence community, they compare the process to a champagne bottle: you shake it and shake it until the cork is thrown up into the sky. Arafat is the cork. The bottle is being shaken today by Israel, the United States, Europe, and especially Saudi Arabia and Egypt. The aim is to shake the bottle without breaking it and without spilling too much champagne (or blood).[22]

Thus, Labor and Sharon share an understanding of the situation and what it implies: Sharon is fully aware that in the near future there is no hope to find an alternative collaborative leadership to replace Arafat and grant a "lawful" face to Sharon's plans. Therefore, the Israeli Army will have to continue doing the job itself for the time being, with the support of the Labor Party and the blessing of the United States. This entails reoccupying the Area As in the West Bank and Gaza Strip in order to stay there for about a year,[23] thus allowing enough time to liquidate any resistance, break the spirit of the people, increase the number of settlements, pave more bypass roads, consolidate the buffer zones, and ultimately find an alternative leadership. Only then will Sharon be ready to begin talks about a long-term interim agreement.[24]

Like his American boss, Sharon also feels obliged to pretend that all these oppressive means are necessary for peace and that, at the end of the day, the Palestinians will be granted a "state." This, however, will come after years of a long-term interim agreement and a temporary Palestinian state without final borders and without any promises regarding the final settlement.

Sharon described to visitors from the American Jewish Committee his vision for the long road to a Palestinian state:

A Palestinian state is inevitable, but it has to be reached gradually. First, there is a need to copy the Afghanistan model: a temporary government that will be nominated for one year under the command of a chief executive, so all steps of reform will be under tight control. The minister of finance of the temporary government will report how the money is being spent, and the minister of education will be responsible for granting the right education to children and for excluding incitement from textbooks.[25]

The long-term U.S.-Israeli cooperation, confirmed again this month, indicates the integration of the Zionist colonialist project within the "international war on terror" launched by the United States, vis-à-vis the liquidation of Arab and Palestinian nationalism. The "democratic reforms" they seek to implement in Palestine are but another stage in this long term war, destroying what remains of the liberation and resistance of national forces in Palestine and the Arab world.

The Rise of Localized Popular Resistance Formations: Jenin Camp and the Future of Palestinian Political Activism[*]

Linda Tabar

In February 2003, Mahmoud Abbas delivered the most serious public critique of the Intifada by a senior PA official. The secretary-general of the PLO and a top former negotiator under Arafat during Oslo denounced the militarization of the uprising and called for a "total halt to all armed operations."

"I have always said I'm against the use of arms," states Abbas, "I think it was a mistake to use arms during the Intifada and to carry out attacks inside Israel. But I am not against the use of stones in resisting the Israeli occupation, nor am I against the use of peaceful means."

By launching a critique of the Intifada, while neglecting to contextualize this as an anticolonial uprising—which is directed as much at the Israeli occupation as it is against the Oslo process and the apparent

---

* Linda Tabar is a Ph.D. candidate at the School of Oriental and African Studies, University of London, and a researcher working with Muwatin, the Palestinian Institute for the Study of Democracy. She also recently supervised an oral history project in Jenin camp for Shaml, the Center for Refugee and Diaspora Studies. This article first appeared in *Between the Lines* no. 21, March 2003.

willingness of the Palestinian leadership to concede Palestinian national rights—Abbas conveniently absolves the PA of any responsibility in this discussion, excludes Oslo from accepted parameters of debate, and levies a damning critique on the popular resistance forces.

Made in the lead-up to the talks between the Palestinian political factions in Cairo, the intent of Abbas's pronouncements is barely concealed: the talks in Cairo are to be focused on reaching an agreement on ways of controlling the Intifada.[26] The leadership and trajectory of the Palestinian national agenda are not up for debate, nor is a post-Oslo national consensus on offer.

Responding to Abbas's comments and subsequent calls for a ceasefire, a leader of the Al Aqsa Martyrs Brigades [a Fateh paramilitary group] in Jenin stated:

> What does it matter to us if the leadership of Fateh and Hamas meet? We already have factional unity [between political parties] on the ground. Our goal is to fight the occupation as long as it exists on our land. The leadership calls for a cease-fire, but they are able to pass the checkpoints in their cars [because they have Israeli permits granted to Palestinian VIPs]. We remain imprisoned in our locality, under daily assault from the Israeli military and its tanks, helicopters, and F-16 fighter planes. The Intifada cannot stop.

This statement reflects the transformations happening on the ground and the new types of political regrouping that cut across traditional party lines. In Jenin, cooperation exists between the armed factions similar to the consolidation of the cross-factional Popular Resistance Committees in the southern part of the Gaza Strip.[27] In the peripheral regions of the 1967 Occupied Territories, in the marginalized communities, particularly the refugee camps and villages in the northern part of the West Bank and the southern part of the Gaza Strip, popular resistance is coalescing around the collaboration that exists between the armed factions operating on the ground.

Though the Intifada erupted as a spontaneous outpouring of mass popular resistance, today it sustains itself largely through the heroic struggle and perseverance of the popular classes in their efforts to throw off the shackles of occupation and Israel's colonial control, as reembedded through the Oslo process.

Oslo turned out to be a "process" minus the "peace." It allowed for the deepening of the Manichaean violence of colonialism's politics of compartmentalized spaces—in this case, cantons of "Palestinian territoriality" encircled and imprisoned within a "besieging cartography" of Israeli checkpoints, elaborate permit systems, settlements, and bypass roads.[28] It is important to recognize that Oslo succeeded in part because it was based upon what French social theorist Jean Baudrillard calls "simulacrum": when reality no longer precedes representation but structures of representation create their own reality—a "hyperreal."[29] Throughout the Oslo period, the volatile transformations on the ground and Israel's colonial impasse were congealed by the projection of "state building" as the linear horizon under which all other contradictions were to be subsumed.

Although the Intifada provides the occasion for the Palestinian leadership to throw off the yoke of Oslo and redefine the Palestinian national agenda, the contrary has occurred. The popular classes and marginalized social groups, particularly the refugees, continually attempt to transgress these boundaries and look beyond Oslo. Yet since the Intifada began, these social actors have found themselves enveloped within a perilous vacuum. Not only has the PA shunned the command role of the Intifada, relating to the uprising as a matter of "primarily tactical significance," rather than backing the uprising as a strategic alternative to the "negotiations;"[30] but the Palestinian intelligentsia, which one scholar rightly described as "*comprador* intellectuals,"[31] and their cohorts within the NGO sphere, have generally been absent from this uprising.

In this context, the rise of localized cross-factional resistance formations is a response *from below* by subaltern groups[32] to the paralysis of the traditional Palestinian national movement and the crisis within Palestinian nationalism exposed by this Intifada. In contrast to the clamor of commentators describing cooperation between the Palestinian factions on the ground as "field alliances" between "unaccountable and undisciplined field operatives," that only serve Hamas's political program,[33] two observations emerge from Jenin:

First, in the space created *between* Hamas's political posturing and the revolt by the vanguard wing of Fateh (the Al Aqsa Brigades) cross-factional resistance represents an organic formation that is embedded within communities. It attempts to rebuild the fractured national movement around unity forged on the ground. Local activists come together in fluid alliances, as in Jenin, or consolidated structures, as in Gaza, and mobilize the community outside a particular ideology; fusing together Islamists and centrist tendencies, interwoven with support for the use of armed struggle against the occupation and underpinned by a strong local identity that is steeped in local resistance experience.

Second, it follows that while the activation of the armed wings of the political parties has generally been understood in the past in terms of vertical [i.e., hierarchical] relations within each party, during this Intifada the armed factions have also become part of a horizontal formation that incorporates the voiceless and unorganized into an inchoate rebellion from below. The unified support among the armed factions in Jenin (both camp and city) for the use of armed struggle and suicide operations is significant because it registers the popular protest of unorganized classes with the impact that Oslo has had on the Palestinian national movement. Factional unity on the ground between the Al Aqsa Brigades [Fateh], Izz el Din al Qassam [Hamas], Saraya al Quds [Islamic Jihad] and to a lesser extent the Brigades of the Martyr Abu Ali Mustapha [PFLP] has split the national political center. As it works to build a front against the Oslo elite, cross-factional resistance has created a strategic dilemma for the PA leadership, forcing it to attempt to eliminate, co-opt, or channel this protest into an alternative strategic agenda.

Jenin Camp: A New Mode of Resistance

One of the untold stories of the Al Aqsa Intifada is the way the "voiceless" and "marginalized" have been independently organizing in order to protect themselves and their own communities. Although born from self-defense, this phenomenon has its own implications and prefigures the potential emergence of new political formations and the onset of new forms of political consciousness.

During the 1987 Intifada, popular committees, created under the rubric of the leadership of Palestinian political parties, mobilized the Palestinian masses and sustained a campaign of civil disobedience.[34] In this uprising, local resistance fighters, in and around Jenin refugee camp, have transformed traditional party structures into a platform for cross-factional decision making, resistance, and collective action. In the spirit of the former popular committees, activists from within the armed factions are acting with more independence toward their central leadership and are mobilizing the residents into a "resistance community." Acting as the nucleus of resistance efforts, the factions cooperate militarily to defend Jenin and also provide relief efforts to the residents of the city.[35]

The Israeli invasion of Jenin camp in April 2002, as part of the so-called Operation Defensive Shield, illustrates this dynamic; far from being dissolved, the factional structures provided the organizational framework upon which cross-factional unity was consolidated. Long before the invasion, personal relations among the *shebab* [literally, the "guys/boys," implying those who are politically active] working within the armed wings of Fateh, Hamas, and Islamic Jihad served as informal networks through which factional unity was initiated, organized, and transformed from something ad hoc into systematic cooperation and joint decision making and planning. Thus, during the invasion, the *shebab*, known and trusted by the families in the camp, incorporated the residents into a "moral community," creating the cohesion necessary for collective resistance. The families not only pledged their commitment to the resistance forces but also provided moral support, sustenance, and shelter for the fighters.

The Intifada and Beyond: Defining the Post-Oslo Political Map from Below

"You may be surprised," says a political leader from the Popular Front for the Liberation of Palestine (PFLP) in Jenin refugee camp, "after the battle in Jenin, my first priority is the people and [local] factions in Jenin, over and above the [central institutions of the] political party." This veteran political activist's comments suggest that cross-factional resistance in Jenin not only is rooted in a popular base but is also transforming the community's "deepest structure of relations and feelings."[36]

"In Jenin," explains a leader from Islamic Jihad, "the lines along which people are organizing have changed—this is transforming people's political views. However, we do not yet have a political structure to embody this new thinking."

Organized resistance in Jenin has overturned traditional ideological divisions, replacing them with a political identity that fuses together previously antagonistic and opposing forces. Unbound by any one particular ideology, this hybrid identity[37] creates the possibility in the future for horizontal mobilization along group lines and around social and political issues—opening up the possibility for the organization of the refugees qua refugees.

In Jenin refugee camp, three palpable changes are evident. First, an emerging local affiliation is fused together with the notion that the "national interest" is no longer sublimated under the authority of the party leadership but that local actors should combine forces in defense of the "national agenda." This represents a deepening of horizontal association and the beginning of a sense of comradeship that transverses political divisions, intersecting and interrupting vertical ties.

Second, Islamist and secularist nationalist groups have joined forces. "We have reached an agreement with the Al Aqsa Brigades," reveals an

activist from Hamas in Jenin camp. "We will work together to end the occupation." However, more important than tactical agreements between Islamist and centrist forces, religious idioms have been transformed into
powerful nodes that buttress and promote an alternative resistance culture
and ideology. In Jenin, local resistance is mediated by *thahirat el-
istish'hadiyeen* or the "rise of martyrdom." A religious idiom, "martyrdom"
infuses a revolutionary ethos into resistance practices; sacrifice and heroism are transformed into modes of social action and ways of reclaiming
subjectivity in the face of "colonialism's rituals of degeneration."[38] Re-
membrance of the martyrs through posters, murals, and necklaces creates
a "cult of *shaheeds*"—a "hidden transcript" inconspicuous to the outsider
yet functioning as a pervasive undercurrent that operates on the political
unconscious, infusing and rejuvenating an autonomous resistance culture.

Third, the division between armed fighters and the civilian population
has been broken down. In Jenin refugee camp, a new moral community has
been constructed out of the experience of collective resistance, forged around
the solidarity between the residents and the cross-factional leadership that
defends the camp. One can imagine a moral community as circumscribed by
a circle, whereby those inside share a common membership and are entitled
to moral consideration, while outsiders are denied this consideration.[39] Just as
Jenin camp is redefined as a moral community, however, the Palestinian nation is also recast as the political horizon and field of vision.

This is an extremely important point. For, while many commentators
have disparagingly looked down upon local resistance formations as the
product of Israel's siege of Palestinian cities, these observers have neglected the dialectical relationship between colonial domination and resistance practices. Each locality, completely sealed by the occupation forces
for most of the Intifada through closures and curfews, has become not
only the site of oppression and humiliation but also a space for alternative
resistance. The point about a new moral community suggests that local
resistance does not succumb to the fragmentation Israel attempts to introduce through siege of Palestinian cities. Local resistance reverses colonial
logic, using the locality as a site from which to launch alternative forms of
resistance simultaneously as it redefines the national as its intended focus,
therefore averting subnational fragmentation.

The resistance groups organized in and around Jenin refugee camp
have joined forces and mobilized residents behind them on two types of
occasions: to defend the camp and the city as a whole from Israeli invasions and to prevent the PA from arresting any of the resistance activists.

When the PA Security Forces arrested Mahmoud Tawalbeh, a local leader of Islamic Jihad, months before the invasion in April 2002, rioting broke out, as all the factions, including the Al Aqsa Brigades, demonstrated their opposition to this arrest. Subsequently, Tawalbeh was released.

The activation of the armed factions and the community behind them on these two occasions represents nothing short of a *negation* that exhibits a glimmer of understanding of the mutuality of interests between the PA and Israel. As Gramsci has argued, it is only through a negation of opposing force relations that the subordinate classes can achieve their own self-conscious group identity.

For the refugees in Jenin camp, therefore, the long-term implications of cross-factional resistance during the Al Aqsa Intifada are not only a deepening of horizontal ties across and within this politically disenfranchised community, but also the potential awakening of refugees as their own political force.

The Quest for Strategy[*]

Azmi Bishara

On September 3, 2002, Muwatin, the Palestinian Institute for the Study of Democracy, hosted a one-day conference in Ramallah entitled "From Occupation to Reform: The Missing File." A wide swath of Ramallah's political, intellectual, and cultural elite attended and participated in the conference, despite the Israeli curfew continuously imposed on the city for the previous three months. Following is a transcript of MK Azmi Bishara's (National Democratic Assembly—Tajamu') keynote speech— significant not merely for its insightful content but also for the degree to which Bishara's opinions are respected within both 1967 and 1948 Palestinian circles.

The Absence of a Strategy for Liberation

I am constantly surprised at how, when the subject of Palestinian strategy is discussed, impatient questioners seek to boil the matter down to "Are you for or against suicide operations?" The reduction of the national strat-

---

*This article first appeared in *Between the Lines* no. 18, October 2002.

egy to this question exemplifies an extreme political poverty in these difficult times, which is also quite tragic.

Allow me to be clear from the start: when we talk about strategy, we
are not talking about various demonstrations, military operations, and the
different steps we ought to take. Many of today's [military] operations are
motivated by vengeance, reaction, or anger and are not a by-product of
any strategy. Likewise, the prevalent discussions regarding the issue of reform [of the PA] are not taking place within a context of strategy, but are
motivated more by questions of [national political] survival and gaining
time.

In this sense, strategy is a continuum—it is not just a collection of in-
dividually distinct steps or operations. It is an intellectual, political, and
even emotional continuum, as well as a question of will. Strategy is also a
question for the leadership, not for individuals. A head of a household has
a strategy, which pertains to the administration of household affairs—but
he is not required to have a political strategy. Likewise, it is not the responsibility of Palestinian intellectuals to formulate a political strategy.
We are talking about the strategy for the leadership of a people. Let us
make this distinction up front so that all discussions do not always degen-
erate into questions of "What is the strategy?" And when discussions do
address the issue of strategy, they must be undertaken with patience and
with the ability to listen rather than with a "give me the summary" approach that is so common. This is because the question of strategy is
wider than the topic of military operations and reform. It is a comprehensive issue that addresses the relationship between the current situation and
the goals we seek to accomplish through political means. We are talking
about political strategies—not about strategies in a laboratory.[40]

The Debate on Military Operations

The question of whether we are "for or against military operations" is
meaningless unless it is known under which strategy these operations take
place and to where these operations will lead. Likewise with reform, the
question is one of "reform in what context?" We must be capable of explaining this in comprehensible terms that people can understand.

Strategy is not only right for the sake of great goals like the "liberation
of the Palestinian people." Our strategy may even serve transitional goals.
There are stages of strategy. The question to be considered, then, is what
are the transitional goals that this strategy will lead toward, and how are

these to be achieved? A political leader must be capable of explaining this, and if he is incapable of doing so, he does not deserve to be a political leader. You cannot be a political leader simply by virtue of continuity or faction—particularly if your political strategy is pushing the people toward death. While death is something basic and exists in struggle, and can even be asked for throughout the course of struggle, it must be explainable. Otherwise we are neither talking about a responsible leadership [nor a responsible society].

I am aware that struggle and liberation require sacrifice, particularly when you are talking about a colonial-settler movement of a nature whose uprooting will be more difficult than any other form of colonization. It is not as though [the Zionists] came within a set mandated period and think in terms of possibly returning [to where they came]. Rather, the nature of this colonialism is such that it says, "I am here so as to remain, so as to take your place." It is clear that ridding oneself of this form of occupation is not possible without a resistance strategy [*strategiyet moqawama*]. This is the principal issue, without which nothing else can be understood.

Reform Versus a Strategy of Resistance

The question of reform must take place within the context of an overall national struggle and within the pursuit for the strategy of liberation from occupation. I do not see a process of incremental reform or for that matter of state building taking place in Palestine that can lead to liberation from occupation without resistance.

[Liberation without resistance] was the presumption of all those who supported Oslo—at least those among them who were not cynical. I am talking about the people who supported Oslo from a position of principle and genuinely believed Oslo could achieve Palestinian national rights. These people argued at the time that "through the Oslo process we are engaging in an incremental process that will lead toward the ending of the occupation" [implying that the need for resistance had ended]. This strategy was based on the idea that after the [1990–91] Gulf War and the establishment of a unipolar American hegemony both regionally and internationally, the Palestinians could begin a process of establishing a state in parts of the West Bank and Gaza. Those who argue this position still believe that despite the passing of many turbulent times, the strategy of the Oslo framework is in principle a constructive one, though it is "presently in need of reform."

I myself am categorically opposed to this strategy. This strategy is completely mistaken and led to giving up liberation. The strategy for liberation must include within it an elementary principle known as resistance [*moqawama*].

What do we mean by *moqawama*?

We mean that the occupation must pay a price to the extent that it is incapable of withstanding it morally, materially, emotionally, politically, economically, and socially. The goal of *moqawama* is not to defeat the occupation militarily. The goal of resistance is not to defeat the occupation in a decisive battle, nor for that matter to pull the occupation into a decisive battle. The goal of resistance is to make the occupation pay the price of its occupation in conditions that those under occupation are capable of withstanding, but taking the continuation of the struggle into consideration at the same time.

The U.S. Call for Reforms and Elections

We cannot infiltrate the American project of "reform." We cannot say that we will exploit the U.S. pressure to reform the PA to implement our own reform. We must see the question of reform in its context. In actuality, there is no real reform taking place. There is reform of the security branches so as to establish a centralized security apparatus capable of interacting with the Americans and the Israelis regarding the issue of "fighting terror." Everything else is a mere sideshow.

Elements within the Palestinian national movement seek to piggyback onto this sideshow so as to infiltrate the reform subject and exploit it. But such aspired-for reform occurs within a contradictory strategy: the strategy of acquiescing to the West, which believes in an incremental process of appeasement in which the U.S. (mainly) and Israel (in secondary fashion) impose their will, insatiably and without end.

Since the [Israeli] invasions of April 2002, the U.S. administration, advertising itself as being responsible for having "saved" the Palestinian leadership from the "raging Israeli bull," has initiated a process of unending blackmail to impose U.S. conditions upon the PA leadership. However, by definition, it is impossible to appease this U.S. administration because it has decisively determined not to deal with the PA leadership. The present Palestinian leadership is unacceptable because it did not behave in the manner expected from it after Oslo. For this reason, the U.S. position is that the change in Palestinian leadership must take place before the [Palestinian] elections [demanded as part of the "reform" plan, which ultimately took place in January 2006, unexpectedly bringing to power Hamas]. They want to place individuals of principal importance to U.S. interests in sensitive positions before the elections. The Americans are not calling for elections to lose them. And it is not by chance, that an expansive campaign of arrests is currently taking place. Israel is arresting the pivotal national political cadre essential to mobilizing for resistance—political leaders as well as field leaders. They already have at least 8,000 prisoners in jail, just as in the 1987 Intifada. This is an essential primary step in preparation for elections. There is a big difference between preparing for elections when these people are in prison and when they are on the streets.

Strategy of Resistance

Now, as previously mentioned, when I speak of a resistance strategy, I am not talking about military operations. The mentality and discourse that "this operation was good" or "no, it was bad" continue to accompany Palestinian armed struggle. We are still measuring our achievements by the number of our martyrs, rather than the losses that have been inflicted upon the occupation. But this is not the point.

I am sorry to say this, but from my modest assessment of the history of the Palestinian struggle, armed struggle was never a strategy. Perhaps it was once a strategy to build a movement. Perhaps it was a strategy to prove that we existed. But armed struggle was never a political strategy to achieve goals and liberation. Yet this [debate over armed struggle as a means for liberation] has yet to be concluded. This has a huge influence upon the existing mental and political culture of entire Palestinian generations raised upon this language. There is a huge responsibility to conclude this part of our history in good faith. If it was a success, let it be concluded as such. If it was a failure, let it be concluded as such. If it was not a strategy, then let it be concluded as such. I am not saying that it was only a failure. I am saying that we must conclude that it was not a strategy for liberation and recognize that Palestinian armed struggle was always governed by different goals in different contexts.

The essential but undeclared principle behind resistance is that the Palestinian people are pulsating with life and are rejecting the status quo: that we are alive—that the situation is not normal—that we refuse to normalize to a situation of occupation—that if we are hurt, we can hurt back. This is a reflex that is a natural instinct. It is evidence of life. But at the same time, it is not sufficient as a political strategy and for a situation as complicated as the Palestinian predicament. Instead we are talking about the formulation of political strategies governed by certain goals and achievements.

Issues That Should Be Confronted in a Strategy of Resistance

When we then sit down to discuss the strategy of resistance, we must take into account the following issues:

First: The Capacity to Make our Adversary Pay the Price

This does not take much accounting. The Palestinian people have already proven that they are capable of making their enemy pay a steep price. I say to you that the Israelis have paid a high price. And don't let cynical people say that the [Palestinian] military operations do not have any influence. On the contrary—they do. Israel, as any other state that respects itself, has the primary task of preserving the security of its citizens. That is the justification for its existence as a state that monopolizes the means of violence. If it is unable to do that, it has an elementary problem.

But this is not sufficient for strategic accounting. The real question is how does it [Israel's inability to provide security to its citizens and the heavy price it has paid as a result of Palestinian military operations] translate politically? What is the political effect of this upon the enemy? Does it lead to a decisive battle where someone's back will be broken [i.e., the Palestinian's]? There is no resistance movement in the world that has such an interest. Are the Palestinians to allow themselves to be drawn into a decisive battle without taking this into account and in a way that has not been studied beforehand? Can we afford that, just because three or four people [a resistance cell] decided it as such? This is incomprehensible and furthermore not acceptable for a national movement that seeks to struggle. This is not up for discussion.

The goal of the national liberation movement must be to splinter the occupiers' society in order to decrease its capacity to withstand the price being paid. If we see that what is being done by the resistance unites the occupiers' society and increases its capacity to pay the price of its occupation—because it enters into a stage of nervous nationalistic chauvinism where its historical complexes are brought to the surface—then things must be stopped and studied. We have a deep national experience that must be studied, and its lessons must be garnered.

Second: The Capacity for Palestinian Society to Withstand the Price It Is Paying

Here we have the experience of the Lebanese resistance [waged against Israel during its occupation of Lebanon from 1982 to 2000], which was being waged in a land where not everybody was supporting it.[41] The Lebanese resistance movement had to constantly maneuver so as to assess to what degree the Lebanese street could withstand what was taking place. Sometimes internal struggles would explode. The situation of the Palestinian liberation movement is better off when compared with that of the Lebanese resistance because [Palestinian] society is behind it. Still, the capacity of a society to remain steadfast and withstand a long-term battle is of utmost import. Is this being taken into consideration when operations are conducted?

Third: The Need for a Political Discourse

Palestinian society must be made aware through a political discourse that explains to it what the goals are. It must know not necessarily every detail of strategy, but rather the broad steps being taken and where they lead, so as to increase its capacity for *sumoud* (steadfastness) and its trust in a responsible leadership. Thus, despite certain ebbs and flows, the people can grasp where it is and where it is going.

Furthermore, there is a political message directed toward the enemy that must be made apparent regarding what precisely the battle is over. The adversary must know this so that he himself may reduce his ability to remain steadfast. If, for example, as in the case of the South Lebanon resistance, Israeli society knows that the battle is for a withdrawal to the international border, it is a great difference from knowing that it will be a withdrawal to Kiryat Shmona [an Israeli settlement near the Lebanese border]. It becomes clear then that the price the society is willing to pay is different in these two circumstances. Likewise, the capacity to remain steadfast is completely different in these two scenarios.

And in general the capacity for a society to withstand losses of its troops is less than its capacity to withstand losses of its civilians. In this sense, it is the opposite from what one might expect. Losses of civilians give the impression in their society that everyone is a possible target. The society therefore concludes that there is no need for discussion or negotiations but that "we have to remain steadfast." However, an attack upon soldiers is an attack upon politics. Soldiers wear an official uniform, which represents the state and its policies. A society can potentially separate it-self from a policy—it can imagine this. Furthermore, its capacity to with-stand losses as a result of a policy is greatly reduced, because it is in theory prepared to change the policies of the state, if it is the state that is targeted.

Fourth: The Message to the World: A Struggle for Liberation

Finally, there is the message to the world, particularly the West. What has taken place in the previous few years is complete confusion over the polit-ical message [of the Intifada] that we have sent.

Precisely at the moment when a sympathizing consensus was in the midst of forming regarding the Palestinian struggle against occupation—as a form of anticolonial resistance and not a question of "terrorism"—the Palestinian political narrative underwent a retreat. One narrative tried to project the Palestinian cause as within Western interests for the region [a reference to the PA narrative in the beginning of the Intifada that sought to improve the conditions of negotiations and suggested that it was in the United States' interests of regional stability to establish a Palestinian state]. In this case even the hint of liberation, progressive values, or de-mocracy was absent.

Another narrative that emerged was one that pushed the framework of the national struggle in the direction of a religious struggle [a reference to the rise of Islamist sloganeering that accompanied Hamas and Islamic Jihad operational participation in the Intifada, and that even elements of Fateh adopted]. It is incomprehensible that an anticolonial, liberation movement will be transformed into a religious struggle. What do Euro-peans [to whom we look to stand with us in solidarity] have to do with this?

Solidarity with a liberation struggle means that there are underdogs—people who are oppressed unjustly and who are fighting against oppres-sion and whose cause is humanitarian and emancipatory. The test, then, is how to frame one's struggle in an understandable humanitarian discourse in a universally comprehensible language. If you cannot do this, there is a problem.

Time for a Popular Intifada

These are times marked by great confusion, made worse by the events of September 11, 2001, and likely to be complicated further if there is a

U.S.-led strike against Iraq. The question that must be asked now relates to the popular horizon of the Intifada. As a result of the continuous invasions, our admission into a period of full reoccupation of the areas once known as Area A, and under the present international conditions, including the positions of the U.S. administration, the importance of the popular character of the Intifada must be underscored. We are living through a period where the Israeli Army dictates the activity of—and has direct authority over—the residents of the West Bank. This makes it incumbent upon Palestinian social forces to think not merely about strategies of resistance but also about the possibility of organizing popular mass struggle, which, in my estimation, will have its own price, but will also bear valuable fruit.

After September 11, the time has come for Palestinian society to return to itself and confront the Israeli military occupation machinery as civilians in the context of a liberation struggle. If a national dialogue is conducted along the basis of "Are we for or against military operations?," the dialogue will fail. The Palestinian national dialogue begins when we sit and discuss what our political goals are and how we can struggle together in a positive manner under one unified leadership. If we can find the organizational context and the enthusiasm for this context, and for its necessity, we will also find the desire to arrive at a collective venture.

Palestinian society should pour into the streets as a besieged oppressed society, posing, for example, the question, "Why should we observe curfew in a collective manner?" If there is a society and it has leadership and organization, this can be implemented within the strategy I have mentioned, capable of combining state building, reform, a political message, and resistance. I realize the situation is complicated. But we must set out to lay the foundations for this strategy.

Israeli Elections 2003 and the Sweeping Victory of Sharon: What Once Was Shall Continue to Be, Only Worse

March 2003

Introduction

The January 28, 2003, general elections in Israel resulted in a massive victory for Ariel Sharon (Likud) and the establishment of the most right-wing government in the history of the state. The Labor Party was decidedly left outside of the newly formed government coalition despite sending clear signals that it was prepared to give up almost all of its conditions for joining it.

The election results indicated the final stages of a long process of deterioration of the Zionist Left, from its former stature as the leader of the Zionist movement before the establishment of the state and its position as the primary constitutor of hegemonic power in political and cultural arenas for decades thereafter. Its dramatic defeat shrank it to dimensions that made it almost an irrelevant political power.

The officially declared reasons for the Labor Party deciding to leave the former Sharon-led unified government, resulting in the call for early general elections, provides sufficient indication of the reasons for its defeat in these elections—namely, the loss of virtually all its political distinctions when compared with the Likud. Labor Party chair Ben Eliezer, who had served as defense minister in Sharon's government, claimed that his decision to withdraw from the Likud government came about because his demand to reduce a small portion of the 2003 budget allocated to the settlements was not met (hence resulting in the Labor Party's failure to vote for it and the collapse of the unified government). However, the real reason for his break from the government stemmed from his fear of political rivals within the Labor Party. The latter had accused Eliezer of acting as a fig leaf for Likud polices, and he feared losing his majority in the coming Labor party primaries.

The hypocrisy of both the accusers and the accused was laid bare: Labor governments were first and foremost responsible for initiating and widening the settlement project both immediately after the 1967 Occupation and during the Oslo years. They also (together with Meretz) initiated and sustained the neoliberal economy in the service of Israeli big capital (see Introduction). This included policies of privatizing services and subcontracting labor, thus lowering living standards to unprecedented levels and hurting the Labor Party's traditional constituency, particularly amongst better-off Ashkenazi workers and small-business owners. Aware of this history, these voters decided to support the Shinui Party instead— a right-wing, overtly racist Ashkenazi party claiming to represent the interest of the petite bourgeoisie. It was clear to all that in addition to sharing the Right's economic vision, the Left also shared its political and "security" positions, as demonstrated through its implementation of the bloody policies of the former unified government.

Mizrahi voters returned to their "home party," the Likud, following their disappointment in the Mizrahi Orthodox party Shas, which had also supported the draconic budget cuts in government expenditures. In doing so, the Mizrahim followed the prevailing security-dominated political culture, trying desperately to prove to the Ashkenazi mainstream their eligibility to join in.

The elections crystallized the political map of Israeli society. The Left coalesced around the misleading discourse of "pragmatism" in its approach to the solution of the 1967 Occupied Territories. However, the rightward move of the Labor Party meant that the actual extreme right-wing policies and ideology pursued by Sharon could now be construed as part of the "political center," with Israeli society securely united around its ever-bloodier war policies.

Israeli Elections 2003: A Massive Victory for the Extreme Nationalist Ashkenazi Bourgeoisie[*]

Tikva Honig-Parnass

The whopping Likud victory in the elections (which doubled its power in the Knesset from 19 to 38 seats, out of a total 120 seats available), together with the astonishing ascendance of the populist, racist, "secular" right-wing Shinui movement (which jumped from 6 to 15 seats) indicates strong support for Sharon's policies in wide strata of Israeli society. That is to say, wide swaths of Israeli society support a prolonged total war against the Palestinian people, which aims at their sociocide ("defeating terror") as a precondition for any political "solution."

Support for Sharon's policies is further evidenced by the Zionist Left's crushing defeat. It was only back in 1996 that these currents, within the government of Shimon Peres, enjoyed the support of 46 percent of Jewish voters (44 Labor Party seats, 12 Meretz seats). Today their numbers are pitifully reduced to 19.6 percent of Jewish voters (19 Labor seats, 5 Meretz seats). This massive decline can primarily be attributed to Israeli society fully turning its back on the so-called "peace camp."

The "Right" Versus the "Radical Right"

Many commentators have attempted to interpret the election results as a victory of the "Center" over the "Left." They point to the fact that the most extreme right-wing parties (the National Religious Party [Mafdal] and the National Unity Party) did not increase their numbers, while the Likud and Shinui did. This interpretation, however, is mistaken or simply cynical. As the progressive commentator Haim Baram emphasizes, what the Likud victory really shows is that "the right nationalist center" [the Likud and Shinui] defeated the Labor Party, which, in contrast to its left-wing image, is actually the "nationalist center"—only somewhat more "pragmatic," particularly with regard to its sensitivity to international public opinion and U.S. foreign policy.[1]

---

[*] This article first appeared in *Between the Lines* no. 21, March 2003.

Meanwhile, Israeli public support for "transfer" (expulsion) of Palestinians is steadily on the rise. Studies show that between 1991 and 2002, the rate of those who support transferring Palestinians in the 1967 Occupied Territories rose from 38 percent to 46 percent, while those who support transferring Palestinian citizens of Israel rose from 24 percent to 31 percent.[2] However, the ever-widening consensus around ethnic cleansing has not found its expression in voting for the extreme right parties that overtly call for transfer. The National Unity Party did not increase its seats, and the fanatic list of Baruch Marzel did not even receive enough votes to secure one Knesset seat.[3] The Israeli voters who support transfer sufficed with the Likud, which in all respects "has never eliminated transfer as a possible idea."[4]

Professor of Political Science Shlomo Avinery correctly emphasizes that what seems to be the weakening of the extreme Right is in fact the general move of the Israeli polity in the direction of the nonextremist Right:

> There is no doubt that many people who wanted to vote for the extreme right parties voted for Likud. The Likud propaganda worked cleverly [being aware of the popularity of Sharon among the extreme right and settlers]. It said, "If you want Sharon, vote Likud and not the National Unity [Party]."[5]

The Zionist "Left"—Labor and Meretz

The enormous defeat of the Zionist Left is the final stage in a long process during which the Labor Party has gradually lost any distinct political identity, increasingly blurring the boundaries between itself and Likud. This process accelerated during their partnership in Sharon's former unified government, set up in 2001. Labor Party ministers willingly gave their consent to and even personally implemented policies of the cruelest war crimes in the Occupied Territories in efforts to repress the Intifada. This strengthened the conviction of many that it is better to vote for the "real Likud," which will "do the job better" than its beta version (Labor), the hypocrisy of whose "peace and moderation" rhetoric has been laid bare. Many of those who withdrew their support for the Labor Party turned to the Likud (which took 12 percent of Labor voters compared with the 1999 election), while others went to Shinui. But they did not vote for Meretz, which they considered "too Leftist." This is no wonder in light of the repeated declarations by Meretz and Labor that "there is no partner on the Palestinian side" and that it was Arafat who rejected former Labor PM Barak's "generous offer" at Camp David 2000 and instead "chose the path of terror."

Nor did Labor (and Meretz) have any alternative socioeconomic policy to offer their potential voters to rescue Israeli society from the unprecedented decrease in living standards, including ever-increasing poverty levels and unemployment due to the policies of the former Likud-Labor unified government. Moreover, the public knows that the social cuts and neoliberal privatization policies of the former Likud-led unified government only continued the measures initially introduced by the Labor Party in the mid-1980s, and since then never challenged in principle even by the self-professed social democrats of Meretz. Thus, it is understandable why both Labor and Likud, together with other partners of Sharon's previous unified government, ignored socioeconomic issues in their election campaigns, concentrating upon "security" issues alone.

The pathetic attempt on the part of Meretz to focus on socioeconomic issues met the justifiable distrust of the victims of the economic disaster, most of whom, among Jewish Israelis, are Mizrahim. Meretz is, at best, a liberal middle-class party that absorbed the remnants of the historic Mapam party without any of the latter's Marxist/socialist discourse. Meretz never represented any of the real interests of the Mizrahi constituency in the past. It therefore gained almost none of their votes in the recent election. As part of its efforts to rid itself of its elitist, Ashkenazi, well-to-do image, Meretz nominated Eitan Kreive to the twelfth seat on its electoral list. Kreive was a leader of the determined and militant disabled people who demonstrated in the winter of 2002 against hard-hitting budget cuts. However, at the last moment, Kreive was replaced by MK Yossi Beilin, a leading figure of the Oslo process and a declared proponent of "free-market economics." (Beilin joined the Meretz list with Yael Dayan, a supposed "extreme dove," after failing to hold a realistic position on the Labor Party list for the Knesset). It was correctly perceived by the public that Meretz preferred Beilin's neoliberal teachings to Kreive's social welfare worldview. Thus Meretz had no chance to mobilize supporters from among those worst hit by the all-too-free economy, because its leaders are among this economic policy's main proponents.

Perhaps the most significant indication of the Zionist Left's loss of its central historic status in Israeli politics was the steady decline of support of Labor and Meretz by youths who voted for the first time. Only 16 percent backed Labor and Meretz in this election, in comparison to 37 percent who voted for them in the 1999 elections and 46 percent in the 1996 elections.

Shinui: The Israeli Version of France's National Front[6]

Meretz and the Labor Party lost many of their supporters among the Ashkenazi bourgeoisie to Tommy Lapid's Shinui party, which they considered a more unequivocal representative of their middle-class interests and their racist, Ashkenazi worldview. Indeed, Shinui is the most blatant right-wing party in Israel's political arena regarding socioeconomic issues. As in the case of Jean Marie Le Pen's National Front movement in France, Shinui misleads the people with populist slogans of the need to rescue the "intermediate class" whose conditions have deteriorated due to those "who don't work" and "live on their account." Shinui identifies the latter in general as the Orthodox, who "don't serve in the army." But this only hides the main target of its racist hatred—namely, Mizrahim, who are the majority of the Jewish working class, and particularly Shas, the only party that identifies itself as Mizrahi.[7] Most Shas supporters, however, *do* serve in the army, as opposed to supporters of the Ashkenazi Orthodox religious party Yahadut Hatora. The latter were not attacked by Shinui throughout the election campaign, despite the fact that Lapid became hoarse by repeatedly shouting "*Rak lo Shas!*" ("Just not Shas!"), as Shinui's main condition for joining the new government after the elections. Shas and the Mizrahim thus served as the scapegoat for the protest of the Ashkenazi lower middle class, which was badly hit by the neoliberal policies of big capital.

Shinui's classist and racist stances are wrapped in the promise of "secularizing Israeli society." The party uses the issues of freedom of and from religion in Israeli society, including demands for public transportation on the Sabbath and for the permitting of civil marriages, to mobilize this constituency. However, when the time came for Shinui to join the government, nothing remained of these slogans.

Lip service was paid to "peace" in the form of a blurred general acceptance of Bush's "road map," conditioned first upon repressing "terror"—a position that fits in well with the "moderate" positions of the Israeli Ashkenazi bourgeoisie who hurried to support Sharon's new government.

Shas and the Mizrahim

The solidarity of Shas members with their fellow Mizrahim did not prevent the decline of the party's power: Shas lost 4 of its 17 seats in the previous Knesset. Most of the non-Orthodox (traditional) Mizrahim, who in the last two election campaigns voted for Shas, have now returned to the

Likud—their "home party"—due to their disappointment with Shas's support of the neoliberal policies of the former unified government. They thus contributed to the wide support Sharon received despite the total failure of his government on all main issues in terms of both stopping the deterioration of the economy and "bringing peace and security" to Israeli citizens by crushing the Intifada and breaking the spirit of the Palestinians.

The wide consensus in Israeli society around "security" as the most important issue, together with the lack of any political party that responds to the oppression of Mizrahim in terms of ethnicity and class affiliation, has brought the very Jewish victims of neoliberalism to vote once again for those who share responsibility for creating their suffering in the first place. Zionism's hegemonic statist ideology, which paved the way for destroying the foundations of any internal social and class solidarity, is ever growing. Along with this, the arrogance of big capital (aware of the workers' helplessness and despair) is increasing. The directorship of Bank Hapoalim, one of Israel's biggest banks, had the nerve to announce the firing of nine hundred employees in the middle of the election campaign. It correctly assumed that this maneuver would not raise any militant solidarity strikes or demonstrations or, for that matter, have any impact at the ballot box. Both big capital and the political establishment seem aware of the fact that the Mizrahim and the poor accept the most extreme "security"-oriented policies together with Israel's militarist culture. In their perception, this approval facilitates their acceptance into "Israeliness," which they willingly trade for any socioeconomic demands.[8] Sharon was therefore not too concerned with the fact that the Mizrahim constitute a substantial part of the Likud constituency when he established his purely Ashkenazi coalition government.

Sharon's Extreme Right-Wing Government Coalition—Labor and Shas Out

The composition of the second Sharon government was established with the support of wide strata of Israeli society, who are well aware of the bloody and destructive military and economic policies it will implemented. The government coalition, which is composed of the Likud, Shinui, the National Religious Party (Mafdal), and the National Unity Party, is the most extreme right-wing government Israel has ever known.

This coalition is also homogeneous in terms of the bourgeois Ashkenazi racism of its partners. Thus the National Religious Party (Mafdal) accepted Shinui's firm condition of excluding Shas from the government, in negotiations that took place the day after the elections. Mafdal represents the religious Ashkenazi middle class, whose support for the settlers and extreme Right has replaced their traditional support for the Zionist colonialist project when it was led by the Mapai party (whose offspring is the present Labor Party). Together with the other part of the secular-extremist Ashkenazi Right (the National Unity Party), Mafdal now supports Likud in its ideological break with its (the Likud's) traditional base of support among "the poor and the believers" (as was declared by the former Likud ideological and political leader, Menachem Begin).[9] Instead, the Likud is confident for the time being that the latter's loyalty to the Right is secure.[10]

The Last Death Throes of Labor's Claimed Distinct Principles

No doubt Sharon feels more comfortable without the prospect for arguments with the new Labor Party chair, Amram Mitzna,[11] in government. Contrary to his Labor Party predecessors in the previous unified government (Peres, Ben Eliezer, and Dalia Yitzik), Mitzna represents the weak remnants of Labor's right-leaning social-democratic discourse and might not have agreed so easily to serve as the fig leaf for some of the bloodiest measures planned by Sharon against the Palestinians. Sharon was indeed in need of the Labor Party's support in general, regarding both his policies toward the Palestinians and his tough economic measures against workers and the poor, to moderate his image internationally and locally. However he was not prepared to pay even the smallest political price for accepting Mitzna's minimal conditions for joining the government coalition, which over time effectively faded away.[12]

Thus, despite the Labor Party's eagerness to join the government, Sharon hurried to conclude a coalition agreement with Shinui, Mafdal, and the National Unity Party. Furthermore, due to the latter's objection to a "Palestinian state," "the actual beginning of negotiations with the Palestinians on the content of Sharon's 'Hertizliya speech' (his support for a 'Palestinian state') will be conditioned on a government decision."[13]

Nor need Sharon fear a "militant opposition," which Mitzna is promising. A large part of the Labor Party, led by the ex-ministers in Sharon's first unified government, regrets the decision to leave the government that led to the elections. They also refuse to remain in the opposition, and appear to be waiting for the first opportunity to join Sharon's government. What is more important is that the Labor Party, headed by Mitzna, does not have a real alternative vision for a solution to the Israeli-Palestinian "conflict." This fact only adds more strength to the already wide consensus around the very Zionist beliefs and presumptions that underlie the support of Sharon's previous policies. These will inevitably bring greater support for even more appalling measures to be used in the prolonged "war on terror." From now on, the sky is the limit for Sharon's bloody war against the Palestinians, which is backed by the United States as well as by most Israelis.

Much of the Same, but Worse: Reflections on the Israeli Elections

Ilan Pappe[*]

Much of the same, but much worse. This seems to be, in a nutshell, the verdict for the results of the last Israeli elections.

It is much of the same, as it is yet another Sharon government, with or without the Labor Party, relying on the support of a majority of the Jewish voters and committed to pursuing the same destructive policies it executed in the last two years.

It is much of the same, as the elections reflect the protracted trend within Israel to exclude the Palestinian minority from the political game as it resonates the continued control of the Israeli Army over the government's policies in the 1967 Occupied Territories. The army command, down to its brigade commanders, is now ruling the life of most Palestinians in the West Bank with force, and it seems a matter of a few months before the same applies to the Gaza Strip. The military can now use whatever means it chooses to maintain the occupation, and thus we are likely to see further bifurcation of the land, the paving of new bypass roads for the settlers, the erection of new army camps (usually on neigh-

* Dr. Ilan Pappe is a senior lecturer in the Department of Political Science at Haifa University and the chair of the Emil Touma Institute for Palestinian Studies in Haifa. He is the author of *The Making of the Arab-Israeli Conflict* (1992), *The Israel/Palestine Question* (1999), and *A History of Modern Palestine: One Land, Two Peoples* (2003). This article first appeared in *Between the Lines* no. 21, March 2003.

borhoods confiscated from the local population), and the establishment of more settlement strongholds. With these old-new policies, all the known facets of life under occupation will persist: daily abuse in the checkpoints, curfews, closures, starvation in the countryside, and economic strangulation in the cities alongside the humiliation of the political leadership in the Muqata'a[14] and the destruction of the social and economic life of the society as a whole.

It is much of the same, as the new government is likely to pursue the same domestic social and economic policies as those of its predecessor—policies that would lead to further polarization of the society, generate more unemployment, lead to the collapse of social services, and prevent economic growth. The absence of any diplomatic initiative on the horizon will accentuate the recession that has already raged under the first Sharon government.

Why Israelis should vote again for such a government is still a valid question, especially in light of its unfulfilled promises to bring personal security to Jewish citizens and its failure to curb the suicide bombs or attacks on civilians. The fifty years of dehumanization of the Arabs and the Palestinians, the militarization of the political system, and the total obedience of academia and media alike to the Zionist ideology—institutions that are expected to provide alternative analysis and criticism—are all partial explanations for the Jewish trend in Israel to vote for nationalist fanaticism, domestic racism, economic adventurism, and social injustice.

But it is worse, both in the sense of what has already taken place in the short time since the elections and in what can happen in the near future.

Ever since the elections there has been a marked escalation in the military operations in the Occupied Territories. A shoot-to-kill policy is now in force in every area under direct Israeli military control. The numbers of Palestinians killed in the West Bank and the Gaza Strip has increased dramatically since the elections in January 2003. Within the war hysteria generated by the American media abroad and the Israeli media at home, the daily slaying of five to six Palestinians (including youths and children) passes almost unnoticed. The only two journalists in the established Israeli media to report such crimes faithfully, Amira Hass and Gideon Levy of *Ha'aretz*, have also desperately been silenced by the warmongering around them. Robert Fisk of the *Independent,* along with conscientious reporters here and there in the British *Guardian* and the French *Libération,* have all tried to attract attention to the brutal reality with various degrees of success; but these are all drops in the sea of words covering the "war on terrorism."

At the center of this new genocidal policy stand two people: Ariel Sharon and Shaoul Mofaz. The first is reincarnated as the epitome of common sense, wise statesmanship, and political wisdom—in short, a centrist; the other as a "professional," namely, devoid of ideology and totally devoted to security and defense. In reality, however, these two are the true successors of the old Zionist Labor movement, Mapai, and its policies of uprooting and colonizing Palestine. The raison d'etre of these policies was incremental takeover, expulsion, and now killing of Palestinians, while executing more dramatic operations at times of war and crises. These actions were traditionally concealed by a discourse of pragmatism, realpolitik, and, if needed, peace.

While negotiating peaceful solutions in the 1930s with the British Mandate government, the Jewish leadership took more land and expanded its stronghold in the country. In the early 1950s, while Israeli diplomats were discussing the fate of the Palestinian refugees, a policy of massive destruction of their homes was carried out while an additional number of Palestinians were evicted by force from their homes inside the Jewish state. Similarly, during the days of the Oslo Accords, the settlement project was extended and the population in the Occupied Territories was subjected to policies of abuse and harassment. The current discourse is that of the "road map"[15]—supposedly a diplomatic avenue—while the direct callous military occupation is spreading and the killing of innocent civilians is increasing.

The deviation from the "gradual policies" was at times of war. In the 1930s, David Ben-Gurion wrote to his son, Amos, that during revolutionary times the Zionist movement can leap forward and forsake more evolutionary and cautious progress. He was referring to the question of "transfer" of the indigenous population. According to Ben-Gurion, massive expulsion could happen only during revolutionary times, namely, the end of the British Mandate. And indeed this historical moment came in 1948, and the ethnic cleansing of Palestine took place.

Around Sharon, Mofaz, and the general command of the army, one can hear the hope and prediction that similar new revolutionary conditions are developing as a result of the imminent American attack on Iraq.

It is indeed difficult to predict how an American invasion would affect the situation in Palestine. But one thing is clear: Israel now has a government that will look at the war as an appropriate historical juncture for taking drastic actions against the Palestinian population. Much depends, of course, on the kind of war the Americans wage on Iraq. If it is a swift military operation, at least to begin with, the repercussions in Palestine will not be immediate or dramatic. A more complicated entanglement could prod Sharon and his ilk to take bolder actions in order to determine by force an old Mapai dream: to have as much of Palestine with as few Palestinians as possible. If, for that matter, 10 percent of Palestine should be called a Palestinian state—namely, a Bantustan—so be it. For whatever policies the new government pursues in the case of Palestine, the present government senses, correctly, that it has wide public support—now that the discourse of transfer has moved from the extreme right to the center.

It is also worse in the new parliamentary constellation. There is massive support for more discriminatory legislation against the Palestinian citizens in Israel. The rule is legislative energy and executive zeal increasing by the day with the aim of totally marginalizing the Palestinian minority. As the Sharon governments (of both 2001 and 2003) are mesmerized by the extreme capitalist ideology adhered to by the captains of the Israeli industrial and financial system, the economic policies of the new government are likely to produce a deeper recession and higher unemployment—the principal victims of which will continue to be the Palestinians in Israel.

So the news from within is that the existential danger to Palestinians living within the boundaries of historical Palestine has dramatically increased as a result of the last elections. For many, it is no longer a question of a potential danger, as the ruthless policies are already in action.

The strategic and tactical questions for those who wish to put an end to this new phase in the destruction of the Palestinian people have not changed as a result of the elections. Although there is a new wave of NGO activity against the occupation and for equality inside Israel, these are low and feeble barricades that are not able to block the tidal wave of further destruction. The need to enlist external pressure so that the efforts of the inside will be empowered in the struggle against this government of evil remains and is more acute than ever before. The veil of silence in the international media of the crimes committed in the Occupied Territories should be removed, and the global civil society's uneasiness with Israeli policies, manifested in the actions taken lately by both European and American peace movements, should turn into effective policies that would render Israel a pariah state as long as its present policies persist.

Why Are Shas and the Mizrahim Supporters of the Right?[16]

An Interview with Sami Shalom Chetrit*

Tikva Honig-Parnass

Q: It is common knowledge that in the last two years, the Shas leadership has shifted to the extreme Right. How do you explain this shift?

A: I don't agree with this analysis regarding the leadership of Shas. One has to differentiate between it and the Mizrahi public. Shas sought to promote the idea that the criterion for determining equality within Israeli identity be one's Judaism alone—without Zionism, without the legend of the pre-1948 Palmach,[17] and without service in the army. Shas addressed Mizrahim, saying, "We don't need anything else except Judaism and don't even need to serve in the army or worship the legend of the Palmach in order to feel as though we are 'good Israelis.'"

Of course, the moment the "security" crisis in Israel escalated, the state demanded that Israelis decide where they stand regarding national loyalty. The Mizrahim realized that Shas's principle of "equality based upon Judaism only," which failed to include a strong Zionist dimension, risked the false sense of equality it aimed to grant them.

Hence, the Shas public almost automatically connects itself to whatever is needed to regain "Israeliness," including shouting "Death to the Arabs!" and hurrying to join the "right-wing" camp, thus strengthening their threatened identity. What is perceived then as Shas becoming more right-wing is but another Mizrahim reaction to the strong threats against their identity.

---

* Dr. Sami Shalom Chetrit was born in Qasr as-Suq, Morocco, in 1960. He moved with his family to Israel in 1963, growing up in the "development town" of Ashdod (the former Palestinian village of Asdud). An activist in oppressed Mizrahi communities on issues related to alternative equal education, community empowerment, and the ideology of Mizrahi radicalization, Chetrit is also a writer and poet. He is the author of *The Mizrahi Struggle in Israel: Between Oppression and Liberation, Identification and Alternative, 1948–2003,* (Tel Aviv: Oved Publishing, 2004). This interview first appeared in *Between the Lines* no. 20, February 2003, and was conducted during the election campaign.

Q: How does this anti-Arabness come to terms with their [the Mizrahim's] Arab origin and heritage?

A: Indeed we should never forget that the Mizrahi Jew has always preserved within himself an Arab identity that can be faced only when alone in the bathroom looking in the mirror. However, it is precisely this Arabness, in a tragic way, that maintains the Mizrahi as anti-Arab and loyal to Ashkenazi Zionism. Thus, by always being obliged to be anti-Arab, the Mizrahi is obliged to be against the Arabness within himself.

This self-hatred becomes even more conspicuous at times like the present, when Arabness is presented as the enemy—not only of Israel, but also of Western humanity as a whole. This is the tragedy of the Mizrahim. No one has to repress or exterminate their identity; they do it themselves.

Thus, given the current crisis in security, we are witnessing a nationalist reconnection among Mizrahim. However, it is not an ideological shift, only a shift in allegiance. This is because when Mizrahim supported Ben-Gurion[18] and the Labor Party in the first decades of the state, they were not more Leftist than they are today. The state-oriented approach that Ben-Gurion represented was also right-wing. In this respect, I don't see any new strengthened rightward ideological orientation among Mizrahim.

Q: You said that we have to differentiate between the Shas leadership and its public. In what way does the leadership differ regarding the 1967 Occupied Territories?

A: Rabbi Ovadia Yosef's[19] worldview has never consisted of a right-wing agenda, in terms of calling for the annexation of the 1967 Occupied Territories. Nor has he ever stood up and said that Israel should expel the Palestinians as part of a political plan or rebuild the Temple, as the Orthodox fanatics demand. Precisely the contrary: he has emphasized that a Jew is forbidden to come close to the Temple Mount [the Al Aqsa Mosque compound].[20] But he is also the only one who gave political justifications in addition to a Halachic[21] commandment that it was necessary "not to irritate the Goyim." This is a kind of realpolitik.

And surely Ovadia Yosef has not established a movement to settle the 1967 Occupied Territories. If you look at the Shas platform, all you find is a general statement saying "We support the war against terror," "We will join Sharon in this battle because he knows how to do it." But this does not make him more right-wing than the Labor Party. Ben Eliezer [Labor] also joined Sharon in the unified government and committed appalling atrocities in the 1967 Occupied Territories as his minister of defense.

Q: The polls show that Shas is going to lose around eight of the seventeen seats it holds in the current Knesset to the Likud. Why are Mizrahim leaving Shas? And why to the Likud?

A: I have always said that 50 percent of those who support Shas are not religious. They have no interest in Shas's religious aim of "Lehahzir Atara leyoshna," which was the original reason for its establishment—namely, to return the authority of oriental Jewish tradition in Halachic decisions and mores to its original status among the Mizrahim, before they were marginalized by the Ashkenazi Orthodox establishment. These people voted Shas only because of their desire to protest against their social, economic, and cultural oppression and discrimination as Mizrahim. And, as I said, in an escalated nationalist period such as the present, when everything regarding nationalism is expressed in the most acute manner, Shas is unable to supply the Mizrahim with a sufficiently stable basis for an equitable identity.

Shas voters are probably deserting to the Likud despite the fact that it does not offer them any solution to their protest. On the contrary, Likud's economic policy is destroying their life. But so was the economic policy of Labor and Meretz—the successors of the Zionist Labor Party, which created their inferior socioeconomic status during its rule from 1948 to 1977, not to mention its central role in introducing and supporting the wild free market thereafter. For now, the Mizrahim joining the Likud is like returning home.

Q: So the Mizrahim never supported the "peace camp" in general and the Oslo Accords in particular?

A: Yes. The Mizrahim have always been ready to serve as soldiers in the "battle" of hate and oppression against Palestinians. The occupation has granted them a way to acquire a cheap nationalist identity. It is actually a shortcut to acquiring an identity that fits the Ashkenazi nationalist identity. The Mizrahim have no place within the Jewish nationalist framework without demonstrating total loyalty to the Zionist hegemony and consistently demonstrating hate—actually self-hate—and superiority over Palestinians.

Let's be honest: What will the Mizrahim gain from the Ashkenazi model of peace known as Oslo or any other initiative within this framework? Nothing! A globalized Israeli economy led by Ashkenazim will flourish; the few industrial enterprises left here will be transferred to the Far East and to Jordan and of course to the 1967 Occupied Territories. The Ashkenazi upper tenth will become increasingly wealthy, to the point that they will kindly agree to satisfy the basic needs of the Mizrahim and the newcomers in the townships and poor neighborhoods [from Ethiopia or from the former Soviet republics] (and even less those of Palestinian citizens) in exchange for social quiet and national loyalty. Privatization will proceed even faster, education and health care will be made conditional on income, and an additional half-million slaving foreign workers will be imported in order to lower the work conditions of Mizrahim and Palestinians alike. Thus, the Mizrahim can only lose from the kind of peace Israel longs for.

Q: On what basis, then, was Shas identified in the past by many radical Mizrahim as a revolutionary movement that had the potential to lead Mizrahi Jews to challenge the Ashkenazi Zionist establishment?

A: I think that the key to understanding this is comprehending the enormous role Arye Deri played in the movement.[22] No doubt he, at least potentially, was more capable of rebelling against the Zionist hegemony than was Rabbi Ovadia Yosef. Indeed, the latter would say, "We the Mizrahim are the true Zionists [and *not* the hegemonic Zionist movement and its ideology], and let no one dare challenge that." But Deri went further and explicitly said, "Zionism brought about the spiritual and cultural extermination of Mizrahi Jewry." Now, whoever is willing to say this stands overtly in opposition to Zionism. And this is much more threatening than Rabbi Ovadia Yosef's position. Yosef therefore no longer wanted Deri to lead Shas because he was a rebel; because Deri was connecting Shas's agenda to the Mizrahi socioeconomic struggle, at least on the level of rhetoric.

Rabbi Yosef is not a Zionist. For him Zionism is only a temporary hostel. All he wants is to be able to carry out his work in peace while gradually building a Jewish community whose life is based on the Halacha: "Work should be done quietly and God will take care." Namely, according to Yosef, the great transformation to a Jewish state based upon the Halacha is inevitable in the future and will come about by God's will, without the need for Deri to "incite the streets."

Ovadia Yosef has no interest in the government after the coming elections, except regarding the budget, which is a necessary condition for Shas continuing its activities on the ground within Mizrahi communities. If you look at these activities, you will find that they consist of simply building a state within a state, in all respects: economic, cultural, and so on.

Q: So what you are saying is that the essential core of Shas is its alienation from the state, despite its calls for "escalating the war against Palestinian terror"?

A: Yes. Shas is not nationalist. For them, a state has a constitution and the legitimacy to enforce a style of life that contradicts Judaism.

But the movement's activists on the ground, in the poverty-stricken neighborhoods, met with a society in distress that lives with a broken, inferior identity that was enabled through Shas to feel equal, albeit up to a certain point. This lasted until the moment of crisis in which Israel is at present, when the question raised is: Are you with *them* or *us*? It is either-or: Are you a nationalist patriot or not?

Q: Until now you have concentrated on the identity issue of Mizrahi Jews. I would like to relate to their class membership and class consciousness. After all, they make up the majority of the Jewish working class. The emphasis, however, of the Shas leadership and often also of the Mizrahim rank and file is on their cultural oppression. Why is there no expressed perception of their class situation or organized demands based on it?

A: We are in times characterized by a nationalist political culture in Israel. Whoever attempts to establish a movement that defines the Mizrahi struggle as a class struggle and to follow the Black Panthers, who were active in early 1970s, will be labeled a traitor.[23] The Black Panthers said, "Either the cake (the state) belongs to everyone, or there should be no cake." So they were persecuted and disappeared.[24] No Mizrahi leader will dare use this language today, knowing that doing so is akin to committing political suicide. Who, then, will show the way? If even Ashkenazi politicians and worker leaders do not dare speak this language, who will do it? Rank-and-file workers and the unemployed can shout and protest, but no one even hears them.

We should remember that class language is universal. It cannot exclude the Arabs from the collective of workers. This is why the Black Panthers and other small groups, who raised class slogans, have disappeared. Speaking in class terms is declaring that you speak on behalf of everyone, the Arabs as well. So again you are a traitor.

Indeed, the nationalist monster has taken over the entire political scene.

Q: Were the Mizrahim ever part of the Zionist Labor movement? What was the approach of the Histadrut to the Mizrahim?[25]

A: Since the mass immigration of Jews from Arab countries to Israel in the early 1950s, Ben-Gurion, and after him the entire Zionist Labor movement, preached that "you cannot wave the security flag and the socioeconomic flag at the same time." And since security is more important, the Mizrahim should delay their demands to improve their economic condition.

However, one should not forget why the Mizrahim were brought here in the first place by the Zionist left government that ruled the state after its establishment. The Mizrahim, like the Palestinians, were not supposed to be here. The presence of both constituted the most difficult problems for Zionism, impeding the implementation of its Eurocentric colonial project in Palestine embodied in the exclusivist Jewish state. However, as Ben-Gurion said, "The state has been established, and the [European] people [the Jews whom the Zionist state was expecting] are gone [in the Holocaust]." There was therefore "no alternative" but to initiate immigration from Arab countries.

Actually, from the beginning, the Mizrahim were allocated to the lower echelons of the Jewish working class—albeit higher than the intentionally proletarianized Palestinians, whose lands were confiscated, among other policies.

The racist dimension was thus combined with class interests: At the beginning there were special departments in the Histadrut for Mizrahi workers (e.g., Department for Oriental Ethnic Groups), along with a special department for Palestinian citizens of Israel (the Arab Department).

Q: This is to say that the Mizrahim were taken care of as "Mizrahim" and thus were excluded from the Ashkenazi community of "workers"?

A: The Histadrut, which was both the employer and a workers' organization, was a tool in the service of the Zionist state as embodied in the dictatorship of Ben-Gurion. Its aim was not to organize the Mizrahi workers as proletarians with class consciousness. On the contrary, its aim was to make them dependent so they would not organize against the state. The historic role of the Histadrut is not comparable to that of any other trade union: it sought to ensure that there would not be any independent organization of workers.

The Histadrut today is a different story altogether. It is an organization composed of a number of powerful committees in the public sector, such as the electric and telephone companies, whose workers have very high salaries and pensions. These are people with an enormous amount of power, who have simply organized to preserve their power without any awareness of class solidarity. The Histadrut does not take care of the interests of what are called the "weak" social layers, even in the most minimal of ways, as it once did in the past. The leader of the Histadrut party, MK Amir Peretz, joined Sharon's government [in the coalition established after the 2001 elections] after he was elected. Imagine: a trade union that joins the government whose aim is to fight against it!

So in this respect I have no hope that this so-called workers' party will mobilize the Mizrahim to vote for it.

Q: There were in the past buds of self-organization of "radical Mizrahim" that the Democratic Mizrahi Rainbow Coalition [HaKeshet Hadimokratit Hamizrachit (hereafter *Keshet*), a group consisting of largely Mizrahi academics, established in 1997], as an all-Mizrahi movement, was supposed to represent. Indeed, as you once wrote, it seemed as though this comprehensive self-organization of Mizrahim combined with an acute political consciousness might lead to radicalization of the Mizrahim masses. What happened to the Keshet and other militant organizations in the past?

A: In the beginning, the radical Mizrahi discourse was promising. It was born out of the explosion of the Mizrahim Black Panthers with its connection to various left movements.[26] From then on, it proceeded, and all kinds of activists initiated organizations such as HILA, *Iton Aher*, and Kedma.[27] What is most attractive is the connection of most of these organizations to the poor neighborhoods and development towns.[28] There was a good atmosphere around these projects; a feeling that at least there was a sort of avant-garde. I don't know whether these were mass movements. What is important is the fact that the activists both worked with the people and were located in the radical and critical fronts in terms of political struggle, Zionism, and so on.

Then came the attempt to establish an umbrella organization for all these separate initiatives in the form of the Democratic Mizrahi Rainbow Coalition. Indeed, many people came to the Keshet from a variety of political backgrounds, such as the Likud and the religious parties. It was fascinating to see what would become of them politically while participating in the same Mizrahi movement. But the academics among the founders of the Keshet, who later became stronger in the movement, took the initiative back to academia, to the Van Leer Institute.[29]

It was originally the sociologist Shlomo Svirski who after having been rejected by the academia, visited poor neighborhoods and radicalized Mizrahi discourse. Svirski's seminal book *Oriental Majority*[30] dealt with the planned allocation of Mizrahi immigrants into the working classes, raising the consciousness of radical Mizrahim. Now many of the new generation of Mizrahi academics have taken this discourse back to the academia and thus deradicalized it.

Mizrahi academics who came to Keshet turned this radical political discourse into a full-fledged academic discourse. Nothing remains of the Mizrahiness of the days of Ella Shohat, which was depicted as "the victim of Zionism."[31] Now Mizrahiness is actually something hybrid. Mizrahiness is considered to influence the Ashkenazim, to mold the Ashkenazi culture.[32] Where is such molding taking place? In the wretched impoverished neighborhoods?

Q: So what you are saying is that what the Keshet really seeks is its share of the Zionist state and ideology?

A: Yes. An additional thing that happened in the Keshet is that in regard to the most serious test—i.e., its position on the Zionist question—it failed. One cannot deny it: the Keshet at present is a Zionist movement. The most conspicuous example of this was seen in its well-publicized efforts to demand reallocation of "state lands" that had been leased to the kibbutzim decades ago.[33] Furthermore, it did not even specify Palestinian citizens as entitled to sharing them, instead saying "all Israeli citizens."

In accordance to privatization plans, most of these lands were meant to pass to the ownership of kibbutzim. The Keshet appealed to the High Court to reallocate these lands to Mizrahim without recognizing the fact that most of these lands had been confiscated from Palestinians and should have been returned to them. They did not even [make the] call to reallocate them equally with Palestinian citizens of Israel. In all other aspects you can also recognize their distance from anti-Zionist positions, including the language and content of the things they write: they are written in a Mizrahi-nationalist language, a kind of socionationalistic version. It makes me shiver.

CHAPTER 7

The Occupation of Iraq: Widening U.S. Hegemony and Its Fallout for Palestine

July 2002–April 2003

Introduction

The drumbeats of an impending U.S. invasion of Iraq were sinisterly welcomed by the Israeli political, military, and media establishments, which foresaw the fruits that an absolute U.S. hegemony in the postwar era would bear for Israel, its watchdog in the region. Unlike left forces internationally, which were protesting in the streets of every major city in Europe and the United States, as well as in Africa, Asia, and Latin America, the Zionist Left and most of the Israeli peace camp remained committed ideologically and politically to their traditional pro-American loyalties, perceiving the United States as the epitome of Western democracy. Rather than raise their voices against the morbid chorus of war-mongering within the Israeli establishment, they made misleading intimations that a settlement with the Palestinians would take place through U.S. enforcement in the postinvasion of Iraq era. In doing so, the Zionist Left also continued to ignore the cynicism of U.S. and Israeli actions on the ground, which were imposing a fait accompli across the 1967 Occupied Territories through the feverish construction of Jewish settlements and bypass roads. It also ignored the tremendous destruction the Israeli Army continued to inflict on the Palestinians, which, in the wake of Operation Defensive Shield upon the West Bank, began to focus increasingly on the Gaza Strip.

Israel's unprecedented raids on Gaza in the run-up to the attack against Iraq were designed to completely eliminate the Palestinians' ability to remain steadfast, thereby extending its policies of sociocide as witnessed in the West Bank during Operation Defensive Shield. Between July 1, 2002 and March 31, 2003, Israel killed no fewer than 356 Palestinians[1] and destroyed 494 homes, 102 water wells, 46 water pumps, 165 greenhouses, 357 irrigation networks,[2] and 120 metal workshops[3] in Gaza alone. Indeed, the run-up to the war on Iraq caused many Palestinians, together with a few genuinely progressive Israelis, to justly fear that the assault upon Iraq might provide the window for Israeli transfer policies to be enacted, as Israel had tried to do in previous war situations.[4] However, while these prewar fears did not materialize, Israel was content to continue with its incremental policies of sociocide with the United States' blessing. Indeed, the joint U.S.-Israeli total wars waged in Iraq and Palestine were tailored to smother both Palestine and Iraq as impediments to U.S. hegemonic interests regionally. This subsequently made the need for the development of a democratic Arab and Palestinian nationalist political project, an existential priority if the Arab world were to survive the new Pax Americana.

As Iraq and the Occupied Territories burned, the culmination of efforts to "reform the PA" were now codified in the form of the Quartet-sponsored[5] "road map to peace."[6] Consistent with the U.S. administration's declared intention to "democratize the Middle East" the "road map" was released by the U.S. State Department on April 30, 2003, only after Arafat agreed to accept the creation of the post of Palestinian prime minister—a post that Mahmoud Abbas (Abu Mazen)[7] was expressly designated by the United States and European Union to fill. Its details outlined a "performance-based" approach, whereby even the tiny "carrots" that the political process dangled before the Palestinians were contingent upon "an unequivocal end to violence and terrorism"; the entire restructuring of the PA security apparatus "aimed at confronting all those engaged in terror and dismantling of terrorist capabilities and infrastructure"; the "confiscation of illegal weapons"; and the resumption of security cooperation with the Israeli Army "with the participation of U.S. security officials." The "road map" required all this to take place before even one Israeli tank redeployed and only then to "restore the status quo that existed prior to September 28, 2000"—the very status quo that ignited the Intifada in the first place. This is to say nothing about what is to be done before "the option of creating an independent Palestinian state with provisional borders" is even discussed.

Although the "road map" left little to be discussed with regard to the terms for final Palestinian submission, the conditions set by the United States for its publication would prove to be ironic. The latter's insistence on creating the position of Palestinian prime minister as a means of marginalizing Arafat and bringing the "moderate" Abu Mazen to power would later bring the Hamas leader, Ismail Hanieh, to power in the January 2006 elections.

Why Israel Pushes for the Strike Against Iraq: Israel's Strategic Policies in the Region[*]

Saleh Abdel Jawwad

An important question that insistently poses itself on the eve of a war against Iraq relates to why Israel and the Zionist lobby in the United States are pushing the war option on the American administration and the American street with all their force. In other words, what are the goals that Israel seeks to achieve in the onset of a full-scale American attack upon Iraq, and what are the proceeds it will garner from the Palestinian file? Furthermore, how can these goals regarding the Palestinians and Iraq be understood in the context of the traditional colonial policies of Zionism before and after the establishment of the state of Israel, toward the region and its periphery?

Weakening the Arab Regional Order

Israel regards a strike against any facet of the Arab regional order, and particularly a chief element of this order, such as Iraq, in the final analysis, as a weakening of this order, which subsequently will have a weakening effect upon the Palestinians. After the Camp David Accords in 1979, Egypt operationally removed itself from the circle of action within the Arab-Israeli conflict, while intertwining its interests with the American orbit. Since then, Israel has shifted its focus to Iraq, given its status as the sole Arab

---

[*] Dr. Saleh Abdel Jawwad is a Professor of History at Birzeit University and lives in El Bireh, near Ramallah in the West Bank. This article first appeared in *Between the Lines* no. 21, March 2003.

country after Egypt to have a powerful combination of ingredients unavailable to other Arab regimes: oil, financial assets, plentiful water supplies, wide expanses of fertile soil, a sufficiently large population, a clear nationalist political trajectory, and a military, industrial, and scientific infrastructure.

Dismembering Iraq

A strike against Iraq carries within its folds the considerable possibility for the dismemberment of the country, even if this is not within the immediate American plans. Such dismemberment is in accordance with how Israel envisions the region—a vision based upon similar representations made by Western orientalists who studied the Middle East at the end of the nineteenth century and throughout the previous century, incorporating their perspectives into Western imperialist and colonialist designs for the region. Such a perspective perceives the region as a mosaic composed of an assortment of ethnicities and cultural and national groupings.[8] Within this framework, Iraq is perceived as a country whose residents can be divided into Sunni, Shiite, Kurd, and Christian groupings distributed across various churches. Likewise, there are powerful regional, denominational, and tribal allegiances concentrated around cities that have particular economic or political interests, such as Baghdad, Tikrit, Basra, Mosul, etc. This mosaic-determining perspective rejects Arab national ideology, and consequently the relationship of Palestinian nationalism to Arab nationalism, while simultaneously justifying Zionist existential legitimacy, based upon the idea of Jewish nationalism, thereby enabling Israel to be a power among the weak.[9]

De-Arabization of the Middle East:
Allying with Anti-Arab Nationalist Forces

Readings in the literature of the Zionist movement—particularly those published at the end of the 1930s after the 1936–39 Palestinian Revolt, which witnessed the beginning of the Arabization of the Palestinian question—indicate that the leaders of the Zionist movement in general and the leaders of the *Yishuv* (the pre-1948 Jewish colonial community in Palestine), in particular, hung their hopes and concerns upon establishing relationships with every ethnic minority within the Arab world and within the non-Arab peripheral countries of the Arab world.

From the end of the 1930s, Ben-Gurion articulated some principles that would become basic indisputable tenets within Zionist understanding:

First, that the Arabs are the primary enemy of the Zionist movement. To confront this chief enemy, it is necessary for Zionism to search for "allies within the East to stand with its allies in the West [whether British or U.S. imperialism]." These "allies of the East" are needed to act as a supplementary force that will support the power of the Zionist project when faced with this (primary) confrontation, which at the end of the day is a "bloody struggle between us and them." Therefore, any grouping or sect that opposes Arab nationalism or declares its preparedness to fight against or resist it is, in reality, an ally of Zionism and helps implement its settlement and state-driven policies.

Second, the Jewish people, who have been subjected to the terrorism and oppression of various governments where they lived, particularly those who lived in Arab countries, perceive as partners and existential allies all minorities and groupings "oppressed" by the Arabs or Muslims. Thus the feeling for the need to free oneself from this oppression is felt in common by both.

These two principles form the basis of what is known as the "Theory of Allying the Periphery." After the establishment of the state of Israel, Ben-Gurion developed this theory to the extent that he sought the creation of a ring of adversaries from among the non-Arab countries that border the Arab world, concentrating particularly on forming strategic relationships with Turkey, Iran, and Ethiopia (known as the "Encirclement Theory").[10] He further thought to expand the links of this encirclement against the Arab world by expanding Israel's relationships with other Asian and African countries. The most recent phase of this policy witnesses Israel's attempt to include India within this strategic encirclement.[11]

Ben-Gurion's theories, which were formulated with other leaders of the Zionist leadership, have provided the philosophy within which an operational program was created for interacting with allies in regard to the Arab world. Against the backdrop of this perspective, Israel has supported secessionist movements in Sudan, Iraq, Egypt, and Lebanon and any secessionist movements in any Arab country that Israel considers an enemy.

The History of Israel's Bloody Interventions in Middle East Politics

Yet the concern over Iraq and Israel's attempts to weaken or prevent it from developing its strengths has always occupied a central objective, particularly after the failure of Zionist plans on the Egyptian front to create allegiances among the Copts. During certain periods, Israel indeed succeeded in gaining a foothold in Iraq by way of forging secret but strong relationships with some leaders of the Kurdish movement. However, it all but completely failed in trying to find allies among the Coptic community in Egypt as a result of the nature of the formation and historical continuity of the Egyptian state, among other reasons.

The Kurds

Communications with the Kurds began at the end of the 1930s and were in place by the end of the 1940s, during which time the Kurds were involved in helping a large part of Iraqi Jewry to reach Palestine on paths that went through Turkey. By the end of the 1950s and the early 1960s, Israel became the primary source of training and arming of the Kurds in their fight against the central government in Baghdad. Throughout this period, the full details of which have yet to be revealed, hundreds of Mossad agents and Israeli military personnel were located throughout northern Iraq under various covers (military advisors, agricultural experts, trainers, doctors, etc.).

Israeli support reached its peak during the Kurdish taking of power in northern Iraq during and after the second Gulf War in 1991, where Kurdish forces were able to take control of the strategically important city of Kirkuk, where some of the main oil fields are located. Nonetheless, the secessionist movement just as quickly collapsed beneath the blows of the Iraqi Army before the United States returned to impose an assortment of changes that permitted once again the end of centralized government rule in northern Iraq and the establishment of an area of far-reaching Kurdish sovereignty.

The Shah of Iran

In similar fashion, Israel supported the shah of Iran in his struggle against Baghdad. The beginning of Israel's relationship with the shah was formed when the Mossad, acting in accord with British and U.S. intelligence departments, worked to bring about the collapse of the democratically elected Iranian leader Mossadeq in 1953. However, the nature and extent of the Israeli role in this remain a mystery to this day. The relationship forged with the shah enabled Iran to be the primary importer of Israeli products before the rise of Khomeini. Israel also played a role in training the SAVAK, the infamous and brutal intelligence service that protected the shah.

Iraq

Likewise, Israel has worked closely to monitor Iraq and has done all in its power to prevent it from developing nuclear capabilities. In this context, Israel destroyed the Iraqi reactor during its assembly in France in 1977 and assassinated an assortment of scientists who worked in the Iraqi nuclear program—most notably the Egyptian scientist Yahya El Mashd. It also assassinated the brainchild of the Iraqi Super Cannon project[12] in Brussels and used aerial bombing to destroy the Iraqi nuclear reactor in 1981. Additionally, and quite infamously, Israel provided arms to Iran during the 1980–1988 Gulf War.

Israeli enmity toward Iraq precedes the Saddam Hussein regime and originated but further deepened after the 1948 War, as a result of Iraq's participation in that war. Iraq was the sole country that participated in the war that refused to participate in the negotiations leading up to the Rhodes Armistice agreement in 1949. Likewise, Iraq sent reinforcements to the Jordanian front in 1967 and actively engaged in the defense of Damascus in 1973.

Wars of Conquest and Attrition

War as an end in and of itself is an ever-present Israeli objective. Sequential wars with the Arab world have formed opportunities to exhaust the Arab world in essential ways, as well as aided in tipping the demographic and/or political situation against the Palestinians and in favor of the Zionist project. Even regional wars in which Israel has not participated have shown that they can directly or indirectly be beneficial to Israel and serve to weaken the Palestinian national movement.

The 1948 War expelled 800,000 Palestinians from their homes, representing 87 percent of the population. According to declassified Israeli documents, the 1956 War was initially planned, particularly relating to the Kufr Qasem Massacre,[13] to facilitate a new wave of expulsion of Palestinians and to bring about the occupation of the West Bank. The 1967 War resulted through direct and indirect ways in the expulsion of 400,000 Palestinians from the West Bank and Gaza Strip and the occupation of those lands. Israel now seeks to finalize its grip on these areas so as to further facilitate its regional powerhouse ambitions. The 1982 War in

Lebanon also resulted in dangerous demographic changes regarding the Palestinian refugee communities in Lebanon. Sharon sought to depopulate the Palestinian presence there owing to the fact that they resided on Israel's northern border, which had become the Achilles' heel of the Jewish state. Of the 450,000 Palestinians living in Lebanon in 1982, no more than 250,000 remain today. (Had the war not taken place, the number of Palestinians in Lebanon would have reached at least 650,000.) This is to say nothing of the social and political subjugation that the Palestinian community in Lebanon underwent as a result of that war.

As for the 1980–1988 Gulf War between Iraq and Iran, the results were also disempowering for the Palestinian cause: the Arab world was split into two camps, Arab resources were squandered, oil income was depleted, and Arab attention was taken away from the Palestinian question.

Finally, the 1990–91 Gulf War resulted in the expulsion of the Palestinian community from Kuwait (numbering roughly half a million), which formed one of the primary arteries of Palestinian income and power in the 1967 Occupied Territories.[14]

Needless to say, a historical and political reading of Zionism and Israel's actions toward the Arab world shows that it has much to gain from the impending U.S. strike against Iraq. Likewise, the Palestinian cause specifically, and the broader cause of Arab nationalism, has much to lose.

Israel's Arrogance Escalates Under Post-Iraq Pax Americana: Blatant Rhetoric and the Impetus for Settlement Construction*

Tikva Honig-Parnass

The first month in the post–Iraq War era has been signified by Israel's increased arrogance in deepening its governance over Palestinian people and lands. While pretending to agree with the hypocritical American initiative to renew "peace talks" through the "road map," Israel has escalated its oppression and killings while tightening the siege around Palestinian towns, villages, and refugee camps and grabbing more Palestinian lands within

---

* This article first appeared in *Between the Lines* no. 22, May 2003.

the framework of the separation wall being erected throughout the West Bank.

The prospect of a "successful" U.S. invasion and occupation of Iraq has signified for many Israelis in the peace camp that resolution of the "Palestinian-Israeli conflict" will be next on the agenda within a Pax Americana framework for the Middle East. Senior liberal commentators and Left politicians have misled the Israeli public by promising that the United States' aspirations to stabilize its hegemony in the region will imply activation of pressure on Israel to accept the "road map." Israel's readiness to make "great sacrifices" as well as its agreement to "a Palestinian state" will ensure the end of the conflict between the two peoples.

This deceptive picture, painted by the Zionist Left, derives from its support for U.S. imperialism and its adherence to neoliberal ideologies and policies. These stances also underlie its support for the declared U.S. "war on terror," which in its eyes justified the occupation of Iraq in the first place. Moreover, the rhetoric of the "global war on terror" has added a new dimension to the arsenal of arguments used by the Zionist Left to back the war against the resistance of the Palestinian people carried out by Sharon and his Labor predecessors, as the local version of the U.S.-led war.

However, nothing that currently occurs in the realm of Israel's savage occupation and its daily oppressive measures, nor within overt and covert diplomatic meetings, could be further from the misleading scenario drawn by the Israeli Left for the post–Iraq War era. On the contrary, Sharon is encouraged to express more blatantly the nature of the "state" he and the United States are "promising" the Palestinians and overtly takes steps on the ground to ensure that nothing that resembles a real state will come about.

The Bantustan as the "Most Appropriate" Solution

The recent pressure the United States exerted upon the Palestinian leadership to have Arafat replaced by Abu Mazen (Mahmoud Abbas) as the condition for publishing the "road map" was meant to set the stage for implementing Sharon's Bantustan vision, albeit at the end of a long and bloody road.

Akiva Eldar, one of the few honest senior Israeli commentators, recently provided evidence of the explicit use of the Bantustan concept by Sharon—a term usually used by radical progressives to describe the nature of the Palestinian state envisioned by the false Palestinian-Israeli peace initiatives that are versions of the Oslo Accords—with the "road map" being the latest progeny of this line of thinking:

> At a dinner in a hotel in Jerusalem at which the former Italian prime minister Massimo D'Alema hosted a number of public figures and ex-politicians, one of the Israeli visitors expressed full confidence in Sharon's peace rhetoric and in his understanding that the solution to the conflict is the establishment of a Palestinian state beside Israel. D'Alema answered that three or four years ago he had a long conversation with Sharon who was in Rome for a brief visit. Sharon explained at length that the Bantustan model was the most appropriate solution to the conflict.[15]

Eldar provides supplementary evidence backing D'Alema's story from a brochure prepared by Benny Allon, the minister of tourism in Sharon's new government (and the leader of the Moledet [Transfer] party), who promotes a "two-state solution": Israel and Jordan. Under the title "The Road to War: A Tiny Protectorate, Overpopulated, Carved Up and Demilitarized" [describing the nature of the future Palestinian state], the Moledet party leader presents "the map of the Palestinian state, according to Sharon's proposal." Eldar adds, "Sharon's map is surprisingly similar to the plan for protectorates in South Africa in the early 1960s. Even the number of cantons is the same—ten in the West Bank (and one more in Gaza)."

Sharon's plan is by no means only his personal vision nor that of the right wing he heads. The ownership rights of this cynical scheme should be justly recognized as belonging to the late Zionist Labor General Yigal Allon, the admired commander of the Palmach in the 1948 War and deputy prime minister for the Labor Party during the 1967 War.[16] Soon after the end of the war, Allon submitted his outline for a Bantustan solution, which subsequently has been adopted in principle by Labor and Likud governments alike. All have worked hard to prepare the ground for this solution by following the planned map of settlement and bypass road construction that aims at ensuring the continued rule of Israel, both directly over the confiscated lands that were declared state lands, and indirectly by encircling almost every single Palestinian community with settlements and military training grounds.

The settlements are thus not just an "obstacle to peace," as the slogan of the Israeli peace camp says: they are the backbone of the very final "peace" planned by Israel and supported by Bush, which will be agreed upon after long years of a "temporary" Palestinian state, necessary in order to prove that it is deserving of a "permanent" Bantustan solution.

The Settlement Layout: Ensuring Total Israeli Control

There is no need to go into the wording of the "road map." As Noam Chomsky emphasized in a recent interview with *Monthly Review*:

> In mid-March [2003], Bush made what was called his first significant pronouncement on the Middle East, on the Arab/Israeli problem. . . . [O]ne sentence, if you take a look at it closely, gives his road map: as the peace process advances, Israel should terminate new settlement programs. . . . That means until the peace process reaches a point that Bush endorses, which could be indefinitely far in the future, until then Israel should continue to build settlements. That's a change in policy. Up until now, officially at least, the U.S. has been opposed to expansion of the illegal settlement programs that make a political settlement impossible. But now Bush is saying the opposite: Go on and settle. We'll keep paying for it, until we decide that somehow the peace process has reached an adequate point.[17]

Nor is there a need to go into the details of the "phases" that according to the "road map" will lead to this final solution, because the plan is doomed to fail even before taking off. The steps taken in the last week of May by the United States to "demand" that Israel accept the "road map" and Sharon's subsequent declaration that he agrees to it are but a spectacle set up to convince the public that the efforts made by these two allies are genuine. Israeli commentators follow Israeli and American intelligence estimates that the prospect of Abu Mazen taking control of the PA to "smash terror" (the condition for implementing the "road map") is meager, "though it is forbidden for Israel to be seen as the one that made him fail."[18]

Indeed, as Chomsky emphasizes, the carte blanche given to continuing the settlement project indicates that both the terms of the "road map" and its chances of taking off are irrelevant. The existing and planned layout of the settlements reveals the political and ideological belief accepted by Likud and Labor alike: namely, that Israel should maintain almost full governance of the entire area west of the Jordan River—for the time being by direct military reoccupation and in the future through a Bantustan state or a number of Bantustan enclaves on the remaining areas ruled by local collaborators.

The hectic pace of ongoing settlement construction, adapted to the aim of sustaining Israel's rule, was recently described by the commentator Danny Rubinstein:

> The wider the destruction of any basic normal life [among Palestinians], which has escalated with the reconquest of the [1967 Occupied] Territories since September 2002, the greater is the development of the settlements. Specifically, the civil and security infrastructure of the settlements in the

West Bank has been greatly strengthened. There is almost full Israeli control over the roads of Judea and Samaria [the biblical names for the West Bank]. The electricity, water, and other service systems of the settlers have become independent and disconnected from the Palestinians'. All planning institutions in the West Bank are at the disposal of the settlers. The Civil Administration of the Defense Ministry, which at the time [of the direct Israeli rule before the establishment of the PA in 1994] took care of civil matters in the [1967 Occupied] Territories, has long been functioning as a tool of the Israeli mechanisms of control across half the area of the West Bank.[19]

Needless to say, removing the settlements is not on Bush's agenda.

The "road map" indeed includes the evacuation of a number of "settlement outposts" (known as " illegal outposts" in Israeli discourse) that have been erected since March 2001. This, however, masks the fact that *all settlements* in the 1967 Occupied Territories are illegal under the Fourth Geneva Convention. However, even the demand to dismantle the outposts has not been implemented. Each time an outpost is dismantled by the army—accompanied by photogenic arguments and confrontations with the settlers—new ones replace it. Since June 2002, when former minister of defense Ben Eliezer (Labor) in the then-unified government, evacuated two outposts, thirty new outposts have been erected.[20]

The outposts[21] play an important role in consolidating Israel's control of the West Bank, which explains the scripted drama in which the army is "helpless" to dismantle them vis-à-vis the "fanatic settlers."[22] Officers estimate that in the majority of cases where outposts were erected, PM Sharon was an active partner to the design of the plans, the selection of the locality, and the timing of the erection of the outpost.[23]

Daniela Weiss, a well-known settler activist and ideologist from Kdumim settlement near Jenin, explains:

> The intention behind erecting outposts is to create a continuum of Jewish settlements along the length and width of the area, to combine between the west of the Shomron [the biblical name used for the north of the West Bank] to its eastern side up to the Jordan Valley, between Jerusalem and Ofra [a settlement just north of Ramallah] and between Ofra and Shilo [a settlement between Ramallah and Nablus], which for a long time has been a block of settlements that spreads to the east. Another intention in erecting the outposts is to create a closing envelope around Arab villages and groups of localities in a way that prevents them from the possibility of expanding and developing. Today there is not one [Jewish] community in the [1967 Occupied] Territories that does not have a ring of strongholds around it that reinforces it.[24]

Meanwhile, Sharon continues hectically enlarging the settlements under the pretext of their "natural population growth." On the morning of

May 21, 2003, the Ministry of Housing advertised the construction of 502 new apartments in Ma'aleh Adumim—the massive settlement that spreads from the east of Jerusalem all the way to Jericho, cutting the West Bank in two. Since the beginning of the year, the government has put 635 new apartments up for sale in various settlements throughout the 1967 Occupied Territories, among them Mitzpe Navo, Maaleh Adumim, Givat Hazayit, Efrat, Ariel, and Elkana.

Long-Term War Against Palestinians Secured Under the "New Middle East"

In the post–Iraq War era, Israel is an active partner in the United States' plans to consolidate its hegemony over the Middle East by continuing its campaign to subdue Syria, Iran, and other countries. The silence Israel was forced to keep before and during the U.S. invasion of Iraq (in order not to hurt the Arab states' support for the United States) has recently been broken. The Israeli establishment has since celebrated the defeat of Iraq, "the greatest threat from the East," with Israeli Foreign Minister Silvan Shalom (Likud) commenting:

> There is here an opportunity for a new Middle East. After the war in Iraq, the rules of the game have changed. Those who adhere to the old rules will be excluded from the game. The United States has proven that it is determined to fight terror. Whoever lied to the United States paid a heavy price. Saddam did . . . and so did Arafat.[25]

Never before has the Zionist state felt so assured in carrying out its long-held vision of smashing Palestinian and Arab nationalism and sharing in the imperialistic hegemony of the Arab world. This is reflected in the fact that the conditions set by Israel for making any concessions with regard to the Palestinians was recently revealed to consist of Palestinians accepting the "Jewishness" and not just the existence of Israel. Sharon is explicit in demanding recognition of Zionism, while the Zionist Left often utters this demand in a casual manner, in the apparently innocent phrase of a "Jewish state." As Sharon said in 2003:

> Like most of the Arabs in the region, Abu Mazen has not recognized the right to erect a Jewish state in its homeland. The end of the conflict will be reached only after the Arabs recognize this.[26]

Sharon admitted that neither Abu Mazen nor any other puppet leader imposed by the United States and Israel can make the Palestinian people accept what is actually Zionism's premise. Nor can Israel rely on the prospect that such change will take place among the Arab people throughout the Middle East. Therefore, underlying Israel's peace posturing is the conviction of the military establishment and Sharon's government that the battle is still long and that there is no chance for any "peace agreement" in the near term:

> "All that is needed is to hold tight for 30 years and not to give up any assets until then," Sharon said to a senior official who served in a key role in the defense establishment. Sharon explained to him that by then, "modern technology will come up with cheap alternative energy sources that will clip the wings of the Arab world and reduce its leverage in the West."[27]

Sharon's proposal for a long-term war to replace the negotiation strategy correlates with Army chief of staff Moshe Ya'alon's assertion that

> this [the continuation of Palestinian resistance] brings us back to the confrontation of the prestate period, the partition proposal, and the War of Independence [1948 War]. . . . The Palestinians have returned us to the War of Independence. Today it is clear that the state of Israel is still an alien element in the region.[28]

Indeed, we are back to the essentials of the conflict between Zionist colonialism and the Palestinian people and their right to their homeland. In the fifty-five years since the Palestinian Nakba, the Jewish state has not fulfilled its vision of eliminating either the Palestinian people or Arab nationalism. Despite its oppressive policies, the state has not succeeded in cutting off the Palestinians who are citizens of Israel from the Palestinian people in the Territories and ending their collective national aspirations. Moreover, while the PLO has long given up the cause of the more than one million Palestinians living in the apartheid version of the Jewish state as part of the Palestinian national agenda, Israel does not exclude them as targets in its full-scale war against the Palestinian people. The grabbing of what remains of Palestinian lands inside Israel and the recent arrest of fifteen senior leaders of the Islamic movement inside Israel, including its head, Sheikh Raed Salah, in addition to the trial of MK Azmi Bishara (see Chapter 4), is the expression of the understanding that the Zionist colonialist war is escalating in the framework of the new Middle East. The camouflaged fascist ideology and culture of power in Israeli society guarantee support for the unrelenting advancement of Sharon, hand in hand with the United States, on their bloody road to hegemony in Palestine and throughout the Arab world. The ongoing physical, social, and cultural destruction of the Palestinian people is only just beginning.

Reflections on Arab Political Activity After Iraq*

Azmi Bishara

On May 14, 2003, the Jerusalem branch of the National Democratic Assembly—Tajamu' held a regional meeting in which party head MK Azmi Bishara discussed "The Arab World After the Aggression Against Iraq." The lecture attempted to address the profound sense of disarray and hopelessness experienced by many anti-imperialist and Arab nationalist forces across the Arab world and within Palestine, as a result of the nature and consequences of the U.S.-led occupation of Iraq. Below is the text of his lecture.

Some might say that we are living in a difficult situation after the U.S.-British aggression against Iraq and the faster than anticipated collapse of the Iraqi regime. Yet irrespective of the reasons for what happened, it is clear that the Arab world has entered a new phase that requires a certain pause to reflect upon this new reality, which will govern us for a considerable period of time. Additionally, it suffices to say that this new reality will also have repercussions upon the Palestinian cause, including the situation of Palestinian citizens inside the Green Line, and the nature of American and Israeli political behavior in the coming period.

The Current Form of Empire: Pax Americana

Today the concept of imperialism has developed and is a subject of consideration not merely in theoretical books, but also on the ground. It is a new type of imperialism, one reminiscent of the Roman Empire, which imposes its war as though it were peace. Tacitus once said, "They create a massacre and call it peace." This is to illustrate what was known as a Pax Romana and today can be termed a Pax Americana. That is, the will of imperialism and the will of the metropole are defining what is "peace and stability," and anything that contradicts this is termed "instability," "terrorism," "barbarism," etc.

But even when compared to the Roman Empire, such massive gaps in technology did not exist between the Romans and their enemies as is wit-

---

* This article first appeared in *Between the Lines* no. 22, May 2003.

nessed today with America and the rest of the world. In the old days, Rome was superior because of its organizational capacities, not its military ones. Today, the current form of empire differs entirely from the past: American imperialism is technologically and quantitatively immensely superior.

Military Intervention Without U.N. Consent

The unilateralism witnessed in the U.S. occupation of Iraq is not new. Since the end of World War II, America has intervened in an armed military manner upon foreign soil no less than two hundred times. It is attempting to impose an international domain that is directly and hierarchically subject to its influence.

America is also imposing new regimes and their policies. . . . Just as today it is enforcing regimes in the Arab world, its most familiar domain of this activity in the past was in Latin America. Those unconvinced that there is nothing new in American politics haven't read Gore Vidal or Noam Chomsky. Recall the question of the United Fruit Company—the monopolistic American food company in Latin America, which acted to change the regime in Guatemala [in 1954] for the simple reason that the Guatemalan government began taxing its produce? What, then, is so new now?

This brings us to another difference that characterizes the United States today: the absence of a second power to counterbalance the United States, which at the very least would confine the wars that it fought to a limited geographical area or would make such wars long and drawn out.

How does all this affect the nature of the wars carried out by the United States? We have just witnessed it [in the U.S. invasion of Iraq]. Shock. The kind of war that lasts just a few days. These are the wars of the modern era with America. Today there is one empire in the world, and that is America. Could anyone with common sense believe that Iraq had a chance of winning this war? If not, then why shouldn't an Iraqi soldier feel the same?

Possibilities for Political Action

What are the prospects of activity in the era characterized by an imperial regime of this nature?

It is clear that the former style of discourse, which still takes place today within classical Arab political movements, is outside this new context. It is necessary that Arab nationalist movements quickly realize that we are confronting a new era, where the political game is in need of new principles to improve Arab societies so they can avoid the dangers of returning to new colonial realities [as is the case in Iraq today].

I will give you an example of the style of the old model and where it led, and how we might transcend this style.

The kind of solidarity [recently witnessed from the Arab world] with Iraq reached the point where at least 4,000 Arab volunteers went to Iraq to fight. This style of solidarity [Arabs going to fight in Iraq] is based upon some sort of vision that exists without testing or looking into the reality on the ground in Iraq. Why did these volunteers go? What did they hope to accomplish? What will happen to them later on? Who decided to send them, and for what goal? In my opinion, these questions are not asked within the political mentality prevalent in anti-imperial movements across the Arab world. They just speak slogans: "There must be volunteers." But they don't ask "Why?" or "For what purpose?"

Likewise, much Arab political activity derives from this same style of thinking: "We must demonstrate" or "We must publish a leaflet." Yet the relationship between the means and the end is a relation that is basically left unstudied. In the Palestinian setting much is done without ever asking the question "What exactly is the benefit?" but is done in the belief that this is how things must be done because it is part of the prevalent political culture. If, for instance, the occupation does something specific, then there is a certain way in which Palestinian forces must respond. The dialectical relationship between a means and end—that a certain action is for a certain purpose and will take us to a certain point—is never carried out. In my opinion this was how the situation was dealt with [by Arab national actors in the Middle East and in Palestine] in regard to Iraq.

The Need for a National Local Agenda

Another issue we must address is the consideration by Arab national movements where they say things like "The issues of Palestine and Iraq are now the main issue of the Arab nationalist movement." But I am of a different opinion. The main national issue of every single nationalist movement throughout the Arab world must be the issues *in their own countries*. The national issue in Egypt should be social and political democracy in Egypt itself and not Palestine. If the issues pertaining to Egyptians are not addressed by the national current within Egypt, there is no way they can be in solidarity with the issue of Palestine. The same is clear for other Arab national movements throughout the Arab world with regard to solidarity with Palestine.

This is not because the issue of Palestine is hierarchically at the top of nationalist priorities. It is true that the issue of Palestine symbolically unites the Arabs, who in these times feel targeted. However, the primary priority of each nationalist group must be to ask itself, What is its importance in its own country? What is its social relevance? What is its political relevance? How can it improve its society within this situation? How is it that we reached a point where a bloody and dictatorial regime [Saddam Hussein's Iraq]—which in the final conclusion was even acting like a monarchical family—had an officially declared ideology of Arab nationalism?

We must study these questions well and what they mean for Arab nationalist ideology across the Arab world.

Who Are "We"?

This takes me to a predicament that might surprise some, owing to the fact that I am an Arab democratic nationalist and that it is my belief that it is our right to dream that the Arab nation can integrate economically and socially. Without such unity, we will, in short, have no place under the sun, and we will remain in a state of social and civil deformity and colonial fragmentation. That is because this process [of national formation] is not complete, and due to the lack of legitimacy of the existing regimes, such deformity will remain.

So when the question "What do we do?" is asked, I counter, "Who are 'we'? Who is it that is asking?" This "we" comprises all the people: from Arafat to the Palestinian opposition, from Ahmed Chalabi[29] to the people of Iraq and to Saddam Hussein.

Rather than wipe out the difference between itself and all the other factions when it asks itself "What do we do now?," the time has come for the democratic nationalist current to differentiate itself from all other currents. To ask itself: What is the difference between itself and the Islamic current? What is the difference between itself and currents that are pro-American? Is the difference between ourselves and those currents allied to American interests one of our blind opposition to the United States as a fait accompli—culturally, civilizationally, and humanly? What is it that precisely differentiates us from the Islamists? Do we share the Islamic interpretation of the United States as crusaders? We are not and should not be just "anti-American." Democrats are not simply against other cultures or nations. Are we supposed to search out our commonality with other currents so that we wipe out our differences, to the extent that we are not able to differentiate between ourselves and so can't even develop a strategy of action? Or is it most important in this stage to search out our uniqueness and to propose plans that differentiate us from the other currents, on the basis of our need for a democratic nature to the construction of prevalently Arab societies?

The Necessity for Nationalist Currents to Solve the Democratic Question

It is no longer possible for the nationalist current to continue its work without solving the democratic question once and for all in its agenda and political culture.

In my understanding, even if democracy's implementation consumes many years, it is worth it because the national current will not be on safe footing until it does this. The national current cannot pursue its agenda without studying *what its internal project is.*

Today I hear the nationalist current talking and saying [that we must work for] "the liberation of Iraq." Very well, then. What is its program for the Iraqi regime afterward? What is its position on the Kurds? Or on social issues? Or on women? Or on economic development? The Islamic current relieves itself [from answering these questions] and says, "Islam is the solution [*Islam huwa al hal*—a traditional Islamic movement slogan]"—and no one dares to ask what that really means.

The democratic agenda of the national current will take time, and I am in no position to give hope to those who are looking for solutions within days. But I am at least saying that this is the beginning of the road. Without a long-term nationalist project in every Arab state, solidarity [with Iraq or Palestine] just becomes a forum for demonstrations of anger that fizzle out. Likewise, the slogans of these demonstrations are just expressions of anger that are raised and then taken away after the demonstrations. They are not raised so as to preserve a long term nationalist project in any Arab state.

Today, it is not possible for us to accomplish any achievements in fighting the policies of the United States by constructing a traditional and conventional army, as was the case in Iraq. We have to make connections with the contradictions within the empire itself, whether it is with its margin, which is today Europe, or, more important and in a concrete manner, the contradictions within America itself. Within American society itself, there are wide swaths of those who will be against a state of permanent war that characterizes the new stage of imperialism. We must engage them and discuss things with them. But on what basis do we wish to discuss things with them today? There must be the simple ABCs of discussion to talk with them, in addition to having credibility.

This above all is how the Zionists have distinguished themselves from us in America and in other places [i.e., through their interaction and connection with Western social movements and formations]. How are we supposed to open up avenues of discourse with African Americans or with the women's movement or with the antiwar movement? Only once the question of our democratic discourse and practice is achieved can there be true solidarity.

Iraq: Opening Opportunities for the Palestinian Cause

In my opinion, the Palestinian cause has been strengthened, not weakened, in the wake of the aggression against Iraq, in contrast to what some people [within the Palestinian national movement] think.[30] These people act as though they are the owners of the "Company of the Palestinian Cause," claiming that because there is no demand for this cause anymore, now is the time to "sell off stock" and make concessions.

But in my opinion, the Palestinian issue has strengthened. Of course we need people to remain steadfast and for there to be a strategy. But internationally, the Palestinian issue has never in its history been this strong. It has become part of the language of justice and legitimacy. Those who were pushing for the war [against Iraq] can't get around the Palestinian issue, and those who are against the war are carrying the Palestinian flag. When has it ever been that one million people are marching in the streets of London carrying the Palestinian flag? Our whole lives the social democracies [within Europe] were with Israel and not with us. All our lives European public opinion has been with Israel, and today it shows sympathy and understanding for the Palestinians.

Look—we knew all along that Iraq was going to fall. Of course we are not happy about it, and it disturbs us to see a new occupation there. But we cannot say that it is the end of the world and that all our options are closed before us as Arab national liberation movements, as Arab nationalist currents, or in general.

In my opinion, the war in Iraq will signify the birth of a new Arab democratic current, just as the Nakba in 1948 was the birth of other currents [i.e., the birth of the modern Palestinian national movement, as well as the rise of other new movements across the Arab world, such as pan-Arabism]. The aggression against Iraq will be the first phase of the birth of a democratic current.

Bad Bargaining

Friends, we call upon the national current not to be stupid once again. It must take its time and be aware of the fact that there is another generation coming. It must understand that its primary importance is to connect the concept of Arab nationalism with the idea of democracy and progressive ideas. If we do not undertake this struggle, it will become nothing. It will lose all the worlds at the same time.

It is not the time for concessions with regard to our national agenda. And in fact nothing will be gained [from such concessions]. Today it seems that they have put Syria on the list [for the same or similar fate as Iraq]. But if Syria makes democratic and economic reforms, it will not need to make "reforms" of its national goals. It will be in affinity with all the democratic forces in the world. It will be able to call upon them in Europe and America, and it will be difficult for Syria to be touched [by U.S. imperialism]. These are the reforms that are required—not reforms of our national convictions against colonialism and against occupation. Some Arab nationalists promote the option of defending dictatorship and corruption in Arab countries and [attempt to] please the Americans and the Europeans with concessions in the Palestinian issue and by giving up anticolonial positions. This is a bad bargain.

The Current of the Future

This is the most important thing in the experience of the National Democratic Assembly—Tajamu'. If this weren't the case, we would have been thrown into prison long ago. The [Israeli] High Court voted 7 to 4 [to allow NDA—Tajamu' to participate in the 2003 elections to the Knesset [see Chapter 4] for the sole reason that we proved ourselves as a democratic current. We are Arabs, but at the same time we are deeply connected to democratic and progressive values and discourse. Without this, we would not be able to remain steadfast for one day in the conditions within Israel. They would get rid of us, *because they know that there is an existential contradiction between Arab nationalism and Zionism.* They also know the kinds of things that we are saying here today. But they cannot touch us [as they want]—not physically, of course (because if they wished to do that they could do that tomorrow), but on the level of our discourse [because we are protected by the strength of our democratic arguments and organizing].

This is the importance of Tajamu', and this is the importance of discourse. We will not make even one concession on principal issues, especially if we seek to live. We are the current of the future upon the Arab stage. Because the alternative to this national democratic presence is not just a nationalist presence that is nondemocratic but the danger of being recruited into the ranks of the Labor Party and Likud, or into the army, or our division into Christians, Muslims, and Druze.

We know that upon our internal setting, without the connection between the national and the democratic with conviction, they [the Israeli establishment] will push us aside and the last dam preventing Israelization will fall. Believe me, there is no economic or social logic to an Arab nationalist current [that is not democratic] for the Arabs "inside" [Palestinian citizens of Israel]. The sole logic will be [our] Israelization. And this means marginalization, just as after the Oslo Accords. In the next elections, we will see 50,000 people going to the Likud party, not just to the Labor Party [a reference to the number of Arabs that voted for the Labor Party before the emergence of NDA—Tajamu' on the Palestinian political party scene inside Israel]. NDA—Tajamu' is the dam that exists, and this is what we must preserve. We will not just work to preserve it, we will also call out to the Arab nationalist currents in the Arab world to come and learn from us and to see what we have done: "This is what we have been able to accomplish within the conditions of Israel." Our task was much more complicated than theirs. At the very least, on the level of ideology, balancing Israeli citizenship with Palestinian nationality has been much more complicated. But if we were able to solve it, so can and must our democrat sisters and brothers in the Arab countries.

The Need for a Political Project—Not Emotional Outbursts

Solidarity is not angry demonstrations where people let out steam for a few days, which sometimes are permitted and other times are not [by respective Arab regimes]. It is the capacity to influence the political process and political decision making. A political party influences politics, not emotions. A demonstration is necessary only if it influences.

We can study ourselves in every country throughout the Arab world: What was the influence of the Arab [nationalist] political project on the decisions of their governments [during the invasion of Iraq]? I tell you: Nothing. It did not influence any decision. It had an influence upon the style of discourse where it became necessary for them [the governments] to sometimes apologize and make lexicographic appeasements to hide their true decisions. But it did not have any influence on the level of the decisions themselves.

But after all, the demonstrations [in the Arab world] are not presenting themselves as a political project. Talk becomes extraneous if a real political project is not proposed. When you propose yourself as a political project, you are forced to educe the means or instruments that I am talking about. But if you are not even initially proposing yourself as a political project that wants to influence political decisions, you are proposing yourself as some sort of romantic atavism from a previous era.

The question in such cases is not one between the means and the ends, which becomes entirely secondary in this case, but one of expressionism: How is it that I can find my own expression rather than my capacity to influence? It is like Walter Benjamin's quotation about the working class during Nazism: "The working class finds its expression, but not its interests." Once subjugated to expressionism and symbolisms, it is as though everything is determined in the realm of words.

What have been the achievements or the extent of influence of this style [of action prevalent within Arab nationalist movements across the Arab world, as well as in Palestine]? Nothing. Yet three quarters of the kind of [Arab nationalist] discourse takes place within this framework.

We witness this kind of thinking and dynamics in the Palestinian setting and particularly in the interaction between the PA and the opposition. The great majority of the [1967 Palestinian political] opposition [parties] actually speak and act in this manner. This is unfortunate, though its cause is noble. It sees itself as preserving the major principles of the Palestinian national movement—something I entirely support. But it is incomprehensible that political discourse takes place in this way—as mere expressionistic discourse.

At the same time, even military operations act in the same way, such as when a certain action takes place on the anniversary of a certain date. So what? [Military] operations are to be conducted within the context of a strategy where these operations are beneficial in pushing the national liberation project forward according to a [previously declared] list of ways: one, two, three, etc. The issue is not expressionistic. And the Palestinian opposition, whose cause is most noble, must study this with all suitable tools.

We have a political current that exists [within the Palestinian national movement] from even before Camp David [in July 2000] that deems that in the wake of the aggression against Iraq, the Palestinians ought to accept what is offered to them. It believes that these were the best conditions that the Palestinians will ever be offered. But Yasser Arafat, as historical political phenomenon, remained steadfast at Camp David—irrespective of our criticism of him. These words can be trusted. Even today we must say that he is the elected president of the Palestinian people. We must acknowledge this because it seems there is a lobby or current [within the PA] that says, "We must learn the lesson of Iraq."

What, then, are the lessons of Iraq? That Palestinians shouldn't occupy Kuwait? That they shouldn't produce chemical weapons? Palestinians can't even make a dictatorship until they have a state. The lesson that they want us to learn is that we should accept America's dictates without discussion. This is in fact the only thing they want us to learn.

But in what way is America threatening the Palestinians? With occupation? We already are occupied. In the context of the Israeli-Palestinian relationship, it is *we* who are demanding that U.N. resolutions be implemented—not the other way around, as was the case with Iraq. In the context of Israel-Palestine, *it is Israel* that has the weapons of mass destruction, and *it is we* who are oppressed. By what logic do we put ourselves in this position and say to ourselves that "We must accept the American dictates"? Rather, we must try to influence American public opinion, because there is a wide consensus there that the Palestinians *are* the underdogs and that Israel is betting on the crazy extremist Protestant revisionist groups.

If we can only understand this and put this together, and search for the appropriate tools. . . . This is tangible talk. I read the American media and the supposed influence of the Israeli lobby, together with those termed the "neoconservatives." These people are actually from the Reagan era, and I don't see them as that new. They have said nothing that [former secretary of state Henry] Kissinger didn't say before them and in worse ways. The only difference is that today America can begin to implement these policies that Kissinger always wanted. Their new wind came after September 11.

But at the same time American public opinion is also still there and can still be talked to. We have to know how to work in this sector and within Europe as well.

CHAPTER 8

Carte Blanche: The Era of Force, Force, and More Force

May–December 2003

Introduction

By summer 2003, Arafat's political capital was entirely spent. Aside from his rather impotent symbolism as an icon of "steadfastness," imprisoned in his Ramallah headquarters, which had been incrementally destroyed by Israel throughout the course of the past year, little remained of his capacity to govern. Israel's scorched-earth policies had driven the Palestinian resistance deep underground, while the world's attention was increasingly focused on the U.S. occupation of Iraq.

It is within this setting that a window of opportunity arose for the political current within the PA that had been marginalized throughout the course of the Intifada, to re-enter the political stage, attempting to re-assert itself. Led by the newly appointed Palestinian Prime Minister Mahmoud Abbas (Abu Mazen) and former Gaza Preventive Security Chief Mohammed Dahlan, this current actively went through the motions of the role-play set out for it by its U.S. masters. Abbas shamelessly took a political tack that openly declared the Intifada "a strategic mistake," while shunning Palestinian resistance as "terrorism." He naively believed these words would bring about the rejuvenation of the "peace process" through the "road map" (see Chapter 7) and ensure the survival of the PA as a political entity.

And indeed, on June 4, 2003, Bush, Sharon, and Abbas re-created the photogenic "peace process" media spectacle at Aqaba, Jordan, publicly de-

claring their commitment to the "road map." Bush's presence symbolized
the U.S.-Israeli accomplishment of fomenting Palestinian-led initiatives
to marginalize Arafat, while backstabbing those who believed in and sac-
rificed for the Intifada. At the same time, neither Bush nor Sharon had
any illusions as to the weakness of Abbas's position. As one Palestinian
commentator described it:

> The Authority has materially ended. The role of Abbas's government will not
> exceed the symbolic and will mean nothing on the ground, where Palestini-
> ans can't even move without the permission of the occupation. . . . Nothing
> remains of any security apparatus or institutions or ministries. This is our re-
> ality, which we are ignoring. The Authority is abstract, symbolic, as is the
> government, which has been transformed into something more similar to an
> NGO to administer the affairs of the people, in the midst of the obstacles
> thrown up by the occupation.[1]

Despite a June 29, 2003, cease-fire declaration by all Palestinian factions, Sharon never officially reciprocated, despite understandings reached
in Aqaba to the contrary. Instead, he ordered the escalation of yet more
provocative assassinations, explicitly declaring a policy of mass assassination of Palestinian leaders and activists without any need for government
confirmation, as had been the case in the past.[2]

Israel's continued killings and oppressive measures succeeded in provoking Hamas revenge operations, thereby creating "proof" regarding
Abbas's inability to "deliver the goods." This, combined with popular
Palestinian disaffection with Abbas's leadership, resulted in the new PM
resigning on September 6, 2003. With "no one to talk to on the Palestinian side," and the need to (preemptively) "defend itself against terror," U.S.
and Israeli maneuvers succeeded in legitimizing an unprecedented and
bloody era of power politics against the Palestinian people.[3] The carte
blanche Israel received in the post–Iraq invasion period could now be
cashed in without the impediments of a false political process it wasn't interested pursuing in the first place. Israel could now blow up entire apartment buildings housing dozens of Palestinian families, under the pretext
that wanted militants had merely slept in them. The senior Israeli political
commentator Aluf Benn succinctly described the nature of Israel's policies
in this era in an October 2003 Ha'aretz op-ed: "Israel's policy in the conflict with the Palestinians can be summed up in ten words: 'What doesn't
work with force will work with more force.'"[4]

State Terror Beneath Big Brother's "Road Map" Wings[*]

Tikva Honig-Parnass

The Israeli government's decision of August 20, 2003, to explicitly declare a policy of mass assassination against Palestinian leaders and activists without any need for government confirmation was taken in the footsteps and with the blessings of the United States. What Noam Chomsky points to regarding recent U.S. "antiterror" policies in Iraq and Afghanistan is also true pertaining to Israel: classifying people it bombs and captures as a new category of "terrorists," who are not entitled to any rights, is a rejection of international humanitarian law dealing with crimes against humanity and war crimes, which were formally criminalized in reaction to the Nazis.[5] However, together with implementing what the Israeli establishment calls its "pinpoint liquidation" policy, Sharon continues to hypocritically declare that he strives to implement the Bush-initiated "road map." Moreover, it is claimed that these mass assassinations are precisely aimed at enabling the implementation of the "road map."

Sharon's False Agreement to the "Road Map" and to Cease-Fire

On June 4, 2003, Sharon and Abu Mazen met in Aqaba, Jordan, where both sides agreed to implement the "road map" and work toward a cease-fire, later achieved on June 29, 2003.[6] However, Sharon immediately began provocations aiming at bringing about the downfall of Abu Mazen, the new Palestinian PM imposed by the United States and European Union as a condition for releasing the "road map" in the first place.

It is difficult to imagine that the United States itself believed that the reform scheme had a chance of working. The United States' silence regarding Sharon's provocations during the cease-fire, at a time when "trust-building steps" were due to be adopted by Israel, indicates its partnership in the Israeli scheme. According to this logic, the deeply flawed "road map" is given lip service as a framework that continues the guise of a "peace process" (thus alleviating international pressure from Europe and

This article first appeared in *Between the Lines* nos. 23–24, September 2003.

the pro-U.S. Arab states), all the while the process is immediately deep-frozen so that Israel and the United States can continue the task of crushing Palestinian resistance. Moreover, Bush is now an enthusiastic supporter of the assassination policy's falling within the boundaries of "Israel's right to defend itself" with "preemptive strikes."

Provocations to Blow Up the Cease-Fire

Based on the agreement reached between Abu Mazen and Sharon regarding implementing the "road map," all Palestinian opposition factions agreed to a cease-fire finally achieved on June 29, 2003. But Israel never officially accepted this cease-fire, arguing that it was only an internal Palestinian agreement that did not obstruct its "defensive" operations. Moreover, Israeli foreign minister Silvan Shalom rejected a proposal made by his Palestinian colleague Nabil Shaath for a permanent *hudna* [Arabic for cease-fire].[7]

While simultaneously rejecting any cease-fire agreement, Israel prepared itself for the coming conflagration in the Occupied Territories as a reaction to its own provocations. Thus the Israeli Army began constructing permanent military positions in areas formerly within Area A[8] (supposedly under the full jurisdiction of the PA, according to the Oslo Accords). It also continued with its other oppressive policies, further emptying the declared cease-fire of its little content. This included the continued suffocation of the population through closures; the razing of hundreds of acres of orange groves and olive orchards; the demolition of houses; and the confiscation of even more land for the construction of hundreds of miles of the Israeli apartheid wall.[9] Meanwhile, other specified "goodwill gestures," such as dismantling outposts and releasing prisoners to facilitate the "road map," turned out to be farces.[10]

No doubt both Israel and the United States were aware of the warning of Palestinian Legislative Council member Hatem Abed El Qader, who clearly said before Abu Mazen set out to meet Bush on July 20, 2003, "If he [Abu Mazen] cannot achieve the lifting of the checkpoints and release the prisoners, he has no chance of remaining in power and will be obliged to resign."[11] However, he achieved neither.

No serious goodwill gestures were made to ease the daily life of the Palestinian population by lifting the checkpoints and roadblocks. Of the approximately 170 checkpoints scattered across the West Bank, no more than five were lifted. Moreover, in the few cases where the dismantling of roadblocks did take place, they were soon replaced by mobile ones, making traffic on West Bank roads even more difficult than before. Thus there was no change for the Palestinians regarding their freedom of movement. Most remained separated from their places of work, school, family, or hospital by a network of checkpoints and bypass roads.

Nor did anything change with regard to the daily killing and mass arrest of military and political activists. Thus for example, on July 3, in Qalqiliya, just three days after the declaration of the cease-fire, special military units killed Mahmoud Shawwar, a Fateh leader, while arresting Ibrahim Yassin, head of the Fateh Tantheem in the city. In this same operation, thirteen other wanted Palestinians were also arrested. On July 9, the Israeli Army killed Iyad Shalmish in the village of Burkin in an operation intended to arrest or kill his brother. On July 15, the army detained nine wanted Palestinians in Jericho. On the same day, an undercover border guard unit arrested an Islamic Jihad activist from the village of 'Ijjeh near Jenin. On August 13, the army arrested seven wanted Palestinians in Nablus. On August 14, Mohammed Sidr, head of the military wing of Islamic Jihad in Hebron, was assassinated.[12]

Israel carefully planned its provocative operations so the resistance forces engaged in the Intifada would have no choice but to break the cease-fire and return to military operations. The expected "major operation" finally took place. On August 19, 2003—more than six weeks after the cease-fire was called and observed by Palestinian factions—twenty-three Israeli adults and children were killed in an attack on a Jerusalem bus in an operation claimed jointly by Hamas and Islamic Jihad.

A Policy of Mass Assassinations: No Agreements with the PA

Despite the Israeli media generally lining up behind government policy, here and there journalists have pointed to the cunning policy of provocations carried out by Sharon during the supposed cease-fire.[13] Just a few days before the attack on the Jerusalem bus, the senior *Ha'aretz* commentator Gideon Samet determined that Sharon was responsible for the imminent failure of the cease-fire, through his provocations (which Samet terms "chronic mistakes"):

> The conception that does not allow any implementation of agreements with the other side has deepened its roots. This is a self-fulfilling prophecy. . . . [The concept's] motives are deep and directed not only toward Palestinians in the 1967 Occupied Territories but also toward those inside Israel. . . . It may lead to another Intifada and to the defeat of the moderate forces in the

PA. It will thus produce an additional incontrovertible argument for its own decisive justification. "Here, it's just like we said: with these Arabs it's impossible to embark on a new path with any map whatsoever."[14]

Samet correctly emphasizes that the violation of the cease-fire and other agreements reached with the Palestinian leadership are the expression of a consistent policy adopted by Israel since the recognition of Oslo's failure took place—namely, to launch a prolonged all-out war on the Palestinian national movement. With respect to the "road map" and the cease-fire, the all-out war has meant not reaching any agreement with what remains of the PA, which, despite its obvious shortcomings as a creation of the Oslo framework, is still connected organizationally, ideologically, and, through its personnel, to the Palestinian national liberation movement embodied in the PLO.

After the attack in Jerusalem, Israel felt secure in continuing its full-scale war against Palestinian nationalism: the next day the Israeli cabinet decided to launch a "change of strategy in the confrontation with the Palestinians."

After a lengthy conversation between Bush and Sharon on August 21, 2003, which secured the latter a green light,[15] the Israeli military junta quickly seized the opportunity to return from the temporary sidetrack of the cease-fire back to the main road of an all-out war. It believed that Sharon would have no problem convincing the world that Abu Mazen would not be capable of doing the job of "uprooting the infrastructure of terror." The conclusion thus reached was that from now on Israel would have to "take care of the terror instead of them [the PA]" because "these people with whom we are working are a bunch of liars. An empire of lies."[16]

This new policy consisted of the aforementioned systematic mass assassinations of leaders and activists in resistance organizations, including not only military leaders but political and ideological leaders as well, "to persecute the heads of terror, one by one."[17] Thus, in the two weeks between August 21 and September 5, 2003, the Israeli Air Force assassinated thirteen Hamas activists in six targeted assassinations in crowded central locations throughout the Gaza Strip. Five other Palestinians were killed in these operations, among them a young girl and an old man, while dozens of others were injured.

The targeting of political leaders had been committed by Israel in the past, going back to the early days of the PLO. But never was it declared so openly and with the expressed moral legitimacy of most intellectuals and journalists. In most cases, these operations would have been kept secret and, if necessary, justified by the pretext that the victim represented "a ticking bomb."[18] Now both the Palestinian leadership and political activists on the ground are included within the enlarged category of "ticking infrastructure," which actually means a permit to kill almost anyone.[19] This, however, could only be initiated in the post–Iraq War era, whereby even the European Union decided, on September 9, 2003, to define the political wing of Hamas as a "terrorist organization."

The Aim: Conflagration

The Israeli military knows exactly where it is heading in adopting the policy of mass assassinations, which, together with the other Israeli provocations, brought about the resignation of Abu Mazen on September 6, 2003. The senior *Yediot Ahronot* commentator Nahum Barnea made it clear: "[Sharon] will continue to go down the route that will inevitably lead to absolute destruction of any governance in the [1967 Occupied] Territories, returning back, as in a time machine, to 1967—to the military government, to being responsible for millions of Palestinians and to terror without limits."[20]

However, as is typical of most Israeli self-proclaimed progressive Zionists, Barnea sees the 1967 Occupation as the root cause of the "conflict," and hence sees in some form of territorial compromise *in the 1967 Occupied Territories* a means of solving it. He thus ignores what the Israeli chief of staff himself, Moshe Yaalon, confirmed recently: that the Intifada, and the necessity to "win it," are the equivalent of the "existential danger" Israel confronted in 1948.[21] Sharon repeated this line in his meeting with the heads of the political establishment of India, declaring that "Israel has been fighting terror for 120 years"—thus seeing the present "war against Palestinian terror" as the continuity of the Zionist colonization project.

Indeed we are back not to 1967 but to pre-1948 and to the fundamental contradiction between Zionism and the Palestinian national movement. The "principal" decision that the Israeli cabinet made September 9, 2003, to "remove" Arafat, and the Israeli Left's "pragmatic" short-term arguments against it, signifies that it is the Israeli Right, rather than the Zionist Left, that is ready to openly recognize the existential nature of this contradiction. On the other hand, it is the Zionist Left that is still faithful to its traditional adherence to a humane veneer, as expressed now in its insisting on keeping Arafat as the fake symbol of Palestinian sovereignty.

Redefining Equality as Rejecting "the Jewish State"

An Interview with NDA—Tajamu' MK Azmi Bishara[*]

Toufic Haddad

Q: In light of Sharon's policies and his deliberate escalations, which have already brought about the end to the cease-fire and are destined to make the "road map" fail, what are Sharon's real plans?

A: Sharon believes in power politics: that it is possible to impose, to dictate, and to change political structures by using power.

On the one hand, Sharon believes that Israel cannot annex the West Bank and Gaza with their populations. On the other hand, he firmly believes that the Palestinians should not get the West Bank and Gaza within the borders of June 4, 1967, and that this can be prevented if Israel knows how to use power.

We should remember that at the end of the 1970s, Sharon was one of the ministers who supported [former Israeli prime minister Menachem] Begin [of the Likud party] in the issue of autonomy for the West Bank and Gaza. Later, in 1988, when King Hussein declared the so-called "disengagement" from the West Bank [i.e., when Jordan withdrew its claims to the West Bank], Sharon revived the autonomy plan in a series of articles he wrote. Autonomy was designated to be established in the densely populated areas that were called the areas of "territorial compromise" by the Yigal Allon Plan, though, in that plan, autonomy was to be given to Jordan (see Introduction).

I think he [Sharon] still believes in this model [of autonomy], but there are two changes there; we can discuss how deep they are.

First, Sharon is willing to call the "autonomy" a "state." Namely, to accept the idea of Palestinian "statehood," but without changing the areas that have been designated for the "autonomy." Sharon still believes in "demographic separation" from these areas—the principle that underlined Allon's plan—but he is willing to call this entity a "state."

---

[*] This article first appeared in *Between the Lines* nos. 23–24, September 2003.

Second, Sharon understands the need to cooperate more with the United States and to actually integrate within the U.S. strategy; not to say "no" to the United States, but try to change its decisions from within. That's why he accepted—without really accepting—but at least nominally accepted the "road map" (see Chapter 7). He knows that he cannot work with the U.S. the way he worked with it in Lebanon [in 1982], where the relationship between him and the U.S. administration was actually very tense. At that time, the U.S. was actually turning against him, because it had not been informed of the plans to "change the regime" in Lebanon and because Sharon went further [in the invasion and its goals] than the U.S. was willing to digest. In the past, Sharon believed that Israel should put the U.S. in front of a fait accompli. Now he understands very well that it doesn't work. He is older and wiser concerning international politics.

These are the two changes to the model he believed in the past: a "state" and total coordination with the United States.

Now, in the framework of the cooperation with the U.S., Sharon needs to convince the U.S. that the [Palestinian] "state" should be on around 42 percent of the West Bank and should be established over the course of a transitional period of at least fifteen years—not three years [as stipulated by the "road map"] or even five years. The longer, the better. This transitional plan means that the Palestinians don't have to give up the "final status issues" [e.g., the right of return, Jerusalem] as they were asked to by Barak at Camp David, and that these issues can be discussed "later," in the next generation.

That is what the man believes, and I don't think he has anything more to suggest to the Palestinians.

Now, Sharon knows very well that a state on 40 percent of the West Bank and Gaza is not viable. He believes it needs to be connected in a confederate manner to Jordan and is pushing in this way.

As I said, his politics are a power politics; a politics of pressure to reshape the Palestinian political and security elite. Not necessarily the leadership—because it is not a leadership anymore—but to reshape an elite that will be able to "give and take" in the direction of implementing what I have just said. That's what he's after, and he has been very consistent with that since the 1980s.

Q: To what extent are his policies supported by the United States?

A: Well it depends on what we mean when we say "the United States." It is better to say the "current U.S. administration [of George W. Bush]" because its way of thinking and the neoconservatives who have risen to power in this administration are very close to Sharon's way of thinking. This includes not only their rise after the [year 2000] elections in the U.S. but also their rise after the events of September 11, 2001. The increase and influence of the neoconservatives thereafter made the U.S. more open to accepting not only Sharon's policies but also, in a way, globalized Israeli security doctrines. For example, conceptions such as "preemptive strike" or "preventive war" are actually Israeli concepts, including [depicting and] understanding "terrorism" as the "main enemy."

Israel's central doctrine was to divide the world into "terrorists" and "antiterrorists" in order that it [Israel] could be on the side of Russia, India, and the U.S. *together.* "Everybody is fighting terrorism." This has enabled Israel to break its own isolation: Israel is on one side, and the entire Arab world is on the other. The fact that the U.S. accepted the division of the world between "terrorists" and "those who fight terrorists" was a breakthrough for Israel internationally, as well as in the U.S. itself.

This made the alignment between Israel and the U.S. look more like an alignment between the Israeli Right Wing and the U.S., which was not the case in the past. Usually the translator of U.S. interests "into Hebrew" was the Labor Party—not the Likud. There was always tension between Likud governments (like [PMs] Menachem Begin and Yitzhak Shamir [who opposed any territorial concessions]) and the U.S. establishment. Sharon personally was persona non grata in the U.S. But now the U.S. administration is leading the U.S. in the direction of cooperation with the Israeli Right Wing—no longer with [the state of] Israel itself. This is a new situation.

Sharon as the Son of the Zionist Labor Establishment

Q: This raises the question as to what extent are Sharon's policies different from those of the Israeli Labor Party.

A: It depends. Historically, if you take the Labor party of Moshe Dayan[22] or Golda Meir[23] or Ben-Gurion, you would say that Sharon represents continuity with this current. In this sense, Sharon may claim their heritage and find historical clues to his own development in them. He may say, "The way I talk is the same way Ben-Gurion talked." And this, of course, is true. He is not a revisionist. He does not come from the Jabotinski tradition of revisionism.[24]

But the [historic] Labor Party went in at least two or three directions: Rabin could claim continuity [with the historic Labor Party]. So could Barak. The question, then, is what is the difference between Sharon and Rabin? Or between him [Sharon] and Barak? Or between him and the historic Labor Party?

Sharon is, no question, a son of the Labor Party historically—a son of the way of thinking of Mapai [of which the Labor Party is the offspring]. At the time of Unit 101[25] and during his service in the Paratroop Brigade, Sharon was closer militarily and in his way of thinking to Moshe Dayan.

Ben-Gurion made a lot of statements praising Sharon as *the* Hebrew soldier—the quintessential Hebrew soldier. Ben-Gurion wanted Israel to build the *sabra* [the image of the "new Israeli generation"—the assumed prime of Zionism], the "courageous commander who leads his battalion physically in battle" and who doesn't respect conventions of war. No "Diaspora minority mentalities," etc.

Now, if you take the concept of "territorial compromise," this is a Labor concept and one that Sharon is ready to accept. Likewise with the concept of "demographic separation" [from the Palestinians, which is used as justification for territorial concessions]. Even the wall that is now being built and that was initiated by Labor MKs was eventually accepted by Sharon. Revisionists in the Likud are against this. Many of the second generation of the Herut party (of which the Likud is the offspring) also do not accept the wall because it is "dividing Eretz Israel." Sharon has no problem dividing Eretz Israel. He is "a man of bulldozers." This also comes from Labor.

Like the old Labor Party, Sharon is ready to accept the "road map" and to speak its language, while at the same time he makes promises to "uproot," to build settlements, and so on. Even someone like Rehavam Ze'evi[26] always claimed that he [Ze'evi] was a continuum of Mapai. He always quoted the historical Mapai leaders to justify his positions. He said, for instance, that "transfer is an idea of Ben-Gurion." I came across a quotation from Moshe Dayan from 1952 where he says, "The destiny of the Palestinians inside Israel [i.e., the Palestinian citizens of Israel] will be like the rest. We should transfer them." This was 1952, when they were already citizens.

To summarize, Sharon's mentality—his lexicon, his words, his actions, his way of thinking—are all from the Hagana.[27] It's the Zionist establishment language, and that's what he is. This is also why he has more understanding with Shimon Peres [Labor] than with Netanyahu [Likud]. He feels more at home with people like Peres.[28]

The Intifada

Q: I would like to change subject a little and ask you to discuss the current Intifada. Of course everyone is aware of the Intifada as an antioccupation movement. But to what extent, in your opinion, does this Intifada include elements attempting to address critical issues of the Palestinian national movement from within and the damaging effects of the Oslo process on the trajectory of the national movement—to the extent that the Intifada has a subtext that shows a loss of faith in the Oslo process and the PA leadership as a whole?

A: We don't know exactly when it picked up in the way you frame it, but there is no question that this is in the subtext of the Intifada, and that is why people who want now to declare the failure of the Intifada are calling to go back to Oslo or even worse than Oslo.

Still, I think that the situation is contradictory. This is so because at the beginning of the Intifada, the PA or elements within it seemed to be interested in and ready to push the people out into the streets to protest against [then-PM] Barak's policies. They also saw it as a way to give support to the Palestinian leadership that was isolated after Camp David in July 2000, because it had said "no" to Clinton, which was considered "unacceptable" internationally (see Introduction).

But the same Palestinian leadership did not want to say "no" because they could imagine what the repercussions of saying no to Clinton were. Therefore, in order not to have to say "no," they did not want Camp David in the first place. They wanted to continue with the phased plan [of · the Oslo process] and didn't want to be faced with the package deal of Barak and Clinton that said "Either-or."

So in that sense, there was a gap, or at least there was no coordination between the leadership's means and goals and the real results. They wanted people out in the streets to support them in their position regarding issues such as East Jerusalem and settlements, although it seems that they accepted the blocs of settlements [i.e., that Israel could annex them] as well as the concept of "territorial exchange" [i.e., exchanging land inside the West Bank for lands inside the Green Line]. Irrespective, the [Palestinian] leadership did not want this crisis, and they cannot forgive Barak, who pushed for it. But when the PA called for help internationally and called for the Palestinian people to give them support, *it was the position of the Palestinian people that came out and not only the position of the leadership.*

From this point on, they [the PA] could not control the process that was unleashed by the Intifada.

Now, it got out of their hands in two directions. First was the Islamic movement and the factions that were never supporters of Oslo [mainly Hamas, Islamic Jihad, and the PFLP]. This was their opportunity to go out into the streets. Second, you had the popular dimensions of the Fateh movement, which were divided into two. There were the leaders of the first Intifada who were not given shares in the leadership [once Oslo was signed] and hence used this opportunity to express their anger against the leadership who came from outside [the Occupied Territories, primarily from Tunis]—not because they agreed or did not agree to Camp David but because they felt that they were excluded by them [the PA]. Second, there were also more authentic elements [in Fateh] that were closer to the people and who genuinely did not agree with what was going on [with Oslo and the trajectory of the PA]. These elements united and became explosive.

On a third level, there was also, of course, Israel's very harsh reaction, which was entirely unexpected. Barak used planes [to suppress the Intifada] for the first time since the 1967 War. This produced a reaction that was of a much wider nature than the opposition of the anti-Oslo factions. There is proof of this: people *joined* the factions in order to commit suicide bomb attacks—*[they did] not [make] suicide bomb attacks because they were in the factions*. There is this idea that people in Hamas make suicide bomb attacks. No. Many people join Hamas to carry out suicide bomb attacks because they want to take revenge on the Israelis. And if Fateh would take them, they would go to Fateh as well. They ask about it in the mosque: "Do you know someone who will send me [on a military mission]?" And no one answers, until six months later when a response comes back. The person is then approached by someone who says, "Do you still want to carry out an operation?"

This kind of dynamic developed because of the terrible oppression, the closures, and so on. People wanted revenge and wanted Israeli society to pay a price. It was felt that this kind of action was perhaps the only weapon the Palestinians had to deter Israel. Many people at that time believed in this because they felt that they didn't have anything more to lose.

Then there was the question of the Palestinian security apparatuses. Yasser Arafat wanted to hold the stick at both ends: first of all, not to lose the Intifada to Hamas and to make sure his own people were there. On the other hand, he did not want to totally lose the way of Oslo but to have that option open as well. That is why the security apparatuses *as apparatuses* did not fight. Despite the fact that they were bombed, raided, destroyed—as apparatuses, they never fought. Ramallah [the headquarters of the PA] was invaded [in Operation Defensive Shield], and they never fought. Jenin was invaded, and they did not fight. The Palestinians from the security apparatuses who participated in the battle of Jenin were individuals who *left* the apparatuses and joined the resistance. If people from the security apparatuses integrated into the Intifada, they did so *as individuals*.

This is very important: Ramallah was invaded, and the security apparatuses were at home in their pajamas. What did that mean? What kind of apparatuses were they supposed to be then? These questions are meaningful for the future of the Palestinians, for their collective memory, and for their sense of trust [of a body like the PA].

At the same time, because of the fact that individuals from the security forces joined in the struggle, you can't say that they [all those who work in the PA] are traitors. But you can say something about the system as a system [which did not fight] and about its significance and function [which was not designed to protect Palestinian society].

In this sense, the Intifada raised all these issues and did away with a lot of illusions. But it has not yet—I'm sorry to say—presented any kind of *alternative way*. The dynamic that I have explained pushed the people into two directions: either the rejectionist direction (which includes being ready to die in order to make the enemy pay the price) or the direction of those who want the Intifada to be proven a failure and preach that we are defeated. These people want the Palestinians to conclude from this so-called defeat that we should go back and accept what we did not accept in the past.

This duality is preventing the development of any real alternative strategy from the Intifada, which is what we always wanted from it.

1948 Palestinians

Q: Assuming that Israel is not interested in giving up the West Bank and is in fact actively engaged in creating a collection of cantons, where do the 1948 Palestinians fit into Israel's comprehensive plans?

A: We know that from the Israeli side, we are already integrated into their answer. When Israelis think of "demographic separation," they think about us too. They conclude that if demographic separation is not implemented, the Palestinians from both sides of the Green Line will become one unit. They also have us in mind when they put up the wall because if there is continuity and intermixing [between 1967 and 1948 Palestinians], it is very hard to control the radicalization and the transition of young people—at least as individuals—to armed resistance. Even if there is no radicalization of the Palestinian masses [in Israel], Israel cannot control the issue with individual young people.

So this is very important for them. After the events of October 2000 (in which thirteen Palestinian citizens were killed by the police), they have given a lot of thought to the Palestinians who are Israeli citizens. And we believe that they have reached some decisions and are already fulfilling plans concerning the issue. For example, they have diagnosed us [the NDA—Tajamu'] as a danger and have tried with all their means to fight us. The fact that we had a strategy and a clear vision meant that we could stand up to them, keep our movement together, and maintain it among the Arab minority inside Israel. But this is only one example.

Persecution and Racism Escalate

Israel is very interested in fighting the current that is trying to unite the Arabs in Israel into one Arab identity. They are trying to divide them into at least three, four, or five identities, thereby making them demographically easier to absorb and co-opt into the Israeli system, the same way they did to the Druze [community]. They think it is a very successful model to extend, for example, to Christians or to Bedouins—that is, to forge alliances with minorities inside the Palestinian minority itself against the majority. They invented this model and have been very aggressive with it.

They bring out their so-called Arab academics, whom they regularly put on Israeli television and radio to attack us. They also work with people who are dependent on them economically—such as local Arabic newspapers, whose publications are all dependent on advertisements from Israeli ministries. For a time, they tried to deprive them of their advertisements in order to co-opt them into toeing the line of incitement against the national movement inside. Theoretically, the papers can remain nationalistic; practically, they must be against everything that is nationalistic and democratic among the Arabs inside Israel. And they succeeded in co-opting them [the newspapers]. They [the newspapers] always encourage skepticism and are against struggle or any idea or movement that is interested in building something through struggle.

In these conditions it was a miracle that we succeeded in actually doubling our seats in the [January 2003] elections—after Iraq; after this psychological depression; after the fact that there is no attractive Arab political project; after the fact that we are economically dependent on Israel; and that "there are no options for the Intifada"; and that the Abbas/Dahlan [PA] leadership is now sitting with [Israeli Minister of Defense Shaoul] Mofaz like friends, while we claim they are war criminals—all this made it very hard to mobilize people for struggle.

We are a minority that lives as Israeli citizens with Israeli rights with Israeli institutions in the Israeli economy. But it is very important to maintain and keep the national Arab identity alive; to give it democratic depth; to keep the solidarity with the West Bank and Gaza going; to keep up our cultural interactions with the Arab world—through our Web site, through our newspapers, through our theoretical and political writings. Because in the end, we believe there *is* a contradiction with the Arabs in Israel [and Zionism] *if they remain Arabs and Palestinians* and organized in the right way. This will be the contradiction of the future.

Today we face a very harsh power politics inside Israel. They are now using the situation after the war against Iraq to implement things that they did not implement in the past—for example, destroying and demolishing houses [of the Palestinian citizens in Israel] in quantities that have never been seen before—ten in one day in the Negev. It's as if they are testing us to see what our reaction will be.

Israel is trying to strike at our self-confidence. But if you do not resist it, you encourage it to do more and you acquiesce to the politics of power. You have to convince Israel that the politics of force do not work with you, by not obeying. *Not by obeying.* This is the challenge that we face, and we are trying to give the people a better example of how to behave in these times of crisis.

This is *the* most right-wing Knesset since 1948. The atmosphere in the parliament is overtly racist. The new thing is that they don't hide it [anymore]. Racists today go around and *say* they are racist. There is an automatic and immediate majority against everything that we suggest in the Knesset—even if it is the most banal civil rights issue. They don't want us to go back to our constituency with any achievements. They want the people to understand that "through these people [the Palestinian MKs], you will get nothing. If you have some rights, it will not be through these people but will be through us—through the Likud, through Labor."

The incitement against us does not stop either. People like Minister of Education Limor Livnat [Likud] will openly use racist categories in the Knesset [justifying her discriminative policies]. It wasn't like this in the previous two or three Knessets. And it's not as though they are "losing their nerve." It stems from too much self-confidence as a result of the fact that they do not anticipate any criticism from the United States. They know very well that they are warmly embraced by the White House and the Congress, so they do what they want. And they pick up on the model of internal policies of the U.S. in its "war on terror," saying "Even in the U.S. the concept of civil rights is relativized." They are totally unrestrained.

1948 Palestinians and the Question of Palestine

Q: At least since Oslo, the question of the Palestinians in Israel has been left completely outside the equation of the broader Palestinian national question. What is your position on that?

A: The logic of Oslo was the logic of accepting the West Bank and Gaza as "Palestine" and addressing the question of what to do about the occupation of these lands. It was not about solving the whole Palestinian issue. Now, whether the Palestinians in Israel were worried or disillusioned [about their noninclusion in Oslo] . . . I don't think the Palestinians in Israel ever demanded that the PLO include them. The majority of Palestinians in Israel were [at the time] voting for Israeli [political] parties and running for election. There were, of course, some Palestinians [inside Israel] who thought they were part of the PLO and who joined the political factions—but we are talking about a few hundred. In general, though, there *wasn't* a demand for the Palestinians in Israel to be included in Oslo.

If you ask me retroactively whether this was wrong, I will tell you that the motivation of many of the Arabs in Israel was "Leave us alone. We want to be Israeli citizens." The Communist Party was leading this direction, calling for the equality of Palestinians inside Israel without really defining equality as the state of the citizens. It accepted the Jewish state without even problematizing the concept.

But it is [also] better that we were not included [in Oslo]. And I said this at the time: including the Arabs in Israel in the negotiations would have meant subjecting them to the balance of power between the PLO and Israel. This would transform our issue from a civil issue inside Israel (which is calling for equal citizenship, etc.) into an external issue caught within the (im)balance of forces. The Arabs in Israel will then be the weakest point in the negotiations. They may be used not only for "land swaps" but for "population swaps"—for instance, "[Israel] gets the Arabs in Israel, and you get the settlers."

This is because the logic of the Oslo negotiations was not "negotiations between a national liberation movement and an occupying power," but *between two sides.* The whole logic was a logic of drawing symmetries and equations. It was not a decolonization process but a negotiated process between "two violent sides," "two radicals," "two moderates." Everything was a kind of [false] symmetry.

But the case of the Palestinians as citizens is stronger than their case as a subject of negotiations between "two sides" of "Palestinians and Israelis" when the balance of power is totally to the benefit of Israel. We would have lost from this. The Palestinian cause would lose, the Palestinians inside Israel would lose—everyone would lose.

Our strong point is the fact that we struggle within the framework of citizenship, of being "inside"—not an issue that belongs to the "other [Palestinian] side," that is not recognized as a "national liberation movement," and that is the weaker side in the negotiations. This is the logic of Oslo, and I don't think that we should have been a part of this logic.

Tajamu' and National Collective Rights

Q: Tajamu' calls for collective rights as a national minority inside Israel. Can you explain precisely what that means?

A: Any old-fashioned classical liberal would say that collective rights is a nonsensical term because all rights are individual and if you say "collective rights" you relativize the individual rights inside this collective. We say no. These are two sets of rights that complement each other. One individual right is the right to have a national identity, and this should be maintainable through what we call [collective] cultural rights. The Arabs in Israel are not immigrants asked to integrate into the new society but indigenous people whose land has been stolen.

Liberalism developed in three phases. One phase was the phase of "civil rights." The second phase was when leftists, ex-leftists, and ex-socialists tried to find a compromise with liberalism by adding "social rights" [such as the right to an adequate standard of living, health, and education] to the [civil] rights of the individual. Now we have "cultural rights" [such as the right to have autonomy over the educational system of the Palestinian minority in Israel]. This is the third development we are trying to add to the rights of the individual: civil rights, social rights, cultural rights.

Israel does not believe in social rights and cultural rights. It so happens that there is an attempt to create a bill of rights inside Israel that will include social rights. Whether it will pass or not, I don't know. Israel seems to be going in the opposite direction—in the direction of wild capitalism, giving up even those social rights it has maintained for a long time.

As a national minority, we are saying "We *have* national minority rights and cultural rights." I can't accept, for example, that the minister of education—who may be from the [right-wing] National Religious Party [Mafdal]—determines what kind of Arab history I will study or what kind of curriculum will be taught in my schools. The curriculum in the Arab schools should be Arab and be determined by Arabs.

But this is not the only thing. We also demand to be able to represent ourselves as Arabs in all institutions of this country that conduct planning—particularly planning of lands—not only so that our land is not confiscated but so we have a say concerning the future of these lands and what will be built there. What kind of industrial zones? What kind of development? Development inside Israel right now means Judaization, namely, bringing Jewish immigrants and developing things for them. We are considered an obstacle on the way to this "development."

By demanding this and by working to develop other similar demands, we help the Arabs in Israel maintain themselves as a national group. This is very important because we might express our opinion as individuals but we don't do this as a group. What we are saying to the Arab public is "Even if Israel does not accept this, we should behave this way. We should be building our institutions so that we can have a say and so that the world can hear us."

There is a lot of discussion between us [Tajamu'] and the other Arab parties because some accuse us of separatism, of irredentism, of nationalism, of being isolationists. We say, "We are democrats." We are the ones who coined the whole concept of the "state of all its citizens." Thus, on the one hand, we do say, "We want to be citizens," but on the other, we are challenging the [Jewish] state, saying, "We are a national group." Israel is dealing with us as though we were three religions or as tribes. The only collective rights that we have in Israel are religious rights regarding how we marry or divorce, etc. [through religious courts, as in the Jewish sector]. This is the only collective right that Israel recognizes. But we say, "We have national rights as a minority." They say, "You are not a national minority, you are a group of [different] minorities." That is why we are called "the minorities [*miutim*]." We are not called "the *national* minority."

It is very important to raise these demands, as it is a kind of identity building. All identities are constructed. Training the people to demand these things is a process of identity construction. Even if you do not achieve some of the things, at least you present yourself as Arabs in a progressive way and not anymore as religious groups.

This is very important in secularizing the population and keeping a modernist identity for the Arabs in Israel—one that is institutionalized and at the same time civil.

We are not nationalists in the sense that we are ideologically nationalist. Of course not. We are *nationals*, not nationalists. We are Arabs. But we are Arab progressive democrats. We believe in coexistence and living with Jews. We are for organizing Arab society in a progressive way. We are for equality between women and men. We are for social rights. We are actually a part of the antiglobalization movement. We are against all kinds of folklore and orientalist authenticity nonsense. We are against fundamentalism. We are progressive democrats, but we also say "For God's sake, there *is* something called an Arab identity." That's all. I mean, 95 percent . . . *99 percent* of the Jews in Israel consider themselves Zionist. They consider themselves nationalists. We are not. We do not believe that nationalism is an [acceptable] ideology. We think democracy is an ideology. We think liberalism is an ideology. And so on. But we think we have to keep our Arab identity. The Arab minority in Israel has the right to organize itself as a national minority in order not to collapse into tribes—as they [the U.S.] are now trying to do in Iraq.

Q: Given this concept and what you formerly said concerning the economic dependency of Palestinians in Israel on the Israeli economy, to what extent can you do this without addressing class dimensions?

A: It's very hard. We do not think we can separate the class struggle of the Arabs in Israel from the class struggle in general. However, the problem is that the class struggle in Israel is totally nationalized and Zionized. It's divided between the poor and the so-called aristocracy of the wage workers—like, for instance, the wage workers of the electricity company.[29]

This is the only case where I am for privatization because it is a monopoly for the aristocracy of the proletariat. The people who work there are actually the owners. They work there and bring their sons to work there, and *they* are blocking any employment of Arabs. And they raise the prices when there is no competition. It's a monopoly: it's a case not of socialism but of a capitalist bureaucracy—that's all.

Many similar things are blocking solidarity between Arab and Jewish workers. Arab workers are not integrated into the heavy industries. They are not in the weapons industry; they are not in the airline industry. The [13] big committees of the workers do not include Arabs because Arabs are not employed in these industries. But if you take the more professional trade unions—for example, the teachers' unions—the Arabs are there. And we do not suggest that the Arabs separate so they can make their own class struggle. It's the same status, the same wages, so they should make the same struggle.

In the end, the whole equality struggle of the Arabs in Israel—in any single question—is a kind of class struggle. Because the majority of Arabs in Israel *are* poor and *are* under the poverty line. Of course it is not organized as a class struggle, though it definitely integrates into the class struggle. At the same time, it is not what dogmatic communists would call "class struggle" because the big workers' committees, which are said to be "leading the class struggle" in this country, actually struggle for their own benefit as privileged groups that are exclusive and do not include Arabs at all.

Two States or a Binational State?

Q: To what extent are you pushing the binational agenda in the context of the current circumstances, whereby Israel controls the entirety of historic Palestine from the river to the sea and is developing a sophisticated apartheid regime with different forms of control across it? Isn't it time to push this agenda?

A: There is no way to push it as a political program from where we stand. Its time will come only when this Palestinian leadership fails. Today the discussion among them [the PA] is one of "who leads," but it hasn't failed yet. There aren't calls from the Palestinian side to the Tajamu' saying "Come and have branches of the Tajamu' in the West Bank and Gaza. Let's make a binational movement. Let's cross the Green Line and make the same political organizations." Before this happens, it makes no sense to call for it. Binationalism without social, political agents on the ground is only an idea: an interview here, an article there. Are there Israeli and Palestinian masses, social agents—social movements—that are raising binationalism? I say no. There are not.

The way the issue of a Palestinian state is now raised is not the Palestinian state the Palestinian people are asking for—it is George Bush's Palestinian state and Sharon's Palestinian state—as I described it at the beginning of this interview. The Palestinian state is no longer a Palestinian national project.

The Intifada doesn't raise binationalism: the Intifada raises nationalism. The Intifada raises separation. It's against occupation. It wants to separate and to have its own entity. The Israeli reaction to it is walls, separation. If you want binationalism, you have to take the Israeli side into consideration. Binationalism cannot survive unless it is an Israeli/Palestinian project. If it's only a Palestinian project, it's not binationalism. The logic of the Intifada would change very much if it became binational with binational goals. Binational goals wouldn't create suicide bombs against buses. And it's not only the Palestinian Authority. Among the Palestinian masses, the mood is still national. National—Islamic. Not binational.

The Right of Return

Q: I agree. But with the collapse of Oslo, you hear a clear call for the basic tenets of the national movement: the right of return, the call for self-determination, the end of occupation. There is a gaping lack of leadership as to harvesting what those goals might mean. If you are talking in a serious way about the right of return, you have to begin to think seriously about options other than two states.

A: No one in the PA leadership is talking about the right of return in a serious way. What kind of right of return? The right of return was originally put forward in the sense of the liberation of Palestine. Is anyone today raising the issue of the right of return to Israel, to become citizens of Israel? Nobody is seriously raising this. Is it a return in the framework of a binational state? Nobody is saying that either. There is this kind of declaration that "We won't give up the right of return to our village"—the romantic use of the concept—and there is the lip service use whereby the concept is attached to the list of Palestinian demands as a kind of cliché. This is lip service. This is not real.

Q: But on a deeper level, it does exist because—

A: Let's see. Because there are a lot of young people's movements around the world speaking about right of return. I agree.

Q: But it's not just around the world: you can begin with the high participation of refugees in this Intifada as an indication that they are still fighting for their rights.

A: Okay. Very good. But the high participation of refugees in this Intifada exists anyway because of class elements. Usually the refugees are the incubators of the national movement. They are the ones who struggle—for anything, not only for the right of return. They are the people who struggle against occupation and not only for the right of return.

People who *are* for the right of return and who support not giving up this right are responsible today for framing the issue politically. The Palestinian leadership will not be able to do this. These people [who support the right of return] must say how [it is possible]. This is very important, because if you do not put it into the political model, you will actually not be answering people like Sari Nusseibeh [who calls for abandoning the right of return and establishing a Palestinian state]. They [people like Nusseibeh] are speaking politics.

The people who call for the right of return will have to say either "There is a place for the right of return in the framework of a two-state solution," (after all, the Zionists accepted the Partition Plan [of 1947, which called for the division of the land into two states, one Arab, the other Jewish], when the Palestinians composed 47 percent of the population of the [proposed] Jewish state), or "Yes, you are right, there is no place for the right of return in a two-state solution, but there is a place for it in the framework of a binational state. And we accept such a framework." This must be done—now. The political questions can't be ignored anymore. People like Nusseibeh must be answered.

The right of return reopens the issue of sovereignty of the state of Israel and what kind of sovereignty [regarding its right to determine its exclusivist Jewish citizenship], etc. If we do not address these issues, we are not speaking seriously about the right of return. Many of the people who support the right of return are very conscious and political, and I sympathize with them very much. They should lead. Let them lead. I want them to lead. Let them ask the questions and address them. Not only abroad but also in Palestine. They must participate in reopening the question and setting the agenda: the right of return, how, and in what political framework. It is very important.

CHAPTER 9

From Arafat's Death to the Disengagement Spectacle

January 2004–September 2005

Introduction

Although the sudden death of Yasser Arafat in November 2004 provided a moment of reflection for the national movement to consider its reconstitution and realignment, the internal Palestinian setting was not favorable to this end. The destruction Israel had unremittingly unleashed on the Palestinians and the historical accumulation of mismanagement portended ominously for the national movement and particularly for Fateh. As the internal Palestinian setting increasingly showed signs of power struggles against the old PA order, Israel's policy of destroying the Palestinian people and national movement continued with numbing brutality, resulting in more than 1,100 Palestinians killed between January 2004 and August 2005 (the beginning of the Israeli unilateral disengagement from Gaza). A majority of these were killed in vicious sustained raids launched against various cities and refugee camps in the Gaza Strip.

Preparations to disengage from Gaza unilaterally, finally confirmed by a Knesset vote on the matter, indicated the plan's goals: to permanently lock up the 1.4 million Palestinians there and throw away the key—to separate Gaza from the West Bank for good, definitely cutting it off from the rest of the world, creating a cheaper form of occupation there. On the other hand, the highest levels of Sharon's government were frankly admitting that the disengagement was a U.S.-Israeli scheme aimed at gaining legitimacy for continuing other parts of the "unilateral project." This entailed locking up the remaining, fragmented parts of the West Bank between the apartheid wall, to the west; and the Israeli-colonized and -controlled Jordan Valley, to the east.

The widely publicized goal of "legitimately" doing away with the semblance of a negotiated solution and replacing it with the "unilateral" approach, based on the pretext that there is "no partner for peace," did little to deter the Zionist Left from hailing the "disengagement" and depicting Sharon as a champion of peace—this despite the fact that Arafat was out of the picture and the compliant Abu Mazen had been "elected" as his successor. Moreover, Labor and Meretz provided the crucial support for passing the plan to "disengage" from Gaza in the Knesset, thus giving the international community the go-ahead to celebrate what was, in essence, a significant step in the total war against the Palestinian people, aimed at accelerating their sociocide.

The "disengagement" exposes the regroupment of Israel's traditional political forces around the tenets of Labor Party "pragmatism," and is expressed by the formation of Sharon's Kadima Party. Together with the Labor Party and Meretz, a new Zionist consensus has been constituted, with only the marginal messianic Right outside its redrawn boundaries.

Arafat's Death, Fateh's Future

Toufic Haddad

After forty years as the figurehead of the modern Palestinian national movement, Yasser Arafat died on November 11, 2005, in a hospital bed in Paris. His passing leaves enormous questions for the future of the Palestinian national movement, not least those associated with filling the void in the decision making and authority for which he was so well known. Though Arafat's legacy will be marked by some important achievements, he had equally as many failures and shortcomings, which will have lasting effects on the national movement for years to come. In the category of the former, he can be attributed with having played a considerable role in crystallizing a defiant Palestinian identity and national movement from the demoralized and fragmented Palestinian people after the Nakba in 1948 and the humiliating Arab defeat to Israel in the 1967 War. With respect to the latter, however, he must also be credited with being so cynical and unprincipled in his ruling that his true historic accomplishments have been greatly undermined, given that the strategies he embarked upon have largely led the Palestinian national movement into a dead end.

This is not the place to go into a comprehensive evaluation of Arafat's life works. Nor should Israel, the United States, and the reactionary Arab regimes be let off the hook for their responsibility in the shortcomings of the Palestinian movement today. It is nonetheless relevant to note that Arafat's most lasting legacy is likely to be felt through the institutions of the national movement and political orientation that he built over the years. These were constructed on a strategic footing that attempted to integrate the Palestinian movement within the regional and international ruling class order. His strategy, which began in the early to mid-1970s, "peaked" in the Oslo process and petered out by the time of his death, held that Palestinian liberation—or at least "statehood"—could come from marketing itself as beneficial to the interests of "regional stability" and was therefore *not* structurally contradictory to Western capitalist interests. But despite his best efforts, this task was always fraught with impossibility, owing to the fact that the Palestinian national movement itself was forged within a cultural and historical crucible that was catalyzed by conceptions of pan-Arabism, anticolonialism, and anti-Zionism. These ideologies and sentiments were (and remain) antithetical to the architecture of Western domination of the region, which is based on support for Israel (as a dependent client state) and pro-U.S. satellite states in the Arab world (Jordan, Egypt, the Gulf States), which respectively shun any genuine Arab nationalist, let alone democratic, agendas. Once imperialism had used Arafat for the purpose of recognizing Israel's right to exist, renouncing Palestinian resistance as terrorism, and having him act as the local cop to smother Palestinian dissent, it simply did away with him, despite his desperate efforts to the contrary.

In the end Arafat was a middle-class pragmatist who removed the spirit of liberation from the national liberation movement, though cynically keeping its lingo. In its place he left a wasteland of a national bureaucracy consisting of overlapping, inefficient, undemocratic structures dependent on Gulf petrodollars and EU and U.S. government aid, and with little sense of direction as to how liberation could be achieved once his strategies and tactics failed or canceled themselves out.

With Arafat's passing, the coming period is sure to be formed by the contradictions and intricacies of the domestic and international settings

that Arafat oversaw during his lifetime. This bears particular consequences for the future of Fateh, the movement Arafat cofounded, remaining its uncontested head until his death. Indeed, questions related to the
future of the PLO, as well as the Palestinian Authority (PA), are also inti-
mately connected to these developments, given that both consist of
Fateh-dominated bureaucracies.

Fateh's Future

The challenges Fateh faces today derive from the kind of organization
Arafat constructed over the years. Since its founding, Fateh has never been
bound by a distinct theoretical political ideology. Instead, its ability to re-
cruit and retain members consisted of its distinct *lack* of an ideology beyond
calling for the achievement of the main Palestinian tenets (the right to self-
determination, the right to statehood, the right of return, etc.), in addition
to its domination over the financial resources of the national movement.
The lack of ideology and strategy of liberation weaving together its variegated constituency—(composed of different generations of Fateh activists,
different strata of social elites; different experiences of struggle, (whether
diasporic or local); and different class interests—had been a hallmark of
Arafat's leadership style over the years. For Arafat, ideology, or confining
the Palestinian movement to one liberation ideology, was limiting and bur-
densome. He preferred instead to cherry-pick ideas from many different
movements, both reactionary and progressive. Thus, as David Ignatius of
the *Washington Post* writes describing Arafat's historical relationship with
the CIA, it was "a way of playing all possible sides of the game. In the early
1970s, when the covert relationship with the United States began, he was
simultaneously in contact with the CIA and the KGB, with the radical
Egyptians and the conservative Saudis."[1] This "tactic" was seen as a way to
create opportunities in various spheres, providing options in the complicated and often antagonistic social and political setting that the national
movement found itself in upon its post-1967 launching.

The legacy of this style carried on into the current Intifada. Whatever
his motivations for doing so, Arafat oversaw simultaneous yet contradictory political currents within his own party. On the one hand, he allowed
for the development of an armed resistance wing within Fateh once the
Intifada began and refused (for the most part) to crack down on resistance
groups, as demanded of him by Israel, the United States, and the European Union. On the other hand, Arafat repeatedly sought to return to the

Oslo framework (whether in the form of the Tenet Plan or the "road map"), despite the fact that these frameworks only gave legitimacy to a false "peace process," were clearly dead ends, and represented the same logic that had led to the Al Aqsa Intifada in the first place. The incongruence between the two strategies resulted in Israel being granted great freedom to exploit the contradictions between each current, making great strides in destroying the Palestinian national movement and society due to the lack of a cohesive Palestinian strategy or discourse.

Now that Arafat is dead, no one is able to negotiate disputes among his followers, and his successors have no clear strategy for how the party should move forward. Perhaps it is more accurate to say that the diverse currents within Fateh that Arafat presided over can lay equal claim to representing the continuity of his legacy, even though many of these currents have contradictory worldviews, with their respective tactics.

The Politics of Chaos

The social, political, and class contradictions Arafat oversaw within Fateh were already beginning to reveal themselves in the months leading up to his death. They have become more pronounced in the context of Israel's scorched-earth policies during the Intifada; Israel's deliberate destruction of institutions related to national and social cohesion; its continual assassination of experienced cadre within the national movement; and its isolation of Arafat himself within his compound since 2002, thereby preventing him from traveling or exercising any real leadership. A few examples illustrate the state of Fateh and cast shadows upon the ability of the movement to survive the death of its founder.

On July 16, 2004, Gaza police superintendent Ghazi Jabali was abducted from his car by a group calling itself the Jenin Martyrs Brigades.[2] The Brigades, which is composed largely of disaffected Fateh security personnel, promptly took him to Bureij refugee camp in Gaza's midsection, announced a state of emergency, and took up positions throughout the streets and rooftops preparing for any attempt to storm the camp. The group's leaders warned they would open fire if any PA police officers attempted to enter the camp's grounds. They also demanded that if Jabali were to be released unharmed, he had to be removed from his position and tried for crimes of corruption and abuse of authority.

Jabali's name has long been synonymous with corruption in Gaza. He was rumored to be connected with several PA-held monopolies that control the Gaza economy, in addition to extortion and even drug racketeering. But these accusations have never been proven, as he was never brought before a judge. Jabali, after all, *was* the law in Gaza, or at least he thought he was. Popular revulsion toward him, however, went beyond critiques of his personal lifestyle, also centering on his political—or rather "security"—role in the PA. His forces were infamous for attacking several popular Palestinian demonstrations, including the storming in 1995 of Al Najah University campus (where a protest against PA arrest campaigns was being held), and the attack on Deheisheh refugee camp near Bethlehem in 2000 (where residents were protesting PA police brutality).

It took several hours of tense negotiations among the Jenin Martyrs Brigades, Gaza security, and Fateh elites before Jabali was finally released, with more than a little egg on his face. A spokesman of the Jenin Martyrs Brigades identifying himself as Abu Iyad would later comment on Al Jazeera television, "We abducted Jabali with the goal of striking at one of the main heads of corruption in the Authority. Since the PA doesn't put an end to this kind of corruption, we took it upon ourselves to do some accounting of our own. We had given it [the PA] years to do something about it, but to no avail." Jabali was dismissed from his position the day after his captors released him—an unprecedented accommodation on behalf of the PA.

The kidnapping of Jabali immediately prompted a wave of similar acts of vigilantism throughout the Gaza Strip, with some isolated incidents taking place even in the West Bank.[3] The abductions, in turn, brought about the resignation of the head of Gaza's intelligence (Amin El Hindi) and Preventive Security Services (Rashid Abu Shbak), both of whom cited "the dissipation of security" (*al infilat al amni*). The resignations symbolized the degree to which the "security" institutions created by Oslo, are increasingly perceived as symbols of political and financial corruption and impediments to the national movement overall. Moreover, they also showed how sections of the Fateh grass roots are prepared to organize against them in the form of inchoate alternative formations loosely associated with the official party but distinct from it politically.

It should come as no surprise to see the issue of corruption acting as the lightning rod for popular discontent, particularly within Fateh. This is not merely because of the existence of corrupt high-ranking figures in the PA—such as Ahmed Qurei' (Abu Ala), the former top negotiator, who is not only rumored to be a kingpin in the local tobacco market but is also under investigation by the Palestinian Legislative Council due to one of his companies allegedly selling Egyptian cement to Israel for the construction of the apartheid wall. Under Arafat, the question of corruption within the PA wasn't an anomaly inasmuch as it was systemic and a means of governance—a deliberate tool of garnering power and consolidating position. The economic monopolies distributed among the Palestinian elite by Arafat (some of whom came back to Palestine with the PLO, some of whom are local West Bankers and Gazans) were a system of patronage that kept the security and economic elites loyal to Arafat himself while competing among themselves for power and influence. They provided him maneuverability in times of crisis in terms of finances, influence, and power while acting collectively as a self-correcting system that ensured that any one individual could not transcend his horizontal positioning vis-à-vis others in favor of a more privileged vertical position closer to Arafat himself.[4]

This style of governance, however, meant that Arafat needed these people even more in recent years in the context of his excommunicated status internationally and the fact that this class (the PA's economic/security elites) were courted by the United States and Europeans because they are known for their lack of politically principled stands and their petty infighting for power. With Arafat's passing, Fateh has now been forced to look at itself in the mirror, and the style and contradictions embedded in Arafat's historical modes of leadership are rising to the surface. These tools were employed first and foremost within Fateh, then applied to the broader movement in the context of the PLO and other national movement actors. The question of corruption has thus served to open a Pandora's box of wider and deeper divisions within Fateh, related in part to the future trajectory of the party in the wake of the failed "Oslo process" experience and the brewing class divide within Fateh between the more resistance-motivated grassroots parts of the movement and the elite, state-inclined PA bureaucracy. The tension is already showing signs that it may very well tear the movement apart.

In a rare interview, Nael Abu Sharekh, a popular and trusted leader in the Nablus branch of the Al Aqsa Martyrs Brigades, made a remarkable series of declarations about the situation inside Fateh, particularly between the PA bureaucrats and elites and the rank-and-file fighters on the ground: "The Al Aqsa Martyrs Brigades—the armed wing of Fateh—is seriously considering breaking off from the movement [Fateh]. The only thing that puts off making a final decision is the feeling within the Brigades that *it* represents the original part of the movement. . . . We have begun to feel a sense of revulsion and nausea because of our belonging to this party, which is led by a bunch of opportunists. We feel this way as a result of their ignoring and abandonment of us."[5]

Abu Sharekh described how the members of the Al Aqsa Martyrs Brigades live in difficult economic conditions and do not receive any financial help from the party—this in addition to the fact that they never feel safe and are constantly in danger of being assassinated by Israel. "Despite repeated letters calling for assistance, the party has abandoned its military wing to an unknown fate. They worry about their own interests, which could be in danger from Israel if they provided any assistance [to us]. They try to get in touch with us only when there is some form of political initiative or a proposal to announce a cease-fire. After that, they cut off relations until a new initiative comes up, or a new cease-fire that serves their interests."

Less than two weeks after giving the interview, Abu Sharekh, together with six other comrades from Fateh, Hamas, and Islamic Jihad, were killed like fish in a barrel as Israeli death squads threw one hand grenade after another into their safe house in the Old City of Nablus.

Presidential Elections 2005

The systemic rifts within Fateh gained prominent expression in the run-up to the January 9, 2005, presidential elections. Secretary-General of Fateh in the West Bank Marwan Barghouti's short-lived candidacy for the presidency, despite his currently serving five life sentences in an Israel prison, was an attempt to give political expression to the disaffected current within Fateh represented by groups like the Al Aqsa Martyrs Brigades, the Jenin Martyrs Brigades, the Popular Resistance Committees, and the Abu Rish Brigades. Not only do these groups feel alienated from the identity and the role they were supposed to play under the Oslo Accords, which essentially cast them as a subcontracted force to ensure Israeli security, they are also alienated from the Fateh party bureaucracy itself. This current is primarily composed of what is known within Fateh as the "third generation," distinguished from the "first generation" of "founding fathers" (of whom only a handful remain) and the "second generation," composed of those who control the bureaucratic structures of Fateh and the PA and who are also largely diasporic in derivation. The "third generation" was institutionally marginalized from the main decision making bodies of Fateh (the Central Committee, the Executive Committee, and the Revolutionary Council) once the diasporic Fateh party returned to erect the Palestinian Authority in 1994. Though its politics are not fully congealed and are subject to influence from below, in principle, this current opposes the negotiated Oslo model, believes in upholding armed struggle as a tool in liberation, and strives for field unity with other factions, including the Islamists, to better coordinate the national movement and its resistance.

Barghouti's decision to nominate himself as an independent candidate to the Palestinian presidency was intended to send a strong message to the bureaucratic, institutional and historical Fateh leadership led by Mahmoud Abbas (Abu Mazen). The latter sees itself as the natural inheritors of Arafat's legacy, considering the long years many of them have been in the Palestinian revolution, and their domination of the main Fateh PLO and PA bodies. But an important reason why they have been able to dominate these bodies is due to the fact that there have not been democratic elections in Fateh since 1988. This has meant that Fateh leaders who might have emerged in either this Intifada or in the previous one have never been represented in these leadership bodies.

Overall, Abu Mazen and his ilk seek to continue the political trajectory of Oslo (now embodied in the defunct "road map"), believing that eventually Israel will be forced to return to negotiations that can yield significant gains for the national movement. They have no strategy to resist the total war that Israel has unleashed against the Palestinian national movement and that has been backed by and coordinated with the United States under the cover of the "war on terror." Instead, Abu Mazen's politics stress the need to "not provide excuses for this war to be ratcheted up" and to end the military nature of the Intifada. This worldview perceives the death of Arafat as opening up the possibility of a "new era" in which the United States might force Israel to come to a settlement.

Though both currents maintained a public face of defiance in the run-up to the elections, the reality of the situation was that they both needed each other more than they cared to admit. Barghouti's current has been weakened throughout the course of the Intifada, with many of its top leaders killed or imprisoned. Furthermore, many Fateh rank-and-file cadres were placed in the schizophrenic position of being split between their loyalty to the Fateh party (whose presidential candidate was officially Abu Mazen) and their support for Barghouti (who ran temporarily as an independent) and his political trajectory. The overwhelming majority of these people, in the end, also still receive their paychecks from the

Palestinian Authority because they are Fateh activists. Barghouti may have been able to win the elections had he pressed on. However, he could not have done so without entirely splintering Fateh—in a socio-political environment that his followers would have found difficult to regroup within. At the same time, Abu Mazen has always suffered from a credibility crisis within the Palestinian national movement, and within Fateh in particular. Unlike Arafat, who even while ill donned military fatigues, emphasizing defiance, however symbolic or misplaced, Abu Mazen is perceived as a soft-spoken technocrat who was never directly associated with the history of Palestinian armed struggle. Instead, his name was associated with financial and political dealings during the Oslo years that tended to sully his image as being corrupt and unduly apt to making political concessions.

The embarrassing public rift within Fateh was eventually resolved with a compromise arrangement that has so far held together. Barghouti agreed to pull out of running for the presidency after receiving guarantees from Abu Mazen that the political mandate of the national movement would be revisited through general elections on all levels of activity: local municipalities, in the Legislative Council, and particularly within Fateh itself. Furthermore, it appears that Barghouti was able to extract certain promises from Abu Mazen, forcing him to disclose publicly that his political platform would not stray from the national tenets supported by the Fateh grass roots. This includes upholding the national "red lines" of the right of return for Palestinian refugees and a full end to the 1967 Occupation, as well as promises that Abu Mazen would fight PA corruption, seek out the protection for militants from all factions, attempt to free political prisoners (including those who were never freed by the Oslo process itself), and improve the democratic functioning of the PA. At the same time, the inability of Barghouti to break from the Fateh elite, thereby maintaining a relationship of dependency on the PA bureaucracy, only delays the resolution of the class and political contradictions within Fateh. Moreover it does not solve the question of Fateh's political identity and the strategies it will need to employ in the wake of the collapse of the Oslo process and now Arafat's death.

Hamas: Waiting in the Wings

Though ultimately Abu Mazen was able to win a majority for presidency (receiving 62 percent of the vote once Barghouti pulled out and endorsed him), the public rift within Fateh, and the larger historical dynamics and schisms within the movement, portend complicated challenges in the future. Moreover, Fateh does not have the luxury of resolving these challenges within a political vacuum but increasingly has to contend with Israel's relentless attacks, on the one hand, and its political opponents within the Palestinian arena, on the other—primarily in the form of the Islamic Resistance Movement—Hamas.

Indeed, the outbreak of the Al Aqsa Intifada and its subsequent sinking of the Oslo process represented a vindication of Hamas's political perspective, which always claimed that negotiations could lead only to political compromise. If the misconduct and financial and political corruption demonstrated by Fateh and the PA during the Oslo years added fodder to Hamas's political and social capital, the limited successes the movement has had in military resistance during this Intifada has helped solidify it as a major political force that can no longer be marginalized or repressed, as had been the case beneath Arafat.

Already during Arafat's final hours, Hamas was calling for its political voice to be heard and for a period of national reconciliation to be reached by carrying out the democratic process. After meeting with then-prime minister Ahmed Qurei' in Gaza in November 2004, a Hamas spokesperson demanded that "we must set up a joint national leadership to make decisions until elections are held. What was permitted to Yasser Arafat is forbidden to others and we must not let interested parties in the PA and PLO control the Palestinian destiny. Arafat derived his authority from being a symbol, but others don't have that privilege."[6]

Hamas's main priority in the upcoming period will be to preserve its gains, avoiding actions that would justify a crackdown against its members while negotiating to have its voice heard as a legitimate partner in the trajectory of the post-Arafat era. An Islamist paper closely associated with Hamas disclosed the party's position with regard to the upcoming general election process: "We must involve ourselves in all facets of life and participate wherever possible because it is illogical for us to undertake jihadist activity against the occupation and to pour into it all of our resources, youth and even leadership and then not to have any ability to influence the direction of political life. Because of this Hamas will raise the banner 'Partners in blood, partners in decision making.'"[7]

On the ground, Hamas is setting its sights on municipal and Legislative Council elections, where it hopes to leverage its influence and power on the political stage in an incremental manner. Both platforms will provide the movement the means through which it can strengthen itself upon the local setting while "legitimizing" its participation in national politics. This is crucial for Hamas given that it is considered relatively new to the Palestinian national political arena and is not a member of the PLO—an isolation that has at times benefited and at times weakened its influence.

During the debacle of the Oslo years, the Islamists began showing their electoral strength in student and trade union elections. But after more than four years of Intifada, the Islamists are poised to pick up considerable support from sectors disaffected by the Fateh-led PA, particularly if it is led by Abu Mazen who claims he will end the Intifada. Indications of this have already begun to surface in the form of the January 27, 2005, municipal elections in Gaza, where Islamists netted seven of ten districts, with an 80 percent voter turnout. Islamists fared more poorly but respectably in similar elections in the West Bank in December 2004, winning eight of twenty-six districts, with thirteen going to Fateh and the rest to independents. After the Gaza elections, Hamas political leader Mahmoud al-Zahhar defiantly declared, "The clear message [the election results relay] to the Zionist entity is that the program of the resistance led by Hamas . . . can carry out achievements in other areas," implying the political sphere.[8]

During the coming period (at least until the Legislative Council elections are held, scheduled for May 2005),[9] Hamas will work hard to try to deepen these "achievements in other areas," perceiving the transitional period of elections in the wake of Arafat's death as instrumental to consolidating its power base, particularly when its "stock" is high. For this reason, it has no real problem in agreeing to observe the cease-fire achieved between Abu Mazen and Sharon at Sharem el-Sheikh on February 11, 2005. From Hamas's perspective, the cease-fire will provide time and opportunities to strengthen its influence in local politics through elections, while attempting to rebuild its networks in the West Bank, which have been severely damaged throughout the course of the Intifada.

The Misleading Disengagement from Gaza: "Unilateralism" Replaces "Peace Process"

Tikva Honig-Parnass

The process of returning to the traditional Zionist approach to the "Palestinian question" as a replacement for the Oslo "years of peace" has rapidly unfolded under overt U.S. protection and the support of the European Union and a number of Arab states. The strategy of launching a long-term war aimed at doing away with the Palestinian national movement and crushing its basic social organization, while waiting for the right circumstances to implement mass expulsion, has now been confirmed by two of the most senior Israeli commentators. Though they predictably blame its necessity upon "Palestinian rejectionism," their frankness could not be more unequivocal. "Since the outbreak of the Intifada," writes Uzi Benziman, "the conception that guides the security establishment is that this conflict is doomed to continue for many generations and that its essence is the eternal refusal, almost religious, of the Palestinians to come to terms with the existence of Israel."[10] Aluf Benn describes what is by now an accepted concept of a war with no end: "At the onset of the fifth year of the Intifada, war has been fixed on the existential condition of the Israelis and Palestinians. No one is speaking anymore about the end of the confrontation and surely not about the solution of the conflict, only regarding the reciprocal 'charging of costs' [i.e., how high a price each side will pay]."[11] Likewise, outgoing chief of staff Moshe Ya'alon repeated his old-time message from 2002[12] in a June 2005 *Ha'aretz* interview,[13] emphasizing that there is no end to the conflict now, nor will there be in the foreseeable future: Israel is still struggling for its right to exist as an independent Jewish state, as it did in 1948, and hence Israelis need to adopt the perception that it will be a "lengthy process" in which "the sword must remain drawn every day." Israeli mothers should tell their sons and daughters that they were born into "a society of struggle."[14]

The "no partner for peace" slogan, initiated by former Labor PM Ehud Barak after the preplanned failure of the July 2000 Camp David summit, has served Sharon well, as he implements his bloody version of total war against the Palestinians. In this regard, Sharon has come to rely on cunning "unilateral" schemes, actually first proposed by a number of

Labor leaders. The year 2005 witnessed the accelerated building of the "apartheid wall" and the building of popular consent for "unilateral disengagement" from the Gaza Strip, which ultimately took place in August 2005. Both the wall and the disengagement were conceived to eternalize Israel's control over what is hoped to be a defeated, atomized Palestinian people.

The strong support given to these plans by the Zionist Left has virtually wiped out what remains of secondary, tactical, or stylistic differences between the two major currents in Zionism, traditionally embodied in the right and left parties and movements.[15]

Israel has felt freer and more confident to carry out its brutal policies in the 1967 Occupied Territories than during any other time in its history. This is not merely a result of the protection the United States has offered it along the way but also because of the lack of any significant pressure exerted by Europe, which in practice has also given a carte blanche to Israel in its "war on terror." Aluf Benn summarizes the international community's indifference to the Palestinian plight:

> At the beginning of the fifth year of the Intifada [October 2004], the international community has become tired of the Israeli-Palestinian bloodletting and filed it in the drawer of chronic conflicts like Kashmir, which are not worth investing energy in. The cliché that quiet in the Holy Land is important for preserving stability in the region and of oil prices has been refuted. The Arab regimes have survived the Israeli occupation of the [1967 Occupied] Territories and the American occupation of Iraq well. Additionally, the prevalent Israeli assumption that it is important to achieve a quick victory in war before the superpowers enforce a cease-fire to the benefit of the Arabs, has collapsed as well.[16]

"The Maneuver of the Century"[17]

The reason for the shift in the international community and its embrace of Sharon lies in the unilateral disengagement plan he devised with the United States. Sharon first announced the plan in a December 2003 speech given at the annual conference hosted by the Hertzliya Interdisciplinary Center,[18] declaring that by October 3, 2005, Israel would unilaterally pull its army out of the Gaza Strip and evacuate the settlements and settlers, including the Gush Katif settlement bloc.[19] He also announced that soon after the Gaza disengagement, four small isolated settlements in the north of the West Bank would be evacuated. No sooner did Sharon decide upon and announce these plans than the image of Israel in the international community changed completely, and not only with respect to the European community. The "unilateral disengagement" plan has reactivated relations between Israel and the pro-American Arab states in the region. According to senior sources in Sharon's office, "The Arab world has already unwillingly come to terms with the existence of Israel, and the only problem now is the Palestinians."[20]

As one progressive researcher rightly concludes, Israel can carry on its brutal policies against the Palestinians "because it feels that finally it has reached the stage where the 'linkage' between the policy of the Arab states and the lot of the Palestinians has been canceled."[21]

The announcement of the disengagement plan has also accelerated many previously ongoing processes within the Israeli political system, culminating in the emergence of a new Israeli political map. We thus witness the regroupment of Israel's traditional political forces, whereby most of the Right and Left have united politically around the strategy of "unilateralism," forming a large consensual bloc against the fanatical Right, composed primarily of the settlers' movement and the parties that represent it—religious and secular alike.

In the post–Iraq invasion era, Israel and the United States no longer need to pretend that they have asked for, let alone received, Palestinian consent to their plans. Unilateral steps, which establish facts on the ground, have replaced the endless talks and negotiations that made up the essence of the strategy of former Israeli governments during the Oslo era. Accordingly, the unilateral disengagement plan aims—and has largely succeeded—to officially bury the Oslo framework. In so doing, it has practically done away with even the "road map" (although the U.S. administration continues to pay lip service to it), not to mention all other plans based on negotiations.[22] Such "peace initiatives" at least claimed to be based in some way upon an agreement negotiated between the PA and Israel. Although since the death in November 2004 of Arafat (who acted as the justification for unilaterally taking these steps in the first place), Sharon has been obliged to "recognize" the new PA leadership under Mahmoud Abbas (Abu Mazen), the only thing actually on offer to this new leadership is "coordination of the withdrawal plan," not reaching any sort of agreement with it.[23]

The Left, which today hails Sharon's disengagement plan, is the very same Left that initiated and actively supported the "political process" of Oslo, both within the international community and the Israeli political spheres. Since the inception of the plan, Shimon Peres—the Israeli "architect of Oslo"—has been secretly meeting with Sharon's people for months, planning the entrance of the Labor Party into Sharon's government.[24] He thus seeks to officially end his own political life project—the Oslo framework—and, with it, abolish the last distinct characteristics of the entire Israeli "peace camp" that supported Oslo and that distinguished it from the Right. The Zionist Left has thus switched to supporting the war strategy of the United States and Sharon, under the pretext of "Sharon's vision for peace" as embodied in the Gaza disengagement—a vision that has been confirmed by senior public figures to be "designed to eternalize war."[25]

The leaders of the so-called Left did not even have the decency to tell the truth to their own public or even to relate to the few liberal commentators like Akiva Eldar, who wrote in *Ha'aretz* as early as September 13, 2004, "The disengagement plan was destined to bury an agreement in the [West] Bank and East Jerusalem that could be accepted by moderate Palestinians. . . . Thus, inevitably [it will] strengthen the motivation to kill Israelis." Neither did they have the decency to disclose that the dismantling of Jewish settlements in Gaza had nothing to do with giving up Israel's control over the Strip or its determination to repress the resistance there, as stipulated in the plan approved by the Knesset in June 2004.[26]

Thus, Israel simply substituted the expensive occupation of Gaza with a cheap occupation, one that in Israel's view exempts it from the occupier's responsibility to maintain the Strip and from concern for the welfare and the lives of its 1.4 million residents, as stipulated in the Fourth Geneva Convention.

Both Right and Left cooperated in hiding from the public the fact that Israel's control of Gaza will continue. They differed only in the extent of honesty in disclosing that the parade of "disengagement" will be a vehicle for mobilizing international public opinion—European support and the consent of the Arab regimes—to Israel's policies in the West Bank.

Indeed, no previous discourse around any "peace plan" has ever reached the level of Orwellian distortion and self-deceit whereby "peace is war" and the most elementary logic is turned on its head.

Straight from the Horse's Mouth: Revealing the Truth Behind the Disengagement Plan

Below are lengthy excerpts of an interview with Advocate Dov Weisglas, Sharon's closest adviser, conducted by Ari Shavit, a senior Israeli analyst. The interview, published in *Ha'aretz* at the beginning of October 2004, served to strengthen popular consent around the dismantling of the settlements in Gaza, which found strong opposition within the Likud.[27] The interview confirms, in fact, that the disengagement plan is designed as a joint U.S.-Israeli scheme to bestow legitimacy on the long-term war launched by Sharon against the Palestinians.

It is important to deconstruct this interview, precisely because the Zionist Left and much of international public opinion have continued to look at the disengagement as a decisive turning point on the road toward a peaceful resolution to the conflict, with Sharon as the Israeli De Gaulle. Furthermore, the real goals behind this "peace" plan, disclosed in this interview, explain the wide support the plan has gained even among forces within the right wing itself.

Moreover, it should be emphasized that Weisglas's arrogant admissions are acknowledged by one of the most influential figures in Sharon's administration, whom Shavit characterizes as "a personal advocate, a family advocate, and a policy advocate. Weisglas is the advocate who for the past thirty months has represented Ariel Sharon vis-à-vis the American mega-authority, the advocate who in the past thirty months, in his official capacity as a senior adviser to the Prime Minister, has almost single-handedly conducted the delicate relationship between the White House and the Sycamore Ranch [Sharon's personal ranch, located in the Negev]. Which is to say, between the United States of America and the state of Israel."

The Palestinians' "refusal" has nothing to do with their national aspirations or the history of the injustice perpetrated against them but with their "religion." Furthermore, given that Israel's official reason for unilateral disengagement is that there is "no partner for negotiations," such an assessment ensures that the current situation, in which Israel "unilaterally" enforces its plans, will remain a long-term condition.

[Weisglas]: "For a great many years the accepted view in the world was that people turned to terrorism because their situation was bad. So that if you make things better for them, they will abandon terrorism. The Palestinian assumption was that when the Palestinian majority gets national satisfaction, they will lay down their arms and the occupiers and the occupied will emerge from the trenches and embrace and kiss. . . . [But] he [Sharon] understood that the ability of a central Palestinian administration to enforce its will on the entire Palestinian society does not exist. He understood that Palestinian terrorism is in part not national at all but religious, and therefore granting national satisfaction will not stop terrorism. [Sharon] insisted that the swamp of terrorism be drained before a political process begins. That was our historic policy achievement.

Aims of the Disengagement Plan

Aim One: To legitimize the wholesale freezing of the political process and the question of a Palestinian state (as stipulated in the Quartet-sponsored "road map") for an indefinite period of time.

Q: If you have American backing and you have the principle of the "road map," [which is not to begin implementation "before terror is eradicated"], why go to disengagement?

A: Because in the fall of 2003 we understood that everything was stuck. And even though according to the Americans' reading of the situation, the blame fell on the Palestinians and not on us, Arik [Sharon's nickname] grasped that this state of affairs would not last. . . . That the U.S. formula would not be enough: that the international community would seek another formula, which would annul the principle that eradication of terrorism precedes a political process. And with the annulment of that principle, Israel would find itself negotiating with terrorism. . . . The result would be a Palestinian state. And all this within quite a short period of time—not decades or even years but a few months.

Instead, Weisglas argues, the disengagement maneuver will delay the peace process for "years to come, perhaps decades."

Q: From your point of view, then, your major achievement is to have frozen the political process legitimately?

A: That is exactly what happened. You know, the term "political process" is a bundle of concepts and commitments. The political process is the establishment of a Palestinian state with all the security risks that entails. The political process is the evacuation of settlements, it's the return of refugees, it's the partition of Jerusalem. And all that has been frozen now. . . . Effectively, this whole package that is called the Palestinian state, with all that it entails, has been removed from our agenda indefinitely. And all this with authority and permission. All with a [U.S.] presidential blessing and the ratification of both houses of Congress.

Aim Two: *To legitimize the consolidation of the Occupation in the West Bank.*

[Weisglas]: Arik doesn't see Gaza today as an area of national interest. He does see Judea and Samaria [the West Bank] as an area of national interest. . . . In regard to the large settlement blocs, thanks to the disengagement plan, we have in our hands a first-ever U.S. statement that it will be part of Israel. In years to come, perhaps decades, when negotiations are held between Israel and the Palestinians, the master of the world will pound on the table and say, "We stated already ten years ago that the large blocs are part of Israel."

What is actually disclosed by Weisglas is a U.S.-Israeli scheme to give up nothing of value in exchange for an explicit promise from the United States to allow Israel to continue controlling the majority of the West Bank. This is explicitly written into the third clause of the first section of the plan, which reads, "It is clear that various regions in the West Bank will remain part of Israel. Israel will annex the central Jewish settlement blocs, towns, security areas, and other lands that Israel has an interest in keeping." For the first time since the annexation of East Jerusalem, the Knesset will approve by law the annexation of parts of Palestinian occupied lands into Israel.[28] But it isn't Sharon who has changed, it's the United States that has officially adopted his political strategy.

[Weisglas]: Sharon has remained loyal to the approach of the Israeli "nationalist camp" [composed primarily of the Likud and smaller parties to its right], which has opposed the Oslo track since its inception. He has long insisted on the principle of "No negotiations till the eradication of 'terror'" [the acceptable code for a prolonged war]. Arik is the first person who succeeded in taking the ideas of the national camp and turning them into a political reality that is accepted by the whole world. After all, when he declared six or seven years ago that we would never negotiate under fire, he generated gales of laughter. Whereas today, that same approach guides the president of the United States. It was passed in the House of Representatives by a vote of 405–7, and in the Senate by 95–5.

The disengagement acts as a device concocted with the U.S. administration with the wink of an eye regarding its implementation.

Q: So you have carried out the maneuver of the century? And all of it with "authority and permission"?

A: When you say "maneuver," it doesn't sound nice. It sounds as if you said one thing and something else came out. But that's the whole point.

After all, what have I been shouting for the past year? That I found a device, in cooperation with the management of the world [the U.S.], to ensure that there will be no stopwatch here. That there will be no timetable to implement the settlers' nightmare [withdrawal of the settlements in the West Bank]. I have postponed that nightmare indefinitely. Because what I effectively agreed to with the Americans was that part of the settlements [in the West Bank] would not be dealt with at all, and the rest will not be dealt with until the Palestinians turn into Finns [peaceful and enlightened people from Finland]. That is the significance of what we did: the freezing of the political process.

Weisglas's victorious summary displays the arrogance of someone who knows that the "world's manager" sees Sharon as the "unilateral" senior executor of its policies.

[Weisglas]: We educated the world to understand that there is no one to talk to. We received a certificate that says: (1) There is no one to talk to. (2) As long as there is no one to talk to, the geographic status quo will remain intact. (3) The certificate will be revoked only when this and this happens—when Palestine becomes Finland. (4) See you then, and bye-bye! What more could have been anticipated? What more could have been given to the settlers?

Enthusiastic Support of the Zionist Left

The blatant details of the truth behind the disengagement plan, which were widely publicized in the Israeli media, did not change the enthusiastic support of the Zionist Left.[29] Like so many times in the past, the Left has rushed to confer legitimacy on a plan that is disastrous for the Palestinians by helping describe it as a great opportunity for peace. This time, however, the plan is being adopted by the man whose hands are stained with more Arab blood than any other Israeli general, and still he is praised by the Labor and Meretz parties as leading "a historic change" that indicates an "an upheaval in Sharon's consciousness."

The Labor Party's aspiration to join Sharon's government was finally realized once the settler and transfer parties left the government due to their objection to the disengagement. Upon losing his parliamentary majority, Sharon turned to the Labor Party to join the government, using its nineteen seats to ensure that the disengagement could still be carried out.[30]

Indeed, the Labor Party joined Sharon's government as his main aid in implementing the disengagement plan in August 2005. Its participation in the government, however, was not conditioned on any specific promises regarding the immediate return to negotiations, the continued evacuation of settlements, or even the dismantlement of "illegal" outposts in the West Bank. Instead, it agreed to define the coalition government as a "continuing government" (not a "new government"), thus releasing Sharon from any obligation to respond to the demands of the parties that join the newly formed government, to change the "basic tenets" of its political platform. The Labor Party thus gave its consent to the original tenets articulated upon the formation of Sharon's first extremist right-wing government in March 2003.[31]

Meretz (Yachad) supported the government from outside.[32] Not only did it support the Knesset vote on the disengagement, it even offered to provide Sharon a parliamentary "safety net" until the disengagement is complete, ensuring that his government does not collapse in the meantime through losing its majority.[33] In a patronizing, colonialist tone, Beilin even turned to Palestinian MKs, calling on them to support the unilateral disengagement plan as well, while paternalistically trying to teach them a lesson in "peace policies:" "This is a moment of truth, and it will be very strange if [political] parties that raise the banner of ending the occupation do not join the peace camp in the vote in the Knesset."[34] It was also no problem for this neoliberal ideologue to call later for supporting the cruelest annual budget ever submitted by Minister of Finance Benjamin Netanyahu in the Knesset vote on the matter—all in the name of keeping Sharon in power for the sake of his "peace plan." Indeed, as a senior commentator of *Ha'aretz* emphasized, "Now, [Beilin] is the most loyal fateful soldier of Sharon. The number one soldier."[35]

Nor did Meretz leaders condition their support of Sharon on the latter's change of approach to Abu Mazen. They thus did not differ from the behavior of the Labor Party ministers in the government who refrained from pressuring Sharon to strengthen the "pragmatic" Palestinian leadership, headed by Abu Mazen. Sharon could thus refuse to talk with Abu Mazen about the "road map," hiding behind statements that the latter is not fulfilling the requirement to dismantle the "terror organizations"—a step that is to be implemented before the most preliminary steps of the "road map" are begun.

Thus, with the support of the Left in his pocket, Sharon could arrogantly demand that the Palestinians accept the central premise of Zionism, emphasizing that the solution to the Israeli-Arab conflict will be possible only when the Arabs recognize the Jewish "right to a homeland, established as a Jewish state, in the Land of Israel." Until that happens—if ever—only slow progress can be made.[36]

The broad consensus Sharon has achieved regarding the unilateral disengagement has helped draw public attention away from the ongoing Israeli operations on the ground. They aim at finishing the process of enclosing what remains of the disconnected swaths of land in the West Bank. At the same time, the frantic daily land grabs for settlement construction in the West Bank continued—including plans to *double* the settler population of the Jordan Valley and complete the fragmentation and closure of the entire West Bank. Meanwhile, the details of the plan to hermetically close off Gaza by controlling its land, air, and sea were fully disclosed in the media throughout the month of June 2005, in fact mocking the very concept of "disengagement."

Indeed, as Professor Ze'ev Sternhell emphasizes, "Arik [Sharon] is now the 'king of Israel,' as the Left has since long given up any commitment to the fundamental values of civilized human beings, so as not to disrupt a historic maneuver."[37]

"One People, One Leader, One Emperor": Redrawing the Boundaries of the Legitimate Zionist Collective

Tikva Honig-Parnass

In the months leading to the disengagement from the Gaza Strip in August 2005, the Israeli political map had the full approval of substantial parts of the Likud and the Zionist Left. This unity of program led to a rift within the Likud party, resulting ultimately in the establishment of a new party—Kadima (Hebrew for "forward"), headed by Sharon himself.

The basis for this schism within the Likud derives from the fact that the Likud ministers in the former coalition government led by Sharon represented two opposing currents regarding their political approaches to the 1967 Occupied Territories. On the one hand are the Likud MKs who followed the political current that represented the ideological continuity of Ze'ev Jabotinski.[38] This current calls for Israel maintaining control over the "entire Eretz Israel" (*Eretz Israel hashlema*) and is led largely by the sons and daughters of the historic leaders of the Herut party (the primogenitor of the Likud party), founded and formerly led by the late Menachem Begin. On the other hand is the more "pragmatist" current, led by Sharon. This current consists of the inheritors of the "security" line that dominated the historic Mapai party (the Eretz Israel Workers' Party) headed by Ben-Gurion.[39] However, in the months prior to the disengagement, part of the first current and their adherents in the rank and file came to adopt Sharon's realpolitik approach, ultimately joining together with the Labor Party as a political bloc aligned against the messianic-religious and secular-fanatical Right.

This cooperation indicates the culmination of the process in which the differences between the historic currents of the Zionist movement have been blurred through the adoption of Mapai's and the Labor Party's "pragmatic" approach to the "conflict"—namely, the understanding that it is impossible to maintain the Zionist state without the support of at least one superpower, entailing making the necessary political "concessions" embodied in Sharon's unilateral approach. Indeed, MK Rubi Rivlin (Likud), the chair of the Knesset, who is of the second generation of former Herut leaders and is opposed to the disengagement plan, is correct in saying "Arik [Sharon] does not represent the movement into which I was born [Herut, the progenitor of Likud]. He is a Mapainik [representing the ideology and policies of the old Mapai party, the progenitor of the Labor Party]. He did not mislead me. I misled myself. I was captive to his charm. I did not see in his ideological deviation a danger."[40]

But realpolitik isn't the only thing guiding Ben-Gurion's disciples in both the Labor and Likud parties regarding their adherence to U.S. dictates. Their joint support for neoliberalism also facilitated their speedy unification into a coalition government. After all, it was the Labor Party that initiated neoliberal economic policies in the mid-1980s, under the Labor-Likud government headed by Shimon Peres and with Baige Shochad, the minister of finance (Labor), leading the charge to dismantle the social welfare state. It was also MK Haim Ramon (Labor), a man who played a central role in establishing the present Likud-Labor unified government, who was responsible for carrying out the last stages of destroying the Histadrut and the remains of organized Jewish worker power, as well as the privatization of the semistate health care system led by the Histadrut.

The battery of various political, economic, and social positions that derive from this worldview, held by both the "pragmatic" Right and Left, which underlies their collaboration in executing the disengagement, are summarized by the progressive political analyst Haim Baram: "This is the true meeting point of most supporters of the disengagement plan: a Jewish chauvinism, a security fixation, lack of any consideration for the Arab factor, support by the American conservative Right, hostility toward the developing states, adoption of [the values of] globalization and the social cannibalism of market forces, and a clear inclination to nuclear weaponry as a deterrent power. The traditional biblical motives involved in their orientation toward the entire Eretz Isreal (*Eretz Israel hashlema*) also exists in their ideological ecology, but its impact is less in comparison to power politics and pragmatic considerations, which are mainly economic and security related."[41]

Disconnecting from the Messianic/Settler Right

With substantial parts of the two main currents of Zionism uniting under one leader and one political mission, the boundaries of the legitimate Zionist collective have been redelineated, leaving the messianic Right clearly outside. The civil disobedience campaigns launched by the settlers and fanatical Right, which became increasingly violent as the disengagement date approached (August 12, 2005), together with the incitement spewed against Sharon, who is depicted as a traitor, has escalated and deepened the rift between the settler parties and both the Left and Right. However, it is not the belief in "Greater Israel" that has delegitimized the settler parties in the eyes of the Zionist Left (nor of course, of the center Right). On the contrary, the Left shares most central premises of Zionism with these forces, including the belief in the "historic right of the Jewish people" to entire "Eretz Israel," given that they have "returned" to their homeland. This is why the Left looks to the annexation of the large settlement blocs and continued Israeli control—albeit indirect—of the West Bank as a "concession" it is willing to pay for "achieving peace." This basic affinity sheds light on the true meaning of what is portrayed by wide sections of the local and international media as "a decisive rift within the nation" around the issue of the unilateral disengagement from the Gaza Strip. But as the progressive commentator Meron Benvenisti emphasizes, this "rift" is "nothing more than an internal Zionist spat."[42] Accordingly, the catchphrases that were the mantra of the Left for years—its readiness to make "painful concessions for peace" and its support for "a Palestinian state with border corrections"—have been appropriated in an Orwellian manner by Sharon himself, contributing to his peaceful image.

But what has actually united the Left and "pragmatic" Right against the settler movement (and their parties) is the latter's blatant challenge to one of the most fundamental principles of Zionism, embodied in their resistance to the disengagement: that is, withdrawing their recognition of the supreme sovereignty of the state of Israel as the embodiment of Zionism and hence as the only source of political legitimacy. In other words, the settlers have violated the maxim "Loyalty to the state, not to the land." Their rebellious discourse and violent confrontations with soldiers and police forces in the months prior to the disengagement from Gaza, embodied these trends, entailing their necessary marginalization by the "sane" majority.

This was the reason for ending the overt brotherhood that Zionist Left politicians and intellectuals expressed toward the settlers and the National Religious Party after the breakout of the Al Aqsa Intifada, resulting in unrelenting attempts on behalf of the Left to create a "dialogue" with them. The most extreme Zionist ideology expressed by the settlers did not seem to constitute a stumbling block in reaching joint "covenants" regarding the basic premises of Zionism, including the nature of the Jewish-democratic state.[43] But the recently growing rift between the Left and religious Zionists (mainly from the National Religious Party) is actually the culmination of a long process that began after the 1967 Occupation and revolves around questions over who has ultimate sovereignty over the state. For decades the senior spiritual and political leadership of the National Religious party saw the erection of a sovereign Jewish state as a positive religious command (*mitzvat asse*). This compelled their cooperation with the Zionist project, since the state was seen as "the beginning of the growth of resurrection." Thus they were loyal supporters of Mapai and Labor governments for decades.

Indeed, the central role conferred on religious institutions and symbols in the state of Israel stemmed from Zionism's need for religious legitimacy for its project, in order to explain its precise choice of Palestine as its target of colonization, when it was already settled by the Palestinian people. It was the state of Israel itself that conferred this role on the religious institutions, enabling them to become state institutions. It was the state that absorbed Halachic laws regarding family affairs into the legal system, together with other religious matters into state functions and practices (such as state observation of the Sabbath and the prevalence of selling kosher meat). This agreed-upon division of labor between the state and religion had no relevance to the state's sovereignty regarding political, economic and social matters, and religious sectors recognized this.[44]

However, after the 1967 Occupation, an ever-growing process of seeing the Halacha as an alternative source of authority to the state in political matters and a tremendous strengthening of messianic elements began to take place among the national religious and settler movements. An expression of this was recently seen in the formation of an unofficial rabbinical entity that overtly seeks to undermine the authority of the Supreme Rabbinate of the State in theory and practice. The very existence of this new institution reveals the extent of alienation these forces feel toward mainstream Zionism and the state.

Moreover, the belief in the supremacy of the Halachic rulings of settler rabbis over army orders (which derive their authority from secular legal systems) has prevailed even among religious nationalist soldiers, who occupy large parts of the command layers of the army. This phenomenon is so extensive that many officers publicly announced that they would refuse orders to evacuate settlements.[45] The rebellious spirit even spread to nonreligious circles of the extreme Right, whose leaders openly challenged the legitimacy of the Knesset decision on the disengagement and called for physically resisting the army's attempts to "uproot Jews from their homes." As Dani Rabinowitz, professor of sociology at Haifa University, notes, "The state of Israel lost its legitimacy in the eyes of the new generation of religious Zionists who attempt to accept the Messianic version of the nationalistic judiciary as an alternative and preferred source of political legitimacy."[46]

Implementing the Political Regrouping: The Establishment of Kadima

After the disengagement took place, a number of Likud ministers who espouse the old "Greater Israel" Herut ideology and who subsequently opposed the unilateral disengagement, began publicly supporting the positions of the "fanatic messianic block," thus opposing Sharon's government, in which they served. Together these forces constituted the only unequivocal opposition to Sharon's disengagement plan within Jewish society in Israel, discounting the miniscule and marginal circles of radical Leftists. But this is the case not only regarding this specific plan. The division of the political map according to the old Zionist political parties no longer reflects the rather broad unification of mainstream Zionism's approach to the "Palestinian question," the Arab world, and the role of the Jewish-Zionist state in the region in the service of U.S. imperialism. The emerging regrouping of Zionist political forces, constituting a massive closing of ranks around Zionist premises and rhetoric, took place on a level that the Zionist state has never experienced in the past. Moreover, its organizational embodiment soon took place.

On November 9, 2005, the former chair of the Histadrut, MK Amir Peretz, won the Labor Party primaries with an astonishing majority against old-time party leader Shimon Peres. Soon after his election, Peretz moved to pull the Labor Party out of Sharon's government, fulfilling his promise to the Israeli Left that he would work to reestablish the Labor Party "as a social democratic, genuine dovish opposition."[47] This move represented the final catalyst needed for Sharon to set out to implement his "big explosion"—namely, to leave the Likud and establish Kadima. This dramatic step brought about the downfall of the Likud-Labor government, opening the way for a Knesset decision to hold general elections on March 28, 2006.

Three of the four ministers who left the Likud, together with Sharon and many Likud party central council leaders who joined Kadima, came from within the close ideological nucleus of the Likud and for decades had adhered to the principle of erecting an entire Eretz Israel from the Mediterranean to the Jordan River. Kadima was also able to attract a significant portion of Likud activists, who, like the rest of their party, were strong opponents of any U.S.-Labor "peace plan" that claimed to consist of Israel's readiness to accept "the partition of the land."

MK Haim Ramon (Labor), who advocated remaining within the Likud-Labor government instead of holding elections, based his argument on what he saw regarding the emerging political map of Israel, articulating it in a manner not yet explicitly admitted by his Labor Party colleagues:

> Only a drunk person would not understand what is happening here. The [old] political map is crumbling, it is an earthquake. Everything moves. The Right [the fanatic right parties] were thrown out [of Sharon's government]. The Likud is fragmented, divided into two parties. Look what happened to Shinui and what is happening to Yachad [Meretz] [which the polls predicted would vanish and shrink, respectively, in coming elections]. And what, now we'll hold elections? . . . Are we [the Labor Party] an alternative? . . . Sharon is carrying out our policy, our platform, we have won. . . . So I think that the opposition today is not us but Uzi Landau [the leader of Sharon's opponents within the Likud and a son of a Herut leader], Epi Eitam [head of the National Religious Party (Mafdal)], and Avigdor Lieberman [head of the extreme secular right party Israel Beitenu]. They are the ones who want to

defeat him [Sharon]. . . . I don't know of any economic or social project that is more important than pulling out of Gaza.[48]

Soon after the withdrawal of the Labor Party from the government and the formation of Kadima, Haim Ramon, Shimon Peres, and a number of central Labor Party leaders joined the new party, whose victory in the coming elections is seen as a fact.

Gaza: Birthing a Bantustan

Toufic Haddad

In the wake of the destruction wrought on the Palestinian national movement in the West Bank after Operation Defensive Shield (March–April 2002; see chapter 5), Israeli strategic military operations have increasingly shifted to the Gaza Strip. This has several causes. The first three years of the Intifada witnessed an Israeli concentrated focus upon the West Bank, due largely to the strategic interests it represented for the Israeli political regime, as articulated in the Allon Plan (see Introduction). The Intifada represented the window of time in which these plans were greatly accelerated and consolidated. In addition to the expansive settlement construction that has taken place throughout the course of the Intifada, Israel has erected no less than 605 closure barriers[49] in the West Bank, designated forty-one roads fully off limits to Palestinian travel, and constructed (or sought to construct) 660 kilometers of separation wall."[50] The West Bank now [September 2005] resembles a massive matrix of contained quadrants controllable from well-defended, fixed military positions and settlements. To make this grid possible, more than 2,730 homes and workplaces in the West Bank have been completely destroyed, and an additional 39,964 others have been damaged since the beginning of the Intifada.[51]

On the other hand, Israel does not see similar interests in the Gaza Strip as envisaged by the Allon Plan and all Israeli plans thereafter. One must recall that the comparable process of ghettoization of the Gaza Strip was *already largely complete by the time the Oslo Accords were signed in 1993*. Israel has subsequently treated the Gaza Strip as an enormous open air prison and a place to which it even "exiles" Palestinians from the West Bank.[52] At the same time, however, Israel could not simply take a "laissez-faire" approach with Gaza, considering the existence of the twenty-two

Israeli settlements there, the geographical continuity the Strip has with the Egyptian Sinai, and, most important, the status Gaza holds as a bastion of national movement activity. With respect to the latter, Gaza represents the most widespread and popularly rooted concentration of Palestinian national resistance activity *anywhere*, whether political or military, despite the extreme limitations in its material conditions. Thus, the total war that Israel has launched on the Palestinian people, designed to liquidate their national, political, and social existence, is quite simply incomplete as long as the Gaza Strip remains the stronghold of such a tenacious nationalist resistance campaign.

Gaza's resistance has always been a headache for Israel; recall that Israel sought to rid itself of the Strip in the 1979 Camp David Accords by ceding it to Egypt. Furthermore, during the 1987 Intifada, Rabin famously wished he would wake up and find that it "had sunk into the sea." The resistance waged in Gaza during the current Intifada has only exacerbated this demand. All Palestinian national factions (with Hamas, Fateh, and the Popular Resistance Committees at the forefront) have engaged in a concerted guerrilla campaign since the Intifada began. With few exceptions,[53] this campaign has been almost exclusively within the confines of the Gaza Strip itself against Israeli Army soldiers and settlers.

And despite the fact that its efficacy vis-à-vis killing Israeli soldiers and settlers has been quite low in comparison to Israelis killed in attacks waged within or from the West Bank, the resistance waged in Gaza has taken place with much higher regularity and on a much higher level of sophistication than that in the West Bank.[54] In fact, the Israeli army Southern Command (responsible for Gaza) disclosed that the number of roadside bombs that exploded in the Gaza Strip in 2003 alone was equal to the number that exploded *throughout the entire eighteen years of Israel's occupation of southern Lebanon.*[55]

This said, it is important not to overestimate the power dynamics at play between the Israeli occupier and the Palestinian resistance. The Israeli Army is considered to be among the strongest armies in the world, while the Gaza fighters are armed mainly with Kalashnikovs, fertilizer bombs, and primitive rockets and mortars. In this sense, one should not exaggerate that Israel has been militarily defeated in Gaza. At the same time, Palestinian resistance is not going away, and, despite the enormous human and financial costs, the resistance destabilized the architecture of Israeli control over the Strip to the extent that it was no longer cost-effective for Israel to remain there under the old arrangement—with up to

8,000 troops and settlers in the midst of 1.4 million Palestinians. Israel has thus reconsidered its former means of control over Gaza in light of its overall strategic priorities (which primarily lie in the West Bank), resulting in a twofold policy: first, to increase the destruction and attacks against the national movement and resistance in Gaza itself; second, to reorganize the occupation in accordance with Israel's long term interests (the Israeli unilateral disengagement plan from Gaza and maneuvers to annex the settlement blocs in the West Bank). Following is a summary of what these policies entail on the ground.

A Policy of Mass Killing and Devastation

The carnage that Israel has increasingly inflicted on the Gaza Strip throughout the Intifada has been remarkable in its seeming invisibility to the outside world. Beit Hanoun, Rafah, Khan Younis, Jabaliya camp, and Gaza City have all become the targets of continuous Israeli assaults, escalating and repeating themselves with numbing regularity. On March 7, 2004, after a routine nighttime meander into Bureij refugee camp that killed fifteen Palestinians, the commander of the Israeli forces in the Gaza Strip, Brigadier General Gadi Shamni, explicitly articulated what the army was doing there. No, it wasn't "retaliating," or "acting in self-defense," or even conducting a "preemptive strike"; it was conducting a "stimulus-and-response operation," the purpose of which is "to stimulate the armed individuals to come out and then kill them off."[56]

What are the options available to Palestinians if this is the ruling logic of the occupation? While many critics have condemned the Intifada for its "militarization" on either pacifist or tactical grounds (arguing that it plays into Israel's hands), few have answers for how to relate to Israeli brutality when the option of nonviolent resistance *is* actually employed and is repeatedly crushed.[57] This is precisely what took place in the midst of Operation Rainbow, an extended "foray" into Rafah refugee camp involving more than a hundred tanks and APCs between May 12 and 24, 2004.[58] The senior Israeli commentator Ben Kaspit described what took place on May 19 when thousands of unarmed Rafah residents marched to the Tel Al Sultan neighborhood, which had been under siege for the previous three days: "'Stop them! Stop them!' shouted [Israeli] officers into their radios, 'You must stop them now!'" Four tank shells were then fired into "a deserted and damaged building, barely standing next to the winding road [presumably to scare the demonstrators away]. The truth is that it's quite fun to shoot like this, in almost clinical conditions, at such a close, station-ary target that isn't shooting back." The tank commander, we are told, "was not yet able to see the spearhead of the demonstration that was making its way toward the bend, yet heard the panicked order to fire."[59] Eight people were killed and fifty wounded, twenty-four of them children.

Israel's use of tank shells as a legitimate form of crowd control is not up for questioning. As Kaspit notes, "the IDF's response to the Palestin-ian demonstration . . . obtained the expected results [the demonstration's dispersal], but at a higher, unexpected price. The operation succeeded, but too many patients died. This was a lapse that the IDF will have to study and correct. In the meantime, they [the army] are marching forward [with Operation Rainbow]. There is no other option. *Halting the operation at this stage will cause a chain reaction. The entire Gaza Strip will rise up and start marching toward IDF tanks with the certain knowledge that it is possible, in this way, to chase out the army.*" [Emphasis added]

Sixty-six residents of Rafah were killed in Operation Rainbow alone;[60] 261 homes (home to 3,352 people) were completely destroyed and an ad-ditional 271 were severely damaged, rendering the homes of an additional 4,069 people unlivable or unsafe.[61]

Israel's policies of wanton killing and destruction reached new heights in Operation Days of Penitence, unleashed on Jabaliya refugee camp and Beit Lahiya in the north of the Strip between September 28 and October 15, 2004.[62] According to the United Nations, approximately 36,000 Pales-tinians were besieged for seventeen straight days while 4,000 others were forced to flee their homes.[63] The assault resulted in at least 103 Palestinian deaths (28 of whom were children); 83 homes, 18 workplaces, and 19 public institutions (including six schools and three mosques) destroyed; and 210 acres of agricultural land completely razed.

Indeed, the level of Israeli repression reached in Gaza makes the dev-astation witnessed in the case of Jenin Camp and Nablus during the March–April 2002 Israeli invasions of West Bank cities look increasingly like "a question of perspective."

Targeting Focal Activists and the Assassination of Sheikh Ahmed Yassin

But there is also method in this madness. Israel has not just concentrated upon sowing random carnage. It has also done all within its power to tar-get, when possible, the key political and field cadres who have worked to advance and improve the organization and quality of the Gaza resistance. These cadres are not as accessible to the occupation as they are in the West Bank, which has been under full and direct Israeli military control since April 2002.[64] Israel therefore primarily focuses upon assassinating activists in Gaza with the use of attack helicopters and missile-fitted unmanned drones. As always in these operations, assassinations continue to be used as an escalatory measure that thickens the fog of "warlike conditions," facilitating yet more bloody maneuvers on the ground.

It would be impossible to go through the 130 key personalities Israel has targeted and killed in Gaza in this period (January 2004–September 2005) or to tell their stories, which are highly significant regarding the Palestinian historical narrative. To the international corporate media, they are anonymous "Palestinian militants" involved in "organizing terror against Israel." To Palestinians in Gaza, they are heroes who, despite all odds, sacrifice their lives to the dream that life not be one condemned to the misery, humiliation, poverty, and injustice of Gaza today.

Nonetheless, it would be incomplete to cover this period without mentioning the assassination on March 21, 2004, of Sheikh Ahmed Yassin, the spiritual leader and founder of Hamas, as well as mentioning that his successor, Abdel Aziz Al Rantisi, was also killed on April 17, 2004.[65] Their deaths, in a nutshell, provide evidence that what Israel seeks to do is not just kill certain leaders but in fact eradicate the organic movements behind them, which incubate Palestinian social and national cohesion and have arisen from previous Israeli attempts to destroy the national movement.

Sheikh Yassin was no difficult target for Israel—a sixty-eight-year-old quadriplegic who was largely deaf and blind. Nonetheless, Israel made him out to be "the godfather of the suicide bombers," who represented a local instantiation of Israel's very own "war on terror"—the crucial framework of logic that has served to "justify" and integrate U.S. and Israeli actions. In the words of Silvan Shalom [Israeli foreign minister in Sharon's Likud government], "We have a global battle against this terrorism. . . . Those extremist organizations, like al-Qaeda, Hamas, Hezbollah, Islamic Jihad, and the others, are motivated by an extreme ideology, to change the world. They are fighting those countries that share the same values as we share, of democracy, of freedom, of human rights, of rule of law. . . . So it's very, very simple. . . . That's why we should do everything we can, because we are protecting our people by fighting against this global phenomenon that is threatening the entire world, and all the democratic countries."[66]

The mileage this line of justification has received in the Western press is mind-boggling, especially considering the nature of the powers that promote it (the Zionist movement and the U.S. ruling classes). Unfortunately, the successes achieved by this alliance can be attributed primarily to the weakness of the international Left and the rote dehumanization of Arabs and Muslims after September 11, 2001 (accepted by most liberals as well), combined with the high level of ignorance and misunderstanding surrounding leaders like Yassin and the movement he founded.

Yassin, a founder of Hamas, was a symbolic leader of a broad political and social current within Palestinian society that represented steadfastness and defiance for the thousands of Palestinians who refuse to give up their rights to self-determination and of return, despite the repeated political and military defeats of the centrist Fateh-led PLO. Hamas's growth must also be seen in the light of the sense of betrayal wide swaths of Palestinians felt after the PLO signed the Oslo Accords and the political and institutional corruption the majority of Palestinians felt this ushered in to the national movement. Neither Yassin nor Hamas has ever had anything to do with any Huntingtonian clash of civilization. Though activists in Hamas may have used similar discourse in the past (always to the detriment of Hamas's cause), Yassin himself was known to be a moderate force within Hamas (and arguably within the national movement overall), confining his demands and that of the party to the Palestinian political center—a full withdrawal to 1967 lines, in exchange for a cease-fire. At the same time, Hamas, like all other Palestinian factions, including the grass roots of the Fateh movement, refuse to concede claims to pre-1948 Palestine and the right of Palestinian refugees to return.

When the prominent Israeli journalist Amira Hass asked what the purpose of the present Intifada was, Yassin responded, "The primary purpose of the Intifada today is to expel the occupation from the 1967 borders. The future will decide the fate of what remains of the soil of Palestine."[67] When Hass pushed Yassin on how "the terrorist attacks inside Israel are strengthening the view of Israelis that you [Hamas] want to 'throw them into the sea,'" Yassin revealed the centrist position he held: "No Palestinian says that we want to throw the Jews into the sea. The Palestinians always say that they want to live on the lands of our forebears and that all of us—Muslims, Jews, and Christians—will live together in the spirit of democracy. But the problem is that the Jews don't want to give the others their rights. They want to establish a racist regime. . . . We have never imposed our principles, nor do we want to dictate them with force. There is no dictate. To each his own religion in a state that will respect all human rights."

No doubt Yassin's political discourse twisted and confused Palestinian national rights with religious language and justifications, obfuscating the genuine nature of Palestinian oppression. But even with this said, his movement's success was based on the defense of Palestinian political and national rights, not Palestinian religious beliefs, and Israel understood that well enough to sign his death warrant.

Disengaging from Gaza: Reorganizing the Occupation

The enormous toll of destruction incrementally leveled against Gaza also served the purpose of preparing the ground for Israel's unilateral disengagement, which ultimately took place between August 15 and September 12, 2005. Through this destruction, Israel sought to convey the unequivocal message that the disengagement did not derive from a concession to Palestinian resistance but was rather the product of Israel's position of strength. Though this may indeed be the case, Palestinian resistance forces have also been keen to point out that were it not for the resistance, Israel would never have considered disengaging from Gaza in the first place. Mohammed Deif, head of the Hamas military wing in Gaza and a five-time survivor of Israeli assassination attempts, released an extended audio recording in the wake of Sharon's decision to disengage, celebrating the victories of Palestinian resistance of all factions and not just Hamas: "The criminal Sharon was elected to smash our resistance in one hundred days. But now the man who once said [the isolated Gaza settlement of] Netzarim was just like Tel Aviv is planning to withdraw from Gaza without anything in return."[68]

Debates over the role of the resistance in bringing about the disengagement have added significance when viewed in the context of Israel's historical policies of controlling Palestinians geostrategically. The predisengagement "borders" of Israel's presence within the Gaza Strip were, from a strategic and military perspective, impractical, cost-ineffective, and, to some extent, indefensible in the long term, when confronted by the daily guerrilla struggle that emerged in Gaza during the Al Aqsa Intifada. These "borders" were made up of at least 45 kilometers of exposed terrain (including the borders of settlements and settlement blocs, military positions and their respective access roads) upon which Israel was required to have a "forward military presence" so as to ensure their basic "defense."[69] With the development of locally engineered medium-range resistance capacities during the present Intifada (mortars and primitive rockets), which were directed at the settlers and the army on a daily basis, Palestinian resistance forces were able to strike at occupation targets from a distance and then escape. This exposed the weaknesses of the predisengagement military and settler map in Gaza, making it untenable. Israel's disengagement plan was in part thus designed to reconfigure the map to give the geostrategic upper hand back to the Israeli army. By removing the settler population and repositioning the Israeli Army primarily on Gaza's borders, while continuing to maintain full control over its land, air, and seas, Israel effectively imposed a containment regime of the Strip that provided less immediate targets for the Palestinian resistance, while obfuscating international opinion regarding the status of Gaza's occupation.[70]

Here it is important to see that the "disengagement," as a tactical redeployment to more effective positions of control, was *not* unprecedented in Israeli policy but actually the *continuation* of similar historical maneuvers. It is precisely the same logic that motivated Israel's geostrategic maneuvers in the wake of the mass uprising of the 1987 Intifada and later embodied in the Oslo Accords. Israel simply used the Oslo Accords to withdraw its military from the major Palestinian population concentrations, repositioning them to the outskirts of the major Palestinian cities, and (again) sold the maneuver as "a step toward peace." The Gaza disengagement is simply a revision of this former map so as to adjust to the new military balance created after almost five years of resistance of a different kind. However, the principle behind both of these tactical maneuvers remains the same: withdrawal from the areas of least strategic significance to Israel, containing these areas, and maintaining their economic, social, and political subjugation in Israel's ever-tightening grip— all, of course, under the banner of "paying the price for peace."[71]

Disengagement Spectacle Subtext

If Israel's intentions through the disengagement were not clear enough— to determine through force a new colonial reality on the ground, a new political reality internationally, and a new Palestinian sociopolitical order—there is something yet more sinister in the way in which the disengagement has been sold to the international community. Meaning that the disengagement's spectacle not only leaves an impossible geographic, demographic, and sociopolitical reality; it also leaves a damaging subtext and false logic that has perhaps more dangerous implications than the wasteland of Gaza itself—a wasteland of 40 percent unemployment rate; 80

percent poverty rate; 5.2 percent annual birthrate; shrinking land reserves, an environmental disaster area, almost no potable water, 75 percent refugee population, with the list going on and on. What could be more damaging than this? The anatomy of the disengagement subtext reads as follows:

False Symmetry

Sharon moved against his extremists; it's time for the Palestinians to move against theirs.

The false parallel between a government-subsidized settler colonial movement and Palestinian national resistance actors from all factions, empowered by all international humanitarian conventions to resist occupation, is designed to build on the dehumanization of Arabs and Muslim in the Western media mind-set. This false symmetry has now become the litmus test for whether "political progress can be made," when in fact Israel has no intention of making any "political progress."

Unrepeatable Trauma

The negative effect of the disengagement upon Israeli society is so severe it cannot reasonably be expected to be repeated.

Functionally this simply means that Israel can continue settlement expansion, while sympathy is aroused for the settler colonial society, not for the colonized society, which suffered (and will continue to suffer) under the occupation's boot.

Israeli "Law and Order" Versus Palestinian Anarchy

Israel used its army and police to carry out a well-organized "disengagement." In the absence of a comparable Palestinian security force regime, Israel has no need to relate to them.

The standard of judging whether this has been achieved can be measured only by the U.S./Israeli-defined criteria of "dismantling the infrastructure of terror"—political arrests of resistance personnel, the confiscation of weapons, the disbanding of all factions who oppose these plans, and so on. Here again Palestinians can prove they are "worthy" enough only by proving how repressive they can be against their own people.

Carte Blanche

Israel has the right to respond severely if Palestinian military operations continue.

This is a rejigged version of the false paradigm witnessed after the Camp David summit in July 2000, whereby "Israeli generosity" was met with Palestinian "rejectionism and terrorism." Today Israel is likewise laying the groundwork for a devastating blow against all those who would continue to oppose and resist the continued occupation of Gaza and the West Bank, even though this occupation is now supposedly less visible to the outside world. For every compliment Israel receives for its disengagement, it functionally receives carte blanche to do what it needs against the Palestinians when they resist the continued occupation of their land. Indeed Israel's top generals have already promised such a harsh and unprecedented response if Palestinian resistance continues.

Normalization of Transfer

With Sharon's decision to forcibly remove the settlers of Gaza, transfer of populations is now functionally legitimized internationally as an acceptable methodology for "paying the price for peace."

If one day the situation arises whereby Israel finds the opportunity to actively transfer Palestinians, on a small or large scale, in the West Bank or even Palestinian citizens of Israel (whether forcefully or "legally"), the international community can "understand" this necessity based on the disengagement's precedent. The refusal of the settlers to leave Gaza has inscribed the logic that "They may not like it, but it is the best for everyone."

Conclusion

Needless to say, the script for the scenarios the disengagement spectacle has erected is already in play. Israeli military chiefs have begun speculating about how Israel's generosity in disengaging has already gone unappreciated and that this may result in "the renewal of terrorist activity," which will necessitate an "Israeli response."[72] No one is talking about how the main valves that control practically every facet of life in the Gaza Strip remain firmly in Israel's hands, only now with the illusion that they are in Palestinian hands.

Finally, we are reminded by the top Israeli commentator Uzi Benziman of what happened in similar episodes in the past. Writing at the end of August 2005, Benziman noted, "On June 5, 1982, five weeks after Israel completed its withdrawal from Sinai in accordance with the peace treaty with Egypt, the IDF invaded Lebanon in what was known as Operation Peace for the Galilee. Was the timing coincidental? Not necessarily. The large-scale Oranim Plan for the invasion of Lebanon had been ready six months before but was not implemented until after the complete evacuation of Sinai."[73]

The point is that after Israel's "disengagement" from Gaza, Israel will have ample political capital, both domestically and internationally, to conduct a wide array of devastating operations not only against the Palestinians and their national movement, but also possibly within other regional arenas. The question hereafter must not be if this capital will be spent but rather where and how it will be spent. Whatever scenario arises, though, the birth of the Gaza Bantustan with wide-scale international blessing has already proven that many, many things that service the agenda of U.S. regional hegemony and Israel are possible today that simply were not possible in previous years.

CHAPTER 10

Expanding Regionally, Resisting Locally: "He Who Wants Peace Prepares for War"

October 2005–November 2006

Introduction

The year 2006 witnessed the widening of the boundaries of legitimate Zionism to encompass even the most extreme, overtly racist right wing in Israel. This wide consensus cut almost completely across the Israeli political spectrum, as common ground was shared regarding the need for a neoliberal economy, a war strategy toward the Palestinians, and the elimination of "radical nationalism" throughout the Middle East.

The results of the Israeli general elections of March 28, 2006, brought the Labor Party in to serve as a senior member of the Kadima government, headed by Ehud Olmert. Soon after, Labor Party Chairman Amir Peretz, the former head of the Histadrut, quickly forgot the promises he had made during the election campaign to reform the "wild" neoliberal economy and transform the Labor Party into a social democratic party. Instead, and with his consent, the government continued to privatize strategic state assets. He also gave approval to further cut government expenditures in the 2007 annual budget, thereby exacerbating preexisting income gaps that make Israel the second worst in this category in the entire Western world.

As defense minister, Peretz also led the U.S.-inspired wars that Israel launched against the Lebanese and Palestinian resistance movements. But the determination and steadfastness of Hezbollah brought about the military defeat of the Israeli Army in the July–August 2006 war and, with it, the failure of Israel to achieve any of its aims: eliminating Hezbollah's resistance capabilities and moral potency in the Arab world and strengthening a pro-U.S./Israel government in Lebanon. This failure, however, did not cause the United States and Israel to give up their aims, only to reformulate how to go about trying to achieve them.

On the Palestinian front, Israel set about using the geographic advantages it acquired as a consequence of the "unilateral disengagement" to choke Gaza into full submission. It was aided in this task by the victory of Hamas in the January 2006 elections and the subsequent financial and political blockade initiated against the Palestinians by the United States, European Union, and Arab states. Hamas's victory was nonetheless an important victory for the popular currents that had launched the Intifada and sustained it from its inception, and quickly turned Gaza into the capital of the reformulating Palestinian national project. The Hamas government's moves to realign the Palestinian movement from within organizationally and politically, combining this within a resistance-inclined framework, immediately placed the Hamas government in Israel's magnified gun sights.

Israel saw the Hamas victory as the opportunity to accelerate the task it had set itself from the beginning of the Intifada: to destroy the Palestinian national movement once and for all. Having largely successfully destroyed Fateh under Arafat, crushed the PA infrastructure in the West Bank, and killed and imprisoned thousands of Palestinian leaders throughout the past six years of Intifada, the time was now ripe to go after the remaining Palestinian national stronghold of Gaza, as the seat of the democratically elected Hamas government and the reformulating national movement.

Following the successful abduction of an Israeli soldier by Palestinian resistance forces in June for the purpose of conducting a prisoner exchange, Israel launched a series of raids against Gaza, resulting in 434 killed (82 of whom were children, and 25 women) between June 25 and November 15, 2006.[1] One such raid (Operation Autumn Clouds) entailed a ten-day blitz into the northern Gaza town of Beit Hanoun, killing 90 Palestinians and destroying 450 homes. Though the Israeli government claimed to have launched the raids to counter the continual rockets Palestinians were firing at southern Israeli towns (in an effort to create deterrence against Israel's continued assassinations and artillery fire), the Israeli media were explicit about the fact that the raids had an entirely different aim, namely, to normalize the direct use of the Israeli Army inside Gaza urban areas after the "disengagement" in preparation for the "large-scale, painful" operation Israel sought inevitably to conduct there. This repeated the precise discourse Israel had used in the run-up to Operation Defensive Shield, launched against the West Bank in March–April 2002, which resulted in hundreds killed and the infrastructure of Palestinian social, political, security, and economic life decimated.

Never before had the differences between the Labor Party and the Right Wing in Israel been blurred to such an extent. By October 2006, the Labor Party leadership resoundingly agreed to the participation of the most overtly racist character in Israeli politics, Avigdor Lieberman, in the Kadima-Labor government.

Lieberman calls, among other things, for stripping the great majority of 1948 Palestinian citizens of Israel of their citizenship (if they "refuse to serve in the army"), transferring them to the walled-up ghettos Israel is creating for the Palestinians in the 1967 Occupied Territories, and sentencing the "traitor" 1948 Palestinian leaders in the Knesset to death. He also calls for the establishment of a presidential regime, as opposed to a parliamentary democracy—a demand that in essence would greatly weaken Israel's formal democratic structure.

The Labor Party's collaboration with Lieberman laid bare the true nature of its traditional "pragmatism"—the very quality that had sanitized Kadima's unilateral "convergence" plan to the world. Though the war against Lebanon in the summer of 2006 canceled this cunning version of a "peace solution," Israel and the United States found greater maneuverability in working for the establishment of a "New Middle East." This joint U.S.-Israel plan redefines the liquidation of the Palestinian national movement and society as part of the war against the axis of evil—thereby enabling the incorporation of full blown methods of warfare against the Palestinians as a direct extension of Israeli and U.S. planned attacks against Syria and Iran.

Thus today's Labor Party, as the product of the historic Zionist labor movement, has peaked in its traditional role of supplying the moral legitimacy for Israel's colonialist policies of dispossession and ethnic cleansing. This final stage of overtly legitimizing the most extreme right-wing elements of Zionism, which it historically opposed, ends the distinct role the Zionist labor movement played in implementing Zionist colonialism. The central premises of its old-time misleading pragmatism have been formally accepted by this extreme wing of Zionism. By now, both definitively agree on the need for a Jewish majority as the defining criteria for engaging in their euphemistically entitled "political compromise," embodied in a cantonized Palestinian entity led by a fully collaborative leadership. This "political compromise," however, is not a compromise with the Palestinians but a compromise with the very ideology of Zionism—temporarily allowing for the presence of Palestinians behind the caging walls of such an entity, until expedient circumstances permit otherwise.

Thus, the process of "kosherizing" Lieberman in fact brings the Zionist Labor movement's role to its logical end. By legitimizing the most extreme margins of the Zionist movement, it challenges the very facade the Zionist Left created to protect and legitimate the cruelest atrocities it practiced against the Palestinian and Arab world for years—the claim that the Zionist project adhered to universal humanistic values and democracy. The decisive majority the new governing coalition enjoys in the Knesset (78 seats in the 120-seat parliament), combined with the moral support provided by enlightened Zionist intellectuals, ensures that Israel's terrifying polices can continue unimpeded.

The redefinition of the Israeli-Palestinian "conflict" in terms of a "war on terror," led by the U.S.-Israeli alliance across the Middle East, confirms that a solution to the question of Palestine can be found only through the deep transformation of the Arab world and the Zionist state. This will be possible only after a sustained battle against U.S.-Israeli hegemony in the Middle East and the treachery of the Arab regimes that oppress their people. At present, this battle is embodied primarily in the resistance struggles of Islamic movements throughout the region, thereby necessitating the tactical support and participation of progressive forces locally, regionally, and internationally toward this common end.

Israeli 2006 Elections: An Umbrella for the War on the Palestinians, Lebanon, and the Entire Middle East

Tikva Honig-Parnass

The major stroke suddenly suffered by Prime Minister Sharon on January 4, 2006, at the start of the general election campaign, brought in Ehud Olmert as his replacement to head-up the newly founded Kadima party.

It also made him the likely future prime minister if predictions regarding Kadima's success at the polls came true. Declaring himself the heir apparent to Sharon's political vision, Olmert called for continuing the policies of unilateralism, this time in the West Bank. Euphemistically called the "convergence" or "realignment" plan, and often interpreted to mean withdrawal from the West Bank, this plan offered nothing more than "a formalization of the program of annexing the valuable lands and most of the resources, including water, of the West Bank, while cantonizing and imprisoning the rest, since he [Olmert] has also announced that Israel will take over the Jordan Valley."[2]

The Labor Party, which continued to support this version of unilateralism in its election campaign, not surprisingly joined the Kadima-led government established after the election. As a senior partner in the government coalition, the Labor Party played a pivotal role in the brutal war launched against Gaza and Lebanon in the summer of 2006. The Labor-Kadima collaboration expressed the wide consensus in Israeli Jewish society about the approach of unilaterally enforcing Israel's dictates as part of the prolonged war strategy adopted after the end of the Oslo negotiation years, while misleadingly presenting its necessity as a consequence of Palestinian rejectionism. The Zionist Left's behavior during the election campaign directly contributed to the disastrous assault later launched against Gaza and Lebanon. It also sheds light upon future scenarios after Israel's defeat in Lebanon—the strengthening of the right wing, for example—and paved the path to Israel playing a more active public role in future U.S.-led catastrophes, including threatened attacks against Iran, which have the potential to set fire to the entire Middle East.

The Election Campaign and Results

A description of the political platforms of the Kadima and Labor parties explains the unfulfilled expectations of both and their collaboration in the coalition government erected after the elections in April 2006.

The Fata Morgana of Amir Peretz

The emergence of Amir Peretz as chairman of the Labor Party and its candidate for prime minister in the March 28 general elections aroused hope among many in the Israeli Left, particularly when compared with Sharon's and Kadima's policies (which the previous Labor Party leadership had, incidentally, also supported). This hope, however, could not rationally base itself on any declared alternative strategy of Peretz and the Labor Party regarding a solution to the Israeli-Palestinian "conflict." From the beginning of the election campaign, it was clear that there were no major differences in this regard between Labor and Kadima. The Labor Party's new chairman declared early on as part of his campaign that "it is Kadima that adopted the Labor Party's position regarding political and security [sic] matters." "So why should the public vote for you?" asked a political commentator from Israeli television Channel 1. "[Because] we are the original," answered Peretz proudly.[3]

The claim of authors' rights to Kadima's political positions was repeated by Meretz MK and spokesperson Zehava Galon, known as the "most leftist" of the Meretz leadership. Galon lamented how "Kadima is now harvesting the fruits" of the wide impact of Meretz's "peace approach" on the Israeli public.[4] The similarity between the Zionist Left's positions and those of Kadima was also pointed out as early as January 28, 2006, in a Ha'aretz editorial: "From the moment that Olmert agreed to open negotiations on a settlement with the Palestinians [which by November 2006 had not taken place], and when Peretz agreed to unilateral steps if these negotiations fail, the two parties have positioned themselves on the same starting line vis-à-vis the Palestinians."

Thus, the January 25, 2006, victory of Hamas in the Palestinian Legislative Council elections gave Peretz the excuse to revive the "no partner" slogan, initially concocted by former Labor Party Prime Minister Ehud Barak,[5] and to support the Olmert government's policy of total war against the Palestinians in the months leading up to the Israeli elections, albeit from the opposition.[6] This included boycotting the Hamas government, ending tax payments to the PA (which Israel collects from Palestinian imports), starving the Gaza Strip, escalating the daily assassinations of Palestinians, and strengthening the siege on the entire 1967 Occupied Territories, turning them into one big prison. This allows the Israeli Left to hide behind the self-contradictory slogan that it seeks "unilateralism with an agreement."[7]

Indeed, wide sections of the Israeli "peace camp," even its radical wings, did not welcome the democratic victory of Hamas. They claimed that Hamas's Islamic worldview contradicted their secular, enlightened self-image. This blocked their ability to recognize the resistance-based essence of Hamas' popularity among wider swaths of Palestinians, well beyond the scope of its religious membership. Nowhere did the Zionist Left bother to respond to analysts like Azmi Bishara, who time and again emphasized that in supporting Hamas, the Palestinian people were declaring that they opposed the former PA policies, which had succumbed to Israeli dictates. Nor did their general political view allow them to relate to the anti-imperialist essence inherent in Hamas's resistance, shared with Hezbollah and other Islamic resistance movements throughout the Middle East. At present, these forces often represent the only significant political forces carrying on this battle.[8] Despite this, most of the Israeli Left refused to see the nationalist rationalism of Hamas's election platform, instead continuing to see the Hamas Charter as proof of the movement's assumed racism and anti-Semitism.[9]

Thus, it was not his "peace" credentials that made Amir Peretz a promising leader for the Left but rather his socioeconomic platform, which misleadingly claimed to fight the most damaging effects of the neoliberal economy. Between the end of 2005 and March 2006, the Israeli Left was captive to the mirage that appeared on the political horizon that promised that the Labor Party would be transformed into a social democratic, authentic" Left party.[10] Many within the Left assumed that there are indeed political elements within the Labor Party and the Zionist Left in general who are loyal to the imaginary past of a "socialist Zionism" and hence are ready to fight against the neoliberal trends that have taken control of the historic Zionist Labor movement.

These false hopes were also based upon promises made by Peretz to his constituency, that he would introduce a law raising the minimum wage to U.S. $1,000 a month, issue new taxes that would target the wealthy, and enlarge government expenditures, rolling back cuts in child allowances, pensions, and so on.[11] Peretz's surprising victory over the old Labor Party leader Shimon Peres in the primaries was interpreted by the representatives of the bourgeoisie in the Labor Party as confirming the possibility that these promised reforms, identified as destructive "neosocialist" steps, might indeed be implemented. Moreover, the immediate desertion of Shimon Peres to Kadima after his defeat brought with it the desertion of 250,000 to 300,000 traditional Labor Party supporters, largely deriving from the well-to-do middle classes, who were estimated to fill up about five seats in the coming Knesset.[12]

The introduction of Avishai Braveman, a professor of economy and president of Birsheva University, into the inner decision-making circles around Peretz was meant to halt this well-to-do middle-class desertion. Braveman, well known for his "moderate" neoliberalism, set out to mitigate the "radical" discourse of Peretz's economic platform. He emphasized that the worldview that underlined it heads toward moderate reforms and not toward a fundamental change in the capitalistic structure of Israel's economy. Peretz hurried to reduce the concerns of the bourgeoisie: "It is possible to keep a free-market [economy] but one that has rules—so it does not bring all of us to operate according to the 'law of the jungle' without restraints."[13]

The diluted socioeconomic message of the Labor Party permitted Kadima and Likud to adopt similar slogans. All three big parties thus came out with "a social agenda," thereby refuting Labor's self-professed unique socioeconomic platform, which had justified voting for it. In fact, anyone in the Left who did not have eyes shut could easily discern that Israel's political map continued to reflect the wide consensus it held in the near past around Sharon's political and economic policies. As Haim Baram warned in January 2006:

> All—from Netanyahu [Likud] on the right, to Peretz on the left—attempt to gather beneath the umbrella of the nationalist center. Even Yossi Beilin speaks about Meretz candidates to the Knesset in terms of future ministers, expressing, in fact, his willingness to participate in a government of political paralysis, and argues for only cosmetic reforms in socioeconomic matters.[14]

Thus again, the Zionist Left's attempts to create a distinct political discourse ended with the disclosure that it is part and parcel of the prevailing racist political culture in Israel. This explains its willingness to join the Kadima-Labor government and its war strategy, as was understood by *Ha'aretz* commentator Gideon Levy. Writing two days before the elections, Levy noted:

> Contrary to appearances, the elections this week are important, because they will expose the true face of Israeli society and its hidden ambitions. More than 100 elected candidates will be sent to the Knesset on the basis of one ticket—the racism ticket. . . . Election 2006 will make this much clearer than ever before. An absolute majority of the MKs in the seventeenth Knesset will hold a position based on a lie: that Israel does not have a partner for peace. An absolute majority of MKs in the next Knesset do not believe in peace, nor do they even want it—just like their voters—and worse than that, don't regard Palestinians as equal human beings. Racism has never had so many open supporters. It's the real hit of this election campaign.
> Nobody is speaking about peace with them, nobody really wants it. Only one ambition unites everyone: to get rid of them, one way or another. Transfer or wall, "disengagement" or "convergence"—the point is that they should get out of our sight. The only game in town, the "unilateral arrangement," is not only based on the lie that there is no partner, is not only based exclusively on our "needs" because of a sense of superiority, but also leads to a dangerous pattern of behavior that totally ignores the existence of the other nation.[15]

Results

Everything Levy predicted came true, and worse. Kadima emerged from the elections as the largest single party, securing 29 seats in the Knesset. But it still needed the Labor Party's 19 seats, Shas's 11 seats, and the Pensioners' Party's (Mifleget Hagimlaim) 7 seats to form a more solid core for its coalition government.[16] Peretz, however, was denied any of the ministries related to socioeconomic policies and instead was nominated minister of defense. This was aimed at ensuring a smooth continuity in policy vis-à-vis economic neoliberalism, backed by the understanding that once Peretz took up his position, he would have to accept the parameters of the hyperneoliberal society that Israel has become. And indeed, in the midst of the war in Lebanon, the government decided to go ahead with the privatization of its oil refineries in Ashdod, selling them for U.S. $764 million (3.25 billion shekels) to one of Israel's biggest capitalists, the Paz Company.[17]

Kadima could also rely on Peretz to faithfully continue its policies of building the apartheid wall in the West Bank, starving Gaza, and daily assassinating Palestinians. In an attempt to make sure that the public understood the meaning of the policy Peretz committed himself to, the general staff of the army disclosed its adherence to an eternal war strategy against the Palestinians, arguing that it represents the continuation of a prolonged confrontation that began with the Zionist colonization of Palestine. In documents leaked to *Ha'aretz* the day before the new government was due to take its oath of office (April 14, 2006), the senior *Ha'aretz* analyst Amir Oren (who has close relations with the military establishment), wrote a report entitled "Will the Sword Strike for Eternity? The General Staff Determines—Yes [it will]." Oren states, "The Qassam [rockets] and [Palestinian] military attacks are not going to end—not this week, not this year, not this decade, and maybe not in this century. As far as the eye can see, this is our life and death. Bloody confrontations without end, in all the generations to come." What has happened in the last six years is the tenth confrontation between Israelis and Arabs since 1929.[18]

Indeed, all throughout the election campaign and two months after the establishment of the Kadima-Labor government, the full siege and starvation of the Gaza Strip continued shamelessly. This was meant to push Hamas into confrontation, allowing for Israel to try to topple and crush the movement given its ascendance to the center of Palestinian resistance. Together with the provocations committed in South Lebanon against Hezbollah, which did not stop after Israel withdrew from most of southern Lebanon in May 2000,[19] Israel, with the blessing of the United States, was waiting for the right circumstances to strike at the advances of the resistance groups both locally (Hamas) and regionally (Hezbollah).

Hence, the abduction of the Israeli soldiers (one in Gaza on June 24, the other in Lebanon on July 12) provided Israel with the opportunity to launch its preplanned assaults, which were seen as the condition for the success of the U.S.-Israeli project for the entire region—namely, to do away with the results of the very U.S. demands for "reform" and "democracy" that, in addition to bringing about the catastrophe of Afghanistan and Iraq, had also brought about the Hamas victory over Fateh in the Palestinian Authority elections and the strengthening of Hezbollah in Lebanon after the "Cedar Revolution" of 2005. They also sought to do away with the enormous acclaim that Hezbollah and its leader, Hassan Nasrallah, have received throughout the region, whose resistance serves as a model for challenging U.S.-Israel hegemony in the region. Hence, Israel's wars against Gaza and Lebanon were launched with the urgency of trying to block the spread of the resistance/democratic processes to U.S. client states in the Middle East.

Black July 2006: The Devastating Assaults on Gaza and Lebanon

The Kadima-Labor government rose to the occasion by launching unprecedented bloody onslaughts on Gaza and Lebanon, led by Amir Peretz as minister of defense and supported by a wall-to-wall consensus within Israeli society. The role of the Left in this unholy alliance was, however, no new phenomenon, as admitted by the senior *Yediot Ahronot* commentator Shimon Shifer: "It is not the first time that precisely a government that consists of 'peace lovers' and not of 'warmongers' from the Right is ready to commit extreme moves that involve great harm to innocent people."[20]

As previously mentioned, the Israeli Army had been preparing for a massive attack on the Gaza Strip for months and was constantly pushing for it.[21] Among other things, Israel's escalated provocations in Gaza aimed at mobilizing support for the plan among the Israeli Left, as well as among international public opinion, including the U.S. Arab client states. The prospect of gaining this support was certainly promising and had been strengthened by hailing the staged disengagement from the Gaza Strip in August–September 2005 as a "withdrawal to recognized international boundaries." This permitted the depiction of the continued Palestinian resistance there as refusing Israel's "goodwill," and contributed a pretext for Israel to go on the rampage.[22]

The provocative steps taken in June 2006 finally brought about the desired pretext. On June 8, Israel assassinated Jamal Abu Samhadana, a senior appointee of the Hamas government, within the context of Israel intensifying its artillery shelling of Gaza and bringing about massive civilian casualties. On June 23, two Gaza civilians, a doctor and his brother, were abducted by the Israeli Army. Only on the next day did the abduction of the Israeli soldier take place—the event Israel considered the casus belli for implementing its plans. Thus, on June 28, Israel's enlarged operation commenced, beginning the destruction of Gaza's civilian infrastructure and the mass detention of the Hamas leadership in the West Bank—totaling 64 democratically elected ministers, parliamentarians, and governors.

Indications of Hamas's preparedness to reach a prisoner exchange agreement were not welcomed by Israel. The agreement, solidified by Egyptian President Hosni Mubarak's envoy General Omar Suleiman, called for a comprehensive cease-fire and the release of the Israeli soldier in exchange for the release of Palestinian prisoners held in Israeli jails—mainly women, children under the age of sixteen, old-time prisoners jailed for more than twenty years, and sick prisoners. Israel demanded, however, that prior to any negotiations, the abducted soldier be released and refused to indicate in advance how many Palestinians it would release.[23] While negotiating, Israel also continued shooting and abducting Palestinians, and bombing and firing shells at their refugee camps with F-16s and tanks. In July alone, 176 Palestinians were killed in what Israel described as Israeli "policing operations," including destroying houses and infrastructure, bombing the main power plant, and making the lives of its 1.4 million residents even more of a living hell than it had been before.[24]

Lebanon

Nor was Israel ready to begin negotiations with Hezbollah regarding the release of the two soldiers it had captured on the northern border. At a news conference held in Beirut within hours of the abductions, Israeli newspapers reported that "Hezbollah's leader Sheikh Hassan Nasrallah explained that its aim was to reach a prisoner exchange where, in return for the two captured Israeli soldiers, Israel would return three Lebanese prisoners it had refused to release in a previous prisoner exchange. Nasrallah declared that 'he did not want to drag the region into war' but added that 'our current restraint is not due to weakness. . . . If they [Israel] choose to confront us, they must be prepared for surprises.'"[25] The Israeli government, however, did not give a single moment for negotiations or even to calmly reflect upon the situation. The cabinet meeting that same day authorized a massive offensive on Lebanon. Moreover, it made sure to target the Lebanese civilian population and infrastructure rather than focusing on Hezbollah targets alone, as had been the case in previous exchanges between the two. Its justification for implementing such a strategy in its preplanned attack was voiced in the cabinet's unanimous agreement that the Lebanese government should be held responsible for the events. Prime Minister Olmert declared, "This morning's events are not a *terror* attack, but the act of a *sovereign state* that attacked Israel for no reason and without provocation." He added that "the Lebanese government, of which Hezbollah is a part, is trying to undermine *regional* stability. *Lebanon is responsible, and Lebanon will bear the consequences of its actions.*" [Emphasis added.][26]

The cynicism expressed in changing the definition of the "enemy" from a "terror organization" to the entire state of Lebanon because "the Lebanese government refuses to actualize its sovereignty in the south of Lebanon" was expressed by "one of the most senior government ministers," who intentionally blurred the distinction between the two, as reported by the *Yediot Ahronot* political commentator Sima Kadmon on July 14, 2006: "At the beginning [of the Israeli attack on Lebanon] it will be bad, but later it will be good. Why good? Because in the [framework of the] war on terror, we could not fully activate our power. But now we can, and we will, and may God have mercy on them."

With his use of the word "now," the unnamed minister expressed his delight at Israel's capacity to legitimize means of war between states. Continuing with his cunning interpretation, the minister explains that "An army has attacked the state of Israel. It is as if Syria had begun an aggression against us. The Hezbollah army has committed an operation against us. And because this organization is dependent upon public support, this is the moment to liquidate it, and to turn Lebanon into a wasteland. After that, things will be good."

The political aim behind targeting the Lebanese people and state while devastating its infrastructure was also openly disclosed—namely, the joint U.S.-Israeli intent to "change the structure of government in

Lebanon and transform it into an ally of the United States, a good neighbor to Israel and a participant in U.S.-oriented alliances in the region."[27] This aim was acknowledged through public declarations of U.S. Secretary of State Condoleezza Rice, who claimed that Israel's catastrophic assault on Lebanon embodied the "birth pangs of the new Middle East." It indicated a departure from past strategy, whereby the United States used to hide its fingerprints on the dirty jobs Israel committed in the service of its imperial master and upon whose hegemony Israel's colonial interests have been dependent.

From the very beginning, official Israeli and U.S. sources were open in admitting that Hezbollah's cross-border raid on July 12, which killed two Israeli soldiers and resulted in the abduction of two more, provided a "unique moment" with a "convergence of interests" among the United States, Israel and pro-U.S. Arab regimes.[28] The United States openly demanded that Israel not agree to a cease-fire and prevented the passage of a cease-fire resolution in the U.N. Security Council until August 11, as it waited for the military situation on the ground to turn irreversibly in Israel's favor. Furthermore, it cynically defended Israel's brutal aggression internationally by claiming that Israel was merely attempting to implement U.N. Security Council Resolution 1559, passed in 2004, which calls, among other things, for the disarmament of Hezbollah and the redeployment of the Lebanese army in the south.

Israeli Liberal Intellectuals: Cheerleaders of the War on Lebanon[29]

Before it became clear what price Israeli soldiers and the civilian population would pay in the war, the Israeli broadcast media, as well as most of the written media, enthusiastically repeated the formulations supplied by state spokespersons. Never before have the media so shamelessly called for the mass destruction and dispossession of a civilian population. Rafi Ginat, the editor in chief of Israel's largest-selling daily paper, *Yediot Ahronot*, pulled no punches in urging the government, on the front page of his paper, to "wipe out villages that host Hezbollah terrorists" and "wash with burning fire Hezbollah terrorists, their helpers, their collaborators, those who look the other way, and everyone who smells like Hezbollah, letting their innocent people die instead of ours."[30]

The media merely conveyed the overwhelming indifference a great majority of the Israeli public felt toward the mass killings and the dispossessions taking place in Lebanon. This is the product of the prevailing political culture, which wholeheartedly adopted Ariel Sharon—the mastermind of the Sabra and Shatila refugee camp massacres—as a champion of peace. "The logic of unilateralism has at last widely been adopted," said Yitzhak Laor, the radical left poet and writer. "Israelis are the only people who count in the Middle East. We are the only ones who deserve to live."[31]

The wide support for the war could not have arisen without the help of the Zionist Left in general and its Zionist left intellectual supporters in particular.

Indeed, the Zionist Left has always supported Israel's wars, seeing each as inevitable, necessary, and just. Still, the 2006 war on Lebanon signified an advanced stage in the process of the left's dehumanization, since it knew even before the assault began that Israel intended to "turn back the clock in Lebanon by twenty years," in the words of Chief of Staff Dan Halutz.[32] Israel's intellectual elite, who continue to present themselves as adhering to universal values of justice and equality, played a central role in articulating the government's misleading narrative in support of the devastation of Lebanon.

Not surprisingly, Hezbollah was described as an existential threat to Israel, and the war against it was framed as a war for Israel's survival. Thus, for example, the playwright Yehoshua Sobol, an old-time faithful supporter of the Israeli peace camp, describes the Hezbollah attack (as well as the "Qassam" missiles from Gaza) as a "declaration that our very being has no right to exist."[33] He admitted that he and the Left in general had been blind to the religious fanaticism and reactionary worldview of Hamas and Hezbollah, which contradicts the Left's supposed progressive secularism and humanity. This allowed for themselves and the public to be misled by the idea that Israel could negotiate a peace solution with them. Moreover, the war was depicted as the continuation of the 1948 War, thus confirming the prevailing discourse of the military and political establishment, which has escalated since the failure of the Oslo track in 2000. In the words of Eitan Haber, who formerly headed the office of the late Yitzhak Rabin and was personally very close to him, "Rabin said once that Israel has only one war in its history, which began in 1948 and has continued until this very day. It is the same war; only its name changes."[34] Moreover, legitimizing the assault on Lebanon in terms of "the second war of Independence" (the 1948 War)[35] was broadened to include the danger Hezbollah posed to the entire enlightened world, as an extension of the axis of evil and not just toward Israel. Yossef Gorni, professor of Jewish history at Tel Aviv University, says:

> In a reality in which Iran threatens the free world, this struggle against its proxy in Lebanon is a war for the existence of the state of Israel in the future. In this respect, though under completely different circumstances, the struggle to create the State itself in the War of Independence [the 1948 War] about sixty years ago and the war taking place today [July 2006] have a common denominator and a common justification: the struggle for our national existence.[36]

The most significant indication of the total moral bankruptcy of the Israeli "peace camp" is the discourse of those Israeli writers who are considered the ideological leaders of Peace Now, the mainstream Israeli peace movement.[37]

The world-renowned author Amos Oz, who was a candidate for the 2006 Nobel Prize and is considered to be the "moral consciousness of the nation," widely respected by progressive circles abroad, played a central role in servicing the political and military establishment. In a July 20 article, during a moment when the destruction of Lebanon was already well under way, Oz described the war as a war of self-defense: "This time [in contrast to the 1982 war against Lebanon] Israel is not invading Lebanon. It is defending itself from a daily harassment and bombardment of dozens of our towns and villages by attempting to smash Hezbollah wherever it lurks." He also argued for the moral superiority of the Israeli Army in contrast to Hezbollah, misleadingly claiming that "Hezbollah is targeting Israeli civilians wherever they are, while Israel is targeting mostly Hezbollah."[38] (The author David Grossman shared this argument in a supportive article for the Lebanon war, published in the U.K. *Guardian* on the same day).[39]

"On the day this article [Oz's article] was published," notes Yizhak Laor, "there were already in Lebanon over half a million refugees and three hundred killed, the great majority of whom were civilians, and entire regions of land destroyed—villages, towns, bridges, schools, hospitals."[40] Only on August 6, 2006, three weeks after the brutal devastation of Lebanon began and after more than one thousand Lebanese had been killed, did Oz, together with two other Israeli "humanist voices" (the authors David Grossman and A. B. Yehoshua) address the Israeli public. They took out a large advertisement in the daily newspaper *Ha'aretz*, calling upon the government to agree to a mutual cease-fire. This took place, however, only after the heroic resistance of Hezbollah and the Lebanese people had collectively repelled Israel's attempts to divide them and they were collectively mobilizing for Lebanon's defense. It also took place after it was well known that the U.N. Security Council was working to adopt a cease-fire declaration and that Israeli officials were involved in its articulation.

The question that occupied the Israeli establishment's mind at the time related to the question as to whether Israel should "widen the operation toward the Litani River" in the few days that remained before the U.N. resolution went into effect. The three humanists objected to this expansion, thus joining large parts of the Israeli media. However, the arguments upon which their call was grounded had nothing to do with morally and politically rejecting Israel's "military operation," which they continued to justify strongly. Instead, it was based on the presumption that the "feasible and reasonable goals of the military action have already been achieved" and that there is no justification "for causing more suffering and bloodshed for both sides for aims that are not feasible." In an effort to deter any idea that symmetry could be drawn between the suffering and bloodshed of "both sides," the writers hastened to add, "The Lebanese nation has no right to demand that its sovereignty be respected if it refuses to enact its full jurisdiction over its territory and citizenry."

The Orientalist and Racist "Left"

In supporting the devastation wrought in Gaza and Lebanon, Israel's icons of humanism are faithful to the Zionist Left's decades-long attribution of legitimacy to the state's aggressive and oppressive policies, in the name of "an existential threat to Israel." This "threat," however, has been identified and equated with the loss of a Jewish majority throughout entire historical Palestine, which would contradict the Zionist model of an exclusivist Jewish state.

The Left's discourse supplies the ideological legitimacy for escalating the hysteria of the "demographic ghost," increasingly prevalent in recent years among politicians and intellectuals in reaction to the determined Palestinian resistance to Israel's policies.[41] It thus allowed the Israeli peace camp to adopt virtually any self-described peace initiative, no matter what its nature and without setting up minimal criteria for what would constitute a genuinely just solution that would end the "conflict." It also allowed for them to uncritically swallow slogans like "there is no partner to peace" after Camp David (July 2000), which served as a pretext for Sharon's "unilateral strategy." Moreover, all the "peaceful" solutions endorsed by the Left have been based upon the premise of demographic segregation as a means of achieving a "Jewish majority"—a majority that has come to be located on ever-expanding areas, "clean" of Palestinians, who would be controlled from the "outside."[42]

However, it has been precisely the Left/Liberal humanist writers who have supplied the moral justification for the dispossession policies that stemmed from the conviction that "there is no partner." Their orientalist discourse and portrayals of Islam and Arab cultural heritage as inherently fanatic and irrational laid the ideological infrastructure for the prevailing conviction about the Palestinians' refusal to make peace. The distorted arguments these writers have used to justify this knee-jerk recalcitrance as infused with apocalyptic dimensions, allowing them to blur the distinction between the loss of the Jewish definition of the state and the Jewish majority within it, on the one hand, to the elimination of the state's actual "existence," on the other. They have thus intimated the possibility of the extermination of Jewish citizens, once they lose their majority. These assumptions do not only underlie the discourse on the prospects for obtaining a peace settlement with the Palestinians, but also underlie this possibility with the entire Arab world.

The author Sami Michael, long acknowledged in Israel as someone who is supposedly genuine about peace, frankly disclosed this orientalist, racist approach underlying his support for a "Jewish majority," in an interview with David Grossman in 1990: "But there's one thing that the Israeli-Arab has not and will not come to terms with and that's that he is a minority."[43] Speaking in the voice of a Palestinian citizen of Israel, Michael explains the antipathy 1948 Palestinians feel about being a minority and toward the Jewish state: "'We look to the future. We, with our birthrate, will again be a majority here. And you, the Jews, are in a crisis, both economic and moral. You are failing. The day will come, and with one good battle, it will all change.' That's still in the back of their minds. 'So why,' the same Arab asks, 'should I wear the suit you've sewn for me, the suit of a minority? I'll just wait.' . . . My ideal would be to reach some kind of joint state, but I don't think that either we or they are ripe for that. And we'd be a minority very quickly—their natural [population growth] has always been larger than ours. Ten years from now, fifty years from now, they'll be the majority and they'll make the decisions. And I, if I've got to be a minority, I'd rather not live in this region. I'm willing to be a minority in the U.S., in Australia, but not in this region, so intolerant of minorities."[44]

In 2004 Sami Michael was serving as the chair of the Association for Civil Rights in Israel (ACRI)—a post whose minimal qualifications should have been a worldview free of biases toward cultural traditions and racist biological premises. However, his reliance on the "national character" of the Arabs to explain the inability to solve the "conflict" has not changed:

> The Arab culture bears a grudge; blood feud is an honor command. It is forbidden to let time blur the memory, to bring to forgiveness and renunciation. A Bedouin who revenged the blood of his father after forty years was scolded: "What is the hurry"? . . . A number of Arab intellectuals condemn the Palestinians who negotiate with Israel, aiming at bringing about peace between the two peoples, and throw at them the terrible accusation "They are apt to reconcile with the loss of Andalusia."[45]

Amos Oz, however, is even clearer in his conclusions regarding the claimed existential danger of losing the Jewish majority. First, Oz explicitly rejects any liberal democratic alternative to a Jewish state with a Jewish majority. He equates the assumed danger created by the supporters of a binational state with an "Islamic occupation" of Israel, as both are presumed to deny the principle of a Jewish majority state:

> I'll tell you something ideological: my Zionism begins and ends in that no human being deserves to experience what my parents and the parents of their parents did. Therefore, in my opinion the Jewish people have the right to be a majority in one small place in this world and that right is not challengeable. It is forbidden for this right to be doubted, not by an Islamic occupation nor by talks about a binational state, according to which there is no difference who will be the majority. The Jews have the right to be a majority in one place in this world, and this right is anchored in the humiliation involved in being an eternal minority everywhere.[46]

And how are the Jews to implement their right? Oz answered this question previously in the context of relating to the 1948 Nakba:

> And if it comes down to: I'm uprooted from my house and you take it from me, or you are uprooted from your house and I take it from you, then it's preferable for me to remain and for you to be uprooted. And if it's going to be that you live and I die, or I live and you die, then it's better that you die. In such a war, our backs are really up against the wall.[47]

This conclusion, drawn from the assumed danger of elimination posed in the 1948 War, carries with it a frightening implication regarding any war in which Israel is involved. It was recently rearticulated against the Lebanese and Palestinians when they were depicted as deserving the "better that you die" alternative. It also integrates well with the imminent catastrophic U.S. plans for the Middle East, in which the senior partnership role of Israel is increasingly being explicitly admitted.

Convergence Agenda Out; New Middle East Agenda In

The determined resistance led by Hamas in the 1967 Occupied Territories, together with the particularly well-organized and efficient resistance of Hezbollah in Lebanon, has resulted in the conviction that the concept of unilateralism in its current form will not do. Namely, the policy that allowed for carrying out the liquidation of the Palestinian nation beneath the misleading "disengagement" plan is insufficient. As a result, the convergence plan that was due to take place in the West Bank was officially shelved on September 15 by Prime Minister Olmert, despite being the plan upon which Kadima had based its election campaign.

Israel thus did away with the cover of a peace plan, or even of maintaining a holding pattern until a peace plan emerges, that used to provide Israel time to continue its liquidation policies. It didn't seem important anymore. To the question "What is your agenda?," Olmert responded, "A prime minister does not need an agenda but only to manage the state."[48]

In claiming "no agenda," Olmert reflects the arrogance of Israel despite the agreed-upon conviction that Israel failed in the war on Lebanon and emerged with the aura of its deterrence power weaker than ever.[49]

And of course no genuine soul-searching has taken place within the Israeli establishment and society at large. The widespread criticism of the war, voiced by reserve officers, public figures from the entire political map, and senior political commentators, has not challenged the decision of the government to launch the assault on Lebanon in the first place, nor for that matter any of the principles of its policies that were responsible for the outbreak of the war. Instead, criticism focused on the faults revealed in the way the war was conducted and the poor functioning of the army and its generals, who could not deliver the goods—the easy victory that they initially expected and promised.[50] The protests were also not able to develop into a mass movement such as that which developed after the 1973 October War, eventually bringing about the first defeat of a Labor Party government in the 1977 general elections.

Israel could thus continue with its policy of liquidating the Palestinian people. What has changed, however, is the emergence of a widened version of "a new Middle East," which seeks to include in its strategy and rhetoric the war against the Palestinians' political, social, and physical existence, as part of the war against "radical nationalism" in the New Middle East. The latter is described by Azmi Bishara as "a new joint U.S.-Israeli adventure, the aim of which is to deliver a debilitating blow to the resistance, both as a domestic and a regional force and movement and as an obstacle to America's bid for complete hegemony over Lebanon."[51]

The determined resistance of Hezbollah and Hamas has brought the Israeli military and political establishment to the conclusion that these movements cannot be uprooted separately from launching a determined war against their political and material supporters within the "axis of evil." The time has therefore come, they emphasize, to strengthen the collaboration with the Arab states that are U.S. allies in this common project that services their joint concerns. According to Foreign Minister Tzipi Livni, "With only military operations, Israel cannot solve its problems in the region. It must cooperate with those Arab governments that have joint interests with Israel. They [the Arab governments] already understand that Israel is not anymore the bully of the neighborhood that wants to take control of any territory, but the *responsible adult*." [Emphasis added.][52]

Israel is playing a central role in the U.S.-led "birth pangs" of this New Middle East, whose next target after the occupation of Iraq and destruction of Lebanon is likely to be "nuclear Iran." Following the Lebanon war, which was presented as the first round in the Israeli-Iranian struggle, the voices of war have only gotten louder. As early as the end of August 2006, Israeli military commentators increased their leaking of information about Israel's preparations for a possible confrontation with Iran, which had begun before the onslaught on Lebanon.[53] On almost a daily basis, the government and media express their conviction that there is an urgent need to impose severe sanctions on Iran insinuating the inevitable need for military attack if diplomacy fails. The most senior Israeli expert on strategic affairs, Ze'ev Schiff disclosed that "in his [October 2006] visit to Moscow, PM Olmert used extraordinarily threatening language. He said that 'the Iranians should be afraid that something they don't want to happen will happen to them. Everyone knows that Israel does not have room to make a mistake in this matter.'" Schiff adds, "The Iranians know this, as do others, and there is no need to expand on it."[54]

The seriousness of Israel's preparations for a coming attack on Iran was also indicated by the admission to the government of the most explicit supporter of this war strategy, Avigdor Lieberman, in October 2006.

Legitimizing the Extreme Right Implications for Local and Regional Axes of Evil

The end of the Israeli-Palestinian "peace" agenda, including the liquidation of the Palestinian people in the context of the war on terror, while eyeing

Iran for future assault, has indeed broadened the existing common denominator between Left and Right in Israel. This common denominator, embodied in the "unilateral" approach, had brought together large parts of the Likud and the Labor Party within the Kadima government, which implemented the "disengagement from Gaza" in 2005, while supported "from the outside" by Meretz. (See Chapter 9.) After the 2006 elections, Olmert's "convergence plan" ("disengagement") was the Labor Party's rationale for participating in the Kadima-Labor government. However, the cancellation of this plan did not bring about any rethinking among Labor Party leaders regarding the issue of remaining in Olmert's government.

Kosherizing Lieberman

The last nail in the coffin of Labor's claim that it represents a distinct political approach came when its leadership decided to stay in the government coalition after the admission of the fascist MK Avigdor Lieberman into the government by PM Olmert on October 24. Lieberman, the founder and chair of the Israel Beitenu party, was offered the position of vice prime minister and "minister for strategic threats." The creation of the latter ministry demonstrates the shared political position of the political and military establishments, which has determined that the most important problems confronting Israel at present are the Iranian threat and the Syrian-Iranian alliance with Hezbollah and Hamas.

Lieberman is an extreme secular right-winger who represents the local version of neoconservatism, combined with Le Pen populism. As a disciple of sheer power politics, he has no need for the traditional Zionist dependency on the Bible and "divine right" to legitimize his blatant war policy. He thus calls upon Israel "to come to terms with its power, to be overt about it [when addressing] its environment [the Palestinians and the Arab world], and to be ready to use it."[55]

Lieberman's desire to condition the granting of civil rights to Palestinians in Israel upon their serving in the Israeli Army, would mean in fact stripping the great majority of Palestinians in Israel of their citizenship. He has openly advocated the transfer of the population concentrated in the area of Um el Fahem to a Bantustan-like future Palestinian entity. In 2002, he also called for the expulsion of any Palestinian citizen of Israel who refused to sign a loyalty oath to the Jewish Zionist state.[56]

This, of course, is not the official policy adopted by the Labor Party, nor by the entire Zionist Left. However, the details of Lieberman's political policies reveal a similarity with the basic principles of the Zionist Left, including Meretz, despite their differences in symbolic and stylistic matters. Both are secularists who believe that state interests are superior to individual human rights. Lieberman has merely carried this logic to its extreme conclusion, rejecting democracy in the quest for "a strong leader" who can impose the "Jewish majority" as a political solution. Azmi Bishara notes:

> He [Lieberman] is trying to change the balance between religion and the state, not to make it more liberal or democratic but more communal and sectarian, though without distinguishing between the two. For Lieberman a Russian need only serve in the army to be treated as a converted Jew. This nationalistic, rather than religious, dimension of conversion is close to the Zionist Left—for example, Yossi Beilin—and it constitutes the basis of dialogue between them, but it is not the only common ground. He also shares with the Left a concern with "the demographic issue" and the need to get rid of the Palestinians in the framework of an agreement in which they give up all their historic demands with the exception of a political entity, which just happens to be an Israeli demand as well. Lieberman clearly wants an entity to be an agent for Israel.[57]

Lieberman's approach is thus different from that of the traditional Israeli Right. Similar to the Israeli Left, he is motivated by demographic and security considerations that lead him to speak about territorial compromise and a Palestinian entity that could absorb the Palestinians.

The Labor Party's agreement to participate in the government together with Lieberman is not only a step that confers legitimacy to the racist party of Lieberman. It has widened the boundaries of legitimate Zionism to include the extreme Right as well—something the latter has long aspired to. The founding of Kadima by Sharon, who separated from the Likud, was presented as his adoption of the "pragmatism" of Mapai, the progenitor of today's Labor Party. It seemed as though the "fanatical Right" had been excluded from the newly widened boundaries of legitimate Zionism, which included the Zionist Left and a substantial part of the Right (see Chapter 9). Now, however, when the true nature of this "pragmatism" is disclosed, the "fanatic Right" publicly adopts it and is subsequently embraced as a legitimate partner in the "mainstream" aims and policies of the Jewish Zionist state. As the progressive political commentator Haim Baram notes:

> The supporters of Lieberman this week [the first week of October 2006] are in fact the natural product of the sharpened trends that were formed by the nationalist statehood of Ben-Gurion [the chair of Mapai and founder of the state]. . . . Most of them are outstanding supporters of the deterrence of nu-

clear weaponry and are disciples of the right-wing philosophy that sees Israel as the spearhead of Western civilization's war against Islam.[58]

The widening consensus emerging around the "Middle East agenda" inevitably strengthens the ideological and political basis for escalating the oppression of the 1967 Palestinians, who are depicted as part of the "Axis of Evil." At the same time, the expressed solidarity of 1948 Palestinians with the Palestinian and Lebanese resistance, and its articulation by NDA—Tajamu' leaders as a model of resistance for all Arabs, enlarges the rift between them and large parts of the Israeli peace camp. The latter have traditionally focused on the 1967 Occupation and did not associate themselves with the democratic struggle waged in Israel, almost exclusively by 1948 Palestinians—namely, their ideological challenge to the Jewish-Zionist state and their daily confrontation with policies of dispossession and marginalization. Moreover, large sections of Israel's self-acclaimed liberals believe that full 1948 Palestinian citizenship rights should be conditioned upon their accepting the premises and policies of the Zionist state. Thus, the latter's solidarity with the resistance in Lebanon was considered by many Zionist liberals as "Israel's Arabs crossing the line"—as the headline of an article by Uzi Benziman, a senior political commentator of *Ha'aretz*, read:

> Organizations that are involved in advancing relations between Jews and Arabs in Israel have from July 12 [the day the two Israeli soldiers were abducted by Hezbollah] been exposed to an ever escalating emotional confrontation in the relations between the two people. While from the vantage point of the Israeli Jew, the second Lebanon war was the most just reaction to an arrogant violation of [Israeli] state sovereignty, in the eyes of the Israeli Arab, the IDF [the Israeli Army] activity was needless, disproportionate, and caused appalling wrongs to his relatives in Lebanon.
>
> In the last war [Lebanon 2006] a line was crossed: Israeli Arabs did not hesitate to display their identification with the enemy overtly and to prefer their connection to them to their commitment to their state, of which they are citizens. . . . [Indeed,] the clash between the loyalty of the Arab citizens to the state and their linkage to the Arab nation (not only to the Palestinian people) is ever aggravating. In essence, it is their refusal to recognize the legitimacy of the Zionist idea—a refusal that has been nourished by the discriminative, stupid, and evil policy of all Israeli governments.[59]

And here comes the unspecified, open-ended warning that carries with it a scary message: "The clash between these two perceptions reignites the question of the capability of Israel's Jews and its Arabs to continue and carry on their lives together on the only basis that has enabled them until present: a joint civil society."

"He Who Wants Peace Should Prepare Himself for War"— While Renouncing Democracy

Much of what Lieberman advocates and stands for has already become a reality in Israel. Responding sarcastically to the weak opposition voices heard from the Labor Party MKs in response to Lieberman's joining the government, Gideon Levy noted, "What exactly will change [with Lieberman's joining the government]? Israel will set out for an unnecessary war? The settlement project will be strengthened? The government will answer negatively to the Syrian peace plan? The racism toward the Arab citizens of Israel will escalate? The occupation army will behave cruelly towards the Palestinians? All this is supplied by the existing government, and Lieberman's joining it will only unmask [its real nature]."[60]

Indeed, its real nature has been unmasked on both the local and regional levels. The military defeat in Lebanon only inspired the government to continue its planned assault on Gaza, which began before the war. With Peretz as minister of defense, the daily killings in and starvation of Gaza, in a U.S.-Israeli effort to bring down the Hamas government and create chaos and civil war, has continued unabated. The concern that there might be established a unified government between Hamas and Fateh, which could be seen as an appropriate partner for talks, only heightened Israeli efforts to provoke countermilitary operations by Palestinian resistance forces.

But Israel's renewed operations on Gaza's southern border with Egypt have not succeeded in stopping the resistance forces from running the blockade imposed by Israel. Nor did Operation Autumn Clouds, launched on Beit Hanoun in the north of the Strip at the beginning of November, stop the firing of primitive rockets toward the southern Israeli towns, even for one day. Indeed, the political and military establishments have often admitted that the military means used by the Palestinian resistance cannot altogether be eliminated by the army. However, alongside the aim of liquidation, which relies upon provoking the Palestinians, the bloodbath the army left behind in Beit Hanoun should be seen in the context of preparations to wage a yet wider "war on terror." "From a military perspective, Operation Autumn Clouds was a live exercise on a model. It included taking over a densely populated urban area for a week, while exacting a high price from the armed Hamas units as part of preparations for wider activity in other regions. The intention was not to stop the Qassams [rockets]. Hence, from the perspective of the goals set by the Southern Command, the operation was very successful."[61]

Moreover, the voices that warn against the threat posed by Iran and the need to prepare against its presumed danger became louder in November. On November 10, Deputy Defense Minister Ephraim Sneh, a Labor "dove," declared that Israel may be forced to launch a military strike against Iran's nuclear program. However, he did so while paying the traditional "Left" lip service to its preference for peace—namely, that he is not "advocating a preemptive strike against Iran," which he considers a last resort, "though even the last resort is sometimes the only resort."

In line with the tendency to depict the Iranian danger in terms of a threat to Israel's very existence, Sneh added that Israel cannot afford "to live under a dark cloud of fear from a leader committed to its destruction." Israel's greatest possible danger could be Iranian President Mahmoud Ahmadinejad's ability "to kill the Zionist dream without pushing a button. That's why we must prevent this regime from obtaining nuclear capability at all costs."[62]

The broadened common denominator of the "war on terror" ensures that large parts of the Left will support any government that implements Israel's active participation in it. The ideological argument for supporting an attack on Iran and other wars that the U.S. and Israel are planning has already been supplied by authors like Amos Oz. Oz hurried to legitimize the "New Middle East agenda" by articulating it in the framework of a war for a "free world." In his thank-you speech given after receiving the Corina Prize for lifetime achievement in literature in Munich, Germany, on September 24, 2006, Oz declared, "The war that is taking place at present is not anymore [a war] between nations but between the fanatics of all sides and the tolerant of all sides."[63]

Moreover, Oz's old-time discourse about "wars of survival," which implies the death of "either us or them," has no doubt paved the way for the dehumanization of wider Israeli sectors, including many on the Zionist Left. Hence, the distance between the rhetoric of the "war on terror" on behalf of the "enlightened" and "humanistic" and those who reject the very values of enlightenment has shrunk, with scarcely a hair separating the two. The total collapse of any commitment to human rights values by many of Israel's intellectual elites is pointed out by Dan Margalit, a leading figure on major Israeli political and cultural programs and talk shows. In his weekly article, published in *Ma'ariv*, on the weekend after the testing of the North Korean nuclear bomb, Margalit demonstrated the rather fast approach of Israeli society toward forsaking democratic values in the era of the "war on terror":

If the world does not react forcefully to what is happening in [North] Korea, Iran, and other countries in the Middle East, and instead acts in [what could be] a second version of the events that took place in Fascist Italy and Nazi Germany in the 1930s, it will pave the way for a war of civilizations.

Hence the enlightened camp should awaken from the helplessness of its Judeo-Christian heritage, one of whose by-products is the lethal combination of hedonism [on the one hand] and of approaching one's enemy with a sense of equality [on the other]. This perception, which has developed primarily within the enlightened academia in the West, assumes that the use of military power is not a solution to problems that arise between opponents in violent conflicts. [But] activation of force is required because the old rules determined by the United Nations after World War Two, and the consciousness that enveloped the United States after dropping two atomic bombs on Japan in 1945, are not valid [anymore] and do not pertain to a situation of confrontation with mad regimes that have broken all shared norms and values [kelim]. . . . The cultured world needs to upgrade the known Roman proverb: He who wants peace (nuclear)—should prepare himself for war (conventional).[64]

Indeed, we are witness to the implementation of the aspiration articulated by the right-wing ideologue Ze'ev Jabotinsky in one of the hymns sung by Betar,[65] the political organization he headed, that "[a] race will emerge here, proud and noble and cruel." This has been possible only with the significant contribution of the Zionist Labor movement, which brought Israeli society to a point where it is prepared to obey the missions it is called upon to fulfill by its unified leadership from "Left" to "Extreme Right"—all on behalf of "Jewish survival." It is the mission first articulated by Zionism's creator, Theodor Herzl, who called upon the future Jewish state to act as the bulwark of "civilization against barbarism," today manifested in the "war on terror," with the "democratic West" struggling against a "fundamentalist" and "fanatical" Arab world. Zionist colonialism, which from its inception aimed at expelling and liquidating the Palestinian people, seeks to achieve this end once and for all in this war, as an extension of the battle against any buds of independent nationalism in the Middle East.

The expansion of the strategies used by Zionism to target all forces who resist U.S. imperialism in the Middle East implies the parallel need to redefine the nature of the battle aimed at the realization of the national rights of the Palestinian people and its necessary condition: the full de-Zionization of the state of Israel. This battle should be seen as part and parcel of a long-term, determined struggle carried out by resistance forces among Palestinians, Israelis, and others throughout the Middle East and beyond for the region's deep transformation, including the struggle for its liberation from U.S.-Zionist hegemony and the collaborative Arab regimes.

The Hamas Victory and the Future of the Palestinian National Movement

Toufic Haddad

The year 2006 will be remembered in history as a year in which two definitive political events took place that have the potential to fundamentally reshuffle the Palestinian national and Arab regional order. First was the sweeping Hamas victory in the January 25, 2006, Palestinian Legislative Council elections, displacing the incumbent Fateh party, which had dominated the Palestinian national setting for almost forty years. Second was the Hezbollah victory over Israel in the July–August war. Though the achievements of both events remain to be consolidated, the political and organizational lessons they taught have left indelible marks on the consciousness of both local and regional constituencies. They also ominously presage that Israel and its U.S. backer will not rest before attempting to roll back these achievements, hoping to definitively inscribe the logic that resistance to their regional hegemony will not be tolerated and that yet further expansion of the repressive means at their disposal will be required to that end. When viewed in the context of the continued U.S. defeats in Iraq and the potential rise of a nuclear Iran, the entire Middle East, with the question of Palestine at its center, now stands at a historic crossroads. The stakes have risen to such a level that it is not irrational to preclude, in both the near and distant future, the possibility of accelerated ethnic cleansing of Palestinians from their lands, the ignition of expanded regional wars, and the possible use of nonconventional weaponry.

In order to assess the confluence and repercussions of these dynamics, it is necessary to explore the events themselves to gain a better understanding of how they came about and what they portend for the future of Palestine and the region at large.

Elections 2006

The Hamas victory was a watershed in the Palestinian liberation struggle because it marked the first time in the modern history of the national movement that a nonmember organization of the PLO displaced the latter as the agent for achieving Palestinian goals. This was an achievement at the same time it was a defeat. It was an achievement because it meant that the Palestinian national movement had not been defeated and was determined to reconstitute itself for the purpose of continuing its struggle toward liberation and achieving its rights. It was a defeat because it marked the colossal failure of the secular national liberation struggle and its inability to invest the enormous historical sacrifices it offered in the framework of a winning strategy.

The Hamas victory must be viewed as the pinnacle of the mass popular movement that began with the Al Aqsa Intifada, to definitively displace the Oslo process paradigm and its infectious repercussions upon the Palestinian national movement. In this respect, it was an achievement in what was a long but, in the end, transitional goal: doing away with the belief that an independent sovereign Palestinian state in the West Bank and Gaza could be erected through U.S. intervention and without contradicting Israel's strategic objectives. Hamas has no illusions that this is possible, nor does it believe that this, given the alignment of regional and local forces, is where the national movement's resources are best placed. Though it will accept the establishment of an independent state in the West Bank and Gaza in the framework of their complete decolonization, it is explicit in articulating that this is not its final goal. Moreover, it understands that if it is to accomplish even this goal, it must lay the foundations for an entirely different national movement that can engage in new forms of struggle, with a different set of pre-assumptions. While it is important to emphasize that Hamas does not have exclusive hegemony over the national movement, the dynamics it has set into play are already forcing other national movement actors to reevaluate their strategy and tactics.

Hamas's victory in the January 25, 2006, elections was no small feat: despite the fact that the elections took place under a brutal occupation and that Israel made no serious concessions to facilitate them; despite the fact that Israel held 11,000 prisoners, many of whom are pivotal national leaders, in its jails; despite the millions of dollars pumped both directly and indirectly into Fateh's campaign by the United States and the European Union in a last-ditch effort to keep the lip service of the "peace process" alive—the Palestinian people resoundingly voted for a different future.

Hamas won a resounding 74 of the parliament's 132 seats, while backing an additional 4 independent candidates who affirmed its program. Fateh was able to muster only 45 seats. Though this commanding majority (59 percent of parliamentary seats) signified, for many political observers, the Islamization of the Palestinian political setting, a closer look at the elections counters this impression, revealing a complicated set of political and organizational issues that accounted for the final results. More than anything, the Hamas victory represented the congealing of certain political undercurrents formerly marginalized within the previous paradigm of the Oslo process. Hamas now operates as an umbrella organization that is leading the national movement and its resistance to the Israeli occupation in association with other Palestinian political actors within Fateh and other factions. Their main contribution to the national movement is embodied in efforts to divest the national movement from its former dependency upon U.S. and EU intervention in their cause, and alternatively to seek to align the movement with forces that have a common interest in an anti-Zionist and anti-U.S. imperial agenda. Gaining a sense for what Hamas is and how its victory in the elections came about sheds light on the possibility for the movement achieving its ends.

The Fateh Defeat

No doubt the clearest message the election results showed was that the Palestinian electorate resoundingly said "No more!" to the ruling Fateh party. Fateh's extended hegemony over Palestinian national decision making and financial resources; its undemocratic decision-making processes vis-à-vis other factions and within the party itself; its poor political calculations and performance; and its latent financial corruption in the end created more enemies than friends within Palestinian society. Ever since the Intifada began, and particularly after the death of Yasser Arafat, the glue that once kept Fateh together dissolved as its contradictions bubbled to the surface.

Fateh had very little it could approach the Palestinian electorate with to convince them to vote for it. Not only had its political strategy to achieve Palestinian rights, as embodied in the Oslo process, failed miserably, but its party elites refused to acknowledge this failure and irrationally maintained loyalty to its framework in the form of support for the U.S.-backed "road map"—a plan conditioned upon full Palestinian submission to U.S./Israeli diktats before the asymmetrical negotiations even begin (see Chapter 7). This despite the fact that Israel had clearly already abandoned this track in favor of "unilateralism" and had gathered support from all major powers of the world to do so.

Under Fateh domination, the Palestinian Authority had ruled the major Palestinian cities by a system of patronage and cronyism, in many cases returning and upholding the rule of local elites who had been displaced in the 1987 Intifada. Its rule was implemented erratically, with no clear division between authorities, oftentimes not even upholding the decisions of its own courts. With the failure of its political project, Fateh itself began to collapse, lacking a revolutionary theoretical framework that could provide it a way forward or, at the very least, mediate the differences within it. The crumbling of Fateh throughout the course of the Intifada has resulted in its variegated constituency dispersing in an assortment of directions, some nationalist (with many joining the resistance), others simply opportunistic and self-serving.

The extent of financial corruption within Fateh began to come to light only recently. A report published by the PA attorney general after the election revealed that an astonishing U.S. $700 million had been plundered from public coffers in fifty different cases under review. While this corruption was facilitated in no unsubtle way by the neoliberal economic regime imposed on the Occupied Territories as a result of the Paris Economic Accord between the PA and Israel in 1994, the corruption scandals were emblematic of what Palestinians perceive as a deeper political corruption within the national movement that had lost focus of its priorities and strategies. No matter what Fateh had sacrificed and contributed historically as the primary founder of the modern national movement, little could be salvaged from that history when the national movement was faced with the serious social and political crisis Palestinian society has undergone under the systematic blows of Israel since the Intifada began, which seek to push the Palestinians to the brink of political and social extinction.

In the end, the Palestinian electorate punished Fateh for its repeated and accumulated failures. This punishment, however, was not supposed to destroy Fateh. A more nuanced investigation of the election results conveys this: of the 66 election seats that were up for grabs through direct party slates (lists), Hamas barely eked out a victory, winning 29 seats to Fateh's 28 seats, with the remaining 9 seats going to four lists of independents and parties on the Left. However, of the 66 remaining seats, which were to be determined through allotted districts, where voters came out to vote for individuals, with a fixed number of seats for each district, Hamas handily beat out Fateh, by 41 to 25. What accounts for the discrepancy was the fact that Fateh was not able to field a unified list of candidates that could meet the many desires of its variegated constituency. In each district where Fateh was forced to field a set number of official candidates, there were inevitably other Fateh members who felt they had been unjustifiably bumped off the official roster and hence ran as independents. The results were devastating for Fateh, as its voter constituency split its ballots among different candidates. Simultaneously, Hamas was able to field a unified list that its smaller but more organized and centralized constituency could vote for collectively.[66]

Ultimately, Fateh was overstretched and trapped in its own web of nepotism. Furthermore, its greatest mistake was to allow for the holding of the Legislative Council elections before it had had time to convene its own sixth Fateh movement conference, which could have put the party more at peace with itself regarding who were its democratically elected representatives. The nonholding of the sixth Fateh conference has been a point of contention within the party for years, given that it was systematically delayed by Arafat himself. The source of the party's former strength (a network of political, economic, social, and revolutionary elites) was now the reason for its demise. Immediately after the election results were finalized, Fateh expelled seventy-five members who had run as independent candidates in the district vote, including many high-ranking members of the Fateh bureaucracy. Grassroots Fateh members also marched en masse in the streets of the West Bank and Gaza demanding the resignation of the Fateh Executive Committee. The repercussions of this internal strife remain unresolved and will likely determine whether Fateh can remain one party or will break apart into smaller, weaker units. Without a new political strategy, however, the latter scenario looks increasingly likely.

The Hamas Victory

Inasmuch as acknowledging the technicalities of how Fateh mishandled the elections is important, overfocusing on them must not lead to a loss of perspective regarding the election results overall; the Hamas victory was not just about negation. Nor was it merely about the oft-cited social welfare network it oversees. Although there are significant socioeconomic reasons behind Hamas's success, this simplification assumes that Palestinians are simply so desperate that they will vote for whoever feeds them and are devoid of any critical political faculties.

Far more significant to Hamas's victory was what it represented politically: a definitive departure from the Oslo model and the humiliating discourse and destructive implications it propagated under Fateh rule.

Palestinians rejected the idea that they had to be a "partner to peace"; that they were the ones who had to prove that they were not terrorists; and that "Israeli security and self-defense" was a legitimate premise in the peace process, necessitating all of Israel's subsequent actions, supported by the United States. Hamas's victory represented a shift of the political ground, whereby, due to its organization and politics, the movement was able to successfully expand its base of support beyond those who support it for ideological reasons to encompass those who want a definitive break from the destructive way things have been operating for so long.

Since its founding in 1987, Hamas has cleverly shadowed all the political areas from which Fateh and the Oslo Accords retreated with respect to Palestinian national rights: the right of return of Palestinian refugees, Jerusalem, and the unity of the entire Palestinian people. In doing so, it was forced to develop into a dynamic, disciplined, centralized party structure that was capable of withstanding not just Israel's attempts to uproot it but also Fateh's desire to marginalize it. Equally as important was the fact that in the struggle to attain these rights, Hamas articulated an alternative strategy to what it saw as the dead end of Oslo and the "honest brokerage" of the United States. Hamas unapologetically preserved and implemented, at times, the Palestinian right to resist, using force as a political tool. This, in the eyes of its U.S., Israeli, and EU detractors, was its gravest sin. Although to many this resistance may have taken controversial forms, the reality of the matter is that Hamas was never unique in its employment of these methods among Palestinian factions and often proved itself to be far more disciplined in its use of them.

Only after politically positioning itself on a firm political base and articulating a program that protected and sometimes implemented a resistance-centered campaign, can Hamas's social work be understood in context. In fact, it is precisely through the consolidation of the first two criteria that Hamas's social welfare networks were transformed from mere charity networks into instruments of political mobilization.

The Hamas Platform

A reading of the political platform of the "Change and Reform" slate (the name Hamas ran under in the elections) sheds further light upon what led this party to power and where it is likely to go in the future.[67] Although the Hamas political platform is no doubt Islamically inspired and infused, its interpretation of Islam and Islamic law (Shari'a) is flexible enough to be able to allow it to incorporate a wide array of national, political, social and civil rights. Hamas also developed a political platform that fused Islamic interpretation and obligations to national and civil principles, arguing that national goals are Islamic ones and vice versa. Thus, for example, its election principles argued that Palestine is "a part of Arab and Islamic lands"; that its "liberation requires joint Palestinian, Arab, and Islamic activity"; and that "what is referred to as 'security coordination' with the occupation is a high national and Islamic crime." It further argued for encouraging "Arab and Islamic unity"; an "end to the besiegement of Arab and Islamic countries"; and challenging the ethnic, sectarian, and regional disputes that divide the nation.

After laying a solid foundation of political positions that it argues are both Islamic and national, it then elaborates in depth upon a wide assortment of political, economic, and social ideas relating to international relations, reform and corruption, public freedoms and human rights, the role and rights of Palestinian Christians, women's rights, youths' rights, the role of education and the media, housing rights, environmental and health standards, agricultural policies, workers rights, and financial dealings.

This sophisticated political platform, combined with the Palestinians' experience of life under Fateh, and quite importantly, the utter failure of Palestinian Left factions to build a distinct, credible secular project, are all reasons Hamas ultimately won. Although no doubt Hamas does not shy from its belief that "Islam is the solution," reductionist portrayals of Hamas as a fundamentalist reactionary movement are misplaced and too often based upon racist, dehumanizing criteria that align with imperialist and Zionist interests.

On the contrary, Hamas's performance in the elections proves that the movement has matured over the years[68] and won the confidence of substantial sectors of the population who expect it to definitively break from the way things were run under Oslo. That is why its platform was confident about calling, among other things, for a "clear division between authorities"; "reform of the legal system"; protecting the independence of the judiciary; improving government transparency and accountability; developing civil society; ending arbitrary arrest and torture; protecting public freedoms "without exception"; and encouraging "a culture of debate and the respect of opinions." It is evident that the majority of Palestinians viewed these positions as crucial priorities for the national movement's survival, irrespective of what these sectors may think about the movement's Islamic derivations.

Defeat for U.S. Imperialism and Zionism:
Countering the Hamas Effect

The Hamas victory was an affront to all the premises that underlay U.S. and Israeli policies during the Intifada and the policies of unilateralism that received wide backing from the international community. Not only did the Hamas victory fly in the face of the Bush administration's efforts to "bring democracy to the Middle East," as though this were to be equated with bringing to power moderate pro-American regimes, it also provided a moral, political, and organizational model that could be looked to by political movements across the region, eager to push for democratic reforms in their respective countries.

The senior Israeli political commentator Aluf Benn immediately recognized the significance of the Hamas victory with respect to its regional repercussions:

> The democratization process that U.S. President George Bush has triggered and the open debate promoted by Arab satellite networks are causing the old frameworks to crumble. The mass demonstrations that led to the Syrians being driven from Lebanon, the elections in Iraq and those in the [Occupied] Territories are merely the beginning. As far as Israel is concerned, the worst stage will come when the democratic wave washes over Jordan, its strategic ally; Egypt, with its modern army and F-16 squadrons; and Syria and its Scud and chemical warhead stores.
>
> Israel saw in Bush's democratization initiative a pretension of naive Americans who had no idea of the reality in the region. . . . The Israelis warned the Americans that that unsupervised Arab democracy will bring the Muslim Brotherhood to power, not pro-Western liberals. But Washington refused to listen and insisted on holding the elections on schedule. The new reality requires both Washington and Jerusalem to reevaluate the situation, before the Hamas effect hits Amman and Cairo. In any case, it will be hard to turn back democratic change and resume the comfortable relations with the old dictatorships."[69]

Israel, the United States, and the European Union immediately set about trying to counter "the Hamas effect." Their initial approach focused on isolating and starving the Hamas government economically and politically beneath the rubric that it was trying to force the movement to accept the same set of political concessions it had extracted from Fateh under Arafat: recognition of Israel, acceptance of the "road map," and disarmament.

But there were indications early on that this approach would never really work, nor was Israel or the United States serious about this happening. From the beginning, the Israeli political and military establishment saw the Hamas victory as a unique opportunity to accelerate its crushing of the national movement, this time with Hamas acting as the ultimate "no partner." Within hours of the election results being released, former Israeli Army Chief of Staff Moshe Ya'alon was chomping at the bit to ratchet up the war against the Palestinians, who were now definitively dehumanized as part and parcel of the "war on terror." He argued that the Palestinian elections ushered in the creation of "Hamastan, Hezbollahstan and al-Qaedastan" in Gaza and that Iran was at Israel's doorstep. Other Israeli political commentators were candid about how the moment of doing away with the Hamas government was fast approaching: "The immediate question on the agenda of Bush and Olmert is whether and when to take action to topple the Hamas government. The reply of the [Israeli] defense establishment is 'Yes' and 'Not yet.' . . . The defense establishment prefers to give Hamas more time to decide whether to go the route of moderation, as the PLO did, or to stick to its guns."[70]

And stick to its guns it did. Despite the increased external pressure for the movement to change its political positions, Hamas remained defiant, attempting to tackle its political challenges head on: "Haven't there been negotiations for ten years? And what were their results?" demanded newly elected Palestinian Prime Minister Ismael Abu Hanieh in a speech in Gaza in June 2006. "When [PA president] Abu Mazen raised the banner of compromise and negotiations—what was Israel's response? We must depart from this path. The Palestinian cause is usurped in its political, security, and financial dimensions. We want to return the Palestinian cause to its legitimate partners, so the people become the source of decision making."[71]

Hamas Foreign Minister Mahmoud al-Zahar was even more explicit regarding what his government's position was toward Israel: "The [Zionist] entity is a foreign body planted on our land. It is a body that has no legitimacy to exist, neither historically nor culturally. There is no way we can normalize relations with it in any scenario. . . . We want the land of Palestine, all of Palestine. From Naqura [in the north, on the Lebanese border] to Rafah [in the south], and from [the Dead] Sea to [the Mediterranean] Sea. We want the return of every Palestinian to every part of Palestine."[72]

On the ground, Hamas began making important political and organizational steps to shore up its position for the task at hand. Despite bitter antagonism from party stalwarts in Fateh, Hamas took pains to achieve political agreements with its main political rival over a national program that attempted to put to rest fears that Hamas would drastically change the historical orientation and political foundation of the national movement itself. Rather than impose an individual party agenda, Hamas sought to build political consensus in an effort to heal and unify the fractured national movement. These positions were eventually formulated in understandings that became known as the National Reconciliation Document, sometimes referred to as the Prisoners' Document, given its origin among high-ranking Palestinian leaders in Israeli prisons.[73] The document outlined a pragmatic program that all major factions can unite under within the context of the needs of the national movement today.

Thus, the document reaffirms the common interest of the different parties "to liberate their land and to achieve their right to freedom, return and independence . . . based upon the historical right of our people to the land of our forefathers, the U.N. Charter, international law, and international legitimacy." It characterizes the national movement as "still passing through a liberation phase with nationalism and democracy as its basic features," thereby cutting against the statist currents that formerly dominated Palestinian discourse and strategy. It also declares that steps will be taken for Hamas and Islamic Jihad to join the PLO as the "sole legitimate representative of the Palestinian people," thereby ensuring a unified framework for the national movement's resources and activity to take place within. It also acknowledges that the Palestinian people have a right to resist, emphasizing the need for this resistance to be focused in the 1967 Occupied Territories. Finally the document calls for the setting up of a "plan toward comprehensive political action to unify the Palestinian political rhetoric," to seek the formation of "a national unity government on a basis that secures the participation of all parliament blocs, especially Fateh and Hamas" and to "work on forming a unified resistance front . . . to lead and engage in resistance against the occupation."

These political achievements were backed up by important organizational steps Hamas made to realign the movement from within. It immediately reshuffled the Palestinian Authority's ministries in an effort to curb and weed out its systemic corruption, resulting in $239 million of PA monies saved.[74] It furthermore recruited the vanguard sections of Fateh, embodied in the Popular Resistance Committees,[75] into the newly formed Executive Force (*Al Quwa al Tanfeethiyyeh*) established by the new Minister of the Interior, Said Siyam. This was seen as necessary by the Hamas government, given the fact that the pre-existing PA security forces were too disparate and functionally tended to act as the personal militias of given Fateh strongmen. Though the formation of the Executive Force resulted in great tensions with the old PA security elite, Hamas saw it as the only means through which it could enforce its rule or, for that matter, address the increasing internal security issues Gaza is confronting as a consequence of the breakdown of a functional system of law after years of Intifada.

Hamas's maneuverings laid the ground for Israel to seek any and all means through which it could reverse these trends.

Beneath the pretext of the continued firing of primitive rockets by Palestinian factions,[76] Israel began shelling the Gaza strip with full blown artillery shells, the first time since the 1967 Occupation that Israel used this method of warfare against the Palestinians. Greatly facilitated by the new geostrategic map set up in the wake of its unilateral disengagement from the Strip in September 2005, Israel fired 5,100 shells at the Gaza Strip from the end of March to mid-May 2006.[77] It also reduced the distance of its artillery fire from Palestinian homes and farmland from 300 meters to 100 meters, ensuring that the lives of the people of the entire northern Gaza Strip were turned into a daily hell, while making certain that casualties became a daily occurrence.[78] The results were immediate and devastating: in the eight months after Israel "disengaged" from Gaza, no fewer than 144 Palestinians were killed, including 29 children.[79]

Israel also made it a point to try to pinpoint the political actors who were crucial for the success of Hamas's strategy. Its assassination of Abu Yusef al Qoqa on March 31 and Jamal Abu Samhadana on June 8—both founders of the Popular Resistance Committees—were deliberate attempts to stop larger sections of the grassroots Fateh movement from breaking from the party bureaucracy and sliding under the Hamas umbrella. Moreover, Abu Samhadana had been specifically designated to head the Interior Ministry's Executive Force and was the highest security official in the new Palestinian government. These acts laid the ground for Hamas to break its policy of not launching resistance operations against Israel—a policy observed for months even before it came to power, in an effort not to provoke unnecessary confrontations that could jeopardize or abort its political ambitions in the elections and after.

The response came on June 24 with a well-coordinated guerrilla attack on Israeli military positions located on Gaza's perimeter. The sophisticated attack, launched by Hamas, the Popular Resistance Committees, and another Fateh splinter group calling itself the Islamic Army, resulted in the death of two Israeli soldiers and the abduction of another. Despite the targeting of strictly military personnel, Israel understood that it had the pretext needed to begin launching its plans to definitively crush the buds of the reorganizing national project from the rubble of what Israel has done to it throughout the Intifada.

Within days of the abduction, Israel bombed Gaza's main power station; destroyed its bridges; abducted sixty-four elected members of local and national Palestinian governance (including eight cabinet members); bombed Gaza's Islamic University, the PA prime minister's office, the foreign minister's office, and dozens of other civil society organizations; and launched wave after wave of ground assaults into all sections of Gaza. The raids killed more than two hundred Palestinians in the first six weeks.

Had it not been for the abduction of two Israeli soldiers on the Lebanon border on July 12, by Hezbollah, and the ensuing war that Israel launched, it is likely that Israel's campaign against Gaza would have continued indefinitely and with yet more unprecedented barbarity.

War Against Lebanon

As with Gaza, Israel exploited the pretext of the Hezbollah abductions to launch a campaign that aligned with a series of its long-standing goals, integrated into the United States' aspirations to consolidate its regional hegemonic interests. Among other factors, the eradication of Hezbollah was seen as necessary to stem the tide of "radical" moral and political victories it had been encouraging throughout the Arab world after it forced Israel to withdraw from south Lebanon in May 2000. Indeed, Hezbollah consciously promoted itself as a model of resistance to Palestinian national movement actors, encouraging Palestinians to take their fate into their own hands and not to wait for U.S. intervention to achieve their rights. "Hezbollah, with its modest capabilities, achieved what several Arab governments, with their organized state armies, did not—as they contented themselves with mere silence about the slaughter of our Palestinian brethren," declared Hezbollah's charismatic leader, Hassan Nasrallah, weeks before the war.[80]

The liberation of south Lebanon in 2000 no doubt played a determining role in inspiring Palestinians to believe that they were not confined to the limitations and bankruptcy of the negotiated process. In this respect it was not an accident that the Intifada erupted a mere four months after Israeli troops withdrew from south Lebanon. Though Israel no doubt instigated and inflamed the Intifada to achieve its wider long-term ends to destroy the Palestinian people and national movement, the Intifada was morally sustained in part by the inspirational vision Hezbollah provided for the Palestinians—that despite material and human losses, it was possible to achieve Palestinian rights through resistance and struggle. The confidence of the Palestinians to resist was further strengthened in the wake of Israel's unilateral withdrawal from Gaza in September 2005. Israel's "unilateral disengagement" vindicated the political tides within the Palestinian national movement that argued that steadfastness and resistance were what had brought it about and that in the future would mark the path toward achieving other Palestinian goals. "Four years of pain [because of the sacrifices of the Intifada] is better than ten years in vain [of negotiations]" became Hamas's political slogan after the "disengagement."

For this reason, snuffing out the flame of resistance was perceived as crucial for Israel to eradicate this sentiment from one of its primary sources. In the midst of the 2006 war in Lebanon, the top Israeli military commentator Ze'ev Schiff was succinct in describing in real terms what was actually at stake in Israel's Lebanon campaign:

> Hezbollah and what this terrorist organization symbolizes must be destroyed at any price. This is the only option that Israel has. We cannot afford a situation of strategic parity between Israel and Hezbollah. If Hezbollah does not experience defeat in this war, this will spell the end of Israeli deterrence against its enemies.

Schiff continued:

> If Israel's deterrence is shaken as a result of failure in battle, the hard-won peace with Jordan and Egypt will also be undermined. Israel's deterrence is what lies behind the willingness of moderate Arabs to make peace with it. Hamas, which calls for Israel's destruction, will be strengthened, and it is doubtful whether any Palestinians will be willing to reach agreements with Israel. Therein lies the link between the fight with Hezbollah and the Israeli-Palestinian conflict.[81]

Although Schiff's account clearly twisted the nature of the struggle among Israel, the Arab states, and the Palestinian national movement,[82] it was evident that the war designed to reassert Israeli deterrence only weakened it further. The inability of Israel to divide Lebanese society against itself or to crush Hezbollah, and the formidable resistance the movement waged to defend Lebanon, were an inspiration to enormous swathes of the Arab and Muslim masses discontented with U.S. and Israeli policies in the region and with their own government's silence and complicity in these affairs.

Horrors to Come

The major setback to Israeli and U.S. regional designs did not, however, mean that the designs themselves were done away with. For the time being, Israel and the United States have "returned to the drawing board" to reformulate how better to approach the situation the next time, hoping that a better-formulated plan will yield more favorable results.

Gaza has now become the obvious target for Israel's attempting to resurrect its "deterrence power." The months of September to November 2006 witnessed a campaign of sustained Israeli political incitement against Gaza, replete with accusations that Israel needed to act quickly against Hamas to counter its potential to internalize any of the lessons it might have learned from Hezbollah's successful defense of Lebanon: "If we do not counter the strengthening of Hamas and the Iranian influence in the Gaza Strip, we will be facing a strategic threat within three to five years and a Lebanon-like reality in the Gaza Strip," warned Yuval Diskin, Head of the Israeli Internal Security Services, Shin Bet.[83] The accusation that tons of explosives and weaponry are being smuggled into Gaza and that an "underground city" is in the process of being constructed there, akin to Hezbollah's bunkers, is meant to lay the foundation for Israel eventually launching what it believes is an inevitable all-encompassing attack upon Gaza in the coming period.

The Israeli military operation, Autumn Clouds, launched at the beginning of November and that resulted in the deaths of more than sixty Palestinians in its first week, was only a prelude to the coming bloody scenario. As the *Yediot Ahronot* correspondent Alex Fishman explains:

> Let there be no mistake. This is not the "large-scale operation." . . . The "large-scale operation"—if given the green light—would be a long-term offensive operation employing a different scope of troops entirely. The Autumn Clouds operation, currently in progress, is still part of the series of defensive operations being carried out against Qassam rocket launchers. . . . The idea is to keep up the incessant activity in an attempt to delay the inevitable and to gain time for what looks like the unstoppable strengthening of Hamas. These operations are simply blocking the dam. But alas, only in fairy tales can a flood be stopped with a single finger.[84]

Fishman continued:

> Autumn Clouds is a targeted operation with limited objectives set for a limited period of time. But it is another step in the direction of concentrating military forces in the Gaza Strip. . . . Operations at the edges of urban areas have now moved into populated areas. . . . Such operations also have a "accustoming" effect. The operations are getting the area and the military forces

used to the IDF presence in the Gaza Strip, each time for a longer period and with larger forces. Meanwhile, the IDF is exercising military tactics in residential areas, and commanders are being trained. . . . [T]there is no chance of a political settlement whatsoever with Hamas. Therefore, we are in the midst of a gradual process toward a large-scale military conflict in the Gaza Strip.

No doubt, in their own regard, all Palestinian factions are engaged in preparing for such scenarios, attempting to synthesize the lessons of years of resistance to Israel during this Intifada and the valuable lessons gleaned from Hezbollah's defense of Lebanon. Speaking at the million-strong victory rally held in central Beirut, Hassan Nasrallah underscored the principles behind the movement's success: "This experience, the experience of the resistance, depends upon faith, precision, and preparedness to sacrifice. It depends upon reasoning, planning, arming, and rational consideration. For we are not a random or chaotic resistance, but a devout, knowledgeable, prepared, trained resistance."

Questions of Strategy

The Palestinian national movement understands well, after years of painful sacrifices, that the process of unifying its ranks, resources, and discourse is long overdue. However, Hamas and Fateh's efforts to rectify their differences and form a unified government continue to be stymied by the existence of the old PA security and former bureaucracy elites who were bumped out of power when Hamas won the elections. Their continual incitement against Hamas and cynical manipulation of the legitimate needs of public sector employees who haven't been paid their salaries because of the economic siege on the Hamas government, are nothing more than a ploy to bring these forces back to power. The United States and Israel are also eager to promote these elites, not so much because they actually wish to make deals with them, more so to further divide and weaken the Palestinian political scene and potentially to incite a civil war.

At the heart of the Fateh-Hamas antagonism, however, is not a question of who controls the PA or who can or cannot pay the bills, but rather a question of strategy. Fateh, despite its failure over the years, still believes in a staged approach focusing on statehood, imposed from without by the United States. It argues that this is the only pragmatic way to achieve a modicum of regional stability for all parties involved—the United States, Israel, the Arab states, and the Palestinians. In this sense, it continues to shun the idea of politically challenging Zionism and U.S. imperialism in the region, seeking instead accommodation and participation with these forces and its Arab state allies. It continues to argue that it is as good a partner as any in the framework of the neoliberal U.S. hegemony over the Middle East and continues to demonstrate a willingness to do this at the expense of the historical national rights of the Palestinians and the genuine democratic self-determination of the Arab people.

Hamas, on the other hand, preserves the elements of a liberation strategy in its outlook, rejecting accommodation to Zionism in the pursuit of Palestinian rights. But the real question for Hamas and the resistance umbrella it is holding is how it seeks to attain its rights. Overall, its tactics vis-à-vis Israel continue to be primarily militarily derived. If it retains this tactic as the primary vehicle of the national movement's struggle, it might be able to deter Israel's planned onslaughts against it, similar in ways to how Hezbollah's preparations, training, and arming were able to repel Israel. Although on the ground this may allow for the Palestinian movement to create a more solid base of operations for itself, it can only encourage (and temporarily at that) the logic of unilateralism and apartheid that Israel is only too happy to erect. Like the Gaza Bantustan that emerged after the "unilateral disengagement," Palestinians would simply be pushed onto land reserves that in the end would remain at the mercy of Israel for their economic and social existence. This is a far cry from achieving Palestinian goals of national liberation, decolonization, and the right of return.

Ultimately, nothing can avoid the fact that in order to fully realize Palestinian national goals, the political struggle to subvert the underpinnings of Zionism and the basis of U.S. imperial hegemony in the region must be tackled head on. Likewise, assembling the forces in Palestine, the Arab world, and abroad, to be able to take up this challenge, is a different project not yet entirely embodied by Palestinian actors, whether from Hamas, the Left, or otherwise. The dialectical transitions that the Palestinian movement is going through today in the wake of Arafat's death, and the rise of Hamas to power, set in the context of the U.S. military bogged down in Iraq and the increasingly assertive anti-imperial currents in Egypt, Lebanon, and Iran, are nonetheless ripe grounds for local and regional experiments in building a political alternative for Palestinian and Arab liberation.

At the same time, these transitions will not take place in a political vacuum. The Israeli–U.S.–Arab client state axis is most certainly not sitting on its hands waiting for such an alternative to arise. Already in the wake of the 2006 Lebanon War, the lessons that Israel and the United

States have learned from this experience are becoming evidently clear. Anthony Cordesman, the top U.S. military strategist who initially disclosed the existence of Operation Field of Thorns before the Intifada erupted (see Introduction) recently gave indications of what this is likely to entail. Speaking at a press conference soon after the cease-fire in Lebanon and after returning from the front lines in the region, Cordesman responded to the question of what the results of the war mean for Israel in the future if it seeks to reassert itself:

> From Israel's viewpoint, you have to use force even more against civilian targets. You have to attack deep. You have to step up the intensity of combat and you have to be less careful and less restrained. And if someone injects into this even one or two crude chemical weapons or radiological weapons, the message and the intensity becomes something which is very difficult to see that can be controlled.[85]

Likewise, the Israeli press has been remarkably forthcoming about the scenarios it is developing to ultimately assert its goal of once and for all entrenching the Jewish state in the heart of the Middle East. The senior *Ha'aretz* political commentator Amir Oren, who has close ties to the military establishment, reported on November 6 on Israel's preparation for a "war initiated by Syria or Hezbollah, separately or together, with backing from Iran. The likelihood is that such a conflagration will erupt in the next two years, peaking in the spring–summer months of 2007.[86]

Oren bases his reports on the "General Staff assessments that have been gathered during a series of meetings in recent weeks," in which Chief of Staff Dan Halutz formulated scenarios for the Israeli Army to consider seriously. Such preparations are seen as needed in light of the "growing sense of 'success' among forces in the region that oppose Israel and the West." According to the Israeli Army, because "hostile Arab states, with Syria at the lead, and paramilitary organizations, prominent among them Hezbollah, have relinquished . . . the possibility of a direct confrontation with Israel," these forces "have opted for a war of continuous attrition, with the deployment of infantry forces heavily equipped with antitank weapons, commando units, ballistic weapons and tunnel access. In countering them, the IDF would like to develop necessary preparedness, partly overt, in an effort to deter them or, in case of failure, to achieve a significant military gain quickly, along parameters determined by the political leadership."

With respect to the Palestinian theater, the assessment is equally as bleak: the Palestinians will continue to attempt "to carry out terrorist attacks, with increasingly overt direction by the Hamas government. . . .

The arming of Hamas in the Gaza Strip in recent months, and the ongoing refusal to accept the terms put forth by the Quartet (recognition of Israel, relinquishing violence, acceptance of previous PLO accords with Israel), lend weight to the adoption of an offensive strategy." This analysis is also sure to permanently inscribe the national liberation movement within the logic of the "war on terror," crucial because of its support within the U.S. ruling class establishment in both the Democratic and Republican wings: "The expected escalation in terrorism [from the Palestinians] also includes the gradual but increasing role of the global Jihadist element and a regional movement operating in Egypt, Jordan, Lebanon and other states affiliated with al-Qaida."

Finally, Israel must also prepare for the possibility that pro-U.S. Arab allies in the region may be seeing their last days. This requires Israel to prepare contingency plans for the existence of "[a]ircraft, naval vessels, missiles, and armored vehicles in armies whose governments have peace treaties with, or do not have immediate hostile policies toward Israel, but who could become immediate threats upon the collapse of their regime, or in-fighting over succession, and the rise of hostile regimes."

Though Israel remains confident that "[t]he United States will try to preserve the principle of 'quality advantage' in favor of the IDF, by making available the most advanced systems to Israel, while delivering to (currently) moderate [Arab] states systems lacking the more sophisticated upgrades," the mere existence of these contingency scenarios is indication of the logic and direction the United States and Israel are heading in.

In these days when the horrors to come are promised by the very logic of the ideology and praxis of the state actors themselves, the imperative to unite and integrate the struggles to liberate the people of Palestine and the Arab world within the worldwide struggle against imperialism, capitalist globalization and it essential arm in this region, Zionist colonialism, couldn't be more apparent or needed. The Al Aqsa Intifada, and most recently the heroic resistance of the Lebanese people against Israel, have shown that history is not predetermined. With the right combination of struggle, organization, and politics, people of limited means can not only repel the reactionary designs of the "masters of the world" but build a world based on a different logic entirely. Today, as has been the case for the past sixty years, the question of Palestine is an inseparable part of the language of liberation, justice, and equality. Now is the time to synthesize these efforts locally, regionally and internationally into a program for Palestinian and Arab liberation and a better world overall, before it's too late.

A Word on Solutions

This book has focused on exposing how present-day Israel is not only a product of the Zionist colonization project, but also an instrument for the further advancement and expansion of this project under the wings of U.S. imperialism. Its goal of eliminating the Palestinian nation is part and parcel of the role that Israel plays as a subcontractor for the interests of U.S. imperialism in the Middle East. This task, which up to now has been successfully accomplished in collusion with the "moderate" Arab states, entails the subversion of any genuine national self-determination or democracy for the people of the region. Within the contemporary ideological framework of the "war on terror," any state that dares to deviate from absolute submission to U.S. rule is doomed to be destroyed.

It is within this context that one must approach the ongoing debates about the question of what is the most adequate political solution to the Palestinian-Israeli "conflict," whether in a "two-state," "binational," or "secular-democratic" framework.

Without getting entangled in the specificities of each solution, an assessment of the present relation of forces locally, regionally, and globally is where this discussion really needs to begin.

This means understanding that an alignment of forces behind the U.S.-Zionist axis blocks any solution that would recognize the national rights of the Palestinian people. Moreover, the daily policies of Israel in the West Bank and Gaza Strip, as well as toward the Palestinian citizens of Israel, continues to prove that the goal of ethnic cleansing, which Zionism adopted since its early days, has remained the real goal underlying these policies. Until a mass expulsion can be enacted, these policies are institutionalizing the annexation of the 1967 Occupied Territories without granting any real human rights to its population. They also continue to deepen the dispossession of 1948 Palestinians, and erode their already second-class, conditional citizenship in the Jewish state. Given this reality, observers should not expect that any solution is imminent under current circumstances.

It goes without saying however that the de-Zionization of Israel is indeed a condition for the realization of the rights of the Palestinian people: to bring about the decolonization of the 1967 Occupied Territories, equality for Palestinian citizens of Israel, and return of the 1948 refugees. It also goes without saying that U.S. support for Israel must be broken before any just solution becomes possible, and that U.S. imperialism regionally must be subverted.

Meanwhile it is important not to lower the ceiling of expectation about what a solution should be on the path to liberation, while simultaneously and consciously working toward building the forces that harbor these interests and are working on a daily basis to realize important transitional elements.

This is why the resistance struggles of the very forces that have the potential to transform this reality have such significance, and why directing energy toward supporting them is so crucial. These struggles are those of the Palestinian people for decolonization of the West Bank and Gaza (represented today in the forces mobilized by the Al Aqsa Intifada and led by Hamas, together with other groupings); the fight for full equality of Palestinian citizens of Israel (led by the NDA-Tajamu' movement); the fight of Palestinian refugees to return (a front that is largely passive, although in different stages of building solidarity alliances throughout the Arab and Western world); the fight of Arab resistance movements against U.S. imperialism and Zionism (represented most prominently in the Iraqi resistance to the U.S. occupation of Iraq, and the Lebanese resistance of Hezbollah against Israel); and the Arab masses opposing their respective illegitimate undemocratic regimes (a front yet to be activated though no doubt in formation).

It is the historical obligation of solidarity forces to support these struggles in their fights against Zionism and U.S. imperialism, while at the same time supporting and building the secular, progressive Left.

Only after envisioning the thorough transformation of the Middle East—whereby the oppression inflicted on the people of the region by U.S. imperialism, the rule of the reactionary Arab regimes, and the status of Israel as a regional power, ends—does the question of a genuine solution become possible.

An independent and democratic Middle East is a requirement for the destructive impact of Western imperialism on the Arab nation and Palestinian people to be done away with.

Therefore if such a fundamental transformation is necessary for a just solution, then why limit our vision for what a solution should be *a priori*? Such a solution could only exist as a series of partial arrangements that are doomed to fail within the current relations of forces. Instead we must strive to achieve this transformation in full, and explore the possibilities it opens up: some form of reunification of the Arab nation in a federation of democratic-socialist states including reconnecting the Palestinians to the broader Arab nation. Only in a united, free Middle East can a political solution that will include the individual and collective rights of Palestinians and Israeli Jews be realized within a political framework that both sides in the "conflict" will agree upon.

We believe that the quest for national identity and cultural heritage does not necessarily imply the need for a separate state apparatus as is often argued. All collective rights, however, can and should be recognized within a political framework, the exact outlines of which are secondary as long as it is achieved by the free decision of the people.

In any case, it is clear that the struggle to find a solution to the question of Palestine is indeed a long one, requiring the unity of all resisting movements in the region, along with building a strong secular left power locally, regionally, and globally. This power must be capable of replacing the present oppressive regimes with just and equal socio-economic structures, thus liberating the people of the region from the forces of globalized capitalism that work hand in hand with U.S. imperialism to enslave them. The Al Aqsa Intifada is a testament to the determined human will to challenge enormous powers of oppression. Let its spirit and its lessons infuse our work for the long road ahead.

The Editors

Contributors

About the Editors

Tikva Honig-Parnass was raised in the prestate Zionist community in Palestine, and fought in its army in the War of 1948. Between 1951 and 1955, she served as the Knesset secretary for the far left Zionist party Mapam. In 1974 she received her Ph.D. in sociology from Duke University and lectured at Tel Aviv University. In 1987, she joined the then anti-Zionist and socialist Alternative Information Center (AIC), which was affiliated with the Israeli branch of the 4th International. From 1989 to June 2000 she edited the AIC English monthly magazine *News from Within*, the last two years of which, she worked together with Toufic Haddad, until they were both fired. In November 2000 she and Haddad co-founded *Between the Lines*, which they co-edited until September 2003.

Tikva Honig-Parnass has been active in the radical antioccupation movements as well as with several attempts of Mizrahi feminists to unite with Palestinian citizens in a joint struggle for democratization of the Jewish-Zionist state. She is now working on her book, *The Jewish-Zionist State in the Left Discourse in Israel*, for Muwatin, the Palestinian Institute for the Study of Democracy.

Toufic Haddad is a Palestinian-American writer and activist who was born and lived in Kuwait until the 1990–91 Gulf War. After studying in the United States, he moved to the West Bank in 1997 and worked at the Alternative Information Center, co-editing the monthly journal *News from Within* with Tikva Honig-Parnass. In November 2000, he co-founded *Between the Lines*, in partnership with Honig-Parnass, co-editing the journal for the following three years. He is also a co-founder of the Beit Jibrin Cultural Center, a progressive educational youth and community center located in Beit Jibrin (Azzeh) refugee Camp (est. 1999), and is a frequent contributor to the *International Socialist Review*.

About the Contributors

Marwan Barghouti is from the village of Kobar near Ramallah. Upon the outbreak of the Al Aqsa Intifada, he was quickly identified as one of its most prominent and charismatic spokespersons. He did so within his capacity as the secretary-general of the Fateh party in the West Bank, a position he has held since 1994. A former student leader of Fateh at Birzeit University, Barghouti was exiled to Jordan in 1987, and was only permitted to return to the Occupied Territories in 1994. In 1996 he was elected to the Palestinian Legislative Council for the district of Ramallah. In April 2002 he was arrested by the Israeli Army where he was tried, convicted, and sentenced to five life sentences. Barghouti refused to recognize the court's legitimacy and demanded instead that "the occupation be put on trial." In December 2004, Barghouti temporarily challenged Fateh head Mahmoud Abbas (Abu Mazen), nominating himself as a candidate in PA presidential elections. Had he remained in the race, public opinion polls showed that he had a good chance of winning the elections.

Dr. Azmi Bishara is a Palestinian citizen of Israel and leads the National Democratic Assembly—Tajamu' party in the Israeli Knesset. Tajamu' initiated the transformation of the political discourse of the Palestinians in Israel, challenging the Jewish–Zionist nature of the state. He frequently writes for *Al Hayat* (London) and *Al Ahram* (Egypt).

Dr. Sami Shalom Chetrit is a radical Mizrahi activist, thinker, poet, writer, and film maker. More information on him and his work can be found at www.authorsden.com/sschetrit.

Dr. Saleh Abdel Jawwad is a professor of History at Birzeit University and lives in el Bireh in the West Bank.

Husam Khader is a refugee from Jaffa whose family was forced into exile in 1948. He grew up in Balata refugee camp in Nablus, and emerged as a leader of the Fateh movement in Nablus. Khader was exiled in 1986 and only returned to Palestine in 1994. In 1996 he was elected to the Palestinian Legislative Council as a member of Fateh for the district of Nablus. He is also the founder and director of the Committee for the Defense of Palestinian Refugee Rights, based in Balata camp. Khader was arrested in March 2003 and sentenced to seven years in prison by an Israeli military tribunal. For more information on his case and the campaign to free Khader, see http://www.hussamkhader.com/english.

Eileen Kuttab is the director of the Women's Studies Center at Birzeit University and an activist in the Palestinian women's movement.

Dr. Yitzhak Laor is a poet, writer, and literary critic. He was born in 1948, and has published fifteen different books including novels, poetry, and essays. He presently writes for the Israeli daily *Ha'aretz* and is the editor of the new critical quarterly *Mita'am*.

Dr. Adi Ophir is a professor of philosophy at the Institute of History and Philosophy of Sciences at Tel Aviv University.

Dr. Ilan Pappe is a senior lecturer in the department of political science at Haifa University and the chair of the Emil Touma Institute for Palestinian studies in Haifa. He is the author of *The Making of the Arab-Israeli Conflict* (1992), *The Israel/Palestine Question* (1999), and *A History of Modern Palestine: One Land, Two Peoples* (2003).

Linda Tabar is a Ph.D. Candidate at the School of Oriental and African Studies, University of London, and is a researcher working with Muwatin, the Palestinian Institute for the Study of Democracy. She also recently supervised an oral history project in Jenin camp for Shaml, the Center for Refugee and Diaspora Studies.

Graham Usher is a journalist based in the 1967 occupied territories and author of *Palestine In Crisis: The Struggle For Peace And Political Independence After* (Pluto Press 1995 and 1997), *Dispatches From Palestine: The Rise and Fall of the Oslo Peace Process* (Pluto Press 1999) and, with John Torday, *A People Called Palestine* (Dewi Lewis Publishing 2001).

Dr. Jamal Zahalqa is among the founders of the National Demo-cratic Assembly—Tajamu', and is the former director of Ahali Center for Community Development based in Nazareth. In January 2003, Zahalqa became a member of Knesset on the NDA—Tajamu' ticket.

Acknowledgments

We would like to thank all the individuals and organizations who supported our work financially and allowed us to continue publishing in the difficult circumstances that we were working under. Without your help and loyalty to our work and message, particularly after we were fired from the Alternative Information Center, we would not have been able to continue. Thank you all. This includes in no special order, Barbara Lubin and the Middle East Children's Alliance, Mizue Aizeki and Layla Welborn, Jonathan Elsberg, Hilt Teuwen of OXFAM Belgium, Mattias Hui, Albert Reiger, Iara Lee, George Gund and Katie McCaffrey, Charles Udry and Page 2, the Collectif Urgence Palestine in Lausanne, Henry Noble and the Freedom Socialist Party, the Galil Foundation, Shirabe Yamada, and Ben S.

We would also like to thank all of our committed subscribers and writers who contributed to the project, making it the unique project that it was. We apologize for not being able to include all the material published in the magazine within this book. Hopefully one day we will be able to find means of doing so. Particular thanks goes out to Graham Usher, Amnon Raz-Krakotzkin, Sami Shalom Chetrit, Heidar Eid, Saleh Abdel Jawwad, Shraga Elam, Saleh el Masri, Allegra Pachecco, Lucy Mair, Shiko Behar, Azmi Bishara, Vijay Prashad, Gilbert Achcar, Islah Jad, Linda Tabar, Khaleda Jarrar, Mufid Qassoum, Naseer Aruri, Yitzhak Laor, Ingrid Jaradat Gasner, Mohammed Jaradat, Erella Shadmi, and Terry Rempel.

Just as important are the many people who helped in different capacities in the production of *Between the Lines*, as well as those who supported us in the years after the magazine stopped publishing, when we were struggling to produce this book. In no special order, this includes Amichai, Hanna and Maya Kronfeld, Sivan and Yuval Parnass-Madar, Tina Beyene, Anthony Arnove, Birgit Althaler and Urs Diethelm, Ala and Azzeh Al Azzeh, the Beit Jibrin Cultural Center and all the friends in Beit Jibrin Refugee Camp, Abu Younis and Umm Younis Al Azzeh, Sami Abu Salem, Abed Asouli, Qassem Kafarneh and the staff of *Ramattan Daily*, Marwa and Azzeh Kafarneh, Mashraqiyyat, Ziad Abbas and Ibda' Cultural Center, Abu Ahmed and his print shop staff, Mizue Aizeki, Layla Welborn, comrades from the International Socialist Organization, Charity Crouse, Alisa Klien and Amy Stamm, Tanya and Ghassan Haddad, Mark Scott, May Jayyousi, Awatef El Sheikh, Tzaporah Ryter, Uda Walker, Mariam Shahin, George Azar, Mounir Kleibo, Diana Buttu, Karma Abu Sharif, Anis and Abed Daraghmeh, Ala Jaradat, Anne and Charles Haddad, and Maria Damelio.

A special thank you goes out to Lance Selfa, Dao Tran, Julie Fain, and Anthony Arnove for their work on the manuscript and finally making it publishable.

We hope we have not left anyone out, and are indebted to you all.

Finally, we dedicate this book to all those, who since the Intifada began, were fighting for liberation, return, justice and peace, but who did not live to see these ideas realized in their lifetime. Your spirit lives on, and so does your fight.

Tikva and Toufic

Notes

Foreword

1. *Between the Lines* was cofounded and coedited by Tikva Honig-Parnass and Toufic Haddad in November 2000. From its inception, it was produced on a volunteer basis, with great help provided by our writers and a circle of individuals and organizations who likewise believed in its mission. It ceased publishing as a consequence of its accumulated debt.

2. "1967 Palestinians" commonly refers to the Palestinians within the 1967 Occupied Territories of the West Bank and Gaza Strip. "1948 Palestinians" commonly refers to the Palestinians who remained inside the newly created state of Israel after 1948 and were later granted Israeli citizenship.

3. The Green Line refers to the 1949 armistice line dividing the newly created state of Israel from the West Bank, then under Jordanian rule, and the Gaza Strip, then under Egyptian rule.

4. Mizrahi Jews are Jews who originate from the Arab world.

5. "Popular classes" refers here to everyone, including day laborers who used to make their incomes working in Israel (often in the service or construction sectors), farmers, public-sector employees within the Palestinian Authority (teachers, ministerial clerks, and even PA security service members), the unemployed, and others. These strata are to be contrasted to "Palestinian elites," who include the local forces who dominate the Palestinian economy (acting often as liaisons for Israeli capitalists), as well as decision makers within PA ministries.

Introduction

1. Abram Leon's theory of Jews as a "people-class" is an attempt to provide a general Marxist interpretation of Jewish history. (See his book *The Jewish Question, a Marxist Interpretation* (New York: Pathfinder, 2002), which includes an illuminating introduction by Nathan Weinstock.) Leon determines that the ascendance of modern capital-

ism in Europe brought about the loss of the specific social and economic functions that Jews played in precapitalist societies as agents of a monetary economy. However, while in Western Europe the loss of their specific function was compensated for by the integration of Jews economically and socially, this phenomenon did not occur in Eastern Europe. The structural weakness of capitalism there prevented the absorption of the Jewish masses who were evicted from their traditional occupations in the economy. Moreover, the local ruling classes, faced with a permanent social and economic crisis, resorted to Jew baiting and persecution, aimed at mutating the spontaneous, elementary anticapitalist sentiment of the masses into anti-Semitism.

The Tel Aviv University historian Shlomo Sand also emphasizes that Zionism was initiated by Eastern European Jewry. However, his analysis emphasizes the fact that only in Eastern Europe did the Jewish community develop the characteristic buds of a national entity. See Shlomo Sand, *Historians, Time and Imagination* (Tel Aviv: Am Oved Publishers, 2004).

2. Shlomo Avinery, *The Making of Modern Zionism: The Intellectual Origins of the Jewish State* (New York: Basic Books, 1981), 5.

3. Shlomo Sand, *Historians,* and Boaz Evron, *The National Accounting* (Or Yehuda: Dvir Publishing, 1998), which was also translated into Arabic by Cairo University Publishing in 1996.

4. These imagined myths, which Benedict Anderson has depicted in other national movements, have been stubbornly clung to by the Israeli academic community, which forcefully rejects any scientific attempt to challenge them. Among the few who do are Sand, Historians, and Evron, *National Accounting.*

5. "Sephardim in Israel: Zionism from the Standpoint of Its Jewish Victims," *Social Text* 19–20 (Fall 1988) (special issue on Colonial Discourse): 1–35.

6. In Hertzel's book *Der Judenstaat* (1896), translated as *The Jewish State: An Attempt at a Modern Solution of the Jewish Question* (London: H. Pordes, 1972), 30.

7. Max Nordau, "Zionist Works," vol. 4, The Zionist Library (Jerusalem: The Executive of the Zionist Organization, 1962), 203.

8. Ze'ev Sternhell, *Nation Building or a New Society? The Zionist Labor Movement (1914–1940) and the Origins of Israel* (Tel Aviv: Am Oved Publishers, 1995). The English version was published as *The Founding Myths of Israel: Nationalism, Socialism, and the Making of the Jewish State* (Princeton, N.J.: Princeton University Press, 1997). Sand, *Historians.* Ilan Pappe, "From the 'Empty Land' to the 'Promised Land' and Back: In the Footsteps of Altneuland," *Mitaam* 1 (January 2005): 79–86. Of course, the civic, secular nationalism that developed in Western Europe and the United States must also be cited for its practices of imperialism and slaveholding, precisely while it was espousing its enlightened ideals of citizenship.

9. In 1977, the Labor Party lost the elections for the first time since the establishment of the state in 1948. It was replaced by the right-wing Likud party, formed from the old Herut party, which absorbed the remains of Hatziyonim Hachadishim (General Zionists). The Likud government was headed by Menachem Begin, the commander of the prestate dissident right-wing militia, Etzel, which was built on the political ideas of Ze'ev Jabontinski, an ideologue of "entire Eretz Israel." In 1925, Jabotinsky formed the World Union of Zionist Revisionists party and the youth movement Beitar. After a decade of opposition to the official Zionist leadership, he and his group seceded from the movement altogether and established the New Zionist Organization, which elected him as president. (See Avi Shlaim, *The Iron Wall, Israel and the Arab World* (New York: W. W. Norton, 2001), 11–13.

10. Gershon Shafir, "Land, Labor and Population in the Zionist Colonization: General and Unique Perspectives," in *Israeli Society: Critical Perspectives,* ed. Uri Ram (Tel Aviv: Breirot Publishers, 1993), 104–20. The article is based on the author's study *Land, Labor and the Origins of the Israeli Palestinian Conflict, 1882–1914* (Cambridge, England: Cambridge University Press, 1989).

11. See the illuminating article by Adam Hanieh, "From State-Led Growth to Global-ization: The Evolution of Israeli Capitalism," *Journal of Palestine Studies* 23, no. 4 (Summer 2003).

12. Gershon Shafir, *Israeli Society*, 5–21. See also Baruch Kimmerling, *Zionism and Territory: The Socio-Territorial Dimensions of the Zionist Politics* (Berkeley 1983), and a summary of his positions in *Immigrants, Settlers, Natives: The Israeli State and Society Between Cultural Pluralism and Cultural Wars* (Tel Aviv: Am Oved Publishing, 2004) and Tamar Guzanski, *The Development of Capitalism in Palestine* (Mifalim Universitayim, 1986), 113.

    Noam Chomsky emphasizes the complexity of the motives behind the dispossess-ing policies that accompany the settlement of the land: "In part they can be traced to chauvinism and 'Exclusivist' ideology, but in part they also reflected the dilemmas of socialists who hoped to build an egalitarian society with a Jewish working class, not a society of Jewish wealthy planters exploiting the natives. The *Yishuv* was thus faced with a profound, never resolved contradiction. The Kibbutzim are a conspicuous case of this contradiction between their adherence to socialism on the one hand and the fact that they were constructed on lands purchased by the Jewish National Fund and from which Palestinians were excluded in principle, lands that were in many instances purchased from absentee landlords with little regard for the peasants that lived and worked on them." See Noam Chomsky, *Middle East Illusions* (Lanham, MD: Row-man & Littlefield, 2003), 13.

13. See Sternhell, *Nation Building*, and Michal Frenkel, "Reselling the Dead Sea: A Re-sponse to Meron Benvenisti," *News from Within* 15, no. 4 (April 1999).

14. Michael Shalev, *Labour and the Political Economy in Israel* (Oxford, England: Oxford University Press, 1992).

15. Sternhell, *Nation Building*.

16. On the supremacy of collective goals in Israeli political culture, see Shmuel N. Eisen-stadt, *Israeli Society in its Transformations* (Jerusalem: Magnes, 1989); Dan Horowitz and Moshe Lisak, *Trouble in Utopia: The Overburdened Polity of Israel* (Tel Aviv: Am Oved Publishers, 1990), chap. 6; Baruch Kimmerling, "Between the Primodial and the Civil Definitions of the Collective Identity: Eretz Israel or the State of Israel?" *Comparative Social Dynamics*, ed. Erik Cohen, et al. (Boulder, CO: Westview Press, 1985); Peter Medding, *The Founding of Israeli Democracy, 1948–1967* (New York: Ox-ford University Press, 1990), chap. 4; Charles Liebman and Don Yehiya, *Civil Reli-gion in Israel: Traditional Judaism and Political Culture in the Jewish State* (Berkeley: University of California Press, 1983), chap. 4.

17. See United Nations General Assembly, A/364, "UNSCOP Report to the General Assembly," September 3, 1947.

18. Gershon Shafir refers to the variety of models of colonialist movements and societies studied by D. K. Fieldhouse, *The Colonial Empires from the Eighteenth Century* (New York: Weidenfeld & Nicolson, 1996), and George Fredrickson, "Colonialism and Racism: The United States and South Africa in Comparative Perspective," in *The Arro-gance of Race* (Middletown, CT: Wesleyan University Press, 1988). Based on them, Shafir differentiates among four types of colonies: "The Military (an occupation colony), the Mixed Colony (namely the mix of the different ethnic groups), the Planta-tion Colony, and finally the Pure Settlement Colony (in which all the population or its majority are strictly European). Unlike the Military Colony the three others are settlement colonies, namely colonies based on the settlement of European popula-tion and on taking control of its economic resources, first of all—the lands." ("Land, Labor," 106).

19. Regarding the Zionist brand of colonialism, see Moshe Machover, "Is it Apartheid?," circulated on his personal list serve November 10, 2004. Available at www .pamolson.org/ArtApartheid.htm. Also Gershon Shafir, *Land, Labor and Population in Zionist Colonization: General and Distinct Aspects in the Israeli Society—Critical Per-*

spectives, ed. Uri Ram (Haifa: Breirot Publishers, 1993), based partially on Gershon Shafir's *Land* and Azmi Bishara, "Separation Spells Racism," *Al-Ahram Weekly*, July 1–7, 2004, http://weekly.ahram.org.eg/2004/697/op2.htm.

20. Gershon Shafir, "Land, Labor."

21. For the concept of ethnic cleansing looming in Zionist thought from its onset, see Nur Masalha, *Expulsion of the Palestinians: The Concept of "Transfer" in Zionist Political Thought, 1882–1948* (London: Pluto Press, 1992); Masalha, *Imperial Israel and the Palestinians: A Politics of Expansion* (London: Pluto Press, 2000). Also, according to his article "For the Record" published in the UK *Guardian* on January 14, 2004, the Israeli historian Benny Morris points to information supplied by released official documents that proves that transfer had been looming in the Zionist thought for decades before it was carried out in 1948. In another article, also published in the *Guardian* ("A New Exodus for the Middle East," October 3, 2002), Morris says that there was no choice but to commit the ethnic cleansing. See also Benny Morris, *1948 and After: Israel and the Palestinians* (New York: Oxford University Press, 1994), 159–211, and its Hebrew version, *Tikun ta'ut: yehudim ve-'aravim be-Eretz Isra'el* (Tel Aviv: Am Oved, 2000); Benny Morris, *The Birth of the Palestinian Refugee Problem Revisited* (Cambridge: Cambridge University Press, 2004). For a critical review of Morris's writings, see Joel Beinin, "No More Tears: Benny Morris and the Road Back from Liberal Zionism," *Middle East Report* 230 (Spring 2004).

It is worth noting that Labor Zionists, including significant currents in the Marxist party of Mapam (the acronym for the Unified Workers' Party), did not view the idea of mass transfer as morally deplorable at any time and their hesitation related only to its political effectiveness.

22. See Ilan Pappe, "From the 'Empty Land.'"

23. On the segregation policies, including the necessity to exclude land and labor from competitive market mechanisms, see Shafir, "Land, Labor." See also Kimmerling, *Zionism and Territory*, and a summary of his positions in *Immigrants, Settlers, and Natives*, and Guzanski, *Development of Capitalism*, 113.

24. The Histadrut was also in charge of "defensive" tasks, which included attacking and expelling Palestinian farmers from land bought by Jewish national institutions.

25. Ben-Gurion early on accepted the concept of partition, understanding that it was vital for gaining a deeper foothold in Palestine. When discussing the tactic of accepting partition (in this case vis-à-vis the partition proposals articulated by the Peel Commission of 1937), Ben-Gurion wrote, "No Zionist can forgo the smallest portion of the Land of Israel. [A] Jewish state in part [of Palestine] is not an end, but a beginning. . . . Our possession is important not only for itself . . . through this we increase our power, and every increase in power facilitates getting hold of the country in its entirety. Establishing a [smaller] state . . . will serve as a very potent lever in our historical effort to redeem the whole country." Benny Morris, *Righteous Victims: A History of the Zionist Arab Conflict* (New York: Vintage Books, 2001), 138.

26. The proposed Arab state had 725,000 Arabs and 10,000 Jews. Jerusalem, designated an international zone, had 105,000 Arabs and 100,000 Jews. The Jewish state had 56 percent of the territory of Palestine and most of the arable land, but Arabs held ownership rights to approximately 90 percent of this land.

27. The secret agreement reached between the Zionists and King Abdullah just twelve days before the U.N. decision on November 29, 1947, which was part of a global strategy to prevent the establishment of a Palestinian state, completed the Zionist scheme. It led to the partition of the Palestinian state, which was never established, between the Zionist state and the Hashemite kingdom. See Simha Flapan, *The Birth of Israel: Myths and Realities*, (New York: Pantheon, 1988); Avi Shlaim, *Collusion Across the Jordan: King Abdullah, the Zionist Movement and the Partition of Palestine* (New York: Columbia University Press, 1988); Ilan Pappe, *Britain and the Arab-Israeli Conflict, 1948–51* (London: Palgrave Macmillan, 1988); Morris, *Birth of Palestinian Refugee*.

28. There is no single authoritative source for the exact number of Palestinian refugees displaced. Badil Resource Center for Palestinian Residency & Refugee Rights estimates this figure at 750,000 to 900,000 and quite valuably qualifies this by comparing the various sources (Palestinian researchers, independent researchers, U.N. documentation, British Foreign Office estimates, U.S. government estimates, and Israeli estimates). See "Estimated Initial Palestinian Refugee Population by Year of Displacement" at www.badil.org/Statistics/population/01.pdf.

29. Gabriel Piterberg, "Mechikot," in *Mitaam* 1 (January 2005), 29–44; translated from *New Left Review*, 10, 2001.

30. Between October 1948 and November 1949, the Israeli Army evacuated the villages of al-Safsaf, Iqrit, Kufr Biram, Kufr 'Anan, Khasas, Jau'neh, Qayttiyeh, al-Ghabasiyya, al-Majdal, and al-Battat and later seized all of their properties. In 1951, the Israeli Army evacuated thirteen villages in the Triangle area and seized their properties. In October 1956, the Israeli Army forced the Palestinian Bedouin tribe al-Bakara to cross the border into Syria. In October 1959, some Bedouin tribes in the Negev Desert were forced to cross the borders into Egypt and Jordan. The lands of all these villages and tribes were confiscated after their cleansing; see Sabri Jiryis, *The Arabs in Israel*, trans. Inea Bushnaq (New York: Monthly Review Press, 1976). For details and maps of the depopulation of Palestinian villages and towns, see Salman Abu Sitta, *From Refugees to Citizens at Home: The End of the Israeli Palestinian Conflict* (London: Palestine Land Society, 2001) and Walid Khalidi, *All That Remains: The Palestinian Villages Occupied and Depopulated by Israel in 1948* (Beirut: Institute for Palestine Studies, 1992).

31. About one quarter of the Palestinian citizens of Israel were made refugees during 1948, though they still were able to remain within the area that became Israel and later acquired Israeli citizenship.

32. Less than 8 percent of the lands within the borders of Israel were owned by Jews before 1948; see Pappe, "From 'Empty Land,'" 79–87.

33. It should be remembered that Israel was admitted to the United Nations (as per U.N. General Assembly Resolution [UNGA] 273 of May 11, 1949) on a conditional basis, pending its compliance with UNGA Resolutions 181 and 194 of December 11, 1948. The former resolution called for the division of Palestine into two states (one Jewish, the other Arab), while the latter stipulated the right of return for Palestinian refugees. Israel's failure to implement either resolution was the basis for arguing that its membership in the United Nations was (is) illegitimate. Moreover, Israel's expansion during the 1948 War into areas beyond the boundaries allocated to the Jewish state subsequent to Resolution 181 further eroded its legitimacy status. This formed the basis for Israel's efforts to win international public opinion by establishing a formal democracy, thereafter claiming to apply equal rights to the Palestinians who remained within its newly created borders.

34. David Kretzmer, *The Legal Status of the Arabs in Israel* (Boulder, CO: Westview Press, 1990), 36.

35. *Oleh* is the Hebrew word used to refer to a Jew immigrating to Israel. Every Jew already settled in the country or born there is deemed to be a person who came to the country as *oleh*. The word literally refers to someone who "ascends" to Jerusalem and the "promised land" and does not just "immigrate" to Israel.

36. For review of the Law of Return and other Basic Laws of the first years of the state, see David Kretzmer, *Legal Status of Arabs*.

37. Other seemingly nondiscriminatory criteria are employed to facilitate different rules or arrangements being applied on national lines. Thus, for example, under the pretext of military service, a wide assortment of rights is denied to Palestinian citizens. For the means used to avoid an apartheid nature of the state through special laws against the Palestinian citizens, see "South Africa, Israel-Palestine, and the Contours of the

Contemporary Global Order," Noam Chomsky interviewed by Christopher J. Lee, *Safundi*, March 9, 2004.

38. Emergency legislation still in use today includes:
    The Press Ordinance (1933)
    Defense (Emergency) Regulations (1945)
    Order for the Extension of the Validity of Emergency Regulations (Foreign Travel) (1948)
    Prevention of Terrorism Ordinance (1948)
    Ship Order (Limitation of Transfer and Mortgaging) (1948)
    Firearms Law (1949)
    State of Emergency Land Appropriation Administration Law (1949)
    Prevention of Infiltration (Offences and Jurisdiction) Law (1954)
    Control of Products and Services Law (1957)
    Emergency State Search Authorities Law (Temporary Order) (1969)
    Extension of Emergency Regulation Law (Legal Administration and Additional Regulations) (1969)
    Extension of Emergency Regulations Law (1973)
    Emergency Powers (Detention) Law (1979)
    Security Service (Combined Version) (1986)
    Registration of Equipment and Its Enlistment to the IDF Law (1987)

39. For the way the Defense Regulations enabled the "security" control of the Palestinian citizens in the first decades of the state, see Ian Lustick, *Arabs in the Jewish State, Israeli Control of a National Minority* (Austin: University of Texas Press, 1980), the Hebrew version being published by Mifras Publishing House, 1985. For the ongoing reliance on these regulations for persecuting the Palestinian leadership in Israel, see "The Case of MK Azmi Bishara," in Chapter 4 in this book. For the use of these regulations against Jewish Israeli dissenters (regarding the trial of Michel Warschawski and the Alternative Information Center in 1986), see "A Political Sentence Against Warschawski and AIC," *News from Within* 5, no. 7, November 29, 1989, and Tikva Honig-Parnass, "The High Court Verdict: Four Warnings to the Israeli Protest Movement," *News from Within* 6, no. 6, July 5, 1990.

40. See Frantz Fanon, *The Wretched of the Earth* (New York: Grove Press, 1963).

41. Giorgio Aganben, *State of Exception* (Chicago: University of Chicago Press, 2005).

42. Baruch Kimmerling, "Neither Democratic nor Jewish," *Ha'aretz*, December 27, 1996.

43. The two laws relating to the monopoly on jurisdiction of the religious establishment in family affairs: Hok Shiput Batai Din Rabaniim, (Nisuim ve gerushim), 1953, and Hok Hadayanim, 1955; other laws that are influenced by Jewish Halacha include the Work Hours and Days of Rest Law and the Freedom of Occupation Law.

44. Baruch Kimmerling, "Religion, Nationalism and Democracy in Israel," *Zmanim* 13, no. 50–51 (1994): 116–32.

45. See Hanieh, "From State-Led Growth" and, by the same author, "Class, Economy, and the Second Intifada," *Monthly Review* 54, no. 5 (October 2002): 29–42; Shlomo Svirski, "Israel in the Global Space," in *The Power of Property*, ed. Dani Filk and Uri Ram (Jerusalem: The Van Leer Institute and Hakibutz Hameuchad Publishing House, 2004), 57–84; Shlomo Svirski and Devora Berenstein, "Who Worked, for Whom and for How Much? The Economic Development of Israel and the Emergence of the Ethnic Division of Labor in Israeli Society," in *Israeli Society: Critical Perspectives*, ed. Uri Ram (Haifa: Breirot Publisher, 1993), 120–48; and Swirski and Berenstein, "Rapid Economic Development," 64–85.

46. Since the mid-1970s, military-related industries became the fastest-growing sector of Israel's economy, and by the early 1980s employed about one quarter of the country's labor force.

47. See Emmanuel Farajun, "Class Divisions in Israeli Society," in *Forbidden Agendas* (London: Al Saqi Books, 1984), 56–69, and, by the same author in this book, "Palestinian Workers in Israel: A Reserve Army of Labor," 77–123.

48. Aziz Haidar, *On the Margins: The Arab Population in the Israeli Economy* (New York: St. Martin's Press, 1995).

49. Svirski and Berenstein, "Rapid Economic Development."

50. As the critical political commentator of *Ha'aretz* newspaper and well-known researcher Meron Benvenisti puts it, the Israeli-Palestinian conflict is viewed in Israeli discourse as "the unfinished business of the 1948 War"; *Ha'aretz*, May 3, 2001. Indeed, the aspiration to conquer the West Bank was strong in wide circles of the Israeli political and military establishment: "Among many officers prevailed the feeling that Ben-Gurion is guilty of not letting us do what we wanted to do in the War of Independence [the 1948 War], and we are waiting for an opportunity to do so [expel the 1948 Palestinians]." Quoted from Tom Segev's book *1967: And the Land Changed Completely*, in Gidi Weitz, *Yediot Ahronot*, June 3, 2005.

51. Noam Chomsky, "At This Moment Israel Is Almost an American Base," *Mitan* 6 (June 2006): 95–101. For a concise history of U.S.-Israel relations, see Chomsky's introduction to *The New Intifada: Resisting Israel's Apartheid*, ed. Roane Carey (London/New York: Verso, 2001), and Lance Selfa, "Israel: The U.S. Watchdog," *International Socialist Review* 4 (Spring 1998), as well as its references. For a more detailed history, see, among many other Chomsky texts, *Fateful Triangle: The United States, Israel, and the Palestinians*, updated ed. (Cambridge, MA: South End Press, 1999), and *Middle East Illusions*, (Lanham, MD: Rowman & Littlefield Publishers, 2003).

52. Also see Israel Shahak, *Israel's Global Role: Weapons for Repression* (with introduction by Noam Chomsky) (Washington, D.C.: Association of Arab-American University Graduates, 1982); Benjamin Beit-Hallahmi, *The Israeli Connection: Who Israel Arms and Why* (New York: Pantheon, 1987); Benjamin Beit-Hallahmi, "U.S.–Israeli-Central American Connection," *The Link* (a publication of Americans for Middle East Understanding, Inc.), 18, no. 4 (November 1985); Jane Hunter, *Israeli Foreign Policy: South Africa and Central America* (Boston: South End Press, 1987).

53. Svirski, "Israel in the Global Space."

54. Palmach is a Hebrew acronym for Plugot Mahatz (storm troopers). It constituted the nucleus of the Zionist paramilitary units established in the *Yishuv* and was the elite of the Zionist army during the 1948 War. Under the full control of the Zionist Labor movement since its inception, Ben-Gurion hurried to dissolve it towards the end of the 1948 War.

55. For a detailed analysis of the Allon Plan in the context of Zionism and U.S. imperialism, see Gilbert Achcar, "Zionism and Peace: From the Allon Plan to the Washington Accords," *Eastern Cauldron* (Monthly Review Press), 205–33. Achcar cites Yigal Allon, *Israël: la lutte pour l'espoir* (Paris: Stock, 1977).

56. See Ibid.

57. This is not to overlook the fact that expulsions were committed in the Golan Heights, the Latrun area (three villages), and the large refugee camps near Jericho. Approximately 300,000 refugees were created by the 1967 War, including around 175,000 UNRWA-registered refugees who became refugees for a second time.

58. The aspiration to expel the Palestinians steadily loomed in Zionist thought after the 1948 ethnic cleansing. According to a book published by the Israeli state archives in May 2005 (see *Ha'aretz*, July 1, 2005), assassinated former Prime Minister Yitzhak Rabin proposed transferring the Palestinians from the West Bank while serving as a major general in the Israel Army in 1956. In 1967, toward the end of the fighting, PM Levi Eshkol nominated a committee whose role was to elaborate upon the possibility

for transferring Palestinians from the Gaza Strip to Iraq. A special office, under the direction of Ada Sireni (a respected "old-timer" member of the Mapai leadership), was established soon after the 1967 War "in order to help Palestinians emigrate." See the interview with Tom Segev on the occasion of the publication of his book *1967: And the Land Changed Completely (1967, ve Ha'aretz shinta et panaiha)* (Tel Aviv: Keter Publishing House, 2005), in Gidi Weitz, *Yediot Ahronot*, June 3, 2005.

59. See Moshe Machover, "Is It Apartheid?," circulated on his personal list serve November 10, 2004. Machover quotes Joseph Weitz in the Histadrut (the Federation of Israeli Trade Unions) daily *Davar*: "This population, which remained 'stuck' to their places, may destroy the very foundation of our state"; "A Solution to the Refugee Problem: A State of Israel with a Small Arab Minority," *Davar*, September 29, 1967. Machover adds, "*Davar* was the Histadrut daily newspaper, in effect, an organ of the Israeli Labor Party. Weitz was a member of that party, an apparatchik who had played a central role in planning the transfer before 1948 and implementing it during 1948/49."

60. Over the years, the Palestinian community inside Israel has dramatically increased its numbers, to the extent that it makes up around 20 percent of the total population today. Furthermore, the Palestinians' national consciousness and resistance to the structural inequality of the Jewish Zionist state has increased tremendously and with it the "demographic hysteria" regarding their higher birthrates, thus "threatening" the erosion of Israel's Jewish majority.

61. Upon his ascendance to power in 2003, Ariel Sharon was successful in convincing a more "pragmatic" part of the Likud to adopt the Labor Party's guiding assumption regarding the necessity to coordinate its policies with the United States through the erecting of a Bantustan state solution on fragmented enclaves of the West Bank, instead of annexing the 1967 Occupied Territories.

62. Today this is seen as implemented through the large Israeli settlement of Ma'aleh Adumim, whose master plan includes an area five times the size of Tel Aviv, extending from the eastern borders of Jerusalem all the way to the Dead Sea. By September 2006 (when these lines were written), the building of a large Israeli police station on the only remaining piece of land that separates Ma'aleh Adumim and Jerusalem is almost finished. It will thus complete the north-south separation of the West Bank.

63. This was also achieved through the arrangement struck by the United States, Israel, the EU, Egypt, and the Palestinian Authority after the unilateral Israeli redeployment (known as "disengagement") from the Gaza Strip in September 2005. Under this arrangement, EU monitors would oversee the direct security of the border crossing in Rafah (the southernmost Gaza city), while Israel would conduct twenty-four hour electronic surveillance of the terminal, with the power to close the terminal or veto any individual who might wish to cross into Egypt.

64. Cited in Achcar, "Zionism and Peace:" "Peace will not come as a result of a 'revolution of hearts' among them [the Arabs], but as the corollary of the balance of forces and a cold political realism. It will be lucidity and the acceptance of reality which will lead them to reconciliation, negotiation and peace." Yigal Allon, 179.

65. By 1985 a third of the Palestinian labor force worked in Israel, almost half in the construction industry. This cheap labor constituted 7 percent of the Israeli labor force.

66. For details of the economic liberalism which has taken place in Israel, see Michael Shalev, "The Contradictions of Economic Reform in Israel," *MERIP Reports,* April 1998.

67. Sammy Smooha, "The Implications of the Transition to Peace for Israeli Society," *Annals of the American Academy of Political and Social Science* 555 (1998): 26–45.

68. Shalev, "Contradictions of Economic Reform."

69. John Mearsheimer and Stephen Walt, "The Israeli Lobby," *London Review of Books* 28, no. 6 (March 23, 2006). Also see George T. Abed, "Israel in the Orbit of America:

Political Economy of a Dependency Relationship," *Journal of Palestine Studies* 16, no. 1 (Autumn 1986): 38–55.

70. For the economic interests in the Oslo Accords, see Shimshon Bichler and Jonatan Nitzan, *From War Profits to Peace Dividends: The Global Political Economy of Israel* (Jerusalem: Karmel Publications, 2001). Also see Shimshon Bichler and Jonatan Nitzan, "The New World Order and Its Old-New Instruments: Prospects for Israeli Society," *News from Within* 11, no. 3 (March 1995).

On the economic factors leading the Israeli capitalist quest for the Oslo Accords, see Efraim Davidi, "Globalization and Economy in the Middle East: A Peace of Markets or Peace of Flags," *Palestine-Israel* 7 (2000): 33. On the Israeli bourgeoisie's suggestion to establish a free trade zone as a means to retain Israeli economic dominance, see Efraim Davidi, "Israel's Economic Strategy for Palestinian Independence," *Middle East Report* 184 (1993): 24.

71. Efraim Davidi, "The Dream and Its Disaster: Israel and Globalization," in *Anti-Globalization of Late Capitalism,* ed. Efraim Davidi (Tel Aviv: Restling Press, 2003), 99–118.

72. Shlomo Ben Ami, *A Room for All* (Tel Aviv: Hakibutz Hameuchad Publishing, 1998), 106. Ben Ami is the former minister in several Labor Party governments.

73. Moshe Machover, "Arafat's Irrelevance," March 2002. The piece was written originally at the indirect request of Seumas Milne, editor of the Comment section of the UK *Guardian* (i.e., a request via a third party, not an explicit commission), but the *Guardian* didn't publish it. It was then circulated to Machover's e-mail list.

74. Only the discordant voices of some critics of the accords, such as Edward Said, Noam Chomsky, and Meron Benvenisti, pointed to this fact. See quotations in Achcar, "Zionism and Peace"; Edward Said, "Comment conjurer le risque d'une perpétuelle soumission à l'État d'Israël," *Le Monde Diplomatique* (Paris), November 1993; Noam Chomsky, "L'accord d'Oslo, vicié au départ," *Courrier international* (Paris), March 3, 1994; and Meron Benvenisti's article in the Israeli daily *Ha'aretz*, May 19, 1994.

75. In 1977, Yigal Allon was quoted as saying "Certainly, if the PLO ceased to be the PLO, we could cease to consider it as such. Or if the tiger transformed itself into a horse, we could mount it. At that moment, we would deserve some headlines in our favor." Cited in Achcar, "Zionism and Peace."

76. Israeli television program *Moked,* September 1, 1993. Quoted in Tikva Honig-Parnass, "The Oslo Agreement: No Recognition of Palestinian National Rights," *News from Within* 9, no. 9 (September 1993).

77. Under Arafat's leadership, the PLO secretly negotiated the Oslo Accords after it became clear, among other reasons, that it was politically and financially isolated as a result of its support of the Iraqi invasion of Kuwait in 1990.

78. For critical analyses of the Oslo Accords, see Edward Said, *Peace and Its Discontents: Essays on Palestine in the Middle East Peace Process* (New York: Vintage, 1996); Achcar, "Zionism and Peace"; Tikva Honig-Parnass, "The Oslo Agreement: No Recognition of Palestinian National Rights"; and Tikva Honig-Parnass, "PLO Recognition of the Jewish-Zionist State," *News from Within* 9, no. 10 (November 1993).

79. Tanya Reinhardt, *Israel/Palestine: How to End the War of 1948* (New York: Seven Stories Press, 2002).

80. Ibid., 192–93.

81. Ben Ami, *A Room for All,* 113. Ben Ami made these comments a few months before the 1998 general elections, which brought the Labor government to power and after which he was designated minister for internal security, something that Davidi, *Dream and Its Disaster,* correctly notes entailed enforcing these "neo-liberal agreements."

82. Quoted in Davidi, *Dream and Its Disaster,* 113.

83. *Ha'aretz*, February 22, 2002.

84. These Israel-PA agreements included the Oslo II Interim Agreement of 1995, the Paris Economic Agreement of 1994, the Hebron Protocol of 1997, and the Wye River Memorandum of 1998.

85. Hebron was actually divided according to the Hebron Protocol of 1997. The H-1 section, approximately 80 percent of the city and housing 115,000 Palestinians, fell into Area A (full PA autonomy); H-2 made up the remaining 20 percent of the land (including the Old City) and housed 35,000 Palestinians and 500 Jewish settlers. During the Al Aqsa Intifada, the Israeli Army again took control of Area H-1.

86. See "Land and Settlements," part of "Facts and Figures," provided by the Palestinian Academic Society for the Study of Academic Affairs (PASSIA)—Jerusalem at www.passia.org/palestine_facts/pdf/pdf2006/6-Land-Settlements.pdf. The 17.2 percent of the West Bank designated as Area A was divided into thirteen noncontiguous entities, resembling, in more ways than one, Native American reservations.

87. Jeff Halper, "Dismantling the Matrix of Control," *News from Within* 15, no. 9 (October 1999).

88. For a summary of how planning was used to disenfranchise Palestinians, see Rafi Segal and Eyal Weizmann, *A Civilian Occupation: The Politics of Israeli Architecture* (London: Verso Books, 2003).

89. See "Land Grab: Israel's Settlement Policy in the West Bank," *Btselem Report*, May 2002. Statistics on settlements are often confusing, given that Israeli human rights groups, which often monitor settlements, tend to differentiate between settlements in the West Bank and settlements in East Jerusalem. At the same time, Palestinian human rights groups have less means and access to the latest information on settlement expansion (such as access to aerial photography, as utilized by the Israeli group Peace Now). Furthermore, Israel often creates a new settlement by building upon a site entirely detached from an existing settlement but labeling the new site as the expanded "natural growth" of the original settlement. With this in mind, updated statistics on settlements can be obtained from www.btselem.org, www.peacenow.org.il/site/en/homepage.asp?pi=25, and www.fmep.org.

90. See "Frequently Asked Questions: Israeli Committee Against House Demolition" at www.icahd.org/eng/faq.asp?menu=9&submenu=1.

91. See Na'ama Carmi, "Oslo: Before and After: The Status of Human Rights in the Occupied Territories," Btselem Information Sheet, May 1999. Sixty-five of these deaths were a result of Israeli settler violence. A copy of the report can be seen at www.btselem.org/English/Publications/Summaries/199905_Oslo_Before_And_After.asp.

92. Important leaders include Ahmed Abu Rish (Fateh Hawks leader, killed in November 1993); Ahmed Abu Ibtihan (Fateh Hawks leader, together with five other comrades killed in March 1994 near Jabaliya Camp in Gaza); Fathi Shikaki (head of the Islamic Jihad, killed in Malta in October 1995); Yehiya Ayyash (Hamas military wing leader, killed in Gaza in January 1996); Muhiyedin al Sharif (head of Hamas military wing in the West Bank, killed in Ramallah in March 1998); and the Awadalla brothers (Adel and Imad, Hamas military wing leaders, killed near Hebron in September 1998). It is also worth mentioning the February 25, 1994, Hebron Massacre in which an Israeli settler killed twenty-nine Palestinian worshipers during an early-morning Ramadan prayer service. The first Palestinian suicide bomb attack took place in Afula forty days later on April 6, 1994.

93. See "Frequently Asked Questions: Israeli Committee Against House Demolition" at www.icahd.org/eng/faq.asp?menu=9&submenu=1.

94. At least twenty-two Palestinians died in captivity in Palestinian Authority prisons, in addition to hundreds more who were tortured. See the reports of the Palestinian Human Rights Monitoring Group during the Oslo era at hwww.phrmg.org. Also see

similar reports of the Palestinian Center for Human Rights in Gaza at www.pchrgaza.org.

95. Clyde Haberman, "12 Die as Arafat's Police Fire on Palestinian Militants," *New York Times*, November 18, 1994. The event was seminal for the PA, consolidating its grip in the Occupied Territories, and particularly in Gaza, where it sought to clamp down on the popular movements of the Intifada after the PLO's return from exile. The PA would later claim that agents provocateur had played a role in the deaths.

96. Perhaps the most glaring example of this tier's joint economic ventures was the opening of a casino in Jericho in 1998. The project was funded by Israeli and PA capitalists, in conjunction with international investors, and was run by an Austrian company. It was unashamedly built just opposite the Palestinian refugee camp of Aqbat Jaber and serviced Israeli and international gamblers. (Local Palestinians were prevented from gambling or even entering unless they worked there.) For more information on the Jericho casino, see Toufic Haddad, "And the Walls Came Tumbling Down: The Jericho Casino," *News from Within*, January 1999.

97. Leila Farsakh, "Under Siege: Closure, Separation and the Palestinian Economy," MERIP Report 217 (Winter 2000). Farsakh cites Ishac Diwan and Radwan Shaban, *Development Under Adversity* (Washington, D.C.: World Bank, 1999), and World Bank, *Poverty in West Bank and Gaza*, unpublished report, 2000.

98. Graham Usher, "The Politics of Internal Security: The PA's New Intelligence Services," *Journal of Palestine Studies* 25, no. 2 (Winter 1996): 21–34.

99. Gilbert Achcar, "Where is the PLO Going: The Long March . . . Backwards," *Eastern Cauldron: Islam, Afghanistan, Palestine, and Iraq in a Marxist Mirror* (New York: Monthly Review Press, 2004), 133.

100. In November 1966, Israel sent an entire armored brigade of nearly four thousand soldiers to attack the West Bank town of Samou' (then under Jordanian rule), killing eighteen Jordanian soldiers. As the historian Norman Finkelstein notes, "The ostensible purpose of the Israeli attack [on Samou'] was to punish King Hussein for, and force him to curb, Palestinian infiltration. Guerillas operating from Jordanian Territory had killed three Israelis in October and early November. Yet leaving to one side that Israel's 'reprisal' policy was not only contrary to international law but counterproductive as well, the fact is that, as Odd Bull, chief of staff of U.N. forces in the Middle East at the time, recalled, 'The Jordanian authorities did all they possibly could to stop infiltration.' A U.N. military observer on the Israel-Jordan border noted even more emphatically that 'Jordan's efforts to curb infiltrators reached the total capabilities of the country.' Indeed until the June 1967 war, more Palestinians were killed by Jordanian soldiers attempting to enter Israel than by the Israelis themselves. And only a few months before the Samu' attack, King Hussein had taken the extraordinary step of arresting most of the PLO staff in Amman and closing its offices." On Israeli provocations in the run-up to the 1967 War, see "To Live or Perish: Abba Eban 'Reconstructs' the June 1967 War," in Norman Finkelstein, *Image and Reality of the Israel-Palestine Conflict* (London: Verso, 2001), 123–49.

In 1997, notes from a 1976 interview with Moshe Dayan conducted by the Israeli journalist Rami Tal were published in *Yediot Ahronot*, confirming that Israel had used provocations against Syria to prepare the ground for ultimately occupying the Golan Heights. According to the published notes, Dayan was unapologetic: "After all, I know how at least 80 percent of the clashes there [on the pre-1967 Israel-Syria border] started. In my opinion, more than 80 percent, but let's talk about 80 percent. It went this way: We would send a tractor to plow some area where it wasn't possible to do anything, in the demilitarized area, and knew in advance that the Syrians would start to shoot. If they didn't shoot, we would tell the tractor to advance farther, until in the end the Syrians would get annoyed and shoot. And then we would use artillery and later the air force also, and that's how it was." See Serge Schmemann, "General's Words Shed a New Light on the Golan," *New York Times*, May 11, 1997.

101. Due to Fateh's "policy of nonintervention," the PLO refrained from deposing the hated Jordanian monarchy in 1970 and replacing it with a democratic state, in so doing likely bringing about a potential revolutionary circumstance throughout the Arab world. The failure to do so, however, subsequently allowed for King Hussein to use the pretext of the PFLP's airplane hijackings (which had precipitated the crisis to begin with) to engineer the exile of the PLO from Jordan. Israel played a role in Black September by threatening to intervene to protect the Jordanian king if Syria moved to stop the massacres.

102. Quoted in Helena Cobban, *The Palestinian Liberation Organization: People, Power and Politics* (Cambridge: Cambridge University Press, 1984), 60–61. Achcar, *Eastern Cauldron,* also has two very valuable essays that document the failed trajectory of the PLO under Fateh and, quite importantly, the failure of the Palestinian Left to offer an alternative. They are "Where Is the PLO Going?: The Long March . . . Backwards," and "Where Is the PLO Going?: The State, the PLO and the Palestinian Left."

103. See "A Dialogue—To Live Together: Moshe Machover and Said Hammami," in *Khamsin—An Anthology. Forbidden Agendas: Intolerance and Defiance in the Middle East*, ed. Jon Rothschild (London: Al Saqi Books, distributed by Zed Press, 1984), 377–400. Hammami was later assassinated in February 1978 in London. Though no organization claimed responsibility for the act, suspicions fell upon the Israeli Mossad or on Abu Nidal's Fateh—The Revolution, a Palestinian splinter faction that had broken away from the PLO. There is also much speculation that the latter group was also deeply penetrated by the Mossad. See Patrick Seale, *Abu Nidal: A Gun for Hire* (New York: Random House, 1992).

104. Ibid., 392–94.

105. *Forbidden Agendas,* 392.

106. Achcar, *Eastern Cauldron.* For a concise summary of the weaknesses and limitations of the PFLP and DFLP, see Mustapha Omar, "The Palestinian National Liberation Movement: A Socialist Analysis," in *The Struggle for Palestine,* ed. Lance Selfa (Chicago: Haymarket Books, 2002), 191–95.

107. The anthropologist Rosemary Sayigh describes how this situation arose: "The absence in 1968–69 of a single solid revolutionary Palestinian movement with cadres trained in mass mobilization should not surprise anyone. At the time, the Palestinian Resistance Movement (PRM [Sayigh's term for the national liberation movement groupings]) was a congery of small scattered clandestine groups that broke into the open before they had completed their merger attempts in a bid to prevent the Arab regimes from submitting to an Israeli dictated peace after the Six Day War [1967]. It was a historic decision, taken prematurely from the point of view of the PRM's own development yet necessary within the Arab context. Upon the newborn PLO resistance framework fell the weight of three sets of problems: sustaining armed struggle against Israel; maintaining a balance of forces within the Arab environment that would give the PRM a minimum of independence; and becoming a government for the oppressed and neglected masses. Given the objective and subjective conditions within which the PRM had to work if it was to exist at all, it can plausibly be argued that it did all that was possible. Others will argue that if the leadership had analyzed the Arab scene more accurately they would not have gambled on spontaneous mass reactions but would have put greater thought and effort into a plan of revolutionary mass organization. If they had done this, the weaknesses that showed up later in the PRM might have been less serious." See Sayigh, *Palestinians: From Peasants to Revolutionaries* (London: Zed Press, 1979), 163–64.

108. Omar, "Palestinian National Liberation Movement," 200–01.

109. The PLO left Lebanon in 1982 (after arriving there in 1970) in the context of the Israeli invasion of Lebanon, an extended Israeli siege of West Beirut, and a spiraling Lebanese civil war.

110. In the late 1970s, Israeli Prime Minister Menachem Begin attempted to establish a network of local collaborators known as the "Village Leagues" (Rawabet al Qura) in an effort to create a leadership that could break local support away from the PLO. The effort failed.

111. The most notable example of such protests was the Tunnel Uprising of September 1996, where upward of eighty Palestinians were killed in the span of three days. Additionally, there were widespread protests in June 1995 regarding the stalled release of Palestinian political prisoners and in March 1997 regarding the building of the Har Homa settlement on Jebel Abu Ghneim near Bethlehem. Regarding the former, see Ziad Abbas, "The Battle for Dignity and Freedom," *News from Within* 11, no. 7 (July 1995); regarding the latter, see Graham Usher, "The Long Shadow of 'Har Homa,'" *News from Within* 12, no. 4 (April 1997).

112. The best-known example typifying both the popular discontent with the negotiated process and the PA's reaction to such protests was the "Leaflet of the 20," released in December 1999. The leaflet was a sharply worded political statement signed by twenty prominent social and political leaders (including members of the Palestinian Legislative Council), representing diverse political backgrounds, including Fateh. The statement called for "the alarm bell to be sounded" because of the high levels of political and organizational corruption in the PA, which was leading the national movement to catastrophe, and the fear that Palestinian national rights were in the process of being sold down the river. The statement resulted in the arrest or house arrest of eight of the twenty signatories, the beating of one member of the Legislative Council (Abdel Jawwad Saleh) in a PA police station, and the shooting and wounding of another (Mu'awiya al Masri). See "The Beginning of Mass Democratic Revolt,?" editorial, *News from Within* 15, no. 11 (December 1999).

113. For informative readings on the retreat of the Palestinian Left both historically and under Oslo, see Achcar, *Eastern Cauldron*; Ali Jaradat, *The Palestinian Left: The Defeat of Democracy* (Rumallah: Muwatin Critical Intervention Series, 1999) (Arabic); Ahmed Qatamesh, ed., *Shedding Light on the Palestinian Left Process and Contrasting It with Other Left Movements* (Rumallah: Munif Al Barghouti Cultural Center, 2005), Publication 8 (Arabic); Sari Hanafi and Linda Tabar, *The Emergence of a Palestinian Globalized Elite: Donors, International Organizations and Local NGOs* (Jerusalem: Institute of Jerusalem Studies and Muwatin, the Palestinian Institute for the Study of Democracy, 2005); Adel Samara, *Epidemic of Globalization: Ventures in World Order, the Arab Nation and Zionism* (Glendale, Calif.: Palestine Research and Publishing Foundation, 2001), 157–75; Imad Sabi', "For the Genuine Repoliticization of the Palestinian Women's Movement: Reflections on Hammami and Kuttab's Article on Strategies Toward Freedom and Democracy in the Palestinian Women's Movement," *News from Within* 15, no. 6 (June 1999).

114. For in-depth analysis of and information on the Tunnel events, see "The Clashes of September 1996: Investigation into the Causes and the Use of Force," Palestinian Center for Human Rights—ICJ, Series Study (7), 1996.

115. Shraga Elam, "'Peace with Violence or Transfer," *Between the Lines* 1, no. 2 (December 2000), 11–15, available at www.acj.org/Jan_17.htm#2. Tanya Reinhart quotes him and elaborates on Cordesman's report in her book *Israel/Palestine* (New York: Seven Stories Press, 2004), 133–35. These military plans were also discussed in the Israeli media over the years, e.g., by the senior military analyst Amir Oren, *Ha'aretz*, November 23, 2001.

116. Anthony H. Cordesman, "Peace and War: Israel Versus the Palestinians, A Second Intifada?—A Rough Working Draft," Center for Strategic and International Studies (CSIS), latest version November 9, 2000, available at www.acj.org/Jan_17.htm#2.

117. Shraga Elam, "Peace." Also see "A Clean Break: A New Strategy for Securing the Realm," A Report Prepared by the Institute for Advanced Strategic and Political

Studies and part of "Study Group on a New Israeli Strategy Toward 2000," available at www.iasps.org/strat1.htm.

118. Such a "green light," to say the least, turned into a demand of the Bush administration, that Israel not agree to a cease-fire but continue with the destruction of Lebanon—a country whose suffering was described as the "birth pangs of a new Middle East" by U.S. Secretary of State Condoleezza Rice. See "Rice Sees Bombs as Birth Pangs," Al Jazeera, July 22, 2006, available at www.informationclearinghouse.info/article14146.htm.

119. Cordesman, "Peace and War," 9.

120. *Jerusalem Post*, August 18, 2000.

121. See Ze'ev Schiff, "Arafat's Violence Dividend," *Ha'aretz*, July 10, 2001. Also Robert Malley and Hussein Agha, "Camp David: The Tragedy of Errors," *New York Review of Books*, August 9, 2001, and Robert Malley and Hussein Agha, "Camp David and After: An Exchange," *New York Review of Books*, June 13, 2002.

122. Akiva Eldar, "His True Face," *Ha'aretz*, June 11, 2004. Eldar cites other Israeli security experts who had in the past expressed similar opinions. These include Ami Ayalon, who was the head of the Shabak (the General Security Services) up until a few months prior to the Intifada, and the Middle East "expert" Mati Shterenberg.

123. See Tikva Honig-Parnass, "PLO Recognition of the Jewish-Zionist State of Israel," *News from Within* 9, no. 10 (November 1993), 12–15.

124. Ze'ev Schiff, "Beilin's Final Agreement," *Ha'aretz*, February 23, 1996.

125. This was confirmed in books by three senior politicians who were involved in the negotiations: Gil'ad Sher, *Just Beyond Reach: The Israeli-Palestinian Peace Negotiations, 1999–2001* (Tel Aviv: Yediot Ahronot Books, 2001); Shlomo Ben Ami, *Quel avenir pour Israel* (Paris: PUF, 2001); and Yossi Beilin, *A Manual for a Wounded Dove* (Tel Aviv: Yediot Ahronot Books, 2001).

126. See Svirski, "Israel in the Global Space." The only trade unions capable of this form of struggle have been the unions granted preference by the Histadrut leadership as early as the 1950s and 1960s—the unions of white collar and public corporations that are yet to be privatized.

127. Nitzan's comments made to Machover "Is it Apartheid" distributed on his private e-mail list serve.

Chapter 1

1. The Sharem el-Sheikh summit was arranged by U.S. President Bill Clinton and convened by Egyptian President Hosni Mubarak. Arafat and Barak were encouraged by representatives of the United States, EU, United Nations, Jordan, and Egypt to keep the peace process going. As time would show, it would fail miserably as the situation on the ground quickly escalated. Over time, these attempts on behalf of the guardians of the regional order would be abandoned in favor of letting sheer military power speak.

2. The Unified National Leadership of the Uprising (Intifada) (UNLU) was the umbrella body composed of the main PLO factions, which served as the underground leadership of the 1987 Intifada. Its main role was to issue leaflets that put forth strategy and tactics.

3. The main PLO factions include Fateh, the Popular Front for the Liberation of Palestine (PFLP), the Democratic Front for the Liberation of Palestine (DFLP), and the People's Party (formerly the Communist Party) in addition to other lesser-known or -active parties: the Popular Front for the Liberation of Palestine—General Command, the Palestinian Democratic Union (FIDA), the Popular Struggle Front, the Palestinian Liberation Front, and the Arab Liberation Front.

4. The Tantheem will be explored more in "The Tantheem Wild Card" in this chapter.

5. This campaign was characterized by a disciplined guerrilla campaign against both the Israeli Army and its mercenary force, the South Lebanon Army (SLA). Inasmuch as Fateh would have liked to imitate Hezbollah's model, neither the conditions within which Fateh was operating nor the composition, structure, and tactics of the party itself were anywhere near to those that existed in Lebanon during the major campaigns of Hezbollah and the Lebanese resistance against the Israeli occupation.

6. See Foreword, Note 3.

7. Usher was almost entirely correct. The unilateral separation plans Israel implemented were actually wider with respect to the areas Israel prepared to annex in the West Bank, as demonstrated by the path of the apartheid separation wall that Israel built incrementally throughout the Intifada. However, with respect to the Gaza Strip, Israel chose to disengage entirely, including from the major settlement bloc of Gush Katif. The Palestinian resistance that developed there was simply too costly for Israel to try and retain these areas; Israel opted instead to withdraw entirely in September 2005.

8. A reference to the fact that the Palestinian resistance waged in the Intifada will increasingly come to resemble the situation in southern Lebanon between the Lebanese resistance and the Israeli Army and its mercenaries (the SLA) between 1982 and 2000.

9. *Yediot Ahronot*, September 7, 1993.

10. These include Jibril Rajoub (Preventive Security, West Bank), Mohammed Dahlan (Preventive Security, Gaza), Toufic Tirawi (Intelligence, West Bank), Amin El Hindi (Intelligence, Gaza), Musa Arafat (Military Intelligence), Haj Ismail (West Bank Chief of Police), and Ghazi Jabali (Gaza Police).

11. This refers to the period of early 1997 when then prime minister Benjamin Netanyahu followed through with the construction of Har Homa settlement, located on Jebel Abu Ghneim near Bethlehem. Popular protests were held throughout the West Bank decrying Israel's continued settlement policy, which was perceived as unilaterally determining negotiations in this case, particularly on the issue of Jerusalem. Har Homa settlement functions to sever Palestinian continuity between Bethlehem and East Jerusalem.

12. Interview with Marwan Barghouti, March 1997, in Graham Usher, *Dispatches from Palestine: The Rise and Fall of the Oslo Peace Process* (London: Pluto Press, 1999), 137.

13. The name "Tantheem," Arabic for "the organization," implies that they are the authentic organization, as opposed to the skewed PA—though both were understood by local Palestinians as being Fateh-led projects.

14. Indeed, Barghouti did nominate himself to replace Arafat, when the Palestinian prime ministerial elections took place in January 2005 after the latter's death. He later withdrew his candidacy, as he was in prison at the time, but used the threat of running to extract concessions from Abu Mazen. See Chapter 9.

15. A reference to the failed Taba summit between Israel and the PA, held from January 21 to January 27, 2001, at Taba in the Sinai Peninsula, in which the "final status" negotiations were held, supposedly building on the Camp David proposals.

16. Bishara is referring to Jewish lynch mobs and vigilante groups who attacked Palestinians in Israel, their property, and their holy sites in the early days of the Intifada. See "Report on Israeli Government and Police Attacks Against Arab Citizens—October 2000" (Arabic) by Mossawa, the Advocacy Center for Arab Citizens in Israel, at www.mossawacenter.org/ar/reports/2000/10/030830.html.

Curiously, an English version cannot be found on the Mossawa site, although the center did publish a similar report entitled "Black October: Israel Slaughters Its Own Citizens," outlining these attacks, available at friendvill2.homestead.com/DocMossawaReport.html.

17. The massacre at Kufr Qassem took place on the eve of the tripartite (Franco-Anglo-Israeli) assault on Egypt in 1956. Forty-eight villagers were killed by the Israeli soldiers on their way home for "violating a curfew" that had been imposed unbeknown to them while they were working their fields.

18. Land Day is commemorated every year on March 30, in memory of the six Palestinian citizens of Israel who were killed in a demonstration that broke out in 1976, protesting a wave of mass land confiscations. Palestinians in the West Bank and Gaza also observe this annual event.

19. The figure for the number of Palestinians killed during the October 2000 uprising of Palestinian citizens of Israel was originally set at fourteen because fourteen people were indeed killed. This figure, however, is generally lowered to thirteen, because one of the October victims was a Palestinian youth from Gaza who was working in Israel at the time.

20. Azmi Bishara was shot with a rubber bullet by Israeli police while at a demonstration against house demolitions in Lydd.

21. The Al Aqsa Intifada marks its commemoration on September 28, 2000, the day Sharon provocatively entered the Al Aqsa compound in Jerusalem. The very next day was a Friday, the Muslim day of prayer, which took place in an atmosphere where hundreds of Israeli police surrounded the compound, overtly expecting a confrontation with worshipers. Seven worshipers were killed on this first day, one of whom was a Palestinian citizen of Israel. See Introduction.

22. This was recently confirmed by Brigadier General Uri Sagie, who was involved in the negotiations with Syria, in an article by Alex Fishman, "We Missed a Peace Agreement with Syria. It Is Unforgivable," *Yediot Ahronot*, September 24, 2004.

23. This is a reference to the term "moderate physical pressure" used to describe Israeli torture techniques made permissible by the Israeli Supreme Court's 1987 Landau Ruling, for use against Palestinian and Arab detainees by the Israeli Army.

24. Abbreviations for the Popular Front for the Liberation of Palestine (PFLP) and the Democratic Front for the Liberation of Palestine (DFLP).

Chapter 2

1. Akiva Eldar, *Ha'aretz*, February 18, 2001.

2. Rehavam Ze'evi (aka Gandhi) was assassinated on October 17, 2001, in a retaliatory attack by the Popular Front for the Liberation of Palestine (PFLP), whose secretary-general, Mustapha Zibri (Abu Ali Mustapha), was killed August 27, 2001, by Israeli Army missiles.

3. Israeli Radio, Channel 2, February 25, 2001.

4. Shlomo Ben-Ami acknowledged even before Camp David 2000 that the Oslo Accords "were founded on a neo-colonialist basis . . . that when there is finally peace between us and the Palestinians, there will be a situation of dependence, of a structured lack of equality between the two entities"; Shlomo Ben-Ami, *A Place for All* (Tel Aviv: Hakibbutz Hameuchad, 1998), p. 106 of the Hebrew version.

5. Dr. Yossi Beilin was one of the initiators of the Oslo Accords. He was later marginalized in the Labor Party, resulting in his departure in December 2003 to the Meretz party (which later changed its name to Yachad—rarely used in Israeli discourse). He was also among the initiators of the "Geneva Initiative" with the top PA negotiator Yasser Abed Rabbo.

6. Quoted in Tom Segev, *Ha'aretz*, February 23, 2001.

7. *Ha'aretz*, February 26, 2001.

8. See Introduction for more on the class structure in Israel.

9. These towns were built in the 1950s and early 1960s, far from the center and close to border areas. They were primarily resided in by Jews who were brought from Arab states in order to strengthen the "legitimacy" of borders that were not yet officially recognized by the United Nations.

10. See interview with Amnon Raz-Krakotzkin in *Between the Lines* no. 4, February 2001.

11. See Amnom Raz-Krakotzkin, "Exile Within Sovereignty: Toward a Critique of the 'Negation of Exile' in Israeli Culture," *Theory and Criticism* no. 4 (Autumn 1993): 23–55.

12. Baruch Kimmerling, "Neither Democratic nor Jewish," *Ha'aretz*, December 27, 1996.

13. Ibid.

14. By 2006, the elements of an explicit Mizrahi challenge to the existing Ashkenazi regime had almost completely disappeared from Shas's discourse, leaving it largely as an ethnic Orthodox movement fighting for its share in the state budget and expressing nonmoderate positions regarding the 1967 Occupied Territories. See the interview with Sami Shalom Chetrit in Chapter 6.

15. See Introduction on its "social constructivism" version—created by the prestate Zionist labor movement. The English version of this book is Ze'ev Sternhell, *The Founding Myths of Israel: Nationalism, Socialism and the Making of the Jewish State*, trans. David Maisel (Princeton, N.J.: Princeton University Press, 1999).

16. Ze'ev Sternhell, *Ha'aretz*, January 26, 2001.

17. *Ma'ariv*, February 9, 2001.

18. At the time, Shas was a politically "moderate" party in the Israeli political arena, calling for Israeli concessions within a peace agreement.

19. The reference here is to a coalition crisis that arose under Barak's government between Shas and Meretz as to whether a large electricity generator was to be transported on a Saturday, the Jewish Sabbath, because there would be less traffic. Shas disagreed because they said it broke the Sabbath. Meretz was furious and threatened to pull out of the coalition.

20. The reference here is to the fact that with the failure of Camp David in June 2000 and the onset of the Intifada, the Labor-led government famously declared that "there was no partner for peace" among the Palestinians. This line all of a sudden proved hollow, when, in January 2001, negotiations resumed in the last month of U.S. President Clinton's tenure, in Taba, Egypt. It therefore made the Israeli claim that there was "no partner" seem absurd, as it was the Labor Party that participated in Taba with the same "no partner" (the PA) and where supposedly some "progress" was made by Israel.

21. Interview with Yossi Beilin by Ari Shavit, *Ha'aretz*, June 14, 2001.

22. Amir Oren, *Ha'aretz*, August 16, 2001.

23. The Sharon-Peres government cabinet meeting of July 4, 2001, decided to "widen" Israel's assassination policy so as to include "not only those who are directly involved in terror operations but also those who send them." See Tikva Honig-Parnass, "Louder Voices of War: Manufacturing Consent at Its Peak," *Between the Lines* no. 8, July 2001.

24. Under the terms of the Oslo Accords, there were supposed to be three stages of redeployment of the Israeli military from the West Bank and Gaza. The first related to the Israeli redeployment from Gaza and Jericho; the second related to the redeployment from the other major Palestinian population concentrations; the third related to Israeli redeployment from the rural areas with the exception of Israeli settlements and the Israeli-designated military areas. In reality, the third redeployment never took place at all and was lumped together with the final status negotiations, against the wishes of the PA negotiators. Even the second redeployment (Oslo II of September 24, 1995) needed several follow-up agreements (the Wye River Memorandum of October 1998 and the Hebron Protocol of January 17, 1997). These endless negotiations and dilemmas over

implementation, among other factors, gave the impression to the Palestinians that the entire process was being used to take as much time as possible, while facts on the grounds were being used to change the reality itself.

25. It took these forces some time to convince Sharon and other Likud leaders to adopt the separation wall plan. The most orthodox elements of the Likud, associated with its Herut party progenitor, objected in principle to the plan, arguing that it would de facto demarcate Israel's borders over land it wanted to annex and "divide the land of Eretz Israel." That is a concession they have historically categorically rejected since its inception. However, as time went on, substantial sections of the Likud accepted the plan and indeed began implementing it on the ground under Sharon's tutelage. Moreover, the conception itself was broadened and incorporated into what became known as the Convergence Plan, drawn up with the establishment of the Kadima party in late 2005, under Sharon and later his successor Ehud Olmert (see Chapter 10).

26. *Ha'aretz*, August 24, 2001.

27. Sima Kadmon, *Yediot Ahronot*, August 24, 2001.

28. Amnon Dankner, *Ma'ariv*, August 31, 2001. Indeed, as time would tell, and as Israel built the wall, the number of Israeli settlers on the western side ballooned. Though the wall is yet to be finished, plans indicate that it will enclose a full 98 percent of the Israeli settler population. See stopthewall.org/FAQs/33.shtml. Furthermore, in February 2006, Israel announced that the Jordan Valley could no longer be accessed by Palestinians, with the infrastructure of strict checkpoints enforcing this. See www.palestine monitor.org/nueva_web/updates_news/pngo/jordan_valley_annexation.htm and stopthewall.org/latestnews/1124.shtml.

29. Amos Harel, *Ha'aretz*, September 6, 2001.

30. Amos Harel and Aluf Ben, *Ha'aretz*, September 6, 2001.

31. On the principle of "separation," see Azmi Bishara, "Separation Spells Racism," *Al Ahram Weekly* no. 697, July 1–7, 2004.

32. See Tikva Honig-Parnass and Toufic Haddad, "The Demographic Danger Haunts the Jewish State," *Between the Lines* no. 9, August 2001.

33. Aluf Ben, *Ha'aretz*, August 19, 2001

34. The Triangle area refers to villages populated by Palestinians who are Israeli citizens that run along the western side of the Green Line. These villages are generally grouped into two parts: the Northern Triangle, which includes the villages of Kufur Qara', 'Ara, Ar'ara, Um el Fahem, Musmus, Baka el Gharbiya, Barta'a, Ein Sahleh, Mu'aweya, Msherfeh, Bayyada, and Ein Ibrahim; and the Southern Triangle (also known as the "Little Triangle"), which includes Kufur Qasem, Tireh, Taybeh, Qalansawa, and Jaljuliyeh.

35. Avirama Golan, *Ha'aretz*, August 23, 2001.

36. Nahum Barnea, *Yediot Ahronot*, September 10, 2001.

37. This portion of the article is based on several sources, including Yair Sheleg's piece in *Ha'aretz* on March 23, 2001 (parts of which published the document it mentions and a number of answers to questions which were referred to by Dr. Uzi Arad, the chairman and guiding spirit behind the convention), and "Policy Recommended by Zionist Elites: Transfer of Palestinians and Blatant Capitalism," *Between the Lines* no. 6, April 2001.

38. Tanya Reinhardt, *Israel/Palestine* (New York: Seven Stories Press, 2002), 204.

39. See Introduction on the post-Oslo return of Israel to a frontal war strategy.

40. For updated information on his case, see www.hussamkhader.org/english/Default.htm.

41. The Jericho casino was forced to shut its doors at the beginning of the Intifada. Israelis were unwilling to go to Jericho, and it is also likely that its owners feared that it could become a target of attack by local Palestinians if it remained open.

42. Quoted from *Palestine Report* 8, no. 13, September 5, 2001.

43. The reference here was to U.S. proposals such as the Mitchell Plan and the Tenet Plan, which were circulating in April 2001 and June 2001, respectively. The former was a general plan put together by former U.S. senator George Mitchell that was intended to explain the causes of "the outbreak of hostilities" and to outline a general framework for how to return things to the negotiating table. The latter was a document written by former CIA head George Tenet designed to provide a more specific plan for doing so, including reciprocal measures that both Israelis and Palestinians needed to carry out. For a copy of the Mitchell Plan, see electronicintifada.net/referencelibrary/keydocuments/doc_page25.shtml; for a copy of the Tenet Plan, see www.yale.edu/lawweb/avalon/mideast/mid023.htm.

44. Khader is referencing Anton Lahad, head of Israel's mercenary army, the South Lebanon Army [SLA], in the former zones of South Lebanon that Israel occupied between 1982 and 2000. Lahad's name is synonymous with Vichy or Quisling—the World War Two–era Nazi collaborators who led the occupation regimes in France and Norway, respectively.

45. The political parties that are members of the PLO, together with Hamas and Islamic Jihad.

46. Gaza International Airport, located in the southernmost corner of the Gaza Strip, was opened on November 24, 1998. Two months after the Intifada's eruption on December 4, 2001, Israel closed it down and destroyed parts of the runway. Though the presence of the Gaza airport sounds as though the Palestinians were enjoying some form of heightened sovereignty, the reality of the matter, as revealed by the Intifada, was that Israel completely controlled the airport's usage, determining who could and could not leave the Gaza Strip through it.

47. Abayat was assassinated, along with two other Tantheem members, in Beit Sahour by a bomb planted in his car on October 18, 2001. The PA refused to publicly acknowledge that it had ceded to local pressure for Abayat's release. The PA's unwillingness to publicly acknowledge what it had done stemmed from the desire not to expose its own weakness, rather than, as Israel claimed, that the PA was playing a duplicitous game and that its jails were a "revolving door."

48. Indeed, these forms of attacks, whereby Palestinian guerrillas attempted to storm well-protected military or settler positions, likely played a role in the Israeli establishment arriving at the conclusion that it needed to withdraw from the Gaza Strip. Of course, Israel ultimately redeployed from Gaza in September 2005, withdrawing its military positions and settler population, although the occupation regime over Gaza was actually strengthened by these actions, not weakened (see Chapter 10). In any case, these military operations were consciously modeled on similar attacks waged by Hezbollah against Israeli targets in South Lebanon, though the Palestinians had nowhere near the level of training or sophistication in weaponry that the former possessed. As the Intifada unfolded, dozens if not hundreds of these operations would continue to be launched in the Gaza Strip, despite the fact that most were unsuccessful and resulted in the fighters' death.

49. *Al Resalah*, October 11, 2001. The PA claimed that its crackdown against the demonstrators was legitimate because they failed to obtain a legal permit.

50. The victims on that day were Abdallah Ifranji (13), Haitham Abu Shamaleh (19, a student from Al Azhar University), and Yousef Al Aqel (21). The Aqel family, which resides in Nusseirat refugee camp, refused to open a mourning tent (*beit azza*), implying that the family sought revenge in blood from the perpetrators of the crime that had killed their family member. Indeed, more than a year later, a Gaza police chief who had supposedly been responsible for opening fire on the Gaza demonstrators that day was kidnapped and killed in Nusseirat camp. Soon after, members of the Aqel family declared, over the refugee camp's mosque loudspeakers, that their revenge was complete.

A mourning tent for Yousef was then opened to the public for three days—the custom once blood revenge is exacted.

51. *Al Hayat Al Jadeeda*, October 9, 2001.

52. *Al Ayyam*, October 9, 2001.

53. *Al Istiqlal* is considered to be the newspaper of the Palestinian Islamic Jihad.

54. Ala Suftawi, editorial, *Al Istiqlal*, October 11, 2001.

Chapter 3

1. See Introduction, Note 58.

2. Review of *Ma'ariv* poll by Hemi Shalev, *Ma'ariv*, January 18, 2002.

3. B. Michael, *Yediot Ahronot*, August 3, 2001.

4. Hadash is the front headed by the Communist Party.

5. *Ha'aretz*, January 30, 2002.

6. Vanunu published classified information about Israel's nuclear reactor in Dimona and was kidnapped by the Israeli Mossad from Italy in 1986. He was released on April 21, 2004, after serving an eighteen-year prison sentence, the first twelve of which were in solitary confinement. Upon his release in 2004, he continued to be prevented from leaving the country. Mustafa Dirani was kidnapped by Israeli commandos from Lebanon in 1994 for his alleged role in the detention of the missing Israeli navigator Ron Arad. Dirani was eventually released with other Lebanese and Arab prisoners in a prisoner exchange with the Lebanese movement Hezbollah. The deal was mediated through Germany, and the prisoners were exchanged for the corpses of three Israeli soldiers and Res. Colonel Elhanan Tennenbaum, who had been abducted by Hezbollah while allegedly in the midst of a drug deal.

7. This was written before the massive Israeli reoccupation of all West Bank cities in the campaign known as Defensive Shield, which took place in March–April 2002. This campaign put an end to the conception of the Area As, as the last vestige of the Oslo Accords (see Chapter 5).

8. Avinery was also the director of the Ministry of Foreign Affairs in Rabin's government.

9. In an interview with Avinery by Ariela Ringel-Hofman in *Yediot Ahronot*, February 1, 2002.

10. In an article entitled "No Pity, No Compassion," *Yediot Ahronot*, January 9, 2002.

11. Peretz would later join the Labor Party and was elected party chairman in November 2005. After the 2006 elections, he became the minister of defense in the Kadima-Labor government, leading the Israeli assaults against Lebanon and Gaza in June–August 2006 (see Chapter 10).

12. See the interview with Sami Shalom Chetrit in Chapter 7.

13. See Yitzhak Laor, "Tears of Zion," *New Left Review* 10 (July–August 2001): 47–61.

14. Dan Margalit, "Another Attempt to Neutralize the Ticking Bomb of the Arabs in Israel," *Ma'ariv*, January 18, 2002.

15. The national religious constituency is composed of right-wing supporters of the settlement movement and is usually politically represented by the National Religious Party (Mafdal).

16. The only report about this meeting was that of Dan Margalit in *Ma'ariv* ("Another Attempt") in which he did not mention the names of the Palestinians who participated, except that of Dr. Man'a.

17. Margalit, "Another Attempt."

18. See Chapter 4 on the trial of MK Azmi Bishara.

19. Sami Shalom-Chetrit, "The Second Jewish-Zionist-Ashkenazi Covenant," *Between the Lines* no. 13, February 2002.

20. "Israel Is Not a State That Has an Army, But an Army to Which a State Is Adjacent" read the headline of an article in *Ma'ariv*, September 6, 2002, by Ben Kaspit; also see "Israel: The Military in Charge?" *Open Democracy*, May 24, 2002, available at www.tau.ac.il/~reinhart/political/24_05_02_Military_in_Charge.html, and Gabi Sheffer, "The Real Pathology," *Ha'aretz* Hebrew weekend supplement, October 13, 2002.

21. Ari Shavit, *Ha'aretz*, August 30, 2002.

22. A reference to a site located in the heart of Nablus, claimed to be the tomb of the biblical Joseph. During Oslo (1993–2000), the site had been used as a religious school (yeshiva) by some Jewish settlers, who would visit it under the protection of joint PA–Israeli Army convoys. However, soon after the Intifada began, both the yeshiva and the Israeli Army presence were evacuated.

23. The famous Israeli general and former minister of defense in various Labor Party governments, including during the 1967 War and the 1973 October War. Dayan was known for his hawkish political positions, which permitted him to quit the Labor Party and participate in Begin's (Likud) government.

24. Shlomo Avinery, *Yediot Ahronot*, September 13, 2002.

25. *Yediot Ahronot*, August 18, 2002.

26. See Tikva Honig-Parnass, "A Society Stripped of Its Democratic and Moral Pretensions," in this chapter.

Chapter 4

1. For a summary of Israeli laws and government decisions passed at the beginning of the Intifada, aimed at stripping 1948 Palestinian citizens of basic rights, see "NDA—Tajamu' Manifesto, September 2002," republished as "Widening the Apartheid Legal System of the Jewish State" in *Between the Lines* no. 18, October 2002. Needless to say, the case of Azmi Bishara was not an isolated incident of persecution. Sheikh Raed Salah, head of the northern wing of the Islamic movement, was arrested on May 13, 2003, and later sentenced and imprisoned for three years, on similar politically motivated charges of "aiding terror." For more on his case, see Jonathan Cook, "The Real Case," *Al Ahram*, May 22–28, 2003, available www.weekly.ahram.org.eg/2003/639/re2.htm.

2. The text of Bishara's speeches in both Um el Fahem and Qirdaha can be found on the Adalah Web site (www.adalah.org) by searching "The State of Israel v. MK Dr. Azmi Bishara."

3. A second charge that was later dropped by the court related to his arranging family visits to Syria for relatives of Palestinian refugees who had been separated from their families since the Nakba in 1948.

4. Quoted in Amnon Raz-Krakotzkin, "No to Dictates, No to War," *Between the Lines* no. 8, July 2001.

5. The front headed by the Communist Party.

6. Excerpts from the interview with MK Mohammad Barakeh by Gidi Weitz, featured in *Kol Ha'ir*, October 5, 2001, and in *Between the Lines* no. 11, October 2001.

7. Ibid.

8. Among others, Adi Ophir, Amnon Raz-Krakotzkin, and Yitzhak Laor.

9. See Azmi Bishara, "Not 'Democracy Defending Itself' but Nationalism Attacking Democracy" in this chapter.

10. On the meaning of national collective rights, see Hassan Jabarin, "Israeliness: On Looking Toward the Future of the Arabs According to Jewish-Zionist Time, in a Space Without a Palestinian Time," *Mishpat ve Memshal* no. 6, 1991, 53–86.

11. Danny Rabinowitz and Khawla Abu Baker, *The Stand-Tall Generation: The Palestinian Citizens of Israel Today* (Jerusalem: Keter Publishing House, 2002).

12. Uzi Benziman, *Ha'aretz*, August 16, 2002.

13. Among others are three laws that govern access to and participation in the Knesset, that prevent family unification, and amendments to the penal law of incitement. See the NDA—*Tajamu'* leaflet of September 2002, republished in *Between the Lines* no. 18, October 2002.

14. The Basic Law: Human Dignity and Liberty of 1992 states that the "purpose of this Basic Law is to protect human dignity and liberty, in order to establish in a Basic Law the values of the state of Israel as a Jewish and democratic state." The formula is repeated in point two of the Basic Law: Freedom of Occupation. "The purpose of this Basic Law is to protect freedom of occupation, in order to establish in a Basic Law the values of the state of Israel as a Jewish and democratic state." Neither law, however, explicitly mentions basic human rights such as the right to equality and the right to freedom of expression. Also, the first law can be changed by a regular majority in the Knesset.

15. See David Kretzmer, *The Legal Status of the Arabs in Israel* (Boulder, CO: Westview Press, 1990).

16. 5746 *Yalkut Hapirsumim 772*. Quoted in ibid., reference no. 38.

17. Azmi Bishara, "Thus an Apartheid Regime Develops," *Between the Lines* no. 1, November 2000.

18. On the meaning of national collective rights, see Hassan Jabarin, "Israeliness." For more on Adalah, see www.adalah.org/eng/index.php.

19. Adalah's Supreme Court Litigation Docket, 2003, issued January 19, 2004.

20. Other motions were filed by right-wing MKs and political parties against Azmi Bishara, 'Abd al-Malek Dahamshe (United Arab List), and Ahmad Tibi (Arab Movement for Renewal), as individual candidates, and against three political party lists: the NDA, the United Arab List, and the joint Democratic Front for Peace and Equality—Arab Movement for Renewal (AMR) list.

21. *Ha'aretz*, December 27, 2003.

22. The CEC approved the candidacy of MK 'Abd al-Malek Dahamshe, as well as the participation of the UAL and the joint Democratic Front for Peace and Equality–AMR list.

23. Adalah's Supreme Court Litigation Docket, 2003, issued January 19, 2004.

24. Uzi Benziman, *Ha'aretz*, January 3, 2003. See also Uzi Benziman's quotation regarding Azmi Bishara featured in "Accusations of Treason Leveled Against MK Bishara, Supported by the Left" in this chapter, taken from Ha'aretz, August 16, 2002.

Chapter 5

1. Statistics on those killed refer to figures obtained from the Palestinian National Data Bank—State Information Services, available at www.pnic.gov.ps/arabic/quds/arabic/shohada_aqsa/quds_list.html.

    Statistics on those assassinated are based on figures provided by the same service, available at www.pnic.gov.ps/arabic/quds/arabic/ivid/martyrs/ivid_11.html.

2. For example on January 14, 2002, Israel assassinated Raed El Karmi, a nationally recognized leader and head of the Al Aqsa Martyrs Brigades in Tulkarem, in order to

ensure that Fateh would break its scrupulously observed cease-fire, maintained for the previous three weeks. This was similar to the provocations of Hamas several months earlier, when Israel killed the top militant Mahmoud Abu Hannoud on November 23, 2001, attempting to force Hamas to break its cessation of attacks within the Green Line, observed since September 11, 2001. The Israeli commentator Danny Rubinstein would write after this latter assassination: "His [Abu Hannoud's] assassination was performed with the explicit intention to provoke Hamas and to bring about retaliatory terror operations by the Islamic organizations" (Danny Rubinstein, *Ha'aretz*, December 25, 2001).

3. The month of February 2002, for example, witnessed the emergence of a pattern whereby Palestinian resistance operations were specifically focused on Israeli military and settler targets. These targets were seen as having wider tactical support within Palestinian society (as opposed to attacks that crossed the Green Line) and to some extent, were believed to provide less of a pretext for Israel to escalate against the Palestinians. They included the following operations:

February 6: Attack on the Jordan Valley settlement of Hamra—Hamas—two settlers and one soldier killed.

February 9: Attack on settler car near Za'tara junction near Nablus—Fateh—one settler killed.

February 10: Attack on IDF Southern Regional Military Headquarters, Birsheva—Hamas—two soldiers killed.

February 15: Destruction of Merkava 3 tank near Netzarim settlement, Gaza Strip—Popular Resistance Committees—three soldiers killed.

February 15: Attack at Surda military check point, North of Ramallah—Fateh—one soldier killed.

February 16: Suicide bomb attack inside Karnei Shomron settlement near Qalqiliya—PFLP—three settlers killed.

February 18: Suicide bomb attack near Ma'aleh Adumim settlement, East Jerusalem—Fateh—one police officer killed.

February 18: Attack near Kissufim settler crossing point, Gaza Strip—Fateh—two soldiers and one settler killed.

February 19: Attack at Ein Arik checkpoint, north of Ramallah—Fateh—six soldiers killed.

February 22: Shooting attack on settler car near Giva't Ze'ev settlement, between Ramallah and Jerusalem—Fateh—one settler killed.

February 25: Shooting attack at Neve Ya'cov settlement, East Jerusalem—Fateh, one police officer killed.

February 25: Shooting attack on settler car near Bethlehem—Fateh—two settlers killed.

February 27: Shooting attack at Atarot settlement industrial area—Fateh—one settler killed.

Despite the emergence of this pattern, because of the lack of centralization of Palestinian resistance forces, the occasional suicide bombing within the Green Line by a given faction would have the effect of destroying the consistency of this trend. It is also important to emphasize that attacks inside the Green Line (often in the form of suicide bombings) were generally carried out as an attempt to find a balance of deterrence or "balance of terror" (in Arabic, *tawazun al ru'b*) for when Israel attacked Palestinian civilians, or instigated renewed hostilities after a provocative assassination. Despite all this, however, the use of these attacks was far less in the overall scope of Palestinian resistance activity, even though they were widely reported in the Western media. Yet even according to Israeli Army statistics, attacks inside the Green Line made up less than 4 percent of the total number of Palestinian resistance operations—and even this statistic includes attacks within Israeli-occupied East Jerusalem, which the Israeli Army classifies as within "the home front." See "Total Number of Terrorist Attacks in the West Bank, Gaza Strip and Homefront since

September 2000" on the IDF Web site:www1.idf.il/DOVER/site/mainpage
.asp?sl=EN&id=22&docid=16703&clr=1&subject=14931&Pos=2&bScope=False.

4. For example, on February 28, 2002, Israel launched Operation Rolling Hell, deliber-
    ately targeting the U.N.-administered refugee camps of Jenin (in Jenin) and Balata
    (in Nablus). Thirty-six people would be killed throughout the course of the next five
    days. The Israeli operation would feature the newly devised army technique of "walk-
    ing through walls" whereby soldiers would smash holes in the walls of refugees'
    homes so as to avoid having to navigate the labyrinth of the refugee camps' alleyways.

5. According to Israeli Army statistics, from the beginning of the Intifada to July 2004,
    there were 131 suicide bombings, out of a total of 22,406 Palestinian attacks. See the
    statistics related to the total number of attacks and the number of suicide bombing
    attacks, as reported by the Israeli Army Web site: www1.idf.il/DOVER/site/
    mainpage.asp?sl=EN&id=22&docid=16703&clr=1&subject=14931&Pos=2&bScope=
    False.

6. Statistics on Palestinians killed relate to the period of March 29 to May 11, 2002, ac-
    cording to the figures provided by the Palestinian National Data Bank—State Infor-
    mation Services, available at www.pnic.gov.ps/arabic/quds/arabic/shohada_aqsa/
    quds_list.html. Statistics on those imprisoned come from estimates by Amnesty In-
    ternational, according to its report "Israel and the Occupied Territories: Mass Deten-
    tion in Cruel, Inhuman and Degrading Conditions," May 29, 2002, press release no.
    001-04. The report is available at www.ppsmo.org/e-website/Others-Press-
    Reports/03Amnesty.htm.

7. In Nablus alone the Israeli Army attacked and destroyed the Al Khadra Mosque
    (more than 1,000 years old; 85 percent destroyed, including its sculpted and inlaid
    mihrab); the Al Kabeer Mosque (1,800 years old; formerly a Byzantine church; 20 per-
    cent destroyed); the Al Satoon Mosque (1,600 years old; formerly a Byzantine church;
    20 percent destroyed, windows shattered); the Greek Orthodox church in the Yasmin
    quarter (400 years old; 40 percent destroyed, including the altar, chandelier, pews,
    Bibles, shattered glass, cracked walls); at least sixty houses of different historical peri-
    ods (1500–1940); Al Shifa Turkish bath (400 years old; hit by three rockets; 50 percent
    destroyed, including the more important historical section of the baths); the eastern
    entrance of the khan (old market) (220 years old; completely destroyed together with
    many supporting arches and arcades above the streets); two soap factories (300 and
    500 years old, respectively); three additional soap factories (between 300 and 500 years
    old); seven Roman water sources (completely destroyed); Al Fatimeya Girls' School
    (over 400 years old; 30 percent damaged); Rashda Girls' School; Jamal Abdelnasser
    Girls' School; Hawwash School; Abdelraheem Mahmoud School; Al Ansari School;
    Zafer Al Masri School; in addition to the Ra's El Ein Kindergarten and scores of
    homes, apartment buildings, and offices. At least 80 percent of the renovated stone-
    paved streets of the Old City were also destroyed. For a more complete overview of the
    destruction, see "Operation Devastation," *Between the Lines* no. 15, May 2002.

8. Excerpts from Moshe Nissim, who drove one of the military bulldozers in Jenin
    refugee camp during the Israeli assault in Operation Defensive Shield, *Yediot Ahronot*,
    May 31, 2002.

9. Text of speech by George W. Bush, June 24, 2002. A copy of the speech is available at
    www.whitehouse.gov/news/releases/2002/06/20020624-3.html.

10. The cynicism of the U.S. reform spectacle was captured well by the Palestinian re-
    searcher Mouin Rabbani, who exposed its absurdity: "Is, for example, Washington
    prepared to countenance a verdict by an independent Palestinian supreme court
    which abolishes military courts and forbids the detention of militants on the basis of
    unsubstantiated Israeli allegations, delivered on the grounds that such practices vio-
    late customary norms of due process? Are Israel and the U.S. prepared to see their fa-
    vorite Palestinians [in the PA] put behind bars or barred from public service on

charges of corruption? Will the international community insist upon municipal elections if the polls predict Hamas control of a substantial number of local councils, thus acquiring the means to further expand its popular base? How will it perceive a legislative assembly empowered to force the executive branch to submit a peace treaty to a national referendum?" (Mouin Rabbani, "Israel Strengthens Apartheid Policies," *Al Ahram Weekly*, May 23, 2002).

11. See Chapter 2, Note 31.

12. The Follow-up Committee is made up of representatives of all sectors of Palestinian society in Israel: political parties, MKs, heads of municipalities, NGOs, and so on. Although recognized as the semiofficial representative of the Palestinian citizens, it is not a democratic body. No real agreed-upon procedures determine its composition and its mandate, and many of its members have not been elected by the constituencies they claim to represent (such as the heads of municipalities, who are often appointed by the Israeli government).

13. See Chapter 1, note 31.

14. Aluf Benn, "U.S. Defense Experts Arrive Here for Strategic Talks," *Ha'aretz*, May 20, 2005.

15. See Vijay Prashad, "Hindutva-Zionism: An Alliance of the New Epoch," *Between the Lines* no. 13, February 2002.

16. See Peace Now settlement report, February 2002, available at www.peacenow.org.il.

17. Akiva Eldar, *Ha'aretz*, June 3, 2002.

18. An Israeli NGO monitoring and reporting upon human rights violations in the Occupied Territories.

19. For the comprehensive findings of this report, see "Land Grab: Israel's Settlement Policy in the West Bank," *B'Tselem Report*, May 2002, available at www.btselem.org/English/Publications/Summaries/200205_Land_Grab.asp.

20. Meron Benvenisti, *Ha'aretz*, May 23, 2002.

21. Shimon Shifer and Orli Azolie, *Yediot Ahronot*, June 11, 2002.

22. Ben Kaspit, *Ma'ariv*, May 31, 2002.

23. Uzi Benziman, *Ha'aretz*, May 31, 2002.

24. The Israeli Army's prospects for liquidating Palestinian resistance in the near future were refuted more than two years later, thus bringing about the "unilateral" plans to erect the wall and disengage from the Gaza Strip.

25. Akiva Eldar, *Ha'aretz*, May 30, 2002.

26. Cairo is a venue where the PA meets and negotiates with the main opposition factions (Hamas, Islamic Jihad, and the PFLP), usually attempting to determine guidelines for the Intifada and particularly for the factions' armed wings. Egypt offered to host these talks so that the opposition faction leadership (often based in Syria) could speak directly with the PA without going through the Israelis.

27. For more on the Popular Resistance Committees in Gaza, see "The Changing Face of Southern Gaza: Popular Resistance Committees," in *Between the Lines* no. 6, July 2001. Toufic Haddad was one of the first to identify the significance of the Popular Resistance Committees. He rightly assessed it as an emerging phenomenon, illustrative of changing forms of political organization from below.

28. Camille Mansour, "Israel's Colonial Impasse," *Journal of Palestine Studies* 30, no. 4 (2001).

29. Jean Baudrillard, *Simulacra and Simulation* (Ann Arbor: University of Michigan Press, 1994).

30. Mouin Rabbani, "The Costs of Chaos in Palestine," *Middle East Report* 224 (Fall 2002).

31. Joseph Massad, "Return or Permanent Exile?" in *Palestinian Refugees: The Right of Return*, ed. Naseer Aruri (London: Pluto Press, 2001) 105–22.

32. A reference to the Subaltern Studies Group founded by Indian historians, who organized and initiated a revisionist reading of Indian nationalist historiography. The group assumed that an investigation of the independent participation of subaltern groups in nationalism would allow for an objective assessment of the role of the nationalist elite and would shed light on the ways in which the elite are implicated in the reproduction of colonial structures of rule. The group's revisionist project revealed subaltern groups looking outside colonial structures of domination and organizing their own revolts, yet waiting in vain for their own nationalist elite to transform these resistance practices into a nationwide movement. See Ranajit Guha, "Introduction," in *A Subaltern Studies Reader, 1986–1995*, ed. Ranajit Guha (Minneapolis: University of Minnesota Press, 1997), and Ranajit Guha, "On Some Aspects of the Historiography of Colonial India," in *Subaltern Studies I: Writings on South Asian History and Society*, ed. Ranajit Guha (Delhi: Oxford University Press, 1994). Article first published in 1982.

33. Mohanned Abdel Hamid, "Why Fateh Doesn't Participate in the Morass of Reform," *Between the Lines* no. 17, August 2002.

34. This was the strategy adopted by the local leadership before it was largely blocked by the PLO in Tunis around 1990–91.

35. The factions distribute monetary assistance to individuals whose houses have been demolished and to the family of the *shuhuda* [martyrs], as well as to families with an injured son/daughter. Although in general these funds are distributed along party lines, the informal linkages among the shebab and between the shebab and the community mean that in practice funds are distributed across faction lines. In particular it is Islamic Jihad which has the most monetary resources available for relief and distributes these funds among the members of the camp, with its own party members having priority. During the Islamic holy month of Ramadan, Islamic Jihad distributed 1,000 coupons, each valued at 100 NIS, or approximately US$22, to families, which could be used at shops in Jenin to purchase food items or basic essentials, such as clothing. A member of the relief wing of Islamic Jihad estimated that they distributed approximately 10,000 NIS to families whose houses had been destroyed since the April 2002 invasion.

36. Raymond Williams, in *The Raymond Williams Reader*, ed. John Higgins (Oxford, England: Blackwell, 2001), 102.

37. Toufic Haddad, "After Two Years of Intifada: Chronicles from the Polity of the Periphery," *Between the Lines* no. 19, December 2002.

38. James C. Scott, *Domination and the Arts of Resistance: Hidden Transcripts* (New Haven: Yale University Press, 1990).

39. David B. Morris, "About Suffering: Voice, Genre, and Moral Community," in *Social Suffering*, ed. A. Kleinman, V. Das, and M. Locke (Berkeley: University of California Press, 1997).

40. Editor's note: Bishara is attempting to cut against the dilettantish approach of many Palestinian intellectuals in his audience regarding their interaction with the Intifada, particularly in the context of the devastation wrought after Operation Defensive Shield. Because many Palestinian intellectuals found themselves entirely outside the struggles of the Intifada on the ground, many were at pains to define their role in the national struggle, particularly since most of them were unaffiliated with any political parties. This tended to lend itself to an impatience and/or a striving to find a role for themselves, sometimes leading them to become involved in misguided positions or initiatives. During his lecture, Bishara indirectly references a full-page advertisement that ran in local Palestinain newspapers in July 2002, funded by the European Union, calling for an end to military operations inside the Green Line, and signed by a host of Palestinain elites.

41. The Lebanese resistance movements against the Israeli occupation of their land were never able to win full backing from Lebanese society, until perhaps the very last years of the occupation, which ended in May 2000.

Chapter 6

1. Haim Baram, *Kol Ha'ir*, January 31, 2003.

2. These studies were done by Professor Asher Arian from the Yaffe Institute for Strategic Research at Tel Aviv University. Reported in Uri As, *Ha'aretz*, January 31, 2003.

3. Marzel was a former member of the openly racist Kach movement, founded by Meir Kahane and now outlawed in Israel.

4. Amnon Barzilai, *Ha'aretz*, January 30, 2003.

5. Interview reported in *Ha'aretz*, January 31, 2003.

6. Shinui, as a party, completely dissolved in the run-up to the March 2006 general elections. It is, however, still telling to briefly describe its political principles to explain why, in the era of the almost complete facistization of Israeli political culture and the homogenization of the Israeli political map, the distinct political organization of Shinui became obsolete.

7. Tommy Lapid, the chair of Shinui, repeatedly declares that he loathes everything connected to what he defines as "Levantine culture."

8. See the interview with Sami Chetrit, "Why Are Shas and the Mizrahim Supporters of the Right?" in this chapter.

9. See more about further developments in the Israeli political map history in Chapter 10.

10. See the interview with Sami Chetrit in this chapter.

11. Mitzna is a reserve general, the former commander of the Israeli Army in the Central District (the West Bank) in the 1987 Intifada and the mayor of Haifa for the ten years previous to the 2003 elections. He was chosen in the Labor primaries to compete against Sharon and the Likud and was known for his "dovish" positions. In the following Labor Party convention, where Shimon Peres was chosen to chair the party, Mitzna was completely marginalized in terms of both party leadership and public exposure.

12. The Labor Party gave up its demand for the immediate and unilateral withdrawal of the Israeli Army from PA Areas A and B—the areas that, according to the Oslo Accords, were under full Palestinian autonomy (the main cities) and those in which Israel retained its military control, respectively. Instead, it made vague references to the advancement of political negotiations, the cessation of tax benefits for the settlements and the inclusion of a declaration promising the implementation of the principles of Bush's speech [of June 24, 2002]—something Sharon had already misleadingly declared he would accept in the form of a "Palestinian state," to come about only after the "crushing of terror." Indeed, Sharon's firmness would serve him well down the road when he ultimately accepted the Labor Party into his government coalition in December 2004, this time, however, without any preconditions on the part of the latter. By that time, both had disclosed their shared political viewpoint as expressed in the political strategy of "unilateralism" (see Chapter 9).

13. Uzi Benziman, *Ha'aretz*, February 28, 2003.

14. The term used to refer to the PA presidential compound, most of which was destroyed during Operation Defensive Shield in April 2002. Despite this, Arafat continued to live and direct the PA from there until his death, though largely as its prisoner. Israel constantly threatened that if he ever left the compound, it would raid it and prevent him from returning.

15. See Tikva Honig-Parnass, "Israel's Arrogance Escalates Under Post-Iraq Pax Americana," in Chapter 7.

16. When Shas was conceived in 1983, it was a small movement whose aim was to disconnect from the Ashkenazi Orthodox *yeshivot* (religious schools), in which the Mizrahim and their learning tradition were discriminated against. Later the party grew and developed its ideology under the absolute spiritual leadership of Rabbi Ovadia Yosef and the political leadership of the charismatic Arye Deri—to whom Shas owed the building of its movement and its ever-growing number of representatives in the Knesset (17 in the 1999 elections).

17. Palmach is a Hebrew abbreviation for Plugot Mahatz (Hebrew for "storm troopers"). The Plugot Mahatz constituted the nucleus of the Zionist paramilitary units established in the *Yishuv* and the elite of the Zionist army during the 1948 War. Under the full control of the left currents of the Zionist Labor movement since its inception, it was dissolved by Ben-Gurion toward the end of the 1948 War. However, it became the symbol of "beautiful [Ashkenazi] Israel," while being promoted as legendary in the Zionist movement narrative.

18. Ben-Gurion was the leader of the Zionist labor movement, who led the pre-1948 *Yishuv* and was the first prime minister of the state of Israel.

19. Rabbi Ovadia Yosef is the highest spiritual authority of Shas, whom all Shas MKs obey on political issues as well. In 2005, the positions of the Shas leadership became more right-wing, including making increasingly vocal declarations against the unilateral disengagement from the Gaza Strip. (See Chapter 9.)

20. According to Jewish tradition, part of the second Temple was built there. What is known as the "Wailing Wall," which is located outside the Al Aqsa Mosque compound, is believed to be the remnants of part of the walls that surrounded the temple. The Al Aqsa Mosque and its surrounding compound are considered to be the third holiest site in Islam after Mecca and Medina. It is believed to be built around the rock from which the Prophet Muhammad ascended into Heaven. According to the agreement reached after the 1967 War, the Islamic waqf is in charge of managing the compound. Jewish extremists object to this agreement and have been committing provocations, hoping to incite the Palestinians to violence, which could end in a change of the status quo in the compound itself and perhaps even in the region.

21. *Halachah*, Hebrew for "law," is the body of Jewish law supplementing the scriptural law and forming especially the legal part of the Talmud. It is the religious body of law, regulating all aspects of life, including religious ritual, familial and personal status, civil relations, criminal law, and relations with non-Jews.

22. Arye Deri played a central role in Shas and the broader Israeli political arena as minister in several governments. He was sentenced to three years in prison for alleged bribery. Since his release in July 2002, he has retired from political life.

23. Chetrit is referring to a rebellion that broke out among young Mizrahim in the early 1970s that called for the transformation of the capitalist Zionist state and for the legitimate rights of all the oppressed, including the Palestinian citizens of Israel. They called themselves the Black Panthers, consciously modeling themselves upon the African-American movement of the same name. See Sami Shalom Chetrit, "30 Years to the Black Panthers," *Between the Lines* no. 6, April 2001.

24. See Chetrit, *Mizrahi Struggle in Israel*, 119–72.

25. The Histradut is the umbrella of unions of Israeli workers that was an arm of the Zionist movement before 1948 and that of the Jewish Zionist state since its establishment. (See Introduction.)

26. A reference to the Israeli Black Panthers' relationship with the then-Socialist anti-Zionist group Matzpen.

27. HILA is a radical Mizrahi NGO that fights for equality in education in development towns and poor neighborhoods. It still functions, and more information can be found at www.hila-equal-edu.org.il. *Iton Aher* (literally, "A Different Magazine") was a radi-

cal Mizrahi magazine; and Kedma was an alternative experimental school that was closed down by the Tel Aviv municipality (see Tamar Barkay and Gal Levy, "Kedma School," *News from Within*, June 1999; Sami Shalom Chetrit, "Huldai, The Duce and the Local Cop," *News from Within*, June 1999). For more information on these initiatives, see www.kedma.co.il (in Hebrew).

28. The "development towns" in peripheral parts of the country along the 1949 armistice lines, with meager living resources, were populated with Mizrahi immigrants. They are now centers of poverty and unemployment.

29. An elite academic interdisciplinary center located in Jerusalem that focuses on culture, theory, and criticism—the name of its quarterly journal. See www.vanleer.org.il/default_e.asp.

30. Shlomo Swirski is *Israel's Oriental Majority* (London: Zed Books, 1989).

31. Referring to Ella Shohat's seminal article, "Mizrahim in Israel: Zionism from the Standpoint of Its Jewish Victims," *Social Text*, Fall 1988, 1–35.

32. Chetrit refers to, among others, to the Introduction to *Mizrahim in Israel: A Critical Observation into Israel's Ethnicity*, ed. Hannan Heve, Yehuda Shenhav, and Pnina Motzafi-Haller (Jerusalem: The Van Leer Jerusalem Institute/Hakibutz Hameuchad Publishing House, 2002), 9–15.

33. In January 2000, Hakeshet Hademokratit Hamizrahit appealed to the High Court of Justice, requesting the cancellation of three decisions made by the Israel Land Council (decisions 717, 727, and 737) dealing with changing the status of agricultural land for the development of industry, commerce, and housing. Keshet claimed that "These decisions contradict the principles of just distribution and social equality, which are the basis of each and every public body in a democratic country. These decisions make it possible for a small public, the agricultural sector comprising only 3 percent of the country's population, to gain economic advantages to the tune of tens of billions of Israeli shekels for land that belongs to the entire public." The truth of the matter is that most of these lands are "state lands" that were confiscated from their Palestinian owners soon after the establishment of the state. They were thereafter given to the kibbutzim on lease, on the condition that they be used for agriculture.

Chapter 7

1. See the monthly reports of the Palestine National Data Bank—State Information Service for this time period at www.pnic.gov.ps/arabic/quds/arabic/ivid/martyrs/Monthly%20report.html.

2. "Report on Israeli Land Sweeping and Demolition of Palestinian Buildings and Facilities in the Gaza Strip, 01st July, 2002–31st March, 2003," a publication of the Palestinian Center for Human Rights, available at www.pchrgaza.org/files/Reports/English/sweepingland9.htm#_ftn2.

3. Figures on the destruction of metal workshops relate only to the period of January and February 2003 and are provided by the "Weekly Report of Israeli Human Rights Violations in the Occupied Palestinian Territories 06–19 February 2003," Palestinian Center for Human Rights, available at www.pchrgaza.org/files/W_report/English/2003/20-02-2003.htm.

4. See Amir Oren, *Ha'aretz*, July 1, 2005. Oren cites a book recently published by the Israeli State Archive entitled *Yitzhak Rabin, Prime Minister of Israel* and edited by Yemima Rosenthal. It documents how the assassinated former Israeli prime minister Yitzhak Rabin proposed transferring the Palestinians from the West Bank while serving as a major general in the Israel Defense Forces in 1956. The transfer suggestion was raised at an IDF staff meeting attended by then–prime minister and defense minister David Ben-Gurion. Rabin proposed initiating a war against Jordan and

using it to deport Palestinians from the West Bank. 'Most of them can be driven out,' said Rabin, then-head of the IDF's Training Division and a week before being appointed GOC Northern Command. 'If the numbers were smaller it would be easier, but the problem can be solved in principle. It would not be a humane move, but war in general is not a humane matter,' he said, according to the book." Furthermore, during the 1967 War, Rabin sent a report as chief of staff to the government, remarking that the army "created the conditions for the Palestinians to escape [as in to avoid being transferred]."

5. The Quartet is composed of the United States, the European Union, Russia, and the United Nations.

6. For a full copy of the Road Map, see www.state.gov/r/pa/prs/ps/2003/20062pf.htm.

7. Abu Mazen had been a former top negotiator of the Oslo Accords and was a senior official in the PLO at the time these articles were writen. He officially became PA prime minister on March 19, 2003, after sustained U.S.-led international pressure to marginalize Arafat resulted in the creation of the position of prime minister itself. Abu Mazen was seen as a more conciliatory, "pragmatic" politician, who had no relation to the historical Palestinian armed struggle. He also negotiated what came to be known as the Beilin–Abu Mazen Agreement in 1995—an informal "peace proposal" that was widely condemned by Palestinian national movement actors as making concessions on all major Palestinian national goals. For more on the Beilin–Abu Mazen Agreement, see Tanya Reinhardt, *Israel/Palestine: How to End the War of 1948* (New York: Seven Stories Press, 2002).

8. Jamil Matar and Ali El Din Hilal, *The Arab Regional Regimes: A Study in Arab Political Relationships*, 3rd ed. (Beirut: Center for Arab Unity Studies, 1983), 30–32.

9. See Israel Shahak, "An Israeli Hegemony over the Entire Middle East," *Jusour* no. 6 (1995).

10. Uri Lubrani, "The Relationships Between Israel and the Countries on the Periphery of the Arab World: Turkey, Iran, Ethiopia," a lecture on the Israeli position regarding Ethnic Communities within the Arab World held at the Center for Strategic Research at Bar Ilan University, Ramat Gan (no date available).

11. Also see Vijay Prashad, "Hindutva-Zionism: An Alliance of the New Epoch," *Between the Lines* no. 13 (February 2002).

12. A reference to a large cannon that Iraq developed in the late 1980s, supposedly with the assistance of a Canadian astrophysicist named Gerald Bull—the eventual victim of assassination in Brussels in 1985.

13. Referring to a massacre conducted by Israeli troops against the village of Kufr Qasem, inside the Green Line. On the eve of the 1956 War, Israel declared a curfew on the village after all its residents had gone to work their fields. Upon their return home, forty-nine were lined up and killed by the Israeli Army for "violating the curfew," which they had been unaware of in the first place. Abdel Jawwad is implying that the massacre at Kufr Qasem in 1956 was designed to play a role similar to that of the massacre at Deir Yassin in 1948, to induce a sense of terror and panic in the remaining Palestinian community inside Israel, resulting in their fleeing or expulsion.

14. Abdel Jawwad also references how in the run-up to the 1990–91 Gulf War, then–Israeli prime minister Yitzhak Shamir (Likud) sought to exploit these events and create a dynamic that would result in expulsion of the residents of the West Bank. On October 8, 1990 (after Iraq had invaded Kuwait but before the U.S. bombardment of Iraq), a small unit of Israeli border patrolmen opened fire on Palestinian demonstrators within the Haram El Sharif/Al Aqsa Mosque compound in Jerusalem, resulting in twenty Palestinians killed. According to Abdel Jawwad, "The massacre resulted, as was required of it, in Palestinian revenge operations in the following weeks, against Israeli civilians, particularly with 'white arms,' in something that became known as

the 'revolution of knives.' This resulted in a negative turn in perception among Israelis who were understanding of the 1987 Intifada. This in turn brought about a consensus that was necessary for any 'exceptional' operations against the Palestinians." See the two-part report by Saleh Abdel Jawwad regarding the Al Aqsa Massacre in the weekly magazine *Al Youm al Sabi'* (The Seventh Day), published in Paris, mid-October 1990.

15. Akiva Eldar, *Ha'aretz*, May 11, 2003.

16. See the Introduction, as well as Gilbert Achcar, "Zionism and Peace: From the Allon Plan to the Washington Accords," *Eastern Cauldron*.

17. See David Barsamian, "Imperial Ambitions," an interview with Noam Chomsky, *Monthly Review* 55, no. 1 (May 2003).

18. Aluf Benn, *Ha'aretz*, May 22, 2003.

19. Danny Rubinstein, *Ha'aretz*, May 19, 2003.

20. Ibid.

21. By June 2005, there were more than 120 outposts. Their construction has not stopped for one day, even a month before the anticipated "unilateral disengagement" from Gaza. For updated information on the outposts, see the Peace Now Web site: www.peacenow.org.il/site/en/peace.asp?pi-58.

22. See "Virtual Evacuation of Virtual Outposts," *Between the Lines* no. 19, December 2002.

23. Amos Harel, *Ha'aretz*, May 16, 2003.

24. Ibid.

25. Quoted in Shalom Yerushalmi, *Yediot Ahronot*, May 5, 2003.

26. Interview with Ariel Sharon by Nahum Barnea and Shimon Shiffer, *Yediot Ahronot*, April 16, 2003. The senior Israeli commentator Aluf Benn confirmed this two years later when summarizing Sharon's vision in 2005: "The solution to the Israeli-Arab conflict will be possible only when the Arabs recognize the 'homeland right' of the Jewish people to erect a Jewish state in Eretz Israel. And till this happens, if at all, only a slow advancement, very slow, can take place." See Aluf Benn, *Ha'aretz*, April 26, 2005.

27. Akiva Eldar, *Ha'aretz*, April 18, 2003.

28. Interview with Ari Shavit, *Ha'aretz*, August 30, 2002. See excerpts of the interview in Tikva Honig-Parnass, "Zionism's Fixation: War Without End" in Chapter 3 in this book.

29. Ahmed Chalabi was the CIA-sponsored Iraqi opposition leader who appeared to have been groomed by the United States to lead Iraq after the overthrow of Saddam Hussein.

30. A reference to elements within the PA who promoted the weakness of the Palestinian position after the U.S. occupation of Iraq.

Chapter 8

1. Abdallah Awwad, "What Is Wanted for Us," *Al Ayyam*, September 4, 2003.

2. For confirmation of the claim of Israel's systematic use of provocations to end this as well as other cease-fire initiatives, which in turn were followed by Palestinian military attacks and suicide operations, see Raviv Druker and Ofer Shelah, *Boomerang* (Jerusalem: Keter Publishing House, 2005), as reported in "A State Inquiry into Sharon et al.," Akiva Eldar, *Ha'aretz*, July 4, 2005.

3. See Eldar, "A State Inquiry." Eldar writes, "*Boomerang* adds spine-chilling revelations . . . about IDF commanders who stoked the fires of the Intifada and carried out something of a military coup. The book confirms that high-ranking intelligence officers marketed the 'no partner' myth to serve the interests of Barak and Sharon, despite there being no support for this in the assessments of military intelligence, the Shin Bet or the Mossad."

4. Aluf Benn, "An Abiding Faith in Force," *Ha'aretz*, October 9, 2003.

5. David Barsamian, "Collateral Language," interview with Noam Chomsky, Znet 16, no. 7/8, July–August, 2003.

6. For more on the Road Map and its stipulations, see the introduction to Chapter 6 (particularly footnote 9) as well as Tikva Honig-Parnass, "The Democratization Reforms Scheme: The United States and Israel Publicly Join Hands on the Road to Liquidating Palestinian Nationalism," in Chapter 5.

7. Shalom Yerushalmi, *Kol Hazman*, August 22, 2003.

8. Ze'ev Sternhell, *Ha'aretz*, August 22, 2003.

9. For the most up-to-date information on the wall and its evolution, from Palestinian sources, see www.stopthewall.org.

10. Israel's promise of prisoner release turned into an act of degradation and humiliation aimed at provoking Palestinians' anger and resistance activities. Most of the 432 released prisoners were scheduled to be released shortly or were administrative detainees (imprisoned without any official charges against them), criminal prisoners, or workers who had entered Israel without a permit, for whom the PA had not even asked release.

11. Danny Rubinstein, *Ha'aretz*, July 21, 2003.

12. Uzi Benziman, *Ha'aretz*, August 22, 2003.

13. See Chapter 8, note 2.

14. *Ha'aretz*, August 13, 2003.

15. Shimon Shifer and Nahum Barnea, *Yediot Ahronot*, August 22, 2003.

16. Ben Kaspit, *Ma'ariv*, Weekend Supplement, August 23, 2003.

17. Aluf Benn, *Ha'aretz*, August 22, 2003.

18. See Saleh Abdel Jawad, "The Israeli Assassination Policy," *Between the Lines* no. 9, August 2001.

19. See Akiva Eldar, *Ha'aretz*, July 4, 2005, where he comments on Raviv Druker and Ofer Shelah's book *Boomerang* (Jerusalem: Keter Publishing House, 2005). Druker and Shelah describe "a process in which members of the highest level of government and the defense establishment turned the 'targeted killings' into wholesale liquidations.

"The book speaks of the licentious use of the threatening term 'highly specific alerts," by means of exploiting an enlisted and intimidated media. The writers charge that the former military advocate general gave a stamp of approval to the light-finger-on-the-trigger policy and was rewarded by becoming the first military advocate general to wear the rank of a major general. They describe a long series of Israeli acts of sabotage on cease-fire initiatives that ended in terror attacks. . . . They accuse ministers Shimon Peres and Ben Eliezer [Labor] of criminal negligence by lending a hand to the deterioration of the situation in the [Occupied] Territories and by standing idly by while Sharon, Mofaz [defense minister], Ya'alon [chief of staff], and Dichter [head of the Shabak] undermined every chance for an easing in the hostilities."

20. Nahum Barnea, *Yediot Ahronot*, September 6, 2003. Israel, however, managed to control the 1967 Occupied Territories while keeping the semblance of the PA as a viable entity, thus avoiding the responsibility of the occupying forces to supply services to

the occupied population. The unilateral disengagement from the Gaza Strip served this specific function. (See Chapters 9 and 10.)

21. See interview with Chief of Staff Moshe Yaalon quoted in Tikva Honig-Parnass, *Zionism's Fixation: War Without End*, in Chapter 3 of this book.

22. Moshe Dayan, a labor leader who later joined the Likud government, was the former Israeli Army chief of staff from 1953 to 1958 and served during different tenures as minister of agriculture, defense minister, and foreign minister.

23. Golda Meir was the prime minister of Israel from 1969 to 1974 and also served as its minister of labor and foreign affairs.

24. Jabotinski was the head of the Betar movement, which separated from the World Zionist Movement in the 1930s. He established the paramilitary organization Etzel in 1937, as an alternative to the official Zionist paramilitary, the Hagana. Jabotinski considered the Hagana to be too restrained in its fight against the British and the Arabs. Jabotinski's tradition is a type of revisionist Zionism that composes the ideological underpinnings of the modern-day Likud party. In 2005, Sharon left the Likud party with a number of its ideological leaders and many followers and established the Kadima party, which won the 2006 elections.

25. Unit 101 was an infamous undercover unit that Sharon established in the early 1950s and that specialized in killing refugees who attempted to return to their lands and raided Palestinian villages across the armistice line, aiming at inciting the situation.

26. Rehavam Ze'evi was a former Israeli minister from the ultra-right-wing Moledet-Transfer party, who was assassinated in October 2001 by the Popular Front for the Liberation of Palestine (PFLP).

27. The largest and main pre-1948 paramilitary branch of the organized *Yishuv*, led by Ben-Gurion and the Labor Zionist Movement on behalf of the World Zionist Movement (alongside the far smaller Etzel and Lehi, which were not under the control of the latter).

28. This affinity explains the future integration of Sharon's Kadima Party with Peres and other Labor Party leaders, as well as the full support Sharon received from the Labor Party regarding his unilateral policies (see Chapters 9 and 10).

29. The electric company workers' committee is one of the "thirteen big committees" in the public sector that the Histadrut supports.

Chapter 9

1. David Ignatius, "Secret Strategies," *Washington Post*, November 12, 2004.

2. The Jenin Martyrs Brigades act as a local subsidiary of the Popular Resistance Committees (PRCs) within Bureij Camp and were established after the Israeli invasion and destruction of Jenin Camp in April 2002, from which the name of the faction he leads derives. They are led by Mahmoud Nashabet, a leader from the first Intifada. For more on the PRCs, see Toufic Haddad, "The Changing Face of Southern Gaza: The Mutaradeen: An Afternoon with the Popular Resistance Committees," Toufic Haddad, *Between the Lines* no. 6, July 2006.

3. On July 30, 2004, members of Al Aqsa Martyrs Brigades in Jenin stormed and burned down the Intelligence (Mukhabbarat) headquarters and the offices of the Jenin governor, Qadura Musa. Zakariya Zubeidi, head of the Jenin Fateh militia, which conducted the raids, commented in an interview with Al Jazeera that "the escalation comes in response to the Mokhaberat creating obstacles for the resistance and collecting information on them rather than providing them protection" (Al Jazeera Web site, July 31, 2004). A day later, similar Fateh militias in Nablus would briefly abduct three Westerners; the abductions occurred one week after Nablus's

deputy mayor was abducted. In all these incidents, the abductees were released unharmed.

4. Graham Usher, "The Politics of Internal Security: The PA's New Intelligence Services," *Journal of Palestine Studies* 25, no. 2 (Winter 1996), 21–34.

5. *Al Quds Al Arabi*, June 11, 2003.

6. "PA Leaders Leave for Paris, Expected to Declare Arafat Dead," *Ha'aretz*, November 8, 2004.

7. "Readings in Hamas's Position Regarding the Presidential Election," *Al Risala*, January 19, 2005.

8. "Hamas Wins Overwhelming Victory in Gaza Vote," *Ha'aretz*, January 29, 2005.

9. The elections were delayed and ultimately held in January 2006.

10. Uzi Benziman, *Ha'aretz*, March 14, 2004.

11. Aluf Benn, *Ha'aretz*, October 6, 2004.

12. Tikva Honig-Parnass, "Zionism's Fixation: War Without End," in Chapter 3.

13. See Ari Shavit, interview with Moshe Ya'alon, *Ha'aretz Weekend Supplement*, June 3, 2005.

14. Also see Akiva Eldar, *Ha'aretz*, June 7, 2005, on Sharon's plans for a prolonged war against the Palestinians.

15. On the ideological and economic reasons behind Israel's return to the original liquidation-and-expulsion approach of Zionist colonization, see the Introduction. The process of reducing the differences between Right and Left in Israel eventually permitted the erection of the Kadima-Labor government, which in July 2006 carried out the bloody war against Lebanon. Defense Minister Amir Peretz of the Labor Party was one of the most hard-line members of the governing cabinet. See Chapter 10.

16. Aluf Benn, *Ha'aretz*, October 10, 2004. On the Arab states' recognition of Israel's prominent status in the region, see Aluf Benn, *Ha'aretz*, December 4, 2004.

17. Phrased as a rhetorical summary question by Ari Shavit in his interview with Dov Weisglas, *Ha'aretz*, October 8, 2004.

18. The yearly gathering of more than three hundred top figures from the academic, security, and political elites organized by the Hertzliya Interdisciplinary Center. The conference discusses what are considered to be the most important issues facing Israel.

19. Gush Katif was the southernmost settlement block in the Gaza Strip, made up of at least eleven individual Israeli settlements, extending 17 kilometers from the Egyptian border along the Gaza Mediterranean coast. For a comprehensive study of Israeli settlements in the Gaza Strip, see "A Comprehensive Survey of Israeli Settlements in the Gaza Strip," Palestinian Center for Human Rights, Series Studies no. 10. The report is available at www.pchrgaza.org/files/S&r/English/study10/Settlements.htm.

20. Aluf Benn, December 12, 2004.

21. Meron Benvenisti, *Ha'aretz*, December 16, 2004.

22. See Tanya Reinhart, *Israel/Palestine: How to End the War of 1948* (New York: Seven Stories Press, 2002), 26–29. The complete text of the Beilin–Abu Mazen understandings is available at www.us-israel.org/jsource/peace/beilinmazen.htm.

23. Danny Rubinstein, *Ha'aretz*, July 4, 2005.

24. Akiva Eldar, *Ha'aretz*, September 13, 2004.

25. MK Labor Efraim Sneh, quoted in "Sharon's Plan Will Eternalize War," *Ha'aretz*, November 10, 2004. Knowing this, however, has not prevented him from supporting the disengagement plan.

26. The third section of the plan clearly states that "Israel will guard and monitor the external land perimeter of the Gaza Strip, will continue to maintain exclusive authority in Gaza air space, and will continue to exercise security activity in the sea off the coast of the Gaza Strip." It also states that "Israel reserves its fundamental right of self-defense, both preventive and reactive, including where necessary the use of force, in respect to threats emanating from the Gaza Strip." Given that this is the framework within which Israel has always carried out its policies against the Palestinians, this essentially means that the mass killing, assassinations, and demolitions can be expected to continue as a continuation of the plan, not as its exception.

The disengagement plan, published by the Israeli cabinet, is available at www.mfa .gov.il/MFA/Peace+Process/Reference+Documents/Revised+Disengagement+Plan+ 6-June-2004.htm.

27. Ari Shavit, *Ha'aretz,* October 8, 2004.

28. Azmi Bishara, "Questions and Answers About Sharon's Disengagement Plan," National Democratic Assembly, parliamentary office statement, October 27, 2004.

29. For the most comprehensive critical review of it, see Sara Roy, "Praying with Their Eyes Closed: Reflections on the Disengagement from Gaza," *Journal of Palestine Studies,* August 2005, and, by the same author, "Gaza Future," *London Review of Books* 27, no. 21, November 3, 2005.

30. Sharon also called upon the small Ashkenazi Orthodox Yahadut Hatora party to join the government.

31. The coalition government at the time included the settlers' and transfer parties of the secular Ha'ichud Halumi and the National Religious Party, Shinui, and the Likud. On the extremist right-wing government established after the victory of the Likud in the 2003 elections, see Tikva Honig-Parnass, "Israeli Elections: A Massive Victory for the Extreme Nationalist, Ashkenazi Bourgeoisie," in Chapter 6.

32. Meretz changed its name to Yachad for the 2001 general elections, when then-MK doves Yossi Beilin and Yael Dayan left the Labor Party after not being elected to leadership positions in its primaries. Thereafter, they joined Yachad but failed to be included among its members who entered the Knesset as a result of the elections. Even though it changed its name, the use of its original name—Meretz—has been retained in public discourse.

33. See Akiva Eldar, *Ha'aretz,* July 4, 2005. Sharon needed the six votes of the Yachad (Meretz) bloc to ensure that he would survive any no-confidence motions brought forward by his political opponents, who included part of the Likud ministers.

34. Yuval Yoaz, *Ha'aretz,* October 24, 2004.

35. Yossi Verter, *Ha'aretz,* November 26, 2004.

36. Aluf Benn, *Ha'aretz,* April 26, 2005.

37. Ze'ev Sternhell, *Ha'aretz,* December 31, 2004.

38. Ze'ev Jabotinski was the chief spokesman for the opposition within the Zionist movement who fought against the mainstream trend of making "concessions" to the British mandate. In 1925 he formed a new party, the World Union of Zionist Revisionists, and the youth movement of Betar. After a decade of opposition to the official leadership of Zionism, he and his group seceded from the movement altogether and established the New Zionist Organization, which elected him president. Jabotinski strongly opposed the partition of Palestine. His growing militancy led him to take over the leadership of the dissident military organization Irgun, which in the 1940s developed into the military underground group Etzel and operated autonomously of the mainstream Zionist military wing—the Hagana, in its military attacks on the British. See Avi Shlaim, *The Iron Wall, Israel and the Arab World* (New York: W.W. Norton & Company, 2001), 11–13.

39. For more insight into this current and Sharon as a continuation of it, see the interview with MK Azmi Bishara in Chapter 8.

40. Nahume Barnea, *Yediot Ahronot*, October 22, 2004.

41. Haim Baram, *Kol Hair*, October 29, 2004.

42. Meron Benvenisti, *Ha'aretz*, June 30, 2005.

43. See Tikva Honig-Parnass, "Zionist Liberals-Left and Right Unite in Defense of the Ashkenazi Jewish State," in Chapter 3.

44. Baruch Kimmerling, "Neither Democratic nor Jewish," *Ha'aretz*, December 27, 1996.

45. See all daily newspapers of the first week of January 2005.

46. Danny Rabinowitz, *Ha'aretz*, November 18, 2004.

47. Akiva Eldar, *Ha'aretz*, November 15, 2005.

48. Ben Kaspit, an interview with MK Haim Ramon, *Ma'ariv*, December 10, 2004.

49. The types of barriers include full-time and partially manned checkpoints, roadblocks (consisting of rows of one-meter concrete blocks), metal gates, earth mounds, earth walls (a long series of earth mounds), and trenches. See United Nations Office for the Coordination of Humanitarian Affairs, humanitarian update April 2005, at www.humanitarianinfo.org/opt/docs/UN/OCHA/ochaHU0405_En.pdf.

50. See B'Tselem: The Israeli Information Center for Human Rights in the Occupied Territories, Statistics on Checkpoints and Roadblocks, www.btselem.org.

51. See property damage assessment in "Four Years Since the Beginning of the Intifada: Systematic Violations of Human Rights in the Occupied Palestinian Territories," Ramallah: Al Haq, September 2004.

52. At least forty-six Palestinians have been forcibly transferred from the West Bank during the Al Aqsa Intifada. This included eighteen who were sent to European countries, while the remainder were exiled to the Gaza Strip. See Al Haq, "Four Years."

53. Overall it should be emphasized that contrary to Western media perceptions, the overwhelming majority of all Palestinian resistance has been confined to the 1967 Occupied Territories themselves. According to Israeli Army statistics, between September 2000 and July 24, 2004, of the 22,406 Palestinian attacks committed during the Intifada, 12,776 (57%) took place in Gaza, 8,741 (39%) took place in the West Bank, and 889 (4%) took place in "the home front" [within the Green Line]—which also surely includes occupied Jerusalem.

The few attacks launched from Gaza outside its borders consisted of launching rudimentary rockets commonly referred to as "Qassams" (though this is a misnomer, as the Qassam rocket is only the name for the Hamas version of the rocket, whereas all factions have their own designs and names for their rockets). But here too, even these attacks (which, according to Israeli statistics, number slightly more than 300) constituted less than 3 percent of the total attacks launched from Gaza. See "General Info and Statistics" on the Israeli Army Web site: www1.idf.il/dover/site/mainpage.asp?sl=EN&id=22&docid=16703.EN&unit=10.

On March 14, 2004, two suicide bombers from Gaza also blew themselves up in the port of Ashdod, killing ten people. Hamas and Fateh claimed responsibility for the attack.

54. To get a sense of the improved level of sophistication of the military resistance in the Gaza Strip, take the example of a military operation Hamas conducted against a military base, located at a key control node dividing Khan Younis from the midsection of the Gaza Strip on June 27, 2004. According to information released by Hamas in an Islamist paper, the idea to blow up the base was developed over the course of a year and a half. Izz el Din el Qassam (the military wing of Hamas) was able to rent out a plot of land 360 meters from the base itself, which was subsequently fenced off, with a very basic roofed structure built upon it. Then, throughout the course of four months,

no fewer than fifteen militants worked day and night to dig a tunnel eight meters below the ground, until they reached just below the base. Thereafter, the militants distributed 1,900 kilograms of explosives in three different locations and promptly blew the base up. In the end, the entire operation (which was filmed and released on video by Hamas), cost upward of $40,000. In addition to the base being destroyed, Israel reported one soldier killed and half a dozen others injured. See *Al Risala*, no. 300, July 8, 2004.

55. "IDF Chief of Staff: Retreat Will Not Solve the Problem," Channel 7 radio (Arutz Sheva), March 8, 2004, quoting Haggai Hubberman, a correspondent for the Israeli settler Web site katif.net.

56. Gideon Levy, "The Victory of Brutality," *Ha'aretz*, March 14, 2004.

57. It is important to note that nonviolent resistance was the overwhelmingly predominant form of resistance practiced throughout the entire 1987 Intifada (resulting in more than 1,500 Palestinian deaths); at the beginning of this Intifada (resulting in hundreds more deaths); and with respect to popular resistance to the Israeli apartheid wall, to land confiscation, and to house demolition (all of which have failed to stop the building of the wall, the confiscation of the land, or the demolition of the houses). This is to say nothing regarding the attempts to resist Israeli colonialism through international forums, such as the United Nations or other international bodies, for example, the International Court of Justice.

58. For a full account of this operation, see "Rafah's New Nakba—A Report on the Violation of Social and Economic Rights in Rafah, May 12–24, 2004" (Arabic), Palestinian Center for Human Rights.

59. Ben Kaspit, "A Signal to Egypt," *Ma'ariv* International English Web edition, May 22, 2004.

60. See statistics on those killed in the month of May 2004, available at www.sis.gov.ps.

61. PCHR, "Rafah's New Nakba."

62. See UNRWA Gaza, "Field Assessment of IDF Operation Days of Penitence," available at www.un.org/unrwa/news/incursion_oct04.pdf.

63. PCHR Weekly Report, October 14–20, 2004.

64. After Operation Defensive Shield in April 2002, Israel maintained direct control of Palestinian cities in the West Bank, conducting raids virtually on a daily basis to arrest and kill activists. Israel does not have the same level of control over the Gaza Strip. That is, the density of Palestinian urban areas and refugee camps makes it largely too difficult and dangerous for Israel to conduct similar raids on the ground, so it prefers to attack from the air. The large ground assaults Israel wages in Gaza are generally focused upon infrastructure and home destruction, rather than against specific activists.

65. The assassination of Rantisi was arguably even more significant for Hamas, as his charisma and leadership were virtually irreplaceable.

66. Interview with Israeli Foreign Minister Silvan Shalom, *Charlie Rose*, PBS, March 23, 2004.

67. Amira Hass, "Balance of Pain," *Ha'aretz*, April 2, 2004.

68. See Izz el Din el Qassam Web site, Mohammed Deif audio recordings.

69. The reference is not to the pre-1967 borders of the Gaza Strip but rather to the former "seam lines" of contact between Israeli settlers and army and the Palestinians *within* the Strip.

70. After the disengagement's completion, Israel controlled Gaza from four well-defined points: the Erez border crossing, the Karni crossing point (where import and export of goods take place), the Rafah border crossing (technically under the control of EU observers but with an Israeli military camera observing the flow of persons and with the ability to veto travel), and the Sufa crossing point. Israel also established a mili-

tary cordon of tanks and armored personnel carriers around the perimeter of Gaza, in addition to a tight aerial and sea observation and besiegement regime of the Strip.

71. The title of the Israeli Ministry of Foreign Affairs document distributed on its Web site and graphically personalizing the "Jewish Communities of Gaza," available at www.mfa.gov.il/MFA/MFAArchive/2000_2009/2005/Paying+the+Price+for+Peace+ +July+2005.htm.

72. The director of military intelligence, Major General Aharon Ze'evi, was already warning in mid-August 2005 that "terrorist activity" might be renewed in April 2006 "if peace talks stall after the disengagement." Likewise, Yuval Diskin, head of the Shin Bet internal security service, cautioned that "the calm prevailing in recent days in the Gaza Strip does not attest to a Palestinian ability to control the area. Immediately after the civilians leave the territory, we will see a gnawing away of the calm."

73. Uzi Benziman, "Dangerous Gimmicks," *Ha'aretz*, August 8, 2005.

Chapter 10

1. See "Weekly Report on Israeli Human Rights Violations in the Occupied Palestinian Territories 09–15 November," no. 44, 2006, Palestinian Center for Human Rights— Gaza, available at www.pchrgaza.ps/files/W_report/English/2006/pdf/weekly%20 report%2044.pdf.

2. Merav Yudilovitch, interview with Noam Chomsky, on *Yediot Ahronot* Web site, August 9, 2006.

3. Reported in Uri Klein, *Ha'aretz*, February 15, 2006.

4. Gideon Allon, interview with Zehava Galon, *Ha'aretz*, February 15, 2006.

5. Barak came up with the "no partner" slogan in September 2000 after the intentional failure of the Camp David summit.

6. After Sharon lost his Knesset majority, Kadima functioned as a temporary government until general elections took place.

7. Azmi Bishara, "Five Thoughts Following the Hamas Victory," *Machsom*, January 30, 2006.

8. See interview with Alex Callinicos, a leader of the Socialist Workers Party, UK, September 18, 2006, available at www.iran-bulletin.org. The interviewer, Ardeshir Mehrdad, is an Iranian socialist and an editor of *Iran Bulletin and Middle-East Forum*.

9. For this position, see the Israeli antioccupation Web site "Occupation Magazine," which presents the entire text of the Hamas charter and refers to Articles 28 and 32 of it, available at www.kibush.co.il/downloads/2006_02_01_The%20Hamas%20 Charter.doc.

10. The words of Ze'ev Sternhell, who was among those misled. See Ze'ev Sternhell, "For the Welfare of All," *Ha'aretz*, December 14, 2005.

11. These promises were made when he left his ten-year post as chair of the Histadrut and former head of the political party Am Echad (One People). They created the expectations that were largely responsible for his victory in the Labor Party primaries.

12. Avirama Golan, *Ha'aretz*, January 10, 2006.

13. Reported by Avraham Tal, *Ha'aretz*, January 20, 2006.

14. Haim Baram, *Kol Hair*, January 20, 2006.

15. Gideon Levy, *Ha'aretz*, March 26, 2006.

16. Likud and Israel Beiteinu won 12 and 11 seats, respectively.

17. Tani Goldstein, *Yediot Ahronot* Web site, July 31, 2006. Goldstein adds that Paz also acquired the stock of the refineries, valued at an additional U.S. $300 million.

18. Amir Oren, *Ha'aretz,* April 13, 2006.

19. See Tanya Reinhart, "Why Israel Will Never Truly Let Go of Gaza," *The Independent Weekly* (Adelaide, Australia), September 9–15, 2006, for details of the provocations made by Israel. Israel refused to release three Lebanese prisoners held in its jails after a previous prisoner exchange; refused to hand over the map of land mines it had planted in southern Lebanon during its eighteen-year occupation; and continued to violate Lebanese land, air, and sea space, sometimes abducting farmers and fishermen.

20. Shimon Shifer, *Yediot Ahronot,* July 14, 2006.

21. Tanya Reinhart, quoting Alex Fishman, senior commentator for *Yediot Ahronot,* in "Why Israel Will Never Truly Let Go of Gaza," *The Independent Weekly* (Adelaide, Australia), September 9–15, 2006.

22. Azmi Bishara, "Channeling the Resistance," *Al Ahram Weekly,* July 6–12, 2006.

23. Danny Rubinstein, *Ha'aretz,* July 14, 2006. By the beginning of November 2006, the abducted soldier was yet to be released.

24. Moreover, due to Israel controlling everything that enters and exits in the Gaza Strip, the power plant continued to be inoperational for months thereafter, making everything from hospitals to refrigeration devices subject to Israel's barbaric policies.

25. Yoav Stern, "Nasrallah: Only Deal Will Free Kidnapped Soldiers," *Ha'aretz,* July 13, 2006.

26. Ze'ev Schiff, *Ha'aretz,* July 14, 2006.

27. Azmi Bishara, "Blackmail by Bombs," *Al Ahram Weekly,* July 20–26, 2006.

28. Robin Wright, "Strikes Are Called Part of a Broad Strategy," *Washington Post,* July 16, 2006.

29. Ran Hacohen, "Israeli Intellectuals Love the War," Antiwar.com, August 7, 2006. Hacohen's critical article on the Israeli liberal elite includes many quotations of their inciting articles in support of the war available at antiwar.com/hacohen/?articleid=9486.

30. Rafi Ginat, *Yediot Ahronot,* July 28, 2006.

31. Yitzhak Laor, "A Tale of Love and Darkness: Propaganda, Narcissism, and the West," *Mitaam, A Periodical for Literature and Radical Thought* 7 (September 2006): 67–91.

32. BBC report, July 12, 2006.

33. *Ma'ariv,* July 21, 2006. Quoted in Hacohen, "Israeli Intellectuals." Sobol repeated his stance in a broadcast interview on Channel 2, the morning of October 8, 2006.

34. Eitan Haber, *Yediot Ahronot,* July 14, 2006.

35. The title of Yosef Gorni's article in *Ha'aretz,* July 30, 2006, quoted below.

36. *Ha'aretz,* July 30, 2006.

37. Peace Now, which was the largest Israeli peace movement, has gradually almost disappeared from the streets since the "failure" of the Oslo track in 2000. Today the movement focuses largely on monitoring and reporting on settlement construction and master plans, as well as the ongoing policies of land confiscation as part of construction of the apartheid wall in the West Bank.

38. Amos Oz, "Why Israeli Missiles Strike for Peace," *Evening Standard,* July 20, 2006. "There can be no moral equation between Hizbullah and Israel. Hizbullah is targeting Israeli civilians wherever they are, while Israel is targeting mostly Hizbullah."

39. David Grossman, "Plans for a Military Victory Over Hizbullah Are a Fantasy," *The Guardian* (U.K.), July 20, 2006, available at www.guardian.co.uk/syria/story/0,,1824533,00.html.

40. Laor, "Tale of Love."

41. See Meron Benvenisti, "Beware the Demographic Demon," *Ha'aretz*, January 27, 2005: "The 'demographic ghost' has come to fully dominate the discourse of 'Left' circles to such an extent that it has begun to take over all public and political discourse in Israel."

42. Meron Benvenisti, "Eight Percent of Their Homeland," *Ha'aretz*, October 6, 2005.

43. David Grossman, *Sleeping on a Wire* (Tel Aviv: Hakibbutz Hameuchad, 1993), 102.

44. Ibid., p. 97.

45. Sami Michael, *Ha'aretz*, September 24, 2004. Andalusia is here "a reference to the flourishing period when various Muslim dynasties ruled over this part of Spain, until 1492 when they were finally defeated and expelled." Indeed, Michael pays lip service to a Jewish culture that also "inscribes deep in its heart its wrongs. . . . Till this day we hate the ancient Egyptians, the Babylonians, Greeks, Romans, the Inquisition in Spain and the pogromists in Hebron early in the last century." However, when the implication of these Jewish cultural traits is raised in regard to the preparedness of Israelis to make concessions to achieve peace, his accusations focus primarily upon the fanaticism of Jewish settlers and right-wing extremists, while steering clear of any critique of Zionist center, let alone left, politicians or intellectuals. He thus implies that Israeli peace plans initiated by progressive Israelis are in accordance with a different, really Jewish cultural tradition, which "poses life above anything else. . . . The Jewish people are still alive because it has disdained empty slogans and chosen life. . . . The Judaism that guarded my people, the tradition which is rooted deep in my soul, both tell me to give up (make concessions) for the sake of life."

46. Amos Oz, *But These Are Two Different Wars* (Jerusalem: Keter Publishing House, 2000), 135. For a critical review of the book, see Yitzhak Laor, "But These Are Two Different Wars," *Ha'aretz*, Sfarim Supplement, May 1, 2003.

47. Ari Shavit, interview with Amos Oz, *Ha'aretz Weekly*, March 1, 2002. Also in Oz, *But These Are Two Different Wars*, p. 134.

48. Yoel Markus, *Ha'aretz*, September 26, 2006.

49. "In Lebanon Israel has lost its deterrent power, the recovery of which was the 'specific' Israeli reason to set out for the U.S. war on Lebanon." Shlomo Ben Ami, *Ha'aretz*, September 7, 2006.

50. See Azmi Bishara, "Precious Clarity," *Al Ahram Weekly*, September 28–October 4, 2006.

51. Bishara, "Blackmail by Bombs."

52. Tzipi Livni, quoted in Nahum Barnea, *Yediot Ahronot*, Weekend Supplement, September 29, 2006.

53. Aluf Ben, *Ha'aretz*, August 25, 2006.

54. Ze'ev Schiff, *Ha'aretz*, November 3, 2006.

55. Azmi Bishara, "Ministry of Strategic Threats," *Al Ahram Weekly*, November 1–7, 2006.

56. *Ha'aretz*, June 28, 2002.

57. Bishara, "Ministry of Strategic Threats."

58. Haim Baram, *Kol Ha'ir*, October 3, 2006.

59. Uzi Benziman, *Ha'aretz*, September 20, 2006.

60. Gideon Levy, *Ha'aretz*, October 15, 2006.

61. Alex Fishman, *Yediot Ahronot*, November 10, 2006.

62. Gil Hoffman and Sheera Claire, interview with Efraim Sneh, *Jerusalem Post*, November 10, 2006.

63. Beni Tziper, *Ha'aretz*, Culture and Literature Supplement, September 29, 2006.

64. Dan Margalit, *Ma'ariv*, The Feast Supplement, September 13, 2006.

65. See Introduction, note 9; Chapter 8, note 23; and Chaper 9, note 38.

66. A small example is telling of the state of Palestinian affairs and why Fateh ultimately fell on its own sword. In the district of Ramallah, five seats were allotted for the parliament, with one being reserved for a Christian, as part of a quota system. Fateh officially fielded five candidates, including one Christian, while Hamas fielded only four candidates. The five Fateh slots were fiercely contested among Fateh's constituency. This is because the basis for Fateh's strength in Ramallah (and indeed everywhere) was not rooted in Fateh's political program but was rather the product of a network of opportunistic alliances with a wide assortment of political elites representing different constituencies and interests. So, for example, the Ramallah district is known for having a high number of refugees from the destroyed Palestinian village of Deir Tarif, near present-day Ramleh inside Israel. One of this constituency's main political representatives historically has been Jamil Al Tarifi, a millionaire contractor who, in the first PA parliament, was a minister of civil affairs for Fateh. Tarifi had become somewhat notorious for having questionable economic relations with Israeli businessmen and was a symbol of corruption even among wide sectors of Fateh. However, in the lawless terrain of the PA, under the Oslo Accords, Tarifi was also seen as someone who, however tainted, could provide protection and influence regarding the daily needs of those he was loyal to and represented. When it came to determining Fateh's official candidates, the party opted not to include Tarifi on the list, fearing it would taint its image. Tarifi, however, wouldn't accept the snub, running an independent campaign that the Deir Tarif constituency of Ramallah still voted for. When the votes were totaled, Tarifi took 16,000 votes, while the official Fateh candidates averaged around 22,500 apiece. The split allowed for the four unified candidates of Hamas to take all seats it ran for, with an average of around 33,000 votes apiece. In almost all districts, similar split votes cost Fateh dearly. Had Fateh been able to field a unified list of candidates with consolidated constituency support, the results of the elections would likely have looked much different and probably much closer to the results of the more evenly divided slate vote.

67. A copy of the Change and Reform slate platform is available in Arabic at www .elections.ps/pdf/hamas_progamme_election.pdf.

68. Hamas evolved from the Islamic Brotherhood movement, which historically has held staunchly anti-Zionist and anticolonialist positions, but also took reactionary positions undermining the Arab Left in the region. The Jordanian branch of the Brotherhood, for example, sided with the Jordanian monarchy in its attempts to crush the PLO during the events of Black September in 1970. Hamas has greatly evolved from its roots, incorporating national liberation notions into its praxis, as evidenced by its recent willingness to join the PLO. Although no doubt a deeper study of its politics and ideology is in order, the movement today operates as a wider canopy, incorporating elements disaffected from the historical national movement and having both progressive and conservative wings within it. For more on Hamas, see Khaled Hroub, *Hamas: A Beginner's Guide* (London: Pluto Press, 2006); Khaled Hroub, *Hamas: Political Thought and Practice* (Washington, D.C.: Institute for Palestine Studies, first published in 1997 in Arabic, English edition 2000); Ziad Abu Amr, *Islamic Fundamentalism in the West Bank and Gaza*, (Bloomington, IN: Indiana University Press, 1994).

69. Aluf Benn, "Wave of Democracy Pits Israel against 'Arab Street,'" *Ha'aretz*, January 29, 2006.

70. Amir Oren, "From Convergence to Submergence," *Ha'aretz*, May 19, 2006.

71. Recordings of Hanieh's speeches are frequently available on Hamas's political Web site, www.palestine-info.info/arabic/index.shtml. This particular speech was posted for his June 16 speech.

72. Mahmoud al Zahar, "We Will Win Any New Elections" (speech), October 21, 2006, available on Hamas Web site.

73. The Prisoners' Document was a manifesto of sorts, drafted on May 11, 2006, by jailed senior Palestinian leaders, representing all major Palestinian factions. It was initially designed to provide a common political and resistance platform for the national movement and was signed by Marwan Barghouti (secretary-general, Fateh); Sheikh Abdul Khaleq al-Natsheh (Hamas), Sheikh Bassam al-Sa'di (Islamic Jihad), Abdul Rahim Mallouh (deputy secretary general of the PFLP), and Mustafa Badarneh (DFLP). The agreement later reached between Fateh and Hamas on June 24 was not the original document but a variant that was revised through negotiations between both parties; available at www.jmcc.org/documents/prisoners.htm.

74. Aljazeera Arabic-language Web site, June 10, 2006.

75. The Popular Resistance Committees were primarily a Fateh-composed faction that formed at the beginning of the Al Aqsa Intifada in Gaza. These forces made up the radical anti-Oslo base within Fateh that broke from their role, often within the PA security services, and aligned themselves with militants from other factions under one large umbrella organization.

76. Though the continued use of these rockets against Israeli targets in the periphery of the Gaza Strip has been criticized tactically, their logic is explained by the Israeli political commentator Gideon Levy: "What would have happened if the Palestinians had not fired Qassams? Would Israel have lifted the economic siege that it imposed on Gaza? Would it have opened the border to Palestinian labourers? Freed prisoners? Met with the elected leadership and conducted negotiations? Encouraged investment in Gaza? Nonsense. If the Gazans were sitting quietly, as Israel expects them to do, their case would disappear from the agenda here and around the world. Nobody would have given any thought to the fate of the people of Gaza if they did not behave violently." Gideon Levy, "Who Started?," *Ha'aretz*, July 9, 2006.

77. Amos Harel, *Ha'aretz*, May 14, 2006.

78. See Association for Civil Rights in Israel (ACRI), "Reducing Safety Zone—A Manifestly Illegal Order," April 23, 2006; available at www.acri.org.il/english-acri/engine/story.asp?id=298.

79. "Israeli Contribution to Conflict Is Forgotten by Leading Papers," FAIR media advisory, July 28, 2006. The report cites the statistics coming from the Israeli human rights organization B'Tselem. See www.fair.org/index.php?page=2928.

80. David Hirst, "The 'Arab System' Is Dying in Lebanon," *The Guardian* (U.K.), July 28, 2006.

81. Ze'ev Schiff, "For Israel, the Conflict in Lebanon Is a Must-Win Situation," *Ha'aretz*, July 27, 2006.

82. Schiff's quotation is deceiving for two primary reasons. First it implies that "Hamas wants to destroy Israel," as though this can be equated with the legitimate desire of all Palestinian factions to end the occupation and the exclusivist Jewish settler colonial arrangement imposed on Palestine. Second, Schiff gives the false impression that the "moderate Arab states" have a policy independent from that of Israel, that were it not for the latter's overwhelming strength, these countries would be in a state of perpetual war with the Jewish state for its eradication. This is historically inaccurate and is too broad a characterization. Jordan, for example, made arrangements with the Zionist movement before 1948 to divide Palestine between itself and the future Jewish state. Moreover, Israel actively came to the defense of the Jordanian monarchy in 1970 to save the regime from Syrian intervention in the events of Black September. If anything, the "moderate Arab regimes" see Israel as part of the same regional order that sustains them in power within the framework of U.S. hegemony. They are well aware that if Israel were to go, they would likely go as well. Israel's strength or "deterrence

power" is directed not at "moderate Arab regimes" but at the anti-Zionist and anti–U.S. imperial forces in the region.

83. "Israel Warns Fateh Could Disappear from Gaza," *Agence France-Presse*, August 20, 2006.

84. Alex Fishman, "Prelude to War," *Yediot Ahronot* English Web site, November 3, 2006.

85. Anthony H. Cordesman, "A Visit to the Israel-Lebanon Front: Lessons of the War and Prospects for Peace and Future Fighting," Center for Strategic and International Studies, August 17, 2006, available at www.csis.org/media/csis/events/060817_cord_transcript.pdf.

86. Amir Oren, "IDF May Face War with Syria, Hizbullah in 2007," *Ha'aretz*, November 6, 2006.

Index

Also from Haymarket Books

Welcome to the Terrordome: The Pain, Politics, and Promise of Sports

Dave Zirin • This much-anticipated sequel to *What's My Name, Fool?* by acclaimed commentator Dave Zirin breaks new ground in sports writing, looking at the controversies and trends now shaping sports in the United States and abroad. ISBN 978-1931859-41-7.

The Communist Manifesto: A Road Map to History's Most Important Political Document

Karl Marx and Frederick Engels, edited by Phil Gasper • This beautifully organized and presented edition of the *Communist Manifesto* is fully annotated, with clear historical references and explication, additional related texts, and a glossary that will bring the text to life. ISBN 1-931859-25-6.

No One Is Illegal: Fighting Racism and State Violence on the U.S.-Mexico Border

Justin Akers Chacón and Mike Davis • Countering the chorus of anti-immigrant voices, Davis and Akers Chacón expose the racism of anti-immigration vigilantes and put a human face on the immigrants who risk their lives to cross the border to work in the United States. ISBN 1-931859-35-3.

Subterranean Fire: A History of Working-Class Radicalism in the United States

Sharon Smith • Workers in the United States have a rich tradition of fighting back and achieving gains previously thought unthinkable, but that history remains largely hidden. In *Subterranean Fire*, Sharon Smith brings that history to light and reveals its lessons for today. ISBN 1-931859-23-X.

Soldiers in Revolt: GI Resistance During the Vietnam War

David Cortright with a new introduction by Howard Zinn • "An exhaustive account of rebellion in all the armed forces, not only in Vietnam but throughout the *world.*"—*New York Review of Books*. ISBN 1-931859-27-2.

Friendly Fire: The Remarkable Story of a Journalist Kidnapped in Iraq, Rescued by an Italian Secret Service Agent, and Shot by U.S. Forces

Giuliana Sgrena • The Italian journalist, whose personal story was featured on *60 Minutes*, describes the real story of her capture and shooting in 2004. Sgrena also gives invaluable insight into the reality of life in occupied Iraq, exposing U.S. war crimes there. ISBN 1-931859-39-6.

The Meaning of Marxism

Paul D'Amato • A lively and accessible introduction to the ideas of Karl Marx, with historical and contemporary examples. ISBN 978-1931859-29-5.

A Little Piece of Ground

Elizabeth Laird • Growing up in occupied Palestine through the eyes of a twelve-year-old boy. Young adult. ISBN 978-1-931859-38-7.

The Dispossessed: Chronicles of the *Desterrados* of Colombia

Alfredo Molano • Here in their own words are the stories of the Desterrados, or "dispossessed"—the thousands of Colombians displaced by years of war and state-backed terrorism, funded in part through U.S. aid to the Colombian government. With a preface by Aviva Chomsky.

Vive la Revolution: A Stand-up History of the French Revolution

Mark Steel • An actually interesting, unapologetically sympathetic, and extremely funny history of the French Revolution. ISBN 1-931859-37-X.

Poetry and Protest: A Dennis Brutus Reader

Aisha Karim and Lee Sustar, editors • A vital original collection of the interviews, poetry, and essays of the much-loved anti-apartheid leader. ISBN 1-931859-22-1.

In Praise of Barbarians: Essays Against Empire

Mike Davis • No writer in the United States today brings together analysis and history as comprehensively and elegantly as Mike Davis. In these contemporary, interventionist essays, Davis goes beyond critique to offer real solutions and concrete possibilities for change. ISBN 1-931859-42-6.

Sin Patrón: Stories from Argentia's Occupied Factories

The lavaca collective, with a foreword by Naomi Klein and Avi Lewis • The inside story of Argentina's remarkable movement to create factories run democratically by workers themselves. ISBN 1-931859-43-4.

Black Liberation and Socialism

Ahmed Shawki • A sharp and insightful analysis of movements against racism, with essential lessons for today's struggles. ISBN 1-931859-26-4.

What's My Name, Fool? Sports and Resistance in the United States

Dave Zirin • What's My Name, Fool? offers a no-holds-barred look at the business of sports today. In humorous and accessible language, Zirin shows how sports express the worst, as well as the most creative and exciting, features of American society. ISBN 1-931859-20-5.

Literature and Revolution

Leon Trotsky, William Keach, editor • A new, annotated edition of Leon Trotsky's classic study of the relationship between politics and art. ISBN 1-931859-16-7.

The Struggle for Palestine

Leading international solidarity activists offer insight into the ongoing struggle for Palestinian freedom and justice. Includes Anthony Arnove, Naseer Aruri, David Barsamian, Paul D'Amato, Phil Gasper, Toufic Haddad, Tikva Honig-Parnass, Rania Masri, Tanya Reinhart, Edward Said, and Ahmed Shawki. ISBN 978-1931859-00-4.

About Haymarket Books

Haymarket Books is a nonprofit, progressive book distributor and publisher, a project of the Center for Economic Research and Social Change. We believe that activists need to take ideas, history, and politics into the many struggles for social justice today. Learning the lessons of past victories, as well as defeats, can arm a new generation of fighters for a better world. As Karl Marx said, "The philosophers have merely interpreted the world; the point however is to change it."

We take inspiration and courage from our namesakes, the Haymarket Martyrs, who gave their lives fighting for a better world. Their 1886 struggle for the eight-hour day, which gave us May Day, the international workers' holiday, reminds workers around the world that ordinary people can organize and struggle for their own liberation. These struggles continue today across the globe—struggles against oppression, exploitation, hunger, and poverty.

It was August Spies, one of the Martyrs who was targeted for being an immigrant and an anarchist, who predicted the battles being fought to this day. "If you think that by hanging us you can stamp out the labor movement," Spies told the judge, "then hang us. Here you will tread upon a spark, but here, and there, and behind you, and in front of you, and everywhere, the flames will blaze up. It is a subterranean fire. You cannot put it out. The ground is on fire upon which you stand."

We could not suceed in our publishing efforts without the generous financial support of our readers. Many people contribute to our project through the Haymarket Sustainers program, where donors receive free books in return for their monetary support. If you would like to be a part of this program, please contact us at info@haymarketbooks.org.

Order these titles and more online at www.haymarketbooks.org or call 773-583-7884.